Steven Murray

CONFIGURING CISCO® ROUTERS FOR BRIDGING, DLSW+, AND DESKTOP PROTOCOLS

THE McGRAW-HILL TECHNICAL EXPERT SERIES

To order or receive additional information on these or any other McGraw-Hill titles in the United States, please call 1-800-722-4726, or visit us at www.computing.mcgraw-hill.com. In other countries, contact your McGraw-Hill representative.

Configuring Cisco® Routers for Bridging, DLSw+, and Desktop Protocols

Tan Nam-Kee

CCIE™ #4307, CCSI™ #98976

McGraw-Hill

New York   San Francisco   Washington, D.C.
Auckland   Bogotá   Caracas   Lisbon   London
Madrid   Mexico City   Milan   Montreal   New Delhi
San Juan   Singapore   Sydney   Tokyo   Toronto

Library of Congress Cataloging-in-Publication Data

Nam-Kee, Tan.
    Configuring Cisco® routers for bridging, DLSW+, and desktop protocols / Tan Nam-Kee.
        p. cm.
    ISBN 0-07-135457-3
    1. Routers (Computer networks)   2. Computer network protocols.   I. Title.
TK5105.543. N36 1999
004.6'2—dc21

                                          99-047517
                                            CIP

McGraw-Hill

A Division of The McGraw-Hill Companies

1 2 3 4 5 6 7 8 9 0   AGM/AGM   9 0 4 3 2 1 0 9

P/N 0-07-135459-X   part of ISBN 0-07-135457-3

The sponsoring editor for this book was Steven Elliot and the production supervisor was Claire Stanley. It was set in New Century Schoolbook by TIPS Technical Publishing.

Printed and bound by Quebecor / Martinsburg.

This study guide and/or material is not sponsored by, endorsed by or affiliated with Cisco Systems, Inc. Cisco®, Cisco Systems®, CCDA™, CCNA™, CCDP™, CCNP™, CCIE™, CCSI™, the Cisco Systems logo and the CCIE logo are trademarks or registered trademarks of Cisco Systems, Inc. in the United States and certain other countries. All other trademarks are trademarks of their respective owners. Rather than put a trademark symbol after every occurrence of a trademarked name, we use names in an editorial fashion only, and to the benefit of the trademark owner, with no intention of infringement of the trademark. Where such designations appear in this book, they have been printed with initial caps.

 This book is printed on recycled, acid-free paper containing a minimum of 50% recycled de-inked fiber.

To my mom, Soh-Eng, and my wife, Hwee-Fern

CONTENTS

Contents

Contents

FIGURES

TABLES

PREFACE

Introduction

Even though IP has become the dominant protocol, applications running on SNA, NetBIOS, IPX, AppleTalk, VINES, DECnet, and ISO CLNS still exist in many enterprise networks. In these multiprotocol environments, networkers often find it exasperating and time-consuming when deploying corporate-wide network applications. The hardest part is making the underlying bridging or routing protocols tick for these network applications.

Currently, not many technical literatures are devoted to configuring Cisco routers for multiprotocol environments. I wrote *Configuring Cisco Routers for Bridging, DLSw+, and Desktop Protocols* to be the book that fills in this gap, using real scenarios in a comprehensive step-by-step implementation approach.

Objectives

The purpose of this book is to make you proficient and dexterous in configuring Cisco routers for multiprotocol environments. By presenting transparent bridging, source-route bridging, DLSw+, IPX, AppleTalk, Banyan VINES, DECnet, and ISO CLNS both conceptually and in the context of practical scenarios, this book aims to foster your understanding of these protocols so that you can integrate them seamlessly in your enterprise network. Whether you are a network administrator, engineer, specialist, or preparing for the CCIE exams, this book systematically lists all the nitty-gritty multiprotocol implementation details for you, reducing your configuration task to less than a chore.

Audience

This book is intended for candidates preparing for the CCIE certification or networking professionals who need to configure and support multiprotocol networks on Cisco routers. The book introduces technical detail progressively in the context of practical scenarios and case studies. No major background in IBM networking or desktop protocols is required.

In addition, the router configurations illustrated in this book can be used to get a connection up and running quickly, or as templates to implement more complex configurations.

Organization of this Book

The book is organized into three parts:

Part 1—Bridging.   Chapter 1 starts with the basic transparent bridging configuration, followed by the implementation of transparent bridging over Frame Relay, X.25, and DDR. The concept of integrated routing and bridging is also illustrated. Likewise, Chapter 2 begins with implementing Source-Route Bridging on Token Ring LANs and Transparent Bridging on Ethernet LANs. Source-Route Translational Bridging is then implemented, enabling source-route stations on the Token Ring LANs to communicate with transparent bridging stations on the Ethernet LANs, and vice versa. Next, Remote Source-Route Bridging over TCP/IP is configured, allowing traffic to be bridged between two remote Token Rings. Chapter 2 also includes the bridging of routable protocols, Source-Route Bridging access control, and performance tuning.

Part 2—IBM Networking: DLSw+.   Chapter 3 thoroughly covers DLSw+ concepts and implementation. This chapter progressively introduces cost peers, backup peers, dynamic peers, border peers, and on-demand peers. In addition, Chapter 3 contains implementation details for configuring DLSw+ over different LAN and WAN media. The concluding section discusses DLSw+ access control.

Part 3—Desktop Protocols.   Chapters 4-8 discuss in detail the concepts and configuration of desktop protocols: Novell IPX, AppleTalk, Banyan VINES, DECnet, and ISO CLNS. Chapter 4 covers IPX RIP, IPX EIGRP, IPXWAN, NLSP, IPX access control, and NetBIOS over IPX. Chapter 5 discusses AppleTalk RTMP, AppleTalk Tunneling, AppleTalk EIGRP, and AppleTalk access control. Chapter 6 illustrates VINES RTP and VINES access control. Chapter 7 focuses on DECnet Phase IV routing, DECnet Level 1 and Level 2 routing, DECnet access control, DECnet Phase V routing, and LAT. Finally, Chapter 8 examines ISO CLNS IS-IS Level 1 and Level 2 routing, ISO CLNS ES-IS, and CLNS access control.

Approach

This book adopts a scenario-based approach, which utilizes representative network topologies as a basis for illustrating the protocols discussed in each chapter. The scenarios are covered in-depth to facilitate learning-by-example, so that you can apply and relate what you have learned from these scenarios to your specific situation. These network scenarios are implemented using different Cisco 2500, 3600, and 4500 series routers running on the Cisco IOS Enterprise Plus feature set version 11.2. The readers are assumed to have some knowledge about the different Cisco router models and the various Cisco IOS feature sets.

— TAN NAM-KEE
CCIE #4307

ACKNOWLEDGMENTS

I wish to acknowledge the following reviewers for their helpful suggestions: Al Banks, Amit Shah, and André Parée-Huff.

In addition, I would like to express my thanks to Steven Elliot, Jennifer Perillo, Franchesca Maddalena, Simon Yates, Clare Stanley, Ruth Mannino, and James Halston, of the editorial staff at McGraw-Hill; and to Robert Kern, Lynanne Fowle, Jeannine Kolbush, Karen Newton, and Jennifer Durham, of the production team at TIPS Technical Publishing.

Finally, special thanks to my family, who put up with my extra work hours for the past six months. This book could not have been written without their support and patience.

ABOUT THE AUTHOR

Tan Nam-Kee (CCIE #4307 and CCSI #98976) is a Cisco certified instructor and has provided extensive Cisco training and customized training to networking professionals from multinational organizations such as Air Lanka, AT&T, Citibank, Compaq, Credit Suisse First Boston, Hewlett Packard, IBM, Merrill Lynch, Telecom New Zealand, and others. He also designs and implements network management solutions for large enterprise networks. Nam-Kee is currently providing consulting services to Global Knowledge Network Private Limited.

Besides being a Cisco Certified Internetwork Expert (CCIE #4307) and Cisco Certified Systems Instructor (CCSI #98976), Nam-Kee is also a Microsoft Certified Systems Engineer (MCSE #926954), SCO ACE, HP OpenView Certified Consultant, Bay Networks Certified Specialist, and Sun Certified Network Administrator. He also holds an M.S. in Datacommunications from the University of Essex, UK, and an M.B.A. from the University of Adelaide, Australia.

ABOUT THE REVIEWERS

As the leading publisher of technical books for more than 100 years, McGraw-Hill prides itself on bringing you the most authoritative and up-to-date information available. To ensure that our books meet the highest standards of accuracy, we have asked some top professionals and technical experts to review the accuracy of the material you are about to read.

We take great pleasure in thanking the following technical reviewers for their insights:

Al Banks (CCNA, CCDA, MCSE) is a network analyst for Southern Farm Bureau Casualty Insurance Company, where he supports a Cisco WAN covering 6 states and provides IBM connectivity to Farm Bureau's state and county offices. In addition, Al maintains Cisco LAN switches for SFB's home office in Ridgeland, MS. Al has been involved in information systems since 1995, specializing in data networking since 1997. He passed the CCIE written exam in June 1999 and is scheduled for the CCIE lab in November 1999.

André Parée-Huff (A+, Network+, Compaq ASE, MCP, MCP+I, MCSE, MCSE+I, CNNA) works for Compaq Computer Corporation's North America Customer Support Center in Colorado Springs, CO, with the Network Support Unit. His responsibilities include support on bridges, routers, switches, hubs, GIGAswitches, and ATMs, for Fortune 500 companies as well as smaller independent companies and local governents.

Amit Shah (CCNA, CCDA) has over 10 years of experience in the networking field and over 7 years in the Cisco networking field. Amit has worked on various large-scale projects, such as SNA to IP migration and Token Ring to Fast Ethernet/VLAN migration. Currently, he is working for RealTech Systems as a network engineer.

Transparent Bridging

Introduction

There is a common saying: "If you cannot route, you bridge." A bridge interconnects LANs to form a single larger logical network at layer 2. Bridging can also separate a congested Ethernet segment into two, segregating the traffic from the initial segment onto the two smaller ones, thus reducing the number of collisions.

When should bridging be chosen over routing? To answer this question, examine what protocols are currently operating in the network and whether these protocols are routable. Routable protocols can be routed or bridged; nonroutable protocols can only be bridged. IP, IPX, Apple-Talk, DECnet, Banyan VINES, and ISO CLNS are routable protocols, while LAT, MOP, NetBIOS, and SNA are nonroutable.

The router functions at the network layer of the OSI Reference Model and uses logical network addresses to make routing decisions. These network addresses can also divide a network into smaller layer-3 logical units to confine local broadcasts. The bridge operates at the data link layer, using MAC addresses to make its forwarding decisions. Bridged networks reside in a single logical network address space; for this reason, bridging helps to conserve network layer addresses. Because there is only one logical network, the bridge must forward (flood) local broadcasts to all connected segments, except the originating one.

For the rest of this chapter, the focus will rest on transparent bridging, which is traditionally used to interconnect or extend two or more Ethernet II or IEEE 802.3 networks into a single logical LAN.

Transparent Bridging Overview

Transparent bridging is predominantly used in Ethernet environments. A transparent bridge does not modify the data frame, does not act as a source or destination for frames, and makes the attached segments appear as a single cable. Frames transmitted between end stations in a bridged LAN carry the MAC address of the source and destination end stations in the source and destination address fields of the frames. The MAC address, or other means of identification of a bridge, is not carried in the frames transmitted between the end stations in the bridged LAN.

Modes of Operation

A transparent bridge has the following modes of operation:

■ Learning

■ Forwarding

■ Filtering

■ Blocking (or Loop Avoidance)

Learning Mode Initially, when the bridge is started, it monitors the source MAC addresses of frames received on each of its ports. The bridge keeps dynamic entries of these addresses and their associated ports in a bridging table (also known as the filtering database). Table entries are automatically removed after a specified time has elapsed since the entries were created or last updated. This aging timer ensures end stations that have moved to a different part of the bridged LAN can still receive frames. The recommended default aging time value by IEEE 802.1D committee is 300.0 seconds and can range from 10.0 to 1000000.0 seconds.

Forwarding Mode When a bridge receives a frame, it searches its bridging table to determine whether an association exists between the destination address and any of the bridge's ports (except the one on which the frame was received). If the table contains such an entry, the bridge will forward the frame out of the correct port specified in the database.

However, if neither the source nor the destination address is found in the table, the bridge will add the source address and its associated port into the table. It then forwards the frame out all ports except the one on which the frame was received. This process is called flooding. If there is a reply from the destination, the bridge will add the source address—which was initially the target destination address—and its associated port into the bridging table. Hence, the bridge will forward subsequent frames out of the designated port.

Note that the bridge will only forward frames to other bridge ports if the receiving port and the transmitting port are both in the forwarding state.

Filtering Mode A bridge will not forward a frame if the source and destination addresses in the bridging table are associated with the same port (meaning both end stations are located in the same segment). This situation is known as filtering and the bridge will discard such frames, conserving overall bandwidth.

However, if both the source and destination stations reside in the same segment, with the destination address unknown to the bridge, the bridge will flood to learn this address. When the destination station replies, the bridge will add the source address together with its associated port to the bridging table. Thereafter, the bridge will filter subsequent frames between the two stations.

Loop Avoidance When more than one path exists between two bridged networks, a bridging loop is formed. Bridging loops are like double-edged swords. The loop provides redundancy, but transparent bridging will fail if there are multiple paths available between any two stations in a bridged network. Thus, a bridge-to-bridge protocol using the spanning tree algorithm retains the benefits of loops and eradicates their problems.

Spanning Tree Algorithm The spanning tree algorithm (STA) was developed by Digital Equipment Corporation (DEC) and later formed the basis of IEEE 802.1D. Note that the Digital algorithm and the IEEE 802.1D algorithm are not compatible. This chapter will use the IEEE 802.1D algorithm as the standard bridging protocol.

The spanning tree algorithm functions like the following:

1. The STA selects the root bridge using the lowest bridge identifier value. That is, the lower the value, the higher the priority. In Figure 1-1, the root bridge is Bridge 1.

2. The STA determines the root port on all the other bridges. A bridge's root port is the port through which the root bridge can be reached with the least total path cost. This value is also known as the root path cost.

3. The STA determines designated bridges and their designated ports. A designated bridge is the bridge on each LAN that provides the lowest root path cost. A designated bridge is the only bridge allowed to forward frames to and from the LAN to which it is attached. Nondesignated bridges (the ones that will create loops) on the same LAN will go into a blocking (or standby) mode, as illustrated in Figure 1-2. The blocked bridge ports will become active when the primary link fails. A LAN's designated port is the port that connects it to the designated bridge.

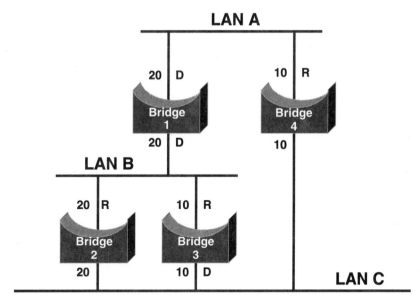

Figure 1-1
Bridged network
before running STA.

D = Designated Port
R = Root Port

There will be situations when two or more bridges happen to have the same root path cost. In such cases, the STA selects the bridge with the highest priority (lowest value) bridge identifier. If the bridge identifiers are also the same, the STA chooses the bridge with the highest priority (lowest value) designated port. Lastly, if the bridge priorities are the same, the STA will use the port identifiers as the tiebreaker. In Figure 1-1, Bridge 3 and Bridge 4 can both reach Bridge 1 (root bridge) with a minimum path cost of 10. In this instance, the bridge identifier is used as the tiebreaker and thus Bridge 3's LAN C port is selected over Bridge 4's.

The spanning tree calculation occurs whenever a topology change is detected, such as during a power cycle or link failure. The calculation requires communication between the bridges and is achieved through configuration messages known as bridge protocol data units (BPDUs). Configuration messages contain important information like the root identifier and the sending bridge's root path cost. These messages also include the bridge and port identifier of the sending bridge and the message age.

Bridges exchange configuration messages at a fixed interval, usually every one to four seconds, equivalent to the hello time. If a bridge fails,

Figure 1-2
Bridged network
after running STA.

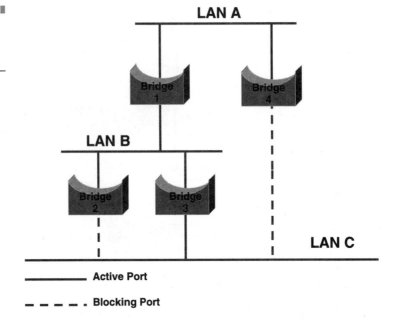

causing a topology change, neighboring bridges will soon detect the lack of BPDUs and initiate the spanning tree recalculation.

All transparent bridge topology decisions are made locally as BPDUs are exchanged between neighboring bridges. Hence, there is no central control on the network topology.

Case Scenario

Figure 1-3 illustrates the overall network scenario that will be referenced throughout this chapter. This enterprise network spans across three sites: Seattle, Portland, and Dallas. The Seattle office is internetworked to the Portland office by X.25, with an ISDN dial-up line that serves as backup in the event the X.25 connectivity becomes unavailable. Similarly, the Portland office is interconnected to the Dallas office through a Frame Relay network. Each site has its Virtual LAN where end systems running on various network protocols (both routable and nonroutable) reside. This scenario implements IP and IPX as the routable protocols. Nonroutable protocols include SNA and NetBIOS. In other words, a routed network

Figure 1-3
The overall network topology.

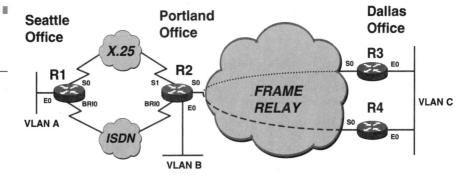

will be implemented for the routable protocols, and a bridged network for the nonroutable ones.

IP Setup

Most enterprises today will have an underlying IP backbone implemented before introducing other network protocols. In Figure 1-4, the enterprise network illustrated in Figure 1-3 is divided into three different routing domains: RIPv2, EIGRP, and OSPF. Code Listings 1-1 through 1-8 illustrate the IP implementation.

Figure 1-4
The overall IP network.

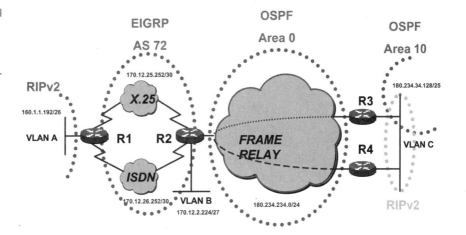

■ ■

Code Listing 1-1

IP configuration for R1.

```
!
hostname C4500-R1
!
username C4700-R2 password cisco
isdn switch-type basic-net3
!
interface Ethernet0
 ip address 160.1.1.193 255.255.255.192
 media-type 10BaseT
!
interface Serial0
 backup delay 10 30
 backup interface BRI0
 ip address 170.12.25.253 255.255.255.252
 encapsulation x25
 bandwidth 56
 x25 address 1701225111
 x25 map ip 170.12.25.254 1701225222 broadcast
!
interface BRI0
 ip address 170.12.26.253 255.255.255.252
 encapsulation ppp
 ppp authentication chap
 dialer map ip 170.12.26.254 name C4700-R2 broadcast 2250295
 dialer idle-timeout 60
 dialer load-threshold 128 either
 dialer-group 1
!
dialer-list 1 protocol ip permit
!
router eigrp 72
 redistribute rip metric 10000 1000 255 1 1500
 passive-interface Ethernet0
 network 170.12.0.0
 no auto-summary
!
router rip
 version 2
 redistribute eigrp 72 metric 3
 passive-interface BRI0
 passive-interface Serial0
 network 160.1.0.0
 no auto-summary
```

1. Code Listing 1-1 illustrates the IP configuration for R1. R1 is a Cisco 4500 series router. The `hostname` command sets the name of the router to C4500-R1. The `username` command uses the host name of R2, for PPP CHAP authentication. Note that the password serves as the authentication key and must be the same for both R1 and R2. The ISDN switch type used is `basic-net3`.

2. The Ethernet interface E0 of R1 is in subnet 160.1.1.192 with a mask of 26 bits. The 10BaseT (instead of the AUI) interface is used.

3. The serial interface S0 of R1 is in subnet 170.12.25.252 with a mask of 30 bits. S0 is connected to a X.25 cloud; therefore, its encapsulation type is X.25. R1's X.121 address is `1701225111`. The `x25 map` command creates a virtual circuit between R1 and R2 for routing IP. The IP and X.121 addresses used by the command are R2's. S0 also uses the backup by ISDN interface BRI0. The `backup delay` command will control the backup link so it will only connect 10 seconds after the primary link is no longer available. The 30 parameter configures the backup link to disconnect after the primary link has reconnected for 30 seconds.

4. The ISDN interface BRI0 (basic rate 2B+D) is in subnet 170.12.26.252 with a mask of 30 bits. Its encapsulation type is PPP, and the PPP authentication protocol used is CHAP. The `dialer map` command is used to call up R2 to establish a PPP connectivity when S0 becomes unavailable. The `dialer idle-timeout` command ensures that the ISDN line will be disconnected if it is idling for 60 seconds. This feature is used as a safeguard against unnecessary ISDN charges when the line is not in use. Initially, when a PPP connectivity is established, only one B channel is used. The `dialer load-threshold` command will bring up the second B channel when the threshold of the first channel has reached approximately 50% (128/255 x 100%). The `either` keyword means that the threshold is applicable to both inbound and outbound traffic. The `dialer-group 1` command refers to the `dialer-list 1` command, and in this case, the list allows all IP traffic to pass. No refining on the dialer-list is required, as the purpose of the BRI0 interface is to backup S0.

5. R1 is running two different routing protocols RIPv2 and EIGRP. RIPv2 spans across interface E0, whereas EIGRP is in autonomous system 72 spanning both S0 and BRI0. Redistribution is required for both routing protocols as R1 is an ASBR. The RIPv2 domain would need to see the routes coming from the EIGRP AS 72 as RIPv2 routes. The EIGRP AS 72 would need to see the routes coming from the RIPv2 domain as EIGRP routes. RIPv2 is used instead of RIP because it supports VLSM. The redistribution process converts all routes coming from EIGRP 72 into RIPv2 routes with a hop count of 3, and all routes coming from RIPv2 into EIGRP's composite metrics. The `passive-interface` command is used to prevent the respective routes within the two routing domains from crossing over to the other. The `no auto-summary` command is used to disable the default auto-summary feature of both protocols.

Code Listing 1-2 shows the IP routing table for R1.

Code Listing 1-2

IP routing table for R1.

```
C4500-R1#show ip route
Codes: C - connected, S - static, I - IGRP, R - RIP, M - mobile, B - BGP
       D - EIGRP, EX - EIGRP external, O - OSPF, IA - OSPF inter area
       N1 - OSPF NSSA external type 1, N2 - OSPF NSSA external type 2
       E1 - OSPF external type 1, E2 - OSPF external type 2, E - EGP
       i - IS-IS, L1 - IS-IS level-1, L2 - IS-IS level-2, * - candidate default
       U - per-user static route, o - ODR

Gateway of last resort is not set

     180.234.0.0/16 is variably subnetted, 2 subnets, 2 masks
D EX    180.234.234.0/24 [170/46482176] via 170.12.25.254, 00:00:02, Serial0
D EX    180.234.34.128/25 [170/46482176] via 170.12.25.254, 00:00:02, Serial0
     160.1.0.0/26 is subnetted, 1 subnets
C       160.1.1.192 is directly connected, Ethernet0
     170.12.0.0/16 is variably subnetted, 3 subnets, 2 masks
D       170.12.26.252/30 [90/46738176] via 170.12.25.254, 00:00:02, Serial0
C       170.12.25.252/30 is directly connected, Serial0
D       170.12.2.224/27 [90/46251776] via 170.12.25.254, 00:00:02, Serial0
```

Code Listing 1-3

IP configuration for R2.

```
hostname C4700-R2
!
username C4500-R1 password cisco
isdn switch-type basic-net3
!
interface Ethernet0
 ip address 170.12.2.225 255.255.255.224
 media-type 10BaseT
!
interface Serial0
 no ip address
 encapsulation frame-relay
 no fair-queue
 frame-relay lmi-type ansi
!
interface Serial0.1 multipoint
 ip address 180.234.234.2 255.255.255.0
 ip ospf network broadcast
 ip ospf priority 255
 bandwidth 56
 frame-relay map ip 180.234.234.3 203 broadcast
 frame-relay map ip 180.234.234.4 204 broadcast
!
interface Serial1
 ip address 170.12.25.254 255.255.255.252
 encapsulation x25
 bandwidth 56
 x25 address 1701225222
 x25 map ip 170.12.25.253 1701225111 broadcast
!
interface BRI0
 ip address 170.12.26.254 255.255.255.252
 encapsulation ppp
 ppp authentication chap
 dialer idle-timeout 60
```

```
dialer map ip 10.1.1.1 name C4500-R1 broadcast
dialer load-threshold 128 either
dialer-group 1
!
dialer-list 1 protocol ip permit
!
router eigrp 72
 redistribute ospf 180 metric 56 1000 255 1 1500
 passive-interface Serial0.1
 network 170.12.0.0
 no auto-summary
!
router ospf 180
 redistribute eigrp 72 metric 200 subnets
 network 180.234.234.0 0.0.0.255 area 0
```

1. Code Listing 1-3 illustrates the IP configuration for R2. R2 is a Cisco 4700 series router. The `hostname` command sets the name of the router to C4700-R2. The `username` command uses the host name of R1, for PPP CHAP authentication. Note the password serves as the authentication key and must be the same for both R2 and R1. The ISDN switch type used is `basic-net3`.

2. The Ethernet interface E0 of R2 is in subnet 170.12.2.224 with a mask of 27 bits. The 10BaseT (instead of the AUI) interface is used.

3. R2 is the hub router in this hub-and-spoke Frame Relay topology. R3 and R4 are spoke routers. For R2, Frame Relay is implemented through a multipoint subinterface S0.1. S0.1 is in subnet 180.234.234.0 with a mask of 24 bits. Note that the Frame Relay LMI type is ANSI. The `frame-relay map` command statically maps the IP addresses of the spoke routers to their respective DLCIs. The `ip ospf network` command sets the OSPF network type to broadcast, since Frame Relay networks are NBMA networks. As R2 is a hub router, the `ip ospf priority` command explicitly sets the priority of S0.1 to be highest so that it can be a DR.

4. The Serial interface S1 of R2 is in subnet 170.12.25.252 with a mask of 30 bits. S1 is connected to the same X.25 cloud as R1; thus its encapsulation type is X.25. R2's X.121 address is `1701225222`. The `x25 map` command creates a virtual circuit between R2 and R1 for routing IP. The IP and X.121 addresses used by the command are R1's.

5. The ISDN interface BRI0 (basic rate 2B+D) is in subnet 170.12.26.252 with a mask of 30 bits. BRI0 encapsulation type is

PPP and the PPP authentication protocol used is CHAP. The `dialer map` command is used to establish a PPP connectivity when R1 makes a call. Note that no ISDN number is supplied here, as R1 will initiate the call. The `dialer idle-timeout` command ensures that the ISDN line will be disconnected if it idles continuously for 60 seconds. This is used as a safeguard against unnecessary ISDN charges when the line is not in use. Initially, when a PPP connection is established, only one B channel is used. The `dialer load-threshold` command will bring up the second B channel when the threshold of the first channel has reached approximately 50% (128/255 x 100%). The `either` keyword means that the threshold is applicable to both inbound and outbound traffic. The `dialer-group 1` command refers to the `dialer-list 1` command, and in this case, the list allows all IP traffic to pass.

6. R2 is running two different routing protocols EIGRP and OSPF. EIGRP spans E0, S1, and BRI0, while S0.1 is in OSPF Area 0. Redistribution is required for both routing protocols, as R2 is also an ASBR. The OSPF domain would need to see the routes coming from the EIGRP AS 72 as OSPF routes. The EIGRP AS 72 would need to see the routes coming from the OSPF domain as EIGRP routes. The redistribution process converts all routes coming from EIGRP AS 72 into OSPF routes with a cost of 200, and all routes coming from OSPF into EIGRP routes with EIGRP's composite metrics.

Code Listing 1-4 shows the IP routing table for R2.

Code Listing 1-4
IP routing table for R2.

```
C4700-R2#show ip route
Codes: C - connected, S - static, I - IGRP, R - RIP, M - mobile, B - BGP
       D - EIGRP, EX - EIGRP external, O - OSPF, IA - OSPF inter area
       N1 - OSPF NSSA external type 1, N2 - OSPF NSSA external type 2
       E1 - OSPF external type 1, E2 - OSPF external type 2, E - EGP
       i - IS-IS, L1 - IS-IS level-1, L2 - IS-IS level-2, * - candidate default
       U - per-user static route, o - ODR

Gateway of last resort is not set

     180.234.0.0/16 is variably subnetted, 2 subnets, 2 masks
C       180.234.234.0/24 is directly connected, Serial0.1
O IA    180.234.34.128/25 [110/1795] via 180.234.234.3, 00:00:02, Serial0.1
     160.1.0.0/16 is subnetted, 1 subnets
D EX    160.1.1.192 [170/2425856] via 170.12.25.253, 00:00:02, Serial1
     170.12.0.0/16 is variably subnetted, 3 subnets, 2 masks
C       170.12.26.252/30 is directly connected, BRI0
C       170.12.25.252/30 is directly connected, Serial1
C       170.12.2.224/27 is directly connected, Ethernet0
```

■ ■

Code Listing 1-5
IP configuration for
R3.

```
hostname C2500-R3
!
interface Ethernet0
 ip address 180.234.34.129 255.255.255.128
 ip ospf priority 0
!
interface Serial0
 no ip address
 encapsulation frame-relay
 frame-relay lmi-type ansi
!
interface Serial0.1 point-to-point
 ip address 180.234.234.3 255.255.255.0
 ip ospf network broadcast
 ip ospf priority 0
 bandwidth 56
 frame-relay interface-dlci 302
!
router ospf 180
 network 180.234.234.0 0.0.0.255 area 0
 network 180.234.34.128 0.0.0.127 area 10
!
router rip
 version 2
 passive-interface Serial0.1
 network 180.234.0.0
 no auto-summary
```

1. Code Listing 1-5 illustrates the IP configuration for R3. R3 is a
   Cisco 2500 series router. The `hostname` command sets the name of
   the router to C2500-R3.

2. The Ethernet interface E0 of R3 is in subnet 180.234.34.128 with a
   mask of 25 bits. The `ip ospf priority` command explicitly sets
   the priority of E0 to zero, the lowest value. This means for that particular area where E0 resides, it will not take part in the DR/BDR
   election. In other words, it will become a DROTHER.

3. R3 is the spoke router in this hub-and-spoke Frame Relay topology.
   The topology is implemented through a point-to-point subinterface
   S0.1. S0.1 is in subnet 180.234.234.0 with a mask of 24 bits. Note
   that the Frame Relay LMI type is ANSI. The `frame-relay`
   `interface-dlci` command defines which DLCI number is associated with S0.1. The `ip ospf network` command sets the OSPF
   network type to broadcast since Frame Relay networks are NBMA
   networks. As R3 is a spoke router, the `ip ospf priority` command explicitly sets the priority of S0.1 to be lowest (zero) so that it
   will never be a DR, will not participate in DR/BDR elections, and
   will become a DROTHER.

4. R3 is running two different routing protocols OSPF and RIPv2. S0.1 is in OSPF Area 0 and E0 is in OSPF Area 10. RIPv2 also spans both S0.1 and E0. Note no redistribution is done here as R3 is using OSPF (administrative distance 110) as the primary routing protocol unless the Frame Relay connectivity between R2 and R3 fails. In normal circumstances, RIPv2 (administrative distance 120) will act as the secondary or backup routing protocol for R3.

Code Listing 1-6 shows the IP routing table for R3.

Code Listing 1-6

IP routing table for R3.

```
C2500-R3#show ip route
Codes: C - connected, S - static, I - IGRP, R - RIP, M - mobile, B - BGP
       D - EIGRP, EX - EIGRP external, O - OSPF, IA - OSPF inter area
       N1 - OSPF NSSA external type 1, N2 - OSPF NSSA external type 2
       E1 - OSPF external type 1, E2 - OSPF external type 2, E - EGP
       i - IS-IS, L1 - IS-IS level-1, L2 - IS-IS level-2, * - candidate default
       U - per-user static route, o - ODR

Gateway of last resort is not set

     180.234.0.0/16 is variably subnetted, 2 subnets, 2 masks
C       180.234.234.0/24 is directly connected, Serial0.1
C       180.234.34.128/25 is directly connected, Ethernet0
     160.1.0.0/26 is subnetted, 1 subnets
O E2    160.1.1.192 [110/200] via 180.234.234.2, 00:23:49, Serial0.1
     170.12.0.0/16 is variably subnetted, 3 subnets, 2 masks
O E2    170.12.26.252/30 [110/200] via 180.234.234.2, 00:23:49, Serial0.1
O E2    170.12.25.252/30 [110/200] via 180.234.234.2, 00:23:49, Serial0.1
O E2    170.12.2.224/27 [110/200] via 180.234.234.2, 00:23:49, Serial0.1
```

Code Listing 1-7

IP configuration for R4.

```
hostname C2500-R4
!
interface Ethernet0
 ip address 180.234.34.130 255.255.255.128
 ip ospf priority 255
!
interface Serial0
 no ip address
 encapsulation frame-relay
 frame-relay lmi-type ansi
!
interface Serial0.1 point-to-point
 ip address 180.234.234.4 255.255.255.0
 ip ospf network broadcast
 ip ospf priority 0
 bandwidth 56
 frame-relay interface-dlci 402
!
router ospf 180
 redistribute rip metric 200 subnets
 network 180.234.234.0 0.0.0.255 area 0
!
router rip
 version 2
 redistribute ospf 180 metric 3
```

```
passive-interface Serial0.1
network 180.234.0.0
no auto-summary
!
```

1. Code Listing 1-7 illustrates the IP configuration for R4. R4 is a Cisco 2500 series router. The `hostname` command sets the name of the router to C2500-R4.

2. The Ethernet interface E0 of R4 is in subnet 180.234.34.128 with a mask of 25 bits. The `ip ospf priority` command explicitly sets the priority of E0 to 255, the highest value. This means for the particular area where E0 resides, it will become the DR.

3. R4 is the spoke router in this hub-and-spoke Frame Relay topology. It is implemented through a point-to-point subinterface S0.1. S0.1 is in subnet 180.234.234.0 with a mask of 24 bits. Note that the Frame Relay LMI type is ANSI. The `frame-relay interface-dlci` command defines which DLCI number is associated with S0.1. The `ip ospf network` command sets the OSPF network type to broadcast, since Frame Relay networks are NBMA networks. As R4 is a spoke router, the `ip ospf priority` command explicitly sets the priority of S0.1 to be lowest (zero) so that it will never be a DR, and thus will not participate in the DR/BDR election, and will become a DROTHER.

4. R4 is running two different routing protocols: OSPF and RIPv2. S0.1 uses OSPF as the routing protocol and is in Area 0. E0 uses RIPv2, which also spans across S0.1. Redistribution is required for both routing protocols as R4 is an ASBR. The OSPF domain would need to learn the routes coming from the RIPv2 domain as OSPF routes. The RIPv2 domain would need to learn the routes coming from the OSPF domain as RIPv2 routes. The redistribution process converts all routes coming from RIPv2 into OSPF routes with a cost of 200, and all routes coming from OSPF into RIPv2 with a hop count of 3. Under normal circumstances, when the Frame Relay connectivity between R2 and R3 is up, R2 will learn the subnet 180.234.34.128 through OSPF. That is, the subnet will be reflected in R2's routing table as an OSPF IA route. However, if the connectivity fails, the route will be reflected as an OSPF E2, since it is now learned via RIPv2.

Code Listing 1-8 shows the IP routing table for R4.

Code Listing 1-8
IP routing table for R4.

```
C2500-R4#show ip route
Codes: C - connected, S - static, I - IGRP, R - RIP, M - mobile, B - BGP
       D - EIGRP, EX - EIGRP external, O - OSPF, IA - OSPF inter area
       N1 - OSPF NSSA external type 1, N2 - OSPF NSSA external type 2
       E1 - OSPF external type 1, E2 - OSPF external type 2, E - EGP
       i - IS-IS, L1 - IS-IS level-1, L2 - IS-IS level-2, * - candidate default
       U - per-user static route, o - ODR

Gateway of last resort is not set

     180.234.0.0/16 is variably subnetted, 2 subnets, 2 masks
C       180.234.234.0/24 is directly connected, Serial0.1
C       180.234.34.128/25 is directly connected, Ethernet0
     160.1.0.0/26 is subnetted, 1 subnets
O E2    160.1.1.192 [110/200] via 180.234.234.2, 00:25:29, Serial0.1
     170.12.0.0/16 is variably subnetted, 3 subnets, 2 masks
O E2    170.12.26.252/30 [110/200] via 180.234.234.2, 00:25:29, Serial0.1
O E2    170.12.25.252/30 [110/200] via 180.234.234.2, 00:25:29, Serial0.1
O E2    170.12.2.224/27 [110/200] via 180.234.234.2, 00:25:29, Serial0.1
```

IPX Setup

The desktop protocol implemented for the enterprise network is IPX. Consider Figure 1-5. The enterprise network illustrated in Figure 1-3 is divided into two different IPX routing domains: IPX RIP and IPX EIGRP. Code Listings 1-9 through 1-16 illustrate the IPX implementation.

Figure 1-5
The overall IPX network.

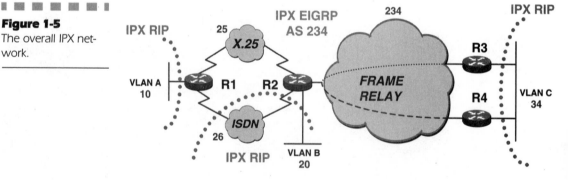

Code Listing 1-9

IPX configuration for R1.

```
hostname C4500-R1
!
username C4700-R2 password cisco
isdn switch-type basic-net3
!
ipx routing 00e0.1e58.6109
!
interface Ethernet0
ipx network 10
!
interface Serial0
 backup delay 10 30
 backup interface BRI0
 ipx network 25
 no ipx split-horizon eigrp 234
 encapsulation x25
 bandwidth 56
 x25 address 1701225111
 x25 map ipx 25.0060.471e.59f8 1701225222 broadcast
!
interface BRI0
 ipx network 26
 encapsulation ppp
 ppp authentication chap
 dialer map ipx 26.0060.471e.59f8 name C4700-R2 broadcast 2250295
 dialer idle-timeout 60
 dialer load-threshold 128 either
 dialer-group 1
!
dialer-list 1 protocol ipx permit
!
ipx router eigrp 234
 network 25
!
ipx router rip
 no network 25
```

Code Listing 1-9 illustrates the IPX configuration for R1. By default, IPX routing is not enabled. Thus, the command ipx routing explicitly enables it and the routing protocol IPX RIP.

1. R1 is running two different routing protocols IPX RIP and IPX EIGRP. E0 is part of IPX network 10 and belongs to the IPX RIP routing domain. No command is required to explicitly enable IPX RIP, since it is the default routing protocol.

2. S0 is part of IPX network 25 and belongs to the IPX EIGRP AS 234. The x25 map command creates a virtual circuit between R1 and R2 for routing IPX. The IPX and X.121 addresses used by the command are R2's. S0 also has ISDN backup via interface BRI0. In an NBMA (X.25) network, to prevent split horizon problem, it should be disabled for the respective IPX routing protocol that is deployed. In

this case, the routing protocol is IPX EIGRP and the command `no ipx split-horizon eigrp 234` is used to disable the split horizon mechanism for the protocol.

3. The ISDN interface BRI0 is part of IPX network 26 and belongs to the IPX RIP routing domain. The `dialer map` command is used to call R2 to establish a PPP connectivity when S0 becomes unavailable. The IPX address, host name, and ISDN number used by the command are R2's. The `dialer-group 1` command refers to the `dialer-list 1` command, and in this case, the list allows all IPX traffic to pass. No refining on the dialer-list is required, as the purpose of the BRI0 interface is to backup S0.

4. To implement only IPX EIGRP on network 25, enable IPX EIGRP for this network using the command `network 25` inside the `ipx router eigrp 234` mode, and disable IPX RIP for this network using the command `no network 25` inside the `ipx router rip` mode.

Code Listing 1-10 shows the IPX routing table for R1.

Code Listing 1-10

IPX routing table for R1.

```
C4500-R1#show ipx route
Codes: C - Connected primary network,    c - Connected secondary network
       S - Static, F - Floating static, L - Local (internal), W - IPXWAN
       R - RIP, E - EIGRP, N - NLSP, X - External, A - Aggregate
       s - seconds, u - uses

6 Total IPX routes. Up to 1 parallel paths and 16 hops allowed.

No default route known.

C          10 (NOVELL-ETHER),   Et0
C          25 (X25),            Se0
E          20 [267008000/1] via       25.0060.471e.59f8, age 00:24:09,
                               1u, Se0
E          26 [267008000/1] via       25.0060.471e.59f8, age 00:24:23,
                               11u, Se0
E          34 [46763776/1] via    25.0060.471e.59f8, age 00:20:52,
                               1u, Se0
E         234 [46738176/0] via    25.0060.471e.59f8, age 00:24:10,
                               1u, Se0
```

Code Listing 1-11

IPX configuration for R2.

```
hostname C4700-R2
!
username C4500-R1 password cisco
!
isdn switch-type basic-net3
ipx routing 0060.471e.59f8
!
interface Ethernet0
 ipx network 20
!
```

■ ■

Code Listing 1-11
(continued)

```
interface Serial0
 no ip address
 encapsulation frame-relay
 no fair-queue
 frame-relay lmi-type ansi
!
interface Serial0.1 multipoint
 bandwidth 56
ipx network 234
 no ipx split-horizon eigrp 234
 frame-relay map ipx 234.0000.0c3e.36ce 203 broadcast
 frame-relay map ipx 234.00e0.1e5f.dd0d 204 broadcast
!
interface Serial1
 encapsulation x25
 bandwidth 56
 ipx network 25
 no ipx split-horizon eigrp 234
 x25 address 1701225222
 x25 map ipx 25.00e0.1e58.6109 1701225111 broadcast
!
interface BRI0
 encapsulation ppp
 ppp authentication chap
 ipx network 26
 dialer idle-timeout 60
 dialer map ipx 26.00e0.1e58.6109 name C4500-R1 broadcast
 dialer load-threshold 128 either
 dialer-group 1
!
dialer-list 1 protocol ipx permit
!
ipx router eigrp 234
 network 234
 network 25
!
ipx router rip
 no network 234
 no network 25
```

1. Code Listing 1-11 illustrates the IPX configuration for R2. By default, IPX routing is not enabled. The command ipx routing explicitly enables it and the routing protocol IPX RIP.

2. R2 is running two different routing protocols: IPX RIP and IPX EIGRP. E0 is part of IPX network 20 and belongs to the IPX RIP routing domain. No command is required to explicitly enable IPX RIP as it is the default routing protocol.

3. S0.1 is part of IPX network 234 and belongs to the IPX EIGRP AS 234. In an NBMA (Frame Relay) network, to prevent split horizon problem, it should be disabled for the respective IPX routing protocol that is deployed. In this case, the routing protocol is IPX EIGRP

and the command `no ipx split-horizon eigrp 234` is used to disable the split-horizon mechanism for the protocol. The `frame-relay map` command statically maps the IPX addresses of the spoke routers R3 and R4 into their respective DLCIs.

4. S1 is part of IPX network 25 and belongs to the IPX EIGRP AS 234. The `x25 map` command creates a virtual circuit between R2 and R1 for routing IPX. The IPX and X.121 addresses used by the command are R1's. In an NBMA (X.25) network, to prevent split horizon problem, it should be disabled for the respective IPX routing protocol that is deployed. In this case, the routing protocol is IPX EIGRP and the command `no ipx split-horizon eigrp 234` is used to disable the split horizon mechanism for the protocol.

5. The ISDN interface BRI0 is part of IPX network 26 and belongs to the IPX RIP routing domain. The `dialer map` command is used to establish a PPP connection when R1 makes a call. Note that no ISDN number is supplied here, as R1 will initiate the call. The IPX address and host name used by the command are R1's. The `dialer-group 1` command refers to the `dialer-list 1` command, and in this case, the list allows all IPX traffic to pass.

6. To implement only IPX EIGRP on network 234 and network 25, we need to enable IPX EIGRP for these networks using the commands `network 234` and `network 25` inside the `ipx router eigrp 234` mode. We need to disable IPX RIP for these networks using the commands `no network 234` and `no network 25` inside the `ipx router rip` mode.

Code Listing 1-12 shows the IPX routing table for R2.

Code Listing 1-12
IPX routing table for R2.

```
C4700-R2#show ipx route
Codes: C - Connected primary network,    c - Connected secondary network
       S - Static, F - Floating static, L - Local (internal), W - IPXWAN
       R - RIP, E - EIGRP, N - NLSP, X - External, A - Aggregate
       s - seconds, u - uses

6 Total IPX routes. Up to 1 parallel paths and 16 hops allowed.

No default route known.

C       20 (NOVELL-ETHER),   Et0
C       25 (UNKNOWN),        Se1
C       26 (UNKNOWN),        BR0
C      234 (UNKNOWN),        Se0.1
E       10 [2195456/1] via       25.00e0.1e58.6109, age 00:23:01,
                        1u, Se1
E       34 [46251776/1] via      234.0000.0c3e.36ce, age 00:23:03,
                        1u, Se0.1
```

Code Listing 1-13
IPX configuration for
R3.

```
hostname C2500-R3
!
ipx routing 0000.0c3e.36ce
!
interface Ethernet0
 ipx network 34
!
interface Serial0
 no ip address
 encapsulation frame-relay
 frame-relay lmi-type ansi
!
interface Serial0.1 point-to-point
 ipx network 234
 no ipx split-horizon eigrp 234
 frame-relay interface-dlci 302
!
ipx router eigrp 234
 network 234
!
!
ipx router rip
 no network 234
```

1. Code Listing 1-13 illustrates the IPX configuration for R3. By default, IPX routing is not enabled. The command `ipx routing` enables it and the routing protocol IPX RIP.

2. R3 is running two different routing protocols: IPX RIP and IPX EIGRP. E0 is part of IPX network 34 and belongs to the IPX RIP routing domain. No command is required to explicitly enable IPX RIP, as it is the default routing protocol.

3. S0.1 is part of IPX network 234 and belongs to the IPX EIGRP AS 234. In an NBMA (Frame Relay) network, to prevent split horizon problem, it should be disabled for the respective IPX routing protocol that is deployed. In this case, the routing protocol is IPX EIGRP, and the command `no ipx split-horizon eigrp 234` is used to disable the split horizon mechanism for the protocol. The `frame-relay interface-dlci` command defines which DLCI number is associated with S0.1.

4. To implement only IPX EIGRP on network 234, we need to enable IPX EIGRP for this network using the command `network 234` inside the `ipx router eigrp 234` mode, and we need to disable IPX RIP for this network using the command `no network 234` inside the `ipx router rip` mode.

Code Listing 1-14 shows the IPX routing table for R3.

Code Listing 1-14

IPX routing table for R3.

```
C2500-R3#show ipx route
Codes: C - Connected primary network,    c - Connected secondary network
       S - Static, F - Floating static, L - Local (internal), W - IPXWAN
       R - RIP, E - EIGRP, N - NLSP, X - External, A - Aggregate
       s - seconds, u - uses

6 Total IPX routes. Up to 1 parallel paths and 16 hops allowed.

No default route known.

C          34 (NOVELL-ETHER),  Et0
C         234 (FRAME-RELAY),   Se0.1
E          10 [2707456/1] via      234.0060.471e.59f8, age 00:24:33,
                         1u, Se0.1
E          20 [267008000/1] via      234.0060.471e.59f8, age 00:24:33,
                         1u, Se0.1
E          25 [2681856/0] via      234.0060.471e.59f8, age 00:24:33,
                         1u, Se0.1
E          26 [267008000/1] via      234.0060.471e.59f8, age 00:24:33,
                         1u, Se0.1
```

Code Listing 1-15

IPX configuration for R4.

```
hostname C2500-R4
!
ipx routing 00e0.1e5f.dd0d
!
interface Ethernet0
!
interface Serial0
 no ip address
 encapsulation frame-relay
 frame-relay lmi-type ansi
!
interface Serial0.1 point-to-point
 ipx network 234
 no ipx split-horizon eigrp 234
 frame-relay interface-dlci 402
!
ipx router eigrp 234
 network 234
!
ipx router rip
 no network 234
!
```

1. Code Listing 1-15 illustrates the IPX configuration for R4. By default, IPX routing is not enabled. The command ipx routing enables it and the routing protocol IPX RIP.

2. R4 is running two different routing protocols IPX RIP and IPX EIGRP. No command is required to explicitly enable IPX RIP, as it is the default routing protocol. Note that the Ethernet interface E0 has no IPX network number here. This is done deliberately to

bridge IPX traffic for this particular interface. For further details, refer to the integrated routing and bridging section.

3. S0.1 is part of IPX network 234 and belongs to the IPX EIGRP AS 234. In an NBMA (Frame Relay) network, to prevent split horizon problem, it should be disabled for the IPX routing protocol deployed. In this case, the routing protocol is IPX EIGRP and the command `no ipx split-horizon eigrp 234` is used to disable the split-horizon mechanism for the protocol. The `frame-relay interface-dlci` command defines which DLCI number is associated with S0.1.

4. To implement only IPX EIGRP on network 234, we need to enable IPX EIGRP for this network using the command `network 234` inside the `ipx router eigrp 234` mode, and we need to disable IPX RIP for this network using the command `no network 234` inside the `ipx router rip` mode.

Code Listing 1-16 shows the IPX routing table for R4.

Code Listing 1-16
IPX routing table for R4.

```
C2500-R4#show ipx route
Codes: C - Connected primary network,    c - Connected secondary network
       S - Static, F - Floating static, L - Local (internal), W - IPXWAN
       R - RIP, E - EIGRP, N - NLSP, X - External, A - Aggregate
       s - seconds, u - uses

6 Total IPX routes. Up to 1 parallel paths and 16 hops allowed.

No default route known.

C        34 (NOVELL-ETHER),  BV1
C       234 (FRAME-RELAY),   Se0.1
E        10 [2707456/1] via      234.0060.471e.59f8, age 00:30:13,
                              1u, Se0.1
E        20 [267008000/1] via     234.0060.471e.59f8, age 09:28:53,
                              1u, Se0.1
E        25 [2681856/0] via      234.0060.471e.59f8, age 00:30:58,
                              1u, Se0.1
E        26 [267008000/1] via     234.0060.471e.59f8, age 00:37:12,
                              1u, Se0.1
```

Basic Bridging Configuration

Transparent bridging is configured on all the routers' interfaces illustrated in Figure 1-3. Code Listings 1-17 through 1-24 illustrate this.

Code Listing 1-17
Bridging configuration for R1.

```
hostname C4500-R1
!
interface Ethernet0
 bridge-group 1
!
interface Serial0
 bridge-group 1
!
interface BRI0
 bridge-group 1
!
bridge 1 protocol ieee
```

1. Code Listing 1-17 illustrates the bridging configuration for R1. The command `bridge 1 protocol ieee` defines the bridge group number as 1 and uses the IEEE 802.1D Spanning Tree Protocol. Note that the Digital Spanning Tree Protocol should be used only for backward compatibility. IEEE and Digital spanning trees are not compatible; hence, we should choose only one. Normally, if the network is homogeneously Cisco, IEEE will be preferred.

2. The command `bridge-group 1` assigns E0, S0, and BRI0 to bridge group 1. This means that nonroutable network protocols can bridge through these interfaces.

Code Listing 1-18 illustrates the bridging information for R1.

Code Listing 1-18
Bridging information for R1.

```
C4500-R1#show spanning-tree

Bridge Group 1 is executing the IEEE compatible Spanning Tree protocol
  Bridge Identifier has priority 32768, address 00e0.1e58.6109
  Configured hello time 2, max age 20, forward delay 15
  Current root has priority 100, address 0060.471e.59f8
  Root port is 2 (Serial0), cost of root path is 17857
  Topology change flag not set, detected flag not set
  Times:  hold 1, topology change 30, notification 30
          hello 2, max age 20, forward delay 15, aging 300
  Timers: hello 0, topology change 0, notification 0

Port 6 (BRI0) of bridge group 1 is down
  Port path cost 15625, Port priority 128
  Designated root has priority 100, address 0060.471e.59f8
  Designated bridge has priority 32768, address 00e0.1e58.6109
  Designated port is 6, path cost 17857
  Timers: message age 0, forward delay 9, hold 0

Port 4 (Ethernet0) of bridge group 1 is forwarding
  Port path cost 100, Port priority 128
  Designated root has priority 100, address 0060.471e.59f8
  Designated bridge has priority 32768, address 00e0.1e58.6109
```

Code Listing 1-18
(continued)

```
Designated port is 4, path cost 17857
Timers: message age 0, forward delay 0, hold 0

Port 2 (Serial0) of bridge group 1 is forwarding
    Port path cost 17857, Port priority 128
    Designated root has priority 100, address 0060.471e.59f8
    Designated bridge has priority 100, address 0060.471e.59f8
    Designated port is 5, path cost 0
    Timers: message age 1, forward delay 0, hold 0
```

Code Listing 1-19

Bridging configuration for R2.

```
hostname C4700-R2
!
interface Ethernet0
 bridge-group 1
!
interface Serial0.1 multipoint
 bridge-group 1
!
interface Serial1
 bridge-group 1
!
interface BRI0
 bridge-group 1
!
bridge 1 protocol ieee
bridge 1 priority 100
```

1. Code Listing 1-19 illustrates the bridging configuration for R2. The command `bridge 1 protocol ieee` defines the bridge group number as 1 and uses the IEEE 802.1D Spanning Tree Protocol.

2. The command `bridge-group 1` assigns E0, S0.1, S1, and BRI0 to bridge group 1. Nonroutable network protocols can bridge out of these interfaces.

3. The command `bridge 1 priority 100` explicitly selects R2 as the root bridge. The default priority value is 32768. R2 is chosen as the root bridge because it has the shortest radius to the rest of the routers, so the entire transparent bridging process will be more efficient. Moreover, physically it is also the hub router in the hub-and-spoke Frame Relay topology.

Code Listing 1-20 illustrates the bridging information for R2.

Code Listing 1-20
Bridging information
for R2.

```
C4700-R2#show spanning-tree

Bridge Group 1 is executing the IEEE compatible Spanning Tree protocol
  Bridge Identifier has priority 100, address 0060.471e.59f8
  Configured hello time 2, max age 20, forward delay 15
  We are the root of the spanning tree
  Topology change flag not set, detected flag not set
  Times:   hold 1, topology change 30, notification 30
           hello 2, max age 20, forward delay 15, aging 300
  Timers: hello 2, topology change 0, notification 0

Port 8 (BRI0) of bridge group 1 is forwarding
   Port path cost 15625, Port priority 128
   Designated root has priority 100, address 0060.471e.59f8
   Designated bridge has priority 100, address 0060.471e.59f8
   Designated port is 8, path cost 0
   Timers: message age 0, forward delay 0, hold 0

Port 2 (Ethernet0) of bridge group 1 is forwarding
   Port path cost 100, Port priority 128
   Designated root has priority 100, address 0060.471e.59f8
   Designated bridge has priority 100, address 0060.471e.59f8
   Designated port is 2, path cost 0
   Timers: message age 0, forward delay 0, hold 0

Port 20 (Serial0.1 Frame Relay) of bridge group 1 is forwarding
   Port path cost 17857, Port priority 128
   Designated root has priority 100, address 0060.471e.59f8
   Designated bridge has priority 100, address 0060.471e.59f8
   Designated port is 20, path cost 0
   Timers: message age 0, forward delay 0, hold 0

Port 5 (Serial1) of bridge group 1 is forwarding
   Port path cost 647, Port priority 128
   Designated root has priority 100, address 0060.471e.59f8
   Designated bridge has priority 100, address 0060.471e.59f8
   Designated port is 5, path cost 0
   Timers: message age 0, forward delay 0, hold 0
```

Code Listing 1-21
Bridging configura-
tion for R3.

```
hostname C2500-R3
!
interface Ethernet0
 bridge-group 1
!
interface Serial0.1 point-to-point
 bridge-group 1
!
bridge 1 protocol ieee
```

1. Code Listing 1-21 illustrates the bridging configuration for R3. The command `bridge 1 protocol ieee` defines the bridge group number as 1 and uses the IEEE 802.1D Spanning Tree Protocol.

2. The command `bridge-group 1` assigns E0 and S0.1 to bridge group 1. Nonroutable network protocols can bridge out of these interfaces.

Code Listing 1-22 illustrates the bridging information for R3.

■ ▪ |

Code Listing 1-22

Bridging information for R3.

```
C2500-R3#show spanning-tree

Bridge Group 1 is executing the IEEE compatible Spanning Tree protocol
  Bridge Identifier has priority 32768, address 0000.0c3e.36ce
  Configured hello time 2, max age 20, forward delay 15
  Current root has priority 100, address 0060.471e.59f8
  Root port is 5 (Serial0.1), cost of root path is 647
  Topology change flag not set, detected flag not set
  Times:  hold 1, topology change 30, notification 30
          hello 2, max age 20, forward delay 15, aging 300
  Timers: hello 0, topology change 0, notification 0


Port 2 (Ethernet0) of bridge group 1 is forwarding
  Port path cost 100, Port priority 128
  Designated root has priority 100, address 0060.471e.59f8
  Designated bridge has priority 32768, address 0000.0c3e.36ce
  Designated port is 2, path cost 647
  Timers: message age 0, forward delay 0, hold 0

Port 5 (Serial0.1 Frame Relay) of bridge group 1 is forwarding
  Port path cost 647, Port priority 128
  Designated root has priority 100, address 0060.471e.59f8
  Designated bridge has priority 100, address 0060.471e.59f8
  Designated port is 20, path cost 0
  Timers: message age 1, forward delay 0, hold 0
```

■ ▪ |

Code Listing 1-23

Bridging configuration for R4.

```
hostname C2500-R4
!
interface Ethernet0
 bridge-group 1
!
interface Serial0.1 point-to-point
 bridge-group 1
!
bridge 1 protocol ieee
```

1. Code Listing 1-23 illustrates the bridging configuration for R4. The command `bridge 1 protocol ieee` defines the bridge group number as 1 and uses the IEEE 802.1D Spanning Tree Protocol.

2. The command `bridge-group 1` assigns E0 and S0.1 to bridge group 1. Nonroutable network protocols can bridge out of these interfaces. Since there are two bridged paths to VLAN C, using spanning tree protocol, one of the bridges' ports (in this case, R4's E0) will go into the blocking state to prevent a loop.

Code Listing 1-24 illustrates the bridging information for R4.

Code Listing 1-24
Bridging information for R4.

```
C2500-R4#show spanning-tree

Bridge Group 1 is executing the IEEE compatible Spanning Tree protocol
  Bridge Identifier has priority 32768, address 00e0.1e5f.dd0d
  Configured hello time 2, max age 20, forward delay 15
  Current root has priority 100, address 0060.471e.59f8
  Root port is 6 (Serial0.1), cost of root path is 647
  Topology change flag not set, detected flag not set
  Times:  hold 1, topology change 30, notification 30
          hello 2, max age 20, forward delay 15, aging 300
  Timers: hello 0, topology change 0, notification 0

Port 2 (Ethernet0) of bridge group 1 is blocking
   Port path cost 100, Port priority 128
   Designated root has priority 100, address 0060.471e.59f8
   Designated bridge has priority 32768, address 0000.0c3e.36ce
   Designated port is 2, path cost 647
   Timers: message age 3, forward delay 0, hold 0

Port 6 (Serial0.1 Frame Relay) of bridge group 1 is forwarding
   Port path cost 647, Port priority 128
   Designated root has priority 100, address 0060.471e.59f8
   Designated bridge has priority 100, address 0060.471e.59f8
   Designated port is 20, path cost 0
   Timers: message age 2, forward delay 0, hold 0
```

Transparent Bridging & Frame Relay

Cisco's IOS supports transparent bridging across Frame Relay networks, allowing bridged packets to be encapsulated in Frame Relay frames for transmission. It is especially useful for sending nonroutable proprietary protocols across these networks. Figure 1-6 zooms into the Frame Relay network where remote transparent bridging is implemented between R2,

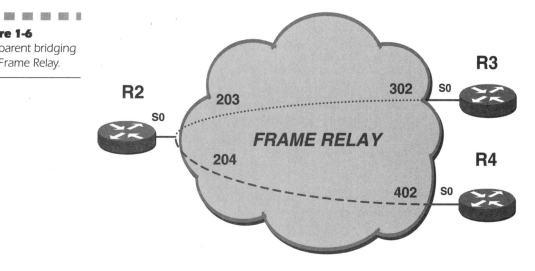

Figure 1-6
Transparent bridging
over Frame Relay.

R3, and R4. Code listings 1-25 through 1-27 illustrate this Frame Relay implementation.

The Frame Relay network illustrated in Figure 1-6 does not support a multicast facility. For R2 the commands frame-relay map bridge 203 broadcast and frame-relay map bridge 204 broadcast are required to define the mapping between R3's and R4's respective MAC addresses and the DLCIs used to bind to these addresses. In the event when a multicast facility is present, these commands will not be necessary, as the facility will be used to learn about the other bridges on the network. The frame-relay map command is not used on point-to-point Frame Relay subinterfaces, but it can be used on multipoint Frame Relay subinterfaces and any physical Frame Relay interfaces (for example S0, S1, etc.). Note that a physical Frame Relay interface is by default multipoint.

Code Listing 1-25
R2 Frame Relay configuration.

```
hostname C4700-R2
!
interface Serial0
 encapsulation frame-relay
 frame-relay lmi-type ansi
!
interface Serial0.1 multipoint
 bandwidth 56
 frame-relay map bridge 204 broadcast
 frame-relay map bridge 203 broadcast
 bridge-group 1
!
bridge 1 protocol ieee
bridge 1 priority 100
```

Code Listing 1-26
R3 Frame Relay configuration.

```
hostname C2500-R3
!
interface Serial0
 encapsulation frame-relay
 frame-relay lmi-type ansi
!
interface Serial0.1 point-to-point
 frame-relay interface-dlci 302
 bridge-group 1
!
bridge 1 protocol ieee
```

Code Listing 1-27
R4 Frame Relay configuration.

```
hostname C2500-R4
!
interface Serial0
 encapsulation frame-relay
 frame-relay lmi-type ansi
!
interface Serial0.1 point-to-point
 frame-relay interface-dlci 402
 bridge-group 1
!
bridge 1 protocol ieee
```

Transparent Bridging & X.25

Cisco's IOS supports transparent bridging across X.25 networks, allows bridged packets to be encapsulated in X.25 frames for transmission, and is especially useful for sending nonroutable proprietary protocols across these networks. Figure 1-7 zooms into the X.25 network where remote transparent bridging is implemented between R1 and R2. Code Listings 1-28 and 1-29 illustrate this X.25 implementation.

Both R1 and R2 use the x25 map bridge command to create a virtual circuit between them for bridging.

Code Listing 1-28
R1 X.25 configuration.

```
hostname C4500-R1
!
interface Serial0
 encapsulation x25
 bandwidth 56
 x25 address 1701225111
 x25 map bridge 1701225222 broadcast
 bridge-group 1
!
bridge 1 protocol ieee
```

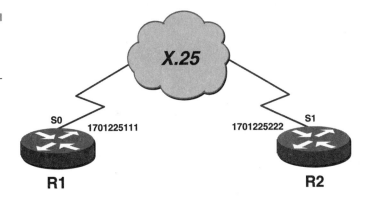

Figure 1-7
Transparent bridging
over X.25.

Code Listing 1-29
R2 X.25 configuration.

```
hostname C4700-R2
!
interface Serial1
 encapsulation x25
 bandwidth 56
 x25 address 1701225222
 x25 map bridge 1701225111 broadcast
 bridge-group 1
!
bridge 1 protocol ieee
bridge 1 priority 100
```

Transparent Bridging & DDR

Cisco's IOS supports transparent bridging over DDR. Figure 1-8 shows the portion of network where remote transparent bridging over DDR is implemented between R1 and R2. Code listings 1-30 and 1-31 illustrate this DDR implementation.

Code Listing 1-30 illustrates the DDR configuration for R1. The dialer map command is used to call up R2 to establish a PPP connectivity when S0 becomes unavailable. The dialer-group 1 command refers to the dialer-list 1 command, and in this case, the list allows all bridged traffic to pass. No refining on the dialer-list is required, as the purpose of the BRI0 interface is to backup S0.

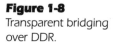

Figure 1-8
Transparent bridging over DDR.

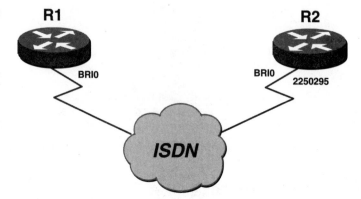

Code Listing 1-30
R1 DDR configuration.

```
hostname C4500-R1
!
username C4700-R2 password cisco
isdn switch-type basic-net3
!
interface BRI0
 encapsulation ppp
 dialer idle-timeout 60
 dialer map bridge name C4700-R2 broadcast 2250295
 dialer load-threshold 120 either
 dialer-group 1
ppp authentication chap
 bridge-group 1
 !
dialer-list 1 protocol bridge permit
bridge 1 protocol ieee
```

Code Listing 1-31
R2 DDR configuration.

```
hostname C4700-R2
!
username C4500-R1 password cisco
isdn switch-type basic-net3
!
interface BRI0

 encapsulation ppp
 ppp authentication chap
 dialer idle-timeout 60
 dialer map bridge name C4500-R1 broadcast
 dialer load-threshold 128 either
 dialer-group 1
 bridge-group 1
 !
dialer-list 1 protocol bridge permit
bridge 1 protocol ieee
bridge 1 priority 100
```

Code Listing 1-31 illustrates the DDR configuration for R2. The `dialer map` command is used to establish a PPP connectivity when R1 makes a call. Note that no ISDN number is supplied here, as R1 will initiate the call. The host name used by the command is R1's. The `dialer-group 1` command refers to the `dialer-list 1` command, and in this case, the list allows all bridged traffic to pass.

Case 1: The X.25 Connectivity between R1 and R2 Fails

Consider Figure 1-9. When the X.25 connectivity between R1 and R2 becomes unavailable, the ISDN backup link will come into effect, with R1 initiating the call.

When this happens, all the routing tables for IP and IPX change. Notice that the IP subnet 170.12.25.252 and the IPX network 25 no longer appear in the tables illustrated in Code Listings 1-32 through 1-39.

Figure 1-9
The X.25 connectivity between R1 and R2 fails.

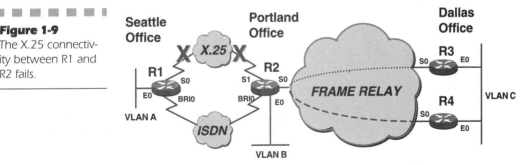

Code Listing 1-32
IP routing table for R1.

```
C4500-R1#show ip route
Codes: C - connected, S - static, I - IGRP, R - RIP, M - mobile, B - BGP
       D - EIGRP, EX - EIGRP external, O - OSPF, IA - OSPF inter area
       N1 - OSPF NSSA external type 1, N2 - OSPF NSSA external type 2
       E1 - OSPF external type 1, E2 - OSPF external type 2, E - EGP
       i - IS-IS, L1 - IS-IS level-1, L2 - IS-IS level-2, * - candidate default
       U - per-user static route, o - ODR

Gateway of last resort is not set

     180.234.0.0/16 is variably subnetted, 2 subnets, 2 masks
D EX    180.234.234.0/24 [170/46482176] via 170.12.26.254, 00:00:27, BRIO
D EX    180.234.34.128/25 [170/46482176] via 170.12.26.254, 00:00:27, BRIO
     160.1.0.0/26 is subnetted, 1 subnets
C       160.1.1.192 is directly connected, Ethernet0
     170.12.0.0/16 is variably subnetted, 3 subnets, 3 masks
C       170.12.26.252/30 is directly connected, BRIO
C       170.12.26.254/32 is directly connected, BRIO
D       170.12.2.224/27 [90/40537600] via 170.12.26.254, 00:00:27, BRIO
```

■ ■

Code Listing 1-33

IPX routing table for R1.

```
C4500-R1#show ipx route
Codes: C - Connected primary network,    c - Connected secondary network
       S - Static, F - Floating static, L - Local (internal), W - IPXWAN
       R - RIP, E - EIGRP, N - NLSP, X - External, A - Aggregate
       s - seconds, u - uses


5 Total IPX routes. Up to 1 parallel paths and 16 hops allowed.

No default route known.

C          10 (NOVELL-ETHER),   Et0
C          26 (PPP),            BR0
R          20 [07/01] via       26.0060.471e.59f8,    40s, BR0
R          34 [08/02] via       26.0060.471e.59f8,    41s, BR0
R         234 [07/02] via       26.0060.471e.59f8,    41s, BR0
```

■ ■

Code Listing 1-34

IP routing table for R2.

```
C4700-R2#show ip route
Codes: C - connected, S - static, I - IGRP, R - RIP, M - mobile, B - BGP
       D - EIGRP, EX - EIGRP external, O - OSPF, IA - OSPF inter area
       N1 - OSPF NSSA external type 1, N2 - OSPF NSSA external type 2
       E1 - OSPF external type 1, E2 - OSPF external type 2, E - EGP
       i - IS-IS, L1 - IS-IS level-1, L2 - IS-IS level-2, * - candidate default
       U - per-user static route, o - ODR

Gateway of last resort is not set

     180.234.0.0/16 is variably subnetted, 2 subnets, 2 masks
C       180.234.234.0/24 is directly connected, Serial0.1
O IA    180.234.34.128/25 [110/1795] via 180.234.234.3, 00:12:35, Serial0.1
     160.1.0.0/16 is subnetted, 1 subnets
D EX    160.1.1.192 [170/40768000] via 170.12.26.253, 00:00:47, BRI0
     170.12.0.0/16 is variably subnetted, 3 subnets, 3 masks
C       170.12.26.252/30 is directly connected, BRI0
C       170.12.26.253/32 is directly connected, BRI0
C       170.12.2.224/27 is directly connected, Ethernet0
```

■ ■

Code Listing 1-35

IPX routing table for R2.

```
C4700-R2#show ipx route
Codes: C - Connected primary network,    c - Connected secondary network
       S - Static, F - Floating static, L - Local (internal), W - IPXWAN
       R - RIP, E - EIGRP, N - NLSP, X - External, A - Aggregate
       s - seconds, u - uses

5 Total IPX routes. Up to 1 parallel paths and 16 hops allowed.

No default route known.

C          20 (NOVELL-ETHER),   Et0
C          26 (UNKNOWN),        BR0
C         234 (UNKNOWN),        Se0.1
R          10 [07/01] via       26.00e0.1e58.6109,     3s, BR0
E          34 [46251776/1] via      234.0000.0c3e.36ce, age 00:13:22,
                                 1u, Se0.1
```

Code Listing 1-36
IP routing table for R3.

```
C2500-R3#show ip route
Codes: C - connected, S - static, I - IGRP, R - RIP, M - mobile, B - BGP
       D - EIGRP, EX - EIGRP external, O - OSPF, IA - OSPF inter area
       N1 - OSPF NSSA external type 1, N2 - OSPF NSSA external type 2
       E1 - OSPF external type 1, E2 - OSPF external type 2, E - EGP
       i - IS-IS, L1 - IS-IS level-1, L2 - IS-IS level-2, * - candidate default
       U - per-user static route, o - ODR

Gateway of last resort is not set

     180.234.0.0/16 is variably subnetted, 2 subnets, 2 masks
C       180.234.234.0/24 is directly connected, Ethernet0
C       180.234.34.128/25 is directly connected, Ethernet0
     160.1.0.0/26 is subnetted, 1 subnets
O E2    160.1.1.192 [110/200] via 180.234.234.2, 00:00:48, Serial0.1
     170.12.0.0/16 is variably subnetted, 3 subnets, 3 masks
O E2    170.12.26.252/30 [110/200] via 180.234.234.2, 00:14:25, Serial0.1
O E2    170.12.26.253/32 [110/200] via 180.234.234.2, 00:14:25, Serial0.1
O E2    170.12.2.224/27 [110/200] via 180.234.234.2, 00:14:25, Serial0.1
```

Code Listing 1-37
IPX routing table for R3.

```
C2500-R3#show ipx route
Codes: C - Connected primary network,    c - Connected secondary network
       S - Static, F - Floating static, L - Local (internal), W - IPXWAN
       R - RIP, E - EIGRP, N - NLSP, X - External, A - Aggregate
       s - seconds, u - uses

5 Total IPX routes. Up to 1 parallel paths and 16 hops allowed.

No default route known.

C        34 (NOVELL-ETHER),  Et0
C       234 (FRAME-RELAY),   Se0.1
E        10 [276864000/2] via      234.0060.471e.59f8, age 00:15:47,
                            1u, Se0.1
E        20 [267008000/1] via      234.0060.471e.59f8, age 00:15:47,
                            1u, Se0.1
E        26 [267008000/1] via      234.0060.471e.59f8, age 00:15:47,
                            1u, Se0.1
```

Code Listing 1-38
IP routing table for R4.

```
C2500-R4#show ip route
Codes: C - connected, S - static, I - IGRP, R - RIP, M - mobile, B - BGP
       D - EIGRP, EX - EIGRP external, O - OSPF, IA - OSPF inter area
       N1 - OSPF NSSA external type 1, N2 - OSPF NSSA external type 2
       E1 - OSPF external type 1, E2 - OSPF external type 2, E - EGP
       i - IS-IS, L1 - IS-IS level-1, L2 - IS-IS level-2, * - candidate default
       U - per-user static route, o - ODR

Gateway of last resort is not set

     180.234.0.0/16 is variably subnetted, 2 subnets, 2 masks
C       180.234.234.0/24 is directly connected, Serial0.1
C       180.234.34.128/25 is directly connected, Ethernet0
     160.1.0.0/26 is subnetted, 1 subnets
O E2    160.1.1.192 [110/200] via 180.234.234.2, 00:01:26, Serial0.1
     170.12.0.0/16 is variably subnetted, 3 subnets, 3 masks
O E2    170.12.26.252/30 [110/200] via 180.234.234.2, 00:16:26, Serial0.1
O E2    170.12.26.253/32 [110/200] via 180.234.234.2, 00:16:26, Serial0.1
O E2    170.12.2.224/27 [110/200] via 180.234.234.2, 00:16:26, Serial0.1
```

■ ▪ |

Code Listing 1-39

IPX routing table for
R4.

```
C2500-R4#show ipx route
Codes: C - Connected primary network,    c - Connected secondary network
       S - Static, F - Floating static, L - Local (internal), W - IPXWAN
       R - RIP, E - EIGRP, N - NLSP, X - External, A - Aggregate
       s - seconds, u - uses

5 Total IPX routes. Up to 1 parallel paths and 16 hops allowed.

No default route known.

C        34 (NOVELL-ETHER),   BV1
C       234 (FRAME-RELAY),    Se0.1
E        10 [276864000/2] via      234.0060.471e.59f8, age 00:17:08,
                            1u, Se0.1
E        20 [267008000/1] via      234.0060.471e.59f8, age 00:17:08,
                            1u, Se0.1
E        26 [267008000/1] via      234.0060.471e.59f8, age 00:17:08,
                            1u, Se0.1
```

The bridging information for R1 and R2 also changes, as illustrated in
Code Listings 1-40 and 1-41.

■ |

Code Listing 1-40

Bridging information
for R1.

```
C4500-R1#show spanning-tree

Bridge Group 1 is executing the IEEE compatible Spanning Tree protocol
    Bridge Identifier has priority 32768, address 00e0.1e58.6109
    Configured hello time 2, max age 20, forward delay 15
    We are the root of the spanning tree
    Topology change flag set, detected flag set
    Times:  hold 1, topology change 30, notification 30
            hello 2, max age 20, forward delay 15, aging 300
    Timers: hello 2, topology change 2, notification 0

Port 6 (BRI0) of bridge group 1 is forwarding
    Port path cost 15625, Port priority 128
    Designated root has priority 32768, address 00e0.1e58.6109
    Designated bridge has priority 32768, address 00e0.1e58.6109
    Designated port is 6, path cost 0
    Timers: message age 0, forward delay 0, hold 0

Port 4 (Ethernet0) of bridge group 1 is forwarding
    Port path cost 100, Port priority 128
    Designated root has priority 32768, address 00e0.1e58.6109
    Designated bridge has priority 32768, address 00e0.1e58.6109
    Designated port is 4, path cost 0
    Timers: message age 0, forward delay 0, hold 0

Port 2 (Serial0) of bridge group 1 is down
    Port path cost 17857, Port priority 128
    Designated root has priority 100, address 0060.471e.59f8
    Designated bridge has priority 32768, address 00e0.1e58.6109
    Designated port is 2, path cost 15625
    Timers: message age 0, forward delay 10, hold 0
```

■ ■

Code Listing 1-41
Bridging information
for R2.

```
C4700-R2#show spanning-tree

Bridge Group 1 is executing the IEEE compatible Spanning Tree protocol
    Bridge Identifier has priority 100, address 0060.471e.59f8
    Configured hello time 2, max age 20, forward delay 15
    We are the root of the spanning tree
    Topology change flag not set, detected flag not set
    Times:  hold 1, topology change 30, notification 30
            hello 2, max age 20, forward delay 15, aging 300
    Timers: hello 1, topology change 0, notification 0

Port 8 (BRI0) of bridge group 1 is forwarding
    Port path cost 15625, Port priority 128
    Designated root has priority 100, address 0060.471e.59f8
    Designated bridge has priority 100, address 0060.471e.59f8
    Designated port is 8, path cost 0
    Timers: message age 0, forward delay 0, hold 0

Port 2 (Ethernet0) of bridge group 1 is forwarding
    Port path cost 100, Port priority 128
    Designated root has priority 100, address 0060.471e.59f8
    Designated bridge has priority 100, address 0060.471e.59f8
    Designated port is 2, path cost 0
    Timers: message age 0, forward delay 0, hold 0

Port 20 (Serial0.1 Frame Relay) of bridge group 1 is forwarding
    Port path cost 17857, Port priority 128
    Designated root has priority 100, address 0060.471e.59f8
    Designated bridge has priority 100, address 0060.471e.59f8
    Designated port is 20, path cost 0
    Timers: message age 0, forward delay 0, hold 0

Port 5 (Serial1) of bridge group 1 is down
    Port path cost 647, Port priority 128
    Designated root has priority 100, address 0060.471e.59f8
    Designated bridge has priority 100, address 0060.471e.59f8
    Designated port is 5, path cost 0
    Timers: message age 0, forward delay 0, hold 0
```

Integrated Routing & Bridging

Using Integrated Routing and Bridging (IRB), a protocol may be both routed and bridged on a given interface. IRB is a Cisco IOS Release 11.2 feature. Specifically, nonroutable protocols will be bridged through the bridged interfaces belonging to the same bridge group, while routable protocols will be routed to other routed interfaces or bridged groups. In other words, IRB enables a packet of the same protocol to be switched between a bridged interface and a routed interface in the same router, and vice versa.

Some of the advantages of IRB are:

- It can be used to interconnect a bridged network and a routed network. This is useful during migration phases when you need to combine both kinds of networks to form a single enterprise network.

- It can be used to conserve logical network addresses for routable protocols. In other words, these protocols are being bridged instead.

- It can optimize network performance by bridging local traffic. A typical example is to use bridging between different VLANs instead of routing.

IRB uses the concept of Bridge-Group Virtual Interface (BVI), which functions like a routed interface that represents a bridge group to a routing domain. The interface number of the BVI is the bridge group number that this virtual interface represents. This number is the link between the BVI and the bridge group.

When a BVI is configured with a network address and routing is enabled, an incoming routable packet entering through a routed interface that is destined for a host in a bridged segment will be processed as follows:

1. The packet is routed to the BVI.

2. The BVI then forwards the packet to the bridging engine.

3. The bridging engine then forwards the packet out of a bridged interface whose bridge group corresponds to the BVI number.

Similarly, packets coming in through a bridged interface that are destined for a host on a routed network will initially be forwarded to the BVI, which will in turn forward them to the routing engine before routing them out the routed interface.

For the BVI to function properly, it must have the necessary addresses and attributes, just like any routed interfaces. The BVI uses the MAC address (the lowest number) from one of the bridged interfaces in the bridge group that its interface number represents.

Code Listing 1-42 illustrates the IRB configuration for R4.

Code Listing 1-42
R4 IRB configuration.

```
hostname C2500-R4
!
ipx routing 00e0.1e5f.dd0d
!
interface Ethernet0
 bridge-group 1
```

Code Listing 1-42
(continued)

```
!
interface BVI1
 ipx network 34
!
bridge irb
bridge 1 protocol ieee
 bridge 1 route ip
 bridge 1 route ipx
 no bridge 1 bridge ip
```

In Code Listing 1-42, R4 is configured to perform IRB specifically for IPX. Notice that `interface BVI1` corresponds to the `bridge-group 1` that is being used throughout the enterprise network. An IPX network number of 34 is assigned to the interface to enable it to perform IPX routing when necessary. IRB is enabled by the command `bridge irb`.

By default, the route/bridge behavior in a bridge group when IRB is enabled is to bridge all packets. In this case, the commands `bridge 1 route ip` and `bridge 1 route ipx` are used explicitly to enable routing on top of the default bridging for IP and IPX. However, in our scenario we need only to route/bridge IPX, and thus the command `no bridge 1 bridge ip` is used explicitly to disable the bridging function for IP. That is, IP packets will be routed and not bridged, whereas IPX packets will be both routed and bridged whenever necessary.

Packets of nonroutable protocols will still be bridged. Note that protocol attributes like network addresses should not be configured on the bridged interfaces, and bridging attributes cannot be configured on the BVI. Notice that E0 has no IPX network number, and the IPX network number for the BVI corresponds to the same network number for VLAN C.

Code Listing 1-43 illustrates the BVI MAC address for R4.

Code Listing 1-43
BVI MAC address for R4.

```
C2500-R4#show interfaces bvi 1
BVI1 is up, line protocol is up
  Hardware is BVI, address is 00e0.1e5f.dd0d (bia 0000.0000.0000)
  MTU 1500 bytes, BW 10000 Kbit, DLY 5000 usec, rely 255/255, load 1/
255
  Encapsulation ARPA, loopback not set, keepalive set (10 sec)
  ARP type: ARPA, ARP Timeout 04:00:00
  Last input never, output never, output hang never
  Last clearing of "show interface" counters never
  Queueing strategy: fifo
  Output queue 0/0, 0 drops; input queue 0/75, 0 drops
  5 minute input rate 0 bits/sec, 0 packets/sec
  5 minute output rate 0 bits/sec, 0 packets/sec
     0 packets input, 0 bytes, 0 no buffer
```

Code Listing 1-43
(continued)

```
Received 0 broadcasts, 0 runts, 0 giants
0 input errors, 0 CRC, 0 frame, 0 overrun, 0 ignored, 0 abort
2474 packets output, 0 bytes, 0 underruns
0 output errors, 0 collisions, 0 interface resets
0 output buffer failures, 0 output buffers swapped out
```

Code Listing 1-44 illustrates the BVI IPX information for R4.

Code Listing 1-44
BVI IPX Information
for R4.

```
C2500-R4#show ipx interface bvi 1
BVI1 is up, line protocol is up
  IPX address is 34.00e0.1e5f.dd0d, NOVELL-ETHER [up]
  Delay of this IPX network, in ticks is 2 throughput 0 link delay 0
  IPXWAN processing not enabled on this interface.
  IPX SAP update interval is 1 minute(s)
  IPX type 20 propagation packet forwarding is disabled
  Incoming access list is not set
  Outgoing access list is not set
  IPX helper access list is not set
  SAP GNS processing enabled, delay 0 ms, output filter list is not
set
  SAP Input filter list is not set
  SAP Output filter list is not set
  SAP Router filter list is not set
  Input filter list is not set
  Output filter list is not set
  Router filter list is not set
  Netbios Input host access list is not set
  Netbios Input bytes access list is not set
  Netbios Output host access list is not set
  Netbios Output bytes access list is not set
  Updates each 60 seconds, aging multiples RIP: 3 SAP: 3
  SAP interpacket delay is 55 ms, maximum size is 480 bytes
  RIP interpacket delay is 55 ms, maximum size is 432 bytes
  IPX accounting is disabled
  IPX fast switching is configured (enabled)
  RIP packets received 6, RIP packets sent 2470
  SAP packets received 3, SAP packets sent 5
```

Code Listing 1-45 illustrates the route/bridge information for R4.

Code Listing 1-45
Route/bridge infor-
mation for R4.

```
C2500-R4#show interfaces irb

BVI1

  Routed protocols on BVI1:
    ipx

Ethernet0
```

■ |

Code Listing 1-45
(continued)

```
Routed protocols on Ethernet0:
   ip         ipx

Bridged protocols on Ethernet0:
   appletalk  clns      decnet     vines
   apollo     ipx       xns

Software MAC address filter on Ethernet0
   Hash Len    Address         Matches  Act    Type
   0x00:  0 a.sffff.ffff.ffff     1903 RCV Physical broadcast
   0x0C:  0 0000.0c07.ac00           4 RCV Interface MAC address
   0x13:  0 00e0.1e5f.dd0d           5 RCV Bridge-group Virtual Interface
   0x2A:  0 0900.2b01.0001           0 RCV DEC spanning tree
   0xC2:  0 0180.c200.0000       54137 RCV IEEE spanning tree

Serial0

Not bridging this sub-interface.

Serial0.1

Routed protocols on Serial0.1:
   ip         ipx

Bridged protocols on Serial0.1:
   appletalk  clns      decnet     vines
   apollo     ipx       xns

Software MAC address filter on Serial0.1
   Hash Len    Address         Matches  Act    Type
   0x00:  0 ffff.ffff.ffff           0 RCV Physical broadcast
   0x13:  0 00e0.1e5f.dd0d           0 RCV Interface MAC address
   0x13:  1 00e0.1e5f.dd0d           0 RCV Bridge-group Virtual Interface
   0x2A:  0 0900.2b01.0001           0 RCV DEC spanning tree
   0xC2:  0 0180.c200.0000           0 RCV IEEE spanning tree
```

Code Listing 1-46 illustrates the BVI MAC address for R3.

■ |

Code Listing 1-46
Route/bridge infor-
mation for R3.

```
C2500-R3#show interfaces irb

Ethernet0

Routed protocols on Ethernet0:
   ip         ipx

Bridged protocols on Ethernet0:
   appletalk  clns      decnet     vines
   apollo     xns

Software MAC address filter on Ethernet0
   Hash Len    Address         Matches  Act    Type
   0x00:  0 ffff.ffff.ffff         665 RCV Physical broadcast
   0x2A:  0 0900.2b01.0001           0 RCV DEC spanning tree
   0x57:  0 0100.5e00.0009        5224 RCV IP multicast
```

■ ■

Code Listing 1-46
(continued)

```
0x58:  0 0100.5e00.0006       0 RCV IP multicast
0x5B:  0 0100.5e00.0005       0 RCV IP multicast
0x5C:  0 0100.5e00.0002   48186 RCV IP multicast
0xC0:  0 0100.0ccc.cccc    2415 RCV CDP
0xC2:  0 0180.c200.0000   18221 RCV IEEE spanning tree
0xC2:  1 0000.0c3e.36ce       4 RCV Interface MAC address

Serial0

Not bridging this sub-interface.

Serial0.1

Routed protocols on Serial0.1:
  ip         ipx

Bridged protocols on Serial0.1:
  appletalk  clns        decnet      vines
  apollo     xns

Software MAC address filter on Serial0.1
  Hash Len    Address      Matches Act      Type
  0x00:  0 ffff.ffff.ffff       0 RCV Physical broadcast
  0x2A:  0 0900.2b01.0001       0 RCV DEC spanning tree
  0xC0:  0 0100.0ccc.cccc       0 RCV CDP
  0xC2:  0 0000.0c3e.36ce       0 RCV Interface MAC address
  0xC2:  1 0180.c200.0000       0 RCV IEEE spanning tree
```

Notice that since IRB is configured in R4, IPX falls under the routed and bridged protocols categories for interfaces E0 and S0.1. Compare this with R3, where IPX corresponds only to the routed protocols category. This is because IPX by default is a routable protocol, and R3 has been configured for IPX routing with the necessary protocol attributes, like IPX network numbers. R3 will not both route and bridge IPX unless IRB is enabled.

Case 2: The Frame Relay Connectivity between R2 and R3 Fails

Consider Figure 1-10. The IP routing table for R2 and R3 changes when the Frame Relay connectivity between them becomes unavailable.

Code Listing 1-47 shows the IP routing table for R2.

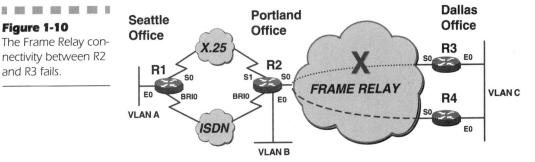

Figure 1-10
The Frame Relay connectivity between R2 and R3 fails.

Code Listing 1-47
IP routing table for R2.

```
C4700-R2#show ip route
Codes: C - connected, S - static, I - IGRP, R - RIP, M - mobile, B - BGP
       D - EIGRP, EX - EIGRP external, O - OSPF, IA - OSPF inter area
       N1 - OSPF NSSA external type 1, N2 - OSPF NSSA external type 2
       E1 - OSPF external type 1, E2 - OSPF external type 2, E - EGP
       i - IS-IS, L1 - IS-IS level-1, L2 - IS-IS level-2, * - candidate default
       U - per-user static route, o - ODR

Gateway of last resort is not set

     180.234.0.0/16 is variably subnetted, 2 subnets, 2 masks
C       180.234.234.0/24 is directly connected, Serial0.1
O E2    180.234.34.128/25 [110/200] via 180.234.234.4, 00:00:06, Serial0.1
     160.1.0.0/16 is subnetted, 1 subnets
D EX    160.1.1.192 [170/2425856] via 170.12.25.253, 00:00:06, Serial1
     170.12.0.0/16 is variably subnetted, 3 subnets, 2 masks
C       170.12.26.252/30 is directly connected, BRI0
C       170.12.25.252/30 is directly connected, Serial1
C       170.12.2.224/27 is directly connected, Ethernet0
```

In Code Listing 1-47, the route entry 180.234.34.128 is now an OSPF E2 route instead of the previous OSPF IA route. This is because once the link between R2 and R3 goes down, the OSPF Area 10 will become disjointed from OSPF Area 0. When this happens, the subnet 180.234.34.128 is no longer learned through OSPF but via RIPv2 instead. RIPv2 serves as a backup routing protocol for R3 so that in the event OSPF becomes dysfunctional, it will take over the routing task. Code Listing 1-48 shows the IP routing table for R3.

Code Listing 1-48
IP routing table for R3.

```
C2500-R3#show ip route
Codes: C - connected, S - static, I - IGRP, R - RIP, M - mobile, B - BGP
       D - EIGRP, EX - EIGRP external, O - OSPF, IA - OSPF inter area
       N1 - OSPF NSSA external type 1, N2 - OSPF NSSA external type 2
       E1 - OSPF external type 1, E2 - OSPF external type 2, E - EGP
       i - IS-IS, L1 - IS-IS level-1, L2 - IS-IS level-2, * - candidate default
       U - per-user static route, o - ODR

Gateway of last resort is not set
```

■ |

Code Listing 1-48
(continued)

```
         180.234.0.0/16 is variably subnetted, 2 subnets, 2 masks
R           180.234.234.0/24 [120/1] via 180.234.34.130, 00:00:07, Ethernet0
C           180.234.34.128/25 is directly connected, Ethernet0
         160.1.0.0/26 is subnetted, 1 subnets
R           160.1.1.192 [120/3] via 180.234.34.130, 00:00:07, Ethernet0
         170.12.0.0/16 is variably subnetted, 3 subnets, 2 masks
R           170.12.26.252/30 [120/3] via 180.234.34.130, 00:00:07, Ethernet0
R           170.12.25.252/30 [120/3] via 180.234.34.130, 00:00:07, Ethernet0
R           170.12.2.224/27 [120/3] via 180.234.34.130, 00:00:07, Ethernet0
```

Similarly, the connectivity failure between R2 and R3 causes R3 to lose its IPX EIGRP functionality, since the router learns the IPX routes over the Frame Relay network using this routing protocol only. When this happens, the default IPX routing protocol, IPX RIP, will take over the routing task. Consequently, the IPX routing table for R3, as shown in Code Listing 1-49, will consist of IPX RIP routes.

■ |

Code Listing 1-49

IPX routing table for R3.

```
C2500-R3#show ipx route
Codes: C - Connected primary network,    c - Connected secondary network
       S - Static, F - Floating static, L - Local (internal), W - IPXWAN
       R - RIP, E - EIGRP, N - NLSP, X - External, A - Aggregate
       s - seconds, u - uses

6 Total IPX routes. Up to 1 parallel paths and 16 hops allowed.

No default route known.

C         34 (NOVELL-ETHER),   Et0
R         10 [10/02] via       34.00e0.1e5f.dd0d,    50s, Et0
R         20 [04/02] via       34.00e0.1e5f.dd0d,    50s, Et0
R         25 [03/01] via       34.00e0.1e5f.dd0d,    50s, Et0
R         26 [04/02] via       34.00e0.1e5f.dd0d,    50s, Et0
R        234 [03/01] via       34.00e0.1e5f.dd0d,    50s, Et0
```

We shall now look at how IRB comes into action. When the connectivity between R2 and R3 becomes unavailable, the bridging path between these routers is lost too. In this case, there is only one path left to VLAN C, and that is through R4. IRB is enabled in R4 and is configured such that IPX traffic is bridged through E0 when the link between R2 and R3 goes down. IPX will not be routed out of E0, as no IPX network number has been configured on this interface. The BVI shares the same IPX network number with VLAN C. IPX traffic will nevertheless be able to route out of interface S0.1. R4 will route IPX packets over from the Frame Relay network and bridge them across to VLAN C. Vice versa, R4 will bridge IPX traffic from VLAN C and route them out to the Frame Relay network. In other words, R4 will bridge IPX traffic destined to VLAN C and route IPX traffic going out to the Frame Relay network. Note that the IPX routing table for all four routers is transparent to this route/

bridge behavior and will still reflect the six different IPX routes respectively.

However, the connectivity failure will cause a topology change for the bridged network and initiate a spanning tree recalculation. The corresponding bridge ports for the bridging path between R2 and R3 are reflected as shown in Code Listings 1-50 and 1-51. R4's bridge port to VLAN C has changed from the blocking state to the forwarding state illustrated in Code Listing 1-52, as there is no longer any physical loop in the bridged network. The state for the rest of the bridge ports remains unchanged.

Code Listing 1-50

Bridging information for R2.

```
C4700-R2#show spanning-tree

Bridge Group 1 is executing the IEEE compatible Spanning Tree protocol
  Bridge Identifier has priority 100, address 0060.471e.59f8
  Configured hello time 2, max age 20, forward delay 15
  We are the root of the spanning tree
  Topology change flag not set, detected flag not set
  Times:  hold 1, topology change 30, notification 30
          hello 2, max age 20, forward delay 15, aging 300
  Timers: hello 2, topology change 0, notification 0

Port 8 (BRI0) of bridge group 1 is forwarding
   Port path cost 15625, Port priority 128
   Designated root has priority 100, address 0060.471e.59f8
   Designated bridge has priority 100, address 0060.471e.59f8
   Designated port is 8, path cost 0
   Timers: message age 0, forward delay 0, hold 0

Port 2 (Ethernet0) of bridge group 1 is forwarding
   Port path cost 100, Port priority 128
   Designated root has priority 100, address 0060.471e.59f8
   Designated bridge has priority 100, address 0060.471e.59f8
   Designated port is 2, path cost 0
   Timers: message age 0, forward delay 0, hold 0

Port 20 (Serial0.1 Frame Relay) of bridge group 1 is down
   Port path cost 17857, Port priority 128
   Designated root has priority 100, address 0060.471e.59f8
   Designated bridge has priority 100, address 0060.471e.59f8
   Designated port is 20, path cost 0
   Timers: message age 0, forward delay 0, hold 0

Port 5 (Serial1) of bridge group 1 is forwarding
   Port path cost 647, Port priority 128
   Designated root has priority 100, address 0060.471e.59f8
   Designated bridge has priority 100, address 0060.471e.59f8
   Designated port is 5, path cost 0
   Timers: message age 0, forward delay 0, hold 0
```

Code Listing 1-51

Bridging information
for R3.

```
C2500-R3#show spanning-tree

Bridge Group 1 is executing the IEEE compatible Spanning Tree protocol
   Bridge Identifier has priority 32768, address 0000.0c3e.36ce
   Configured hello time 2, max age 20, forward delay 15
   Current root has priority 100, address 0060.471e.59f8
   Root port is 2 (Ethernet0), cost of root path is 747
   Topology change flag not set, detected flag not set
   Times:  hold 1, topology change 30, notification 30
           hello 2, max age 20, forward delay 15, aging 300
   Timers: hello 0, topology change 0, notification 0

  Port 2 (Ethernet0) of bridge group 1 is forwarding
     Port path cost 100, Port priority 128
     Designated root has priority 100, address 0060.471e.59f8
     Designated bridge has priority 32768, address 00e0.1e5f.dd0d
     Designated port is 2, path cost 647
     Timers: message age 1, forward delay 0, hold 0

  Port 5 (Serial0.1 Frame Relay) of bridge group 1 is down
     Port path cost 647, Port priority 128
     Designated root has priority 100, address 0060.471e.59f8
     Designated bridge has priority 32768, address 0000.0c3e.36ce
     Designated port is 5, path cost 747
     Timers: message age 0, forward delay 8, hold 0
```

Code Listing 1-52

Bridging information
for R4.

```
C2500-R4#show spanning-tree

Bridge Group 1 is executing the IEEE compatible Spanning Tree protocol
   Bridge Identifier has priority 32768, address 00e0.1e5f.dd0d
   Configured hello time 2, max age 20, forward delay 15
   Current root has priority 100, address 0060.471e.59f8
   Root port is 6 (Serial0.1), cost of root path is 647
   Topology change flag not set, detected flag not set
   Times:  hold 1, topology change 30, notification 30
            hello 2, max age 20, forward delay 15, aging 300
   Timers: hello 0, topology change 0, notification 0

  Port 2 (Ethernet0) of bridge group 1 is forwarding
     Port path cost 100, Port priority 128
     Designated root has priority 100, address 0060.471e.59f8
     Designated bridge has priority 32768, address 00e0.1e5f.dd0d
     Designated port is 2, path cost 647
     Timers: message age 0, forward delay 0, hold 0

  Port 6 (Serial0.1 Frame Relay) of bridge group 1 is forwarding
     Port path cost 647, Port priority 128
     Designated root has priority 100, address 0060.471e.59f8
     Designated bridge has priority 100, address 0060.471e.59f8
     Designated port is 20, path cost 0
     Timers: message age 1, forward delay 0, hold 0
```

Summary

Chapter 1 covered an important aspect of internetworking; that is, bridging. Bridging is useful because it can send and receive nonroutable traffic like NetBIOS and SNA.

Transparent bridging mainly applies to Ethernet environments and uses the spanning tree algorithm to prevent loops. Communication between the bridges is conversed through configuration messages called bridge protocol data units (BPDUs).

Normally, in today's enterprise networks, standard and proprietary protocols are bound to be present. In the case scenario, a routed network and a bridged network were implemented. Transparent bridging can also be configured for different WAN implementations like Frame Relay, X.25, and DDR. Based on these implementations, the concept of integrated routing and bridging, and how routing and bridging can complement and backup each other in a contemporary network, were demonstrated.

References

1. Black, U. *Physical Level Interfaces and Protocols.* Los Alamitos, California: IEEE Computer Society Press, 1988.

2. Digital Equipment Corporation, Intel Corporation, Xerox Corporation. *The Ethernet, A Local Area Network, Data Link Layer and Physical Layer Specifications.* Version 2.0, November 1982.

3. Documentation CD-ROM, Cisco Systems, Inc., 1998.

4. IEEE 802.1D Standard for Local Area Network MAC Bridges, ANSI/ IEEE Standard, October 1985.

5. IEEE 802.3–Local Area Networks Standard, 802.3 Carrier Sense Multiple Access, ANSI/IEEE Standard, October 1985.

6. Miller, M. A. *LAN Protocol Handbook.* San Mateo, California: MT&T Books, 1990.

7. Perlman, R. *Interconnections: Bridges and Routers.* Reading, Massachusetts: Addison-Wesley Publishing Company, Inc., 1992.

8. Stallings, W. *Data and Computer Communications.* New York: Macmillan Publishing Company, 1991.

9. Tannenbaum, A. S. *Computer Networks*, 2nd ed. Englewood Cliffs, New Jersey: Prentice Hall, 1988.

2

Source-Route Bridging

Introduction

The Source-Route Bridging (SRB) algorithm was initially developed by IBM to interconnect multiple physical Token Rings into one logical network segment. This was then proposed to the IEEE 802.5 committee that eventually adopted SRB into the IEEE 802.5 Token Ring specification.

SRB technology is a combination of bridging and routing functions because a source-route bridge can, besides bridging, also make routing decisions based on the content of the MAC frame header. However, the routing function is confined at the MAC layer; this permits the higher-layer protocols to execute their tasks more efficiently and also allows the LAN to be expanded (or extended) transparently to these protocols.

Source-Route Bridging Overview

SRB Operation

With SRB, the entire route to destination is resolved before any data is sent. To achieve this, hosts use explorer packets to locate the destination hosts. SRB uses three types of explorer packets:

- Specific route or local ring explorer
- All-rings/all-routes explorer
- Spanning explorer

Consider Figure 2-1. Assume that initially Host A has some data to send to Host B and does not know whether Host B is on the same or on a different Token Ring segment.

To verify this, Host A sends out a local ring explorer. If the frame returns with a positive indication that Host B has seen it, Host A will presume that Host B is in the same segment. If not, Host A will infer that Host B is on another remote ring segment. In the latter case, Host A sends an all-path explorer to pinpoint the exact remote segment where Host B is located. Each bridge receiving the explorer frame copies the frame onto all outbound ports, and route information is added to the explorer frames as they traverse across the SRB internetwork. Inside the explorer is the Routing Information Field (RIF), which contains a map of the path taken by this explorer packet. After a route is selected, it is

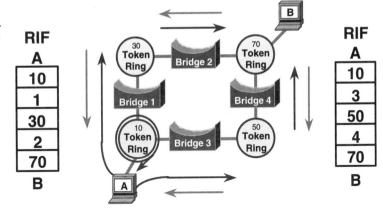

Figure 2-1
A simple SRB Network.

inserted into this field. Note that the presence of routing information within the frame is indicated by the setting of the most significant bit within the source address field, called the routing information indicator (RII) bit, as illustrated in Figure 2-2.

Eventually, when Host A's explorer frames reach Host B, Host B responds to each frame individually by changing the direction bit in the routing control field of the RIF and sending the packet back along the same path on which it has arrived. Host A receives the following two routes to Host B, which are comprised of a series of rings and bridges:

- RING 10 to Bridge 1 to RING 30 to Bridge 2 to RING 70

- RING 10 to Bridge 3 to RING 50 to Bridge 4 to RING 70

When Host A receives back all the response frames, it selects a path based on the suggested criteria defined in the IEEE 802.5 specification. These include:

- First frame received

- Response with the minimum number of hops

- Response with the largest allowed frame size

- Different combinations of the above criteria

Typically the path information contained in the first frame received will be used.

IEEE 802.5 Frame Format

The RIF is part of the IEEE 802.5 Token Ring Frame and is structured as illustrated in Figure 2-2.

The routing information field (RIF) is made up of a two-byte routing control (RC) field and multiple two-byte routing descriptor (RD) fields. Note that the IBM Token Ring specifies a maximum of eight rings and seven bridges (N=18 bytes), whereas the IEEE 802.5 Token Ring specifies a maximum of 14 rings and 13 bridges (N=30 bytes).

The routing control (RC) field consists of the following:

- Type field–three bits
  - Specific route
  - 100 = All rings/all-routes
  - 110 = Spanning route
- Length field–five bits (this field determines the length of the RIF, measured in bytes)
- Direction–one bit (this field determines which way to interpret the RIF)
- Largest frame–three bits (this field indicates the largest frame accepted on route to destination)

Figure 2-2

IEEE 802.5 Token Ring frame format.

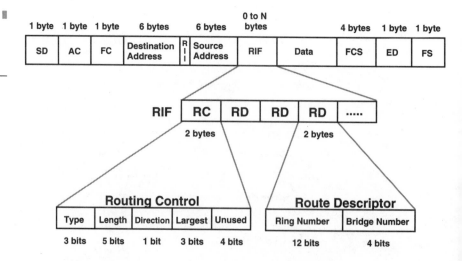

The path to the destination uses a combination of ring and bridge numbers that represent the possible paths the source node might use to send packets to the destination. Each ring number in the RIF field represents a single Token Ring in the SRB network and is denoted by a unique 12-bit ring number. Each bridge number represents a bridge between two Token Rings in the SRB network and is denoted by a unique four-bit bridge number. This information is derived from explorer packets traversing the SRB network, and the routing descriptor (RD) field lists each ring and bridge that are negotiated:

- Ring number–12 bits (defines a unique ring number within the network)

- Bridge number–four bits (defines a unique bridge number connecting two rings)

Case Scenario

Figure 2-3 illustrates the overall network scenario that will be referenced throughout this chapter. This enterprise network spans across two remote campuses: Santa Clara and San Jose. The Santa Clara campus is interconnected to the San Jose campus via a HDLC link. Within the Santa Clara campus, R1 and R2 are interconnected to VLAN 12, and R1 is also attached to RING 1. Similarly, in the San Jose campus, R3 and R4 are interconnected to RING 34, and R4 also internetworks RING 4 and VLAN 4 together.

End systems running on various network protocols (both routable and nonroutable) reside in each LAN (Ethernets and Token Rings). IP is the routable protocol in this scenario, whereas SNA and NetBIOS are the nonroutable ones.

IP Setup

Consider Figure 2-4. The two campus networks are in the same IP EIGRP Autonomous System (AS) 130. This sets up the IP backbone for Remote Source-Route Bridging (RSRB) over TCP/IP between R2 and R3 in later sections. Code Listings 2-1 through 2-8 illustrate this.

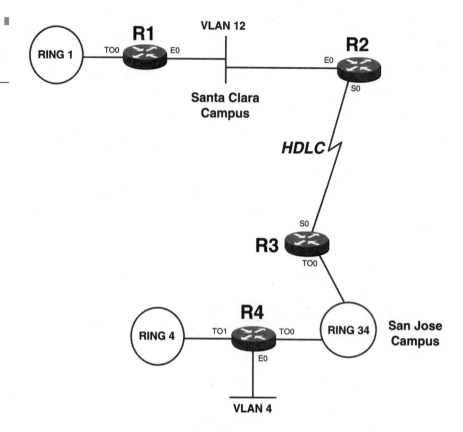

Figure 2-3
The overall network topology.

Code Listing 2-1
IP configuration for R1.

```
hostname C2500-R1
!
interface Ethernet0
 ip address 130.13.12.1 255.255.255.0
!
interface TokenRing0
 ip address 130.13.1.1 255.255.255.0
 ring-speed 16
!
router eigrp 130
 network 130.13.0.0
 no auto-summary
```

1. Code Listing 2-1 illustrates the IP configuration for R1. The Ethernet interface, E0, is in subnet 130.13.12.0 with a mask of 24 bits, belonging to the same subnet as R2's E0.

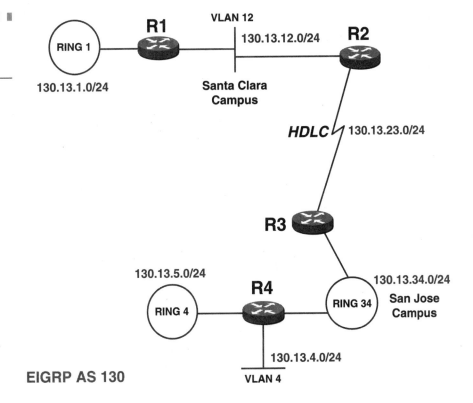

Figure 2-4
The overall IP network.

R1

RING 1

130.13.1.0/24

VLAN 12
130.13.12.0/24

R2

Santa Clara
Campus

HDLC 130.13.23.0/24

R3

130.13.5.0/24

R4

RING 4

RING 34

130.13.34.0/24

San Jose
Campus

130.13.4.0/24

VLAN 4

EIGRP AS 130

2. The Token Ring interface, TO0, is in subnet 130.13.1.0 with a mask of 24 bits. The ring speed is 16 Mbps.

3. R1 is running IP EIGRP. The EIGRP routing protocol is in autonomous system 130 spanning across both E0 and TO0. The no auto-summary command disables the default auto-summary feature of the routing protocol.

Code Listing 2-2 illustrates the IP routing table for R1.

■ ▮ ▮ ▮ |

Code Listing 2-2

IP routing table for R1.

```
C2500-R1#show ip route
Codes: C - connected, S - static, I - IGRP, R - RIP, M - mobile, B - BGP
       D - EIGRP, EX - EIGRP external, O - OSPF, IA - OSPF inter area
       N1 - OSPF NSSA external type 1, N2 - OSPF NSSA external type 2
       E1 - OSPF external type 1, E2 - OSPF external type 2, E - EGP
       i - IS-IS, L1 - IS-IS level-1, L2 - IS-IS level-2, * - candidate default
       U - per-user static route, o - ODR

Gateway of last resort is not set

     130.13.0.0/24 is subnetted, 6 subnets
C       130.13.12.0 is directly connected, Ethernet0
D       130.13.5.0 [90/46284032] via 130.13.12.2, 02:09:47, Ethernet0
D       130.13.4.0 [90/46293504] via 130.13.12.2, 02:10:25, Ethernet0
C       130.13.1.0 is directly connected, TokenRing0
D       130.13.23.0 [90/46251776] via 130.13.12.2, 02:22:36, Ethernet0
D       130.13.34.0 [90/46267904] via 130.13.12.2, 02:18:47, Ethernet0
```

■ ▮ ▮ ▮ |

Code Listing 2-3

IP configuration for R2.

```
hostname C2500-R2
!
interface Ethernet0
 ip address 130.13.12.2 255.255.255.0
!
interface Serial0
 ip address 130.13.23.2 255.255.255.0
 bandwidth 56
!
router eigrp 130
 network 130.13.0.0
 no auto-summary
```

1. Code Listing 2-3 illustrates the IP configuration for R2. The Ethernet interface, E0, is in subnet 130.13.12.0 with a mask of 24 bits, belonging to the same subnet as R1's E0.

2. The Serial interface, S0, is in subnet 130.13.23.0 with a mask of 24 bits. R2 is interconnected to R3 via HDLC through S0.

3. R2 is running IP EIGRP. The EIGRP routing protocol is in autonomous system 130 spanning across both E0 and S0. The no auto-summary command disables the default auto-summary feature of the routing protocol.

Code Listing 2-4 illustrates the IP routing table for R2.

■ |

Code Listing 2-4

IP routing table for R2.

```
C2500-R2#show ip route
Codes: C - connected, S - static, I - IGRP, R - RIP, M - mobile, B - BGP
       D - EIGRP, EX - EIGRP external, O - OSPF, IA - OSPF inter area
       N1 - OSPF NSSA external type 1, N2 - OSPF NSSA external type 2
       E1 - OSPF external type 1, E2 - OSPF external type 2, E - EGP
       i - IS-IS, L1 - IS-IS level-1, L2 - IS-IS level-2, * - candidate default
       U - per-user static route, o - ODR

Gateway of last resort is not set

     130.13.0.0/24 is subnetted, 6 subnets
C       130.13.12.0 is directly connected, Ethernet0
D       130.13.5.0 [90/46258432] via 130.13.23.3, 02:10:19, Serial0
D       130.13.4.0 [90/46267904] via 130.13.23.3, 02:10:56, Serial0
D       130.13.1.0 [90/297728] via 130.13.12.1, 02:22:14, Ethernet0
C       130.13.23.0 is directly connected, Serial0
D       130.13.34.0 [90/46242304] via 130.13.23.3, 02:19:19, Serial0
```

■ |

Code Listing 2-5

IP configuration for R3.

```
hostname C2500-R3
!
interface Serial0
 ip address 130.13.23.3 255.255.255.0
 bandwidth 56
!
interface TokenRing0
 ip address 130.13.34.3 255.255.255.0
 ring-speed 16
!
router eigrp 130
 network 130.13.0.0
 no auto-summary
```

1. Code Listing 2-5 illustrates the IP configuration for R3. The Token Ring interface, TO0, is in subnet 130.13.34.0 with a mask of 24 bits, belonging to the same subnet as R4's TO0. The ring speed is 16 Mbps.

2. The Serial interface, S0, is in subnet 130.13.23.0 with a mask of 24 bits. R3 is interconnected to R2 via HDLC through S0.

3. R3 is running IP EIGRP. The EIGRP routing protocol is in autonomous system 130 spanning across both TO0 and S0. The no auto-summary command disables the default auto-summary feature of the routing protocol.

Code Listing 2-6 illustrates the IP routing table for R3.

Code Listing 2-6

IP routing table for R3.

```
C2500-R3#show ip route
Codes: C - connected, S - static, I - IGRP, R - RIP, M - mobile, B - BGP
       D - EIGRP, EX - EIGRP external, O - OSPF, IA - OSPF inter area
       N1 - OSPF NSSA external type 1, N2 - OSPF NSSA external type 2
       E1 - OSPF external type 1, E2 - OSPF external type 2, E - EGP
       i - IS-IS, L1 - IS-IS level-1, L2 - IS-IS level-2, * - candidate default
       U - per-user static route, o - ODR

Gateway of last resort is not set

     130.13.0.0/24 is subnetted, 6 subnets
D       130.13.12.0 [90/46251776] via 130.13.23.2, 02:11:02, Serial0
D       130.13.5.0 [90/192256] via 130.13.34.4, 02:10:24, TokenRing0
D       130.13.4.0 [90/297728] via 130.13.34.4, 02:11:02, TokenRing0
D       130.13.1.0 [90/46267904] via 130.13.23.2, 02:11:02, Serial0
C       130.13.23.0 is directly connected, Serial0
C       130.13.34.0 is directly connected, TokenRing0
```

Code Listing 2-7

IP configuration for R4.

```
hostname C4700-R4
!
interface Ethernet0
 ip address 130.13.4.4 255.255.255.0
 media-type 10BaseT
!
interface TokenRing0
 ip address 130.13.34.4 255.255.255.0
 ring-speed 16
!
interface TokenRing1
 ip address 130.13.5.4 255.255.255.0
 ring-speed 16
!
router eigrp 130
 network 130.13.0.0
 no auto-summary
```

1. Code Listing 2-7 illustrates the IP configuration for R4. The Ethernet interface, E0, is in subnet 130.13.4.0 with a mask of 24 bits. The 10BaseT interface is used.

2. The Token Ring interface, TO0, is in subnet 130.13.34.0 with a mask of 24 bits, belonging to the same subnet as interface R3's TO0. The ring speed is 16 Mbps.

3. The Token Ring interface, TO1, is in subnet 130.13.5.0 with a mask of 24 bits. The ring speed is 16 Mbps.

4. R4 is running IP EIGRP. The EIGRP routing protocol is in autonomous system 130 spanning across E0, TO0, and TO1. The no auto-summary command disables the default auto-summary feature of the routing protocol.

Code Listing 2-8 illustrates the IP routing table for R4.

Code Listing 2-8
IP routing table for R4.

```
C4700-R4#show ip route
Codes: C - connected, S - static, I - IGRP, R - RIP, M - mobile, B - BGP
       D - EIGRP, EX - EIGRP external, O - OSPF, IA - OSPF inter area
       N1 - OSPF NSSA external type 1, N2 - OSPF NSSA external type 2
       E1 - OSPF external type 1, E2 - OSPF external type 2, E - EGP
       i - IS-IS, L1 - IS-IS level-1, L2 - IS-IS level-2, * - candidate default
       U - per-user static route, o - ODR

Gateway of last resort is not set

     130.13.0.0/16 is subnetted, 6 subnets
D       130.13.12.0 [90/46267904] via 130.13.34.3, 02:11:08, TokenRing0
C       130.13.5.0 is directly connected, TokenRing1
C       130.13.4.0 is directly connected, Ethernet0
D       130.13.1.0 [90/46284032] via 130.13.34.3, 02:11:08, TokenRing0
D       130.13.23.0 [90/46242304] via 130.13.34.3, 02:11:08, TokenRing0
C       130.13.34.0 is directly connected, TokenRing0
```

Basic SRB Configuration

SRB is configured on all the routers' Token Ring interfaces illustrated in Figure 2-5. IBM Token Ring chips on a dual-port bridge can process up to two ring numbers. Therefore, for flexibility and future expansion reasons, the routers are configured as multiport bridges using virtual rings. A virtual ring on a multiport bridge allows the router to interconnect three or more Token Rings since it simulates a logical Token Ring internal to the router. This causes all the Token Rings connected to the router to perceive each other as if they are all on the same ring. The virtual ring is implemented using a ring group. Code Listings 2-9 through 2-11 illustrate this.

Code Listing 2-9
SRB configuration for R1.

```
hostname C2500-R1
!
source-bridge ring-group 12
!
interface TokenRing0
 ring-speed 16
 source-bridge 1 1 12
 source-bridge spanning
```

1. Code Listing 2-9 illustrates the SRB configuration for R1. To take advantage of the virtual ring feature, the Token Ring interface, TO0, is configured to belong to ring group 12.

Figure 2-5
SRB implementation
using ring groups.

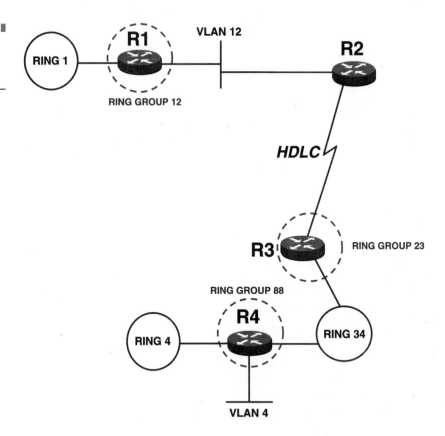

2. Ring group 12 is defined using the global command source-bridge ring-group 12. Note that in this case, the traffic takes an extra hop onto the virtual ring before reaching its destination.

3. To enable SRB and assign the ring group 12 to TO0, the interface subcommand source-bridge 1 1 12 is defined at TO0. The first 1 is the local ring number, Ring 1; the second 1 is the bridge number; and 12 is the target ring number—in this case, ring group 12. Note that all these values are in decimal format.

4. The interface subcommand source-bridge spanning, defined at TO0, manually enables the forwarding of spanning or single-route explorers. This is because spanning tree is not automatically run.

Code Listing 2-10
SRB configuration for
R3.

```
hostname C2500-R3
!
source-bridge ring-group 23
!
interface TokenRing0
 ring-speed 16
 source-bridge 34 3 23
 source-bridge spanning
```

1. Code Listing 2-10 illustrates the SRB configuration for R3. To take the advantage of the virtual ring feature, the Token Ring interface, TO0, is configured to belong to ring group 23.

2. Ring group 23 is defined using the global command `source-bridge ring-group 23`. Note that in this case, the traffic takes an extra hop onto the virtual ring before reaching its destination.

3. To enable SRB and assign the ring group 23 to TO0, the interface subcommand `source-bridge 34 3 23` is defined at TO0. The number `34` is the local ring number, Ring 34; `3` is the bridge number; and `23` is the target ring number—in this case, ring group 23. Note that all these values are in decimal format.

4. The interface subcommand `source-bridge spanning`, defined at TO0, manually enables the forwarding of spanning or single-route explorers. This is because spanning tree is not automatically run.

Code Listing 2-11
SRB configuration for
R4.

```
hostname C4700-R4
!
source-bridge ring-group 88
!
interface TokenRing0
 ring-speed 16
 source-bridge 34 4 88
 source-bridge spanning
!
interface TokenRing1
 ring-speed 16
 source-bridge 4 4 88
 source-bridge spanning
```

1. Code Listing 2-11 illustrates the SRB configuration for R4. To take the advantage of the virtual ring feature, the Token Ring interfaces, TO0 and TO1, are configured to belong to ring group 88.

2. Ring group 88 is defined using the global command `source-bridge ring-group 88`. Note that in this case, the traffic takes an extra hop onto the virtual ring before reaching its destination.

3. To enable SRB and assign the ring group 88 to TO0, the interface subcommand `source-bridge 34 4 88` is defined at TO0. The number `34` is the local ring number, Ring 34; `4` is the bridge number; and `88` is target ring number—in this case, ring group 88. Note that all these values are in decimal format.

4. To enable SRB and assign the ring group 88 to TO1, the interface subcommand `source-bridge 4 4 88` is defined at TO1. The first 4 is the local ring number, Ring 4; the second 4 is the bridge number; and `88` is the target ring number—in this case, ring group 88. Note that the bridge numbers do not necessarily have to match, unlike a dual-port bridge, where matching is mandatory.

5. The interface subcommand `source-bridge spanning`, defined at TO0 and TO1, manually enables the forwarding of spanning or single-route explorers. This is because spanning tree is not automatically run.

Source-Route Translational Bridging

Source-Route Translational Bridging (SR/TLB) permits SRB and transparent bridging (TB) networks to interoperate. SR/TLB enables a source-route (SR) station on Token Ring domains to communicate with TB stations on Ethernet domains, and vice versa.

SR/TLB is implemented via a logical bridge constructed between a specified virtual ring group and a transparent bridge group.

The TB looks like a standard SRB from the viewpoint of an SR station. A ring number (pseudo ring number) and a bridge number associated with a ring group depict the entire transparent bridging domain. Vice versa, the SRB resembles just another port in the bridge group from the perspective of a TB station.

When bridging from an SRB (Token Ring) domain to a TB (Ethernet) domain, the RIFs of the frames are removed but are cached for use by subsequent return traffic.

When bridging from transparent bridging domain to the SRB domain, the router checks whether the packet has a multicast, broadcast, or unicast (single host) destination. If it is a multicast destination, the router will send the packet as a spanning tree explorer. However, if it is a unicast destination, the router will first determine whether there is a path to this destination in the RIF cache. If there is an available path, the router will use it. If no alternative path is found in the cache, the router will send the packet as a spanning-tree explorer.

Note that the Spanning Tree Protocol messages ensure a loop-free topology in the TB domain. Hence they are not interchangeable between the SRB domain and the transparent bridging domain. Therefore, the SRB and transparent bridging domains must not have multiple paths set up in between them.

Figure 2-6 illustrates how SR/TLB is implemented on R1 using pseudo ring 77, and on R4 using pseudo ring 99. These are implemented in Code Listings 2-12 and 2-13.

Figure 2-6
SR/TLB implementation using pseudo rings.

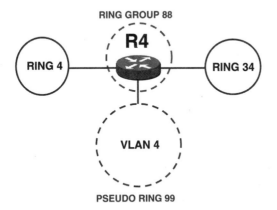

■ |

Code Listing 2-12
SR/TLB configuration
for R1.

```
hostname C2500-R1
!
source-bridge ring-group 12
source-bridge transparent 12 77 1 1
!
interface Ethernet0
 bridge-group 1
!
interface TokenRing0
 ring-speed 16
 source-bridge 1 1 12
 source-bridge spanning
!
bridge 1 protocol ieee
```

1. Code Listing 2-12 illustrates the SR/TLB configuration for R1. TB is configured for interface E0, and SRB is configured on interface TO0. The global command `source-bridge transparent 12 77 1 1` establishes a logical translation bridge between the transparent bridging domain (VLAN 12) and the source-route bridging domain (RING 1).

2. The number `12` is the virtual ring group number created by the `source-bridge ring-group` command to be associated with the transparent bridge group.

3. The number `77` is the pseudo-ring number denoting the transparent bridging domain as RING 77. Note that this number must be unique and not used by any other rings in the source-route bridging domain.

4. The first `1` is the bridge-number created by the `source-bridge ring-group` command. This will be the bridge leading to the transparent bridging domain.

5. The second `1` is the transparent bridge group number created by the `bridge-group` command to tie into the source-route bridging domain.

■ |

Code Listing 2-13
SR/TLB configuration
for R4.

```
hostname C4700-R4
!
source-bridge ring-group 88
source-bridge transparent 88 99 4 1
!
interface Ethernet0
 media-type 10BaseT
 bridge-group 1
!
```

Code Listing 2-13 (continued)

```
interface TokenRing0
 ring-speed 16
 source-bridge 34 4 88
 source-bridge spanning
!
interface TokenRing1
 ring-speed 16
 source-bridge 4 4 88
 source-bridge spanning
!
bridge 1 protocol ieee
```

1. Code Listing 2-13 illustrates the SR/TLB configuration for R4. TB is configured for interface E0, and SRB is configured on interface TO0. The global command `source-bridge transparent 88 99 4 1` establishes a logical translation bridge between the transparent bridging domain (VLAN 4) and the source-route bridging domain (RING 4 and RING 34).

2. The number `88` is the virtual ring group number created by the `source-bridge ring-group` command to be associated with the transparent bridge group.

3. The number `99` is the pseudo-ring number denoting the transparent bridging domain as RING 99. Note that this number must be unique and not used by any other rings in the source-route bridging domain.

4. The number 4 is the bridge-number created by the `source-bridge ring-group` command. This will be the bridge leading to the transparent bridging domain.

5. The number 1 is the transparent bridge group number created by the `bridge-group` command to tie into the source-route bridging domain.

Remote Source-Route Bridging

Remote Source-Route Bridging (RSRB) bridges traffic between two Token Rings from different (or remote) routers. As discussed in the previous sections, virtual rings or ring groups bridge together two or more local rings. These ring groups can be extended between multiple routers so that all the Token Rings on these routers can communicate with each other. These routers must be part of the same ring group (virtual ring) and be peered together in order to pass SRB traffic between them

There are three ways of transporting SRB traffic to remote rings: direct, FST, and TCP encapsulations.

Direct encapsulation is the easiest way of implementing remote peering. In direct encapsulation, the routers that are peered together must be directly attached to each other, which implies that there is a single-hop count limitation and traffic is not routable. When the remote (serial) connectivity tends to "flap" or is not completely stable, TCP encapsulation will be a better option.

Fast Sequenced Transport (FST) uses IP encapsulation. It has an edge over direct encapsulation because there is no hop-count limitation (it is able to extend over multiple hops) and traffic is routable. However, because of the encapsulation of SRB packets in an IP packet, FST has more protocol overhead than direct encapsulation. Moreover, it depends on a network-layer protocol (IP), whereas direct encapsulation only needs layer-2 connectivity (HDLC, LAN LLC).

The TCP encapsulation type is commonly adopted for RSRB. Nevertheless, TCP encapsulation has the highest overhead compared to direct or FST encapsulations. This is because every SRB packet will now be encapsulated within a full IP and TCP header, and as a result, additional CPU cycles are required for maintaining a TCP session for every remote-peer created in the routers. The major advantage of using TCP encapsulation is its reliable delivery of packets, which lightens the recovery burden of end stations in the event a packet is lost or becomes corrupted.

In Figure 2-7, RSRB is configured between R2 and R3 using TCP encapsulation. In other words, SRB packets are tunneled through TCP/IP. Ring group 23 on R3 is extended to include R2 so that all the rings (including pseudo ring 77) on these routers can communicate with each other. Note that R2 and R3 must also be peered together. Code Listings 2-14 and 2-15 illustrate this RSRB implementation.

Code Listing 2-14
RSRB configuration for R2.

```
hostname C2500-R2
!
source-bridge ring-group 23
source-bridge remote-peer 23 tcp 130.13.12.2
source-bridge remote-peer 23 tcp 130.13.34.3
source-bridge transparent 23 77 3 1
!
interface Ethernet0
 ip address 130.13.12.2 255.255.255.0
 bridge-group 1
!
```

Code Listing 2-14
(continued)

```
interface Serial0
 ip address 130.13.23.2 255.255.255.0
 bandwidth 56
!
router eigrp 130
 network 130.13.0.0
 no auto-summary
!
bridge 1 protocol ieee
```

1. Code Listing 2-14 illustrates the RSRB configuration for R2. The `source-bridge ring-group 23` command extends ring group 23, defined initially in R3, to R2.

2. The `source-bridge remote-peer 23 tcp 130.13.12.2` command identifies the IP address to be used by the local router, R2.

Figure 2-7
RSRB between R2
and R3 over TCP/IP.

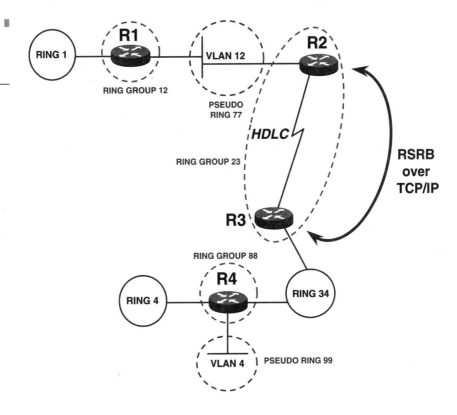

In this case, the IP address of E0, `130.13.2.2`, is adopted. Note that `23` is the ring group number defined earlier by the `source-bridge ring-group` command.

3. The `source-bridge remote-peer 23 tcp 130.13.34.3` command peers to the remote router, R3, which belongs to ring group 23.

4. TB is configured on interface E0. The global command `source-bridge transparent 23 77 3 1` establishes a logical translation bridge between the transparent bridging domain (VLAN 12) and the source-route bridging domain (ring group 23).

5. The number `23` is the virtual ring group number created by the `source-bridge ring-group` command to be associated with the transparent bridge group.

6. The number `77` is the pseudo-ring number denoting the transparent bridging domain as RING 77. Note that this number must be unique and not used by any other rings in the source-route bridging domain.

7. The number `3` is the bridge number created by the `source-bridge ring-group` command that is defined in R3 (this is possible because ring group 23, defined initially in R3, now spans across both R2 and R3). This will be the bridge leading to the transparent bridging domain.

8. The number `1` is the transparent bridge group number created by the `bridge-group` command to tie into the source-route bridging domain.

Code Listing 2-15
RSRB configuration for R3.

```
hostname C2500-R3
!
source-bridge ring-group 23
source-bridge remote-peer 23 tcp 130.13.12.2
source-bridge remote-peer 23 tcp 130.13.34.3
!
interface Serial0
 ip address 130.13.23.3 255.255.255.0
 bandwidth 56
!
interface TokenRing0
 ip address 130.13.34.3 255.255.255.0
 ring-speed 16
 source-bridge 34 3 23
 source-bridge spanning
!
router eigrp 130
 network 130.13.0.0
 no auto-summary
```

1. Code Listing 2-15 illustrates the RSRB configuration for R3. The `source-bridge remote-peer 23 tcp 130.13.34.3` command identifies the IP address to be used by the local router, R3. In this case, the IP address of TO0, `130.13.34.3`, is adopted. Note that 23 is the ring group number defined earlier by the `source-bridge ring-group` command.

2. The `source-bridge remote-peer 23 tcp 130.13.12.2` command peers to the remote router R2, which belongs to ring group 23.

Code Listings 2-16 through 2-22 illustrate the information for the SRB, SR/TLB, and RSRB configured in the previous sections.

Code Listing 2-16

Source-route bridging information for R1.

```
C2500-R1#show source-bridge

Local Interfaces:                                    receive       transmit
              srn bn  trn r p s n  max hops      cnt           cnt         drops
To0             1  1   12 * * f     7  7  7      1157          1414          0

Global RSRB Parameters:
 TCP Queue Length maximum: 100

Ring Group 12:
  No TCP peername set, TCP transport disabled
   Maximum output TCP queue length, per peer: 100
   Rings:
   bn: 1   rn: 1    local  ma: 4007.78fa.bb30 TokenRing0         fwd: 1027
   bn: 1   rn: 77   locvrt ma: 4007.78fa.bbb0 Bridge-group 1     fwd: 1015

Explorers: ------- input -------          ------- output -------
              spanning all-rings   total    spanning all-rings   total
To0              75         15        90        387        0        387

   Local: fastswitched 481      flushed 0     ·  max Bps 38400

               rings      inputs      bursts       throttles    output drops
               To0           90           0               0             0
```

In Code Listing 2-16, VLAN 12 appears as RING 77 in R1's SRB domain (ring group 12).

Code Listing 2-17

Spanning-tree information for R1.

```
C2500-R1#show span

Bridge Group 1 is executing the IEEE compatible Spanning Tree protocol
   Bridge Identifier has priority 32768, address 00e0.1e5f.dd0d
   Configured hello time 2, max age 20, forward delay 15
   Current root has priority 32768, address 0000.0c3e.36ce
   Root port is 2 (Ethernet0), cost of root path is 100
   Topology change flag not set, detected flag not set
   Times:  hold 1, topology change 30, notification 30
           hello 2, max age 20, forward delay 15, aging 300
   Timers: hello 0, topology change 0, notification 0
```

Code Listing 2-17
(continued)

```
Port 2 (Ethernet0) of bridge group 1 is forwarding
    Port path cost 100, Port priority 128
    Designated root has priority 32768, address 0000.0c3e.36ce
    Designated bridge has priority 32768, address 0000.0c3e.36ce
    Designated port is 2, path cost 0
    Timers: message age 2, forward delay 0, hold 0

Port 9 (RingGroup12) of bridge group 1 is forwarding
    Port path cost 10, Port priority 0
    Designated root has priority 32768, address 0000.0c3e.36ce
    Designated bridge has priority 32768, address 00e0.1e5f.dd0d
    Designated port is 9, path cost 100
    Timers: message age 0, forward delay 0, hold 0
```

In Code Listing 2-17, Ring group 12 appears as bridge port 9 in R1's TB domain (bridge group 1).

Code Listing 2-18
Source-route bridging information for R2.

```
C2500-R2#show source-bridge

Global RSRB Parameters:
 TCP Queue Length maximum: 100

Ring Group 23:
  This TCP peer: 130.13.12.2
  Maximum output TCP queue length, per peer: 100
  Peers:                   state    bg lv  pkts_rx  pkts_tx  expl_gn   drops TCP
   TCP 130.13.12.2         -         3        0        0        1        0   0
   TCP 130.13.34.3         open      3      1105     1427      152        0   0
  Rings:
   bn: 3   rn: 77    locvrt ma: 4000.307c.6c73 Bridge-group 1      fwd: 1105
   bn: 3   rn: 34    remote ma: 4007.78fa.7b10 TCP 130.13.34.3     fwd: 1110
```

In Code Listing 2-18, VLAN 12 appears as RING 77 in R2's SRB domain (ring group 23). RSRB is configured on R2; the IP address of the local TCP peer is 130.13.12.2 (the IP address of R2's E0), whereas the IP address of the remote TCP peer is 130.13.34.3 (the IP address of R3's TO0).

Code Listing 2-19
Spanning-tree information for R2.

```
C2500-R2#show span

Bridge Group 1 is executing the IEEE compatible Spanning Tree protocol
    Bridge Identifier has priority 32768, address 0000.0c3e.36ce
    Configured hello time 2, max age 20, forward delay 15
    We are the root of the spanning tree
    Topology change flag not set, detected flag not set
    Times:  hold 1, topology change 30, notification 30
            hello 2, max age 20, forward delay 15, aging 300
    Timers: hello 2, topology change 0, notification 0
```

Code Listing 2-19
(continued)

```
Port 2 (Ethernet0) of bridge group 1 is forwarding
    Port path cost 100, Port priority 128
    Designated root has priority 32768, address 0000.0c3e.36ce
    Designated bridge has priority 32768, address 0000.0c3e.36ce
    Designated port is 2, path cost 0
    Timers: message age 0, forward delay 0, hold 0

Port 6 (RingGroup23) of bridge group 1 is forwarding
    Port path cost 10, Port priority 0
    Designated root has priority 32768, address 0000.0c3e.36ce
    Designated bridge has priority 32768, address 0000.0c3e.36ce
    Designated port is 6, path cost 0
    Timers: message age 0, forward delay 0, hold 0
```

In Code Listing 2-19, Ring group 23 appears as bridge port 6 in R2's TB domain (bridge group 1).

Code Listing 2-20
Source-route bridging information for R3.

```
C2500-R3#show source-bridge
Local Interfaces:                         receive      transmit
            srn bn  trn r p s n  max hops    cnt          cnt        drops
To0         34  3   23 * * f    7  7  7     1533         1307          0

Global RSRB Parameters:
 TCP Queue Length maximum: 100

Ring Group 23:
  This TCP peer: 130.13.34.3
   Maximum output TCP queue length, per peer: 100
   Peers:                 state    bg lv  pkts_rx  pkts_tx  expl_gn  drops TCP
     TCP 130.13.12.2      open        3     1151     1601      291      1   0
     TCP 130.13.34.3      -           3        0        0        0      0   0
   Rings:
     bn: 3   rn: 34   local  ma: 4007.78fa.7b10 TokenRing0        fwd: 1151
     bn: 3   rn: 77   remote ma: 4000.307c.6c73 TCP 130.13.12.2   fwd: 1146

Explorers: ------- input -------       ------- output -------
            spanning  all-rings   total     spanning  all-rings    total
To0            0          0         0          156         0        156

  Local: fastswitched 291      flushed 0        max Bps 38400

          rings     inputs     bursts      output drops
          To0         291         0             0
```

In Code Listing 2-20, VLAN 12 appears as RING 77 in R3's SRB domain (ring group 23). RSRB is configured on R3. The IP address of the local TCP peer is 130.13.34.3 (the IP address of R3's TO0), whereas the IP address of the remote TCP peer is 130.13.12.2 (the IP address of R2's E0).

Code Listing 2-21

Source-route bridging information for R4.

```
C4700-R4#show source-bridge

Local Interfaces:                                  receive     transmit
            srn bn  trn r p s n  max hops           cnt         cnt        drops
To0         34  4   88  * * f    7  7  7           1503        1208          0
To1          4  4   88  * * f    7  7  7            418         663          0

Global RSRB Parameters:
 TCP Queue Length maximum: 100

Ring Group 88:
  No TCP peername set, TCP transport disabled
  Maximum output TCP queue length, per peer: 100
  Rings:
   bn: 4  rn: 34   local  ma: 4006.e278.9a5f TokenRing0          fwd: 1083
   bn: 4  rn: 4    local  ma: 4006.e278.9abf TokenRing1          fwd: 306
   bn: 4  rn: 99   locvrt ma: 4006.e278.9a1f Bridge-group 1      fwd: 779

Explorers: ------- input -------          ------- output -------
           spanning all-rings    total    spanning all-rings    total
To0             303       18       321         119        6       125
To1              83        6        89         339       18       357

   Local: fastswitched 446      flushed 0       max Bps 38400

           rings      inputs      bursts      throttles    output drops
           To0           321           0              0               0
           To1            89           0              0               0
```

In Code Listing 2-21, VLAN 4 appears as RING 99 in R4's SRB domain (ring group 88).

Code Listing 2-22

Spanning-tree information for R4.

```
C4700-R4#show span

Bridge Group 1 is executing the IEEE compatible Spanning Tree protocol
   Bridge Identifier has priority 32768, address 0060.471e.59f8
   Configured hello time 2, max age 20, forward delay 15
   We are the root of the spanning tree
   Topology change flag not set, detected flag not set
   Times:  hold 1, topology change 30, notification 30
           hello 2, max age 20, forward delay 15, aging 300
   Timers: hello 2, topology change 0, notification 0

Port 2 (Ethernet0) of bridge group 1 is forwarding
   Port path cost 100, Port priority 128
   Designated root has priority 32768, address 0060.471e.59f8
   Designated bridge has priority 32768, address 0060.471e.59f8
   Designated port is 2, path cost 0
   Timers: message age 0, forward delay 0, hold 0

Port 15 (RingGroup88) of bridge group 1 is forwarding
   Port path cost 10, Port priority 0
   Designated root has priority 32768, address 0060.471e.59f8
   Designated bridge has priority 32768, address 0060.471e.59f8
   Designated port is 15, path cost 0
   Timers: message age 0, forward delay 0, hold 0
```

In Code Listing 2-22, ring group 88 appears as bridge port 15 in R4's TB domain (bridge group 1).

Bridging of Routed Protocols

In Cisco routers, the default for routed protocols is to ignore RIF information and use protocol-specific information such as IP headers, rather than MAC information, to route datagrams. Without RIF information, a packet cannot be bridged across a SRB network. Therefore, to bridge routed protocols across an SRB network, the RIF information has to be collected and inserted into the routed frames.

In Figure 2-3, RING 34 interconnects R3 and R4. In order to bridge IP packets across this SRB network, the interface subcommand `multiring ip` is applied on interface TO0 of R3 and interface TO0 of R4. This command will enable R3 and R4 to collect and append RIF information to IP packets so that IP packets can be bridged across RING 34 to R3 and R4. In effect, this command converts R3 and R4 into SRB end stations for IP. Code Listings 2-23 and 2-24 illustrate this.

Code Listing 2-23
R3 configuration.

```
hostname C2500-R3
!
source-bridge ring-group 23
!
interface TokenRing0
 ip address 130.13.34.3 255.255.255.0
 ring-speed 16
 source-bridge 34 3 23
 source-bridge spanning
 multiring ip
!
router eigrp 130
 network 130.13.0.0
 no auto-summary
```

Code Listing 2-24
R4 configuration.

```
hostname C4700-R4
!
source-bridge ring-group 88
!
interface TokenRing0
 ip address 130.13.34.4 255.255.255.0
 ring-speed 16
 source-bridge 34 4 88
 source-bridge spanning
 multiring ip
!
router eigrp 130
 network 130.13.0.0
 no auto-summary
```

SRB Access Control

This section outlines the three types of filters typically used to secure SRB networks: NetBIOS access filters, administrative filters, and access expressions (a logical combination of administrative filters). Furthermore, these filters can be used to optimize network performance by reducing redundant or unwanted SRB traffic propagating across the network.

NetBIOS Access Filters

NetBIOS packets can be filtered using two types of filters: station names and byte offset (arbitrary byte patterns in the packet itself).

The following are some rules of thumb to keep in mind when configuring NetBIOS access filters:

- The access lists are always scanned in sequential order (first to last line)

- New additions to the existing NetBIOS access lists are always appended to the end of the list

- The access list parameters (station names) are case-sensitive

- A NetBIOS station name access list and a NetBIOS byte offset access list can have identical names. These two lists are unique by nature and thus bear no resemblance to each other

- The station names included in the NetBIOS station name access lists are matched with the source name field for NetBIOS commands—00 (ADD_GROUP_NAME_QUERY frame) and 01 (ADD_NAME_QUERY frame)—as well as the destination name field for NetBIOS commands—08 (DATAGRAM frame), 0A (NAME_QUERY frame), and 0E (NAME_RECOGNIZED frame)

- If an access list does not contain a particular station name, the default action is to deny the access to that station

To minimize performance overheads, NetBIOS access filters do not examine all packets. Instead, they only examine packets that establish and maintain NetBIOS client/server (or peer-to-peer) connections, thereby effectively blocking new access and unnecessary loading across the router. This means that a new access filter can filter all new sessions immediately, whereas existing sessions could continue for some time before they too are blocked.

Figure 2-8 illustrates a NetBIOS environment whereby four NetBIOS hosts are connected to RING 1 and another four to RING 2. NetBIOS station name filters are implemented in R1 and R4. Code Listings 2-25 and 2-26 illustrate this.

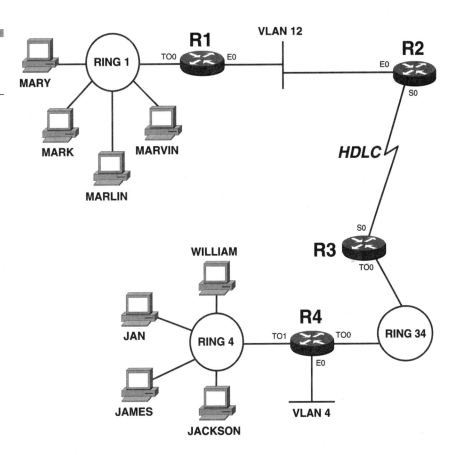

Figure 2-8
A sample NetBIOS scenario.

Code Listing 2-25
NetBIOS station name filter configuration for R1.

```
hostname C2500-R1
!
source-bridge ring-group 12
!
interface TokenRing0
 ring-speed 16
 source-bridge 1 1 12
 source-bridge spanning
 netbios input-access-filter host MLIST
!
netbios access-list host MLIST permit MAR?
```

1. Code Listing 2-25 illustrates the NetBIOS station name filter configuration for R1. The `netbios access-list host MLIST permit MAR?` global command permits NetBIOS packets with station names "MARY" or "MARK" to pass through R1. As this is the only list defined, the NetBIOS stations (Marlin and Marvin) that are not defined are denied implicitly. Note that the question mark, ?, matches any single character that follows after "MAR". In this case, "MAR?" matches "MARY" and "MARK".

2. The interface subcommand `netbios input-access-filter host MLIST` activates the netbios station name filter, MLIST, on TO0 in the inbound direction.

Code Listing 2-26
NetBIOS station
name filter configuration for R4.

```
hostname C4700-R4
!
source-bridge ring-group 88
!
interface TokenRing1
 ring-speed 16
 source-bridge 4 4 88
 source-bridge spanning
 netbios input-access-filter host JLIST
!
netbios access-list host JLIST deny JA*
netbios access-list host JLIST permit *
```

1. Code Listing 2-26 illustrates the NetBIOS station name filter configuration for R4. The `netbios access-list host JLIST deny JA*` global command denies NetBIOS packets with any station names beginning with "JA" (JAN, JAMES, and JACKSON) to pass through R4. The `netbios access-list host JLIST permit *` global command permits NetBIOS packets with any other station names (WILLIAM) to pass through R4. Note that the asterisk, *, matches zero or more sequences of characters that follow after "JA". In this case, "JA*" matches "JAN", "JAMES", and "JACKSON".

2. The interface subcommand `netbios input-access-filter host JLIST` activates the netbios station name filter, JLIST, on TO1, in the inbound direction.

Considering the above configurations, station WILLIAM can only see station MARY and station MARK on RING 1; vice versa, station MARY and station MARK can only see station WILLIAM on RING 4.

Administrative Filters

Generally, a source-route bridge filters frames according to the RIF information in these frames and will not forward a frame back to its originating network segment or to any other network segment that the frame has already traversed. However, SRB frame filtering can be further enhanced by explicitly configuring administrative filters based on the following:

■ *Protocol type*   This is implemented by specifying protocol type codes (refer to Table 2-1 for some of the common protocol type codes) in an access list. This access list is then applied to either IEEE 802.2 encapsulated packets or to SNAP encapsulated packets on the appropriate interface. The sequence in which these elements are specified affects the sequence in which the access conditions are checked. Each condition is tested successively. A matching condition is then used to execute a permit or deny decision. If no conditions match, a deny decision is reached (implicit deny).

TABLE 2-1

Some common protocol type codes

Value (in hex)	Description
0000-05DC	IEEE 802.3
0800	DOD IP
0805	X.25 Level 3
0806	ARP for IP
6003	DECnet Phase IV
6004	DECnet LAT
8035	Reverse ARP
809B	EtherTalk—AppleTalk over Ethernet
80F3	AARP—AppleTalk AARP
80D5	IBM SNA Services over Ethernet
8137-8138	Novell

■ *Vendor code*   Table 2-2 illustrates some sample vendor codes used for administrative filtering.

TABLE 2-2

A list of sample vendor codes

Vendor	IEEE Assigned Addresses (in hex)
Cisco	00 00 0C XX XX XX
Novell	00 00 1B XX XX XX
Wellfleet	00 00 A2 XX XX XX
Intel	00 AA 00 XX XX XX
3Com	02 60 8C XX XX XX
Digital	AA 00 04 XX XX XX

■ *Source address*   This is implemented by assigning an access list that checks the source addresses of Token Ring or IEEE 802 frames going into a particular interface.

■ *Destination address*   This is implemented by assigning an access list that checks the destination addresses of Token Ring or IEEE 802 frames going out a particular interface.

Figure 2-9 illustrates a scenario whereby RING 1 has two Macintoshes (MAC1 and MAC2) running on AppleTalk, and RING 4 has two different batches of PCs—one using Intel's network interface card (NIC) and the other using 3Com's. A protocol-type-code filter is implemented in R1, and a vendor-code filter is implemented in R4. Code Listings 2-27 and 2-28 illustrate these.

Code Listing 2-27

Protocol type code filter configuration for R1.

```
hostname C2500-R1
!
source-bridge ring-group 12
!
interface TokenRing0
 ring-speed 16
 source-bridge 1 1 12
 source-bridge spanning
 source-bridge input-type-list 201
!
access-list 201 deny 0x809B 0x0000
access-list 201 deny 0x80F3 0x0000
access-list 201 permit 0x0000 0xFFFF
```

1. Code Listing 2-27 illustrates the protocol type code filter configuration for R1. The `access-list 201 deny 0x809B 0x0000` command denies AppleTalk data packets (protocol type code 0x809B) to

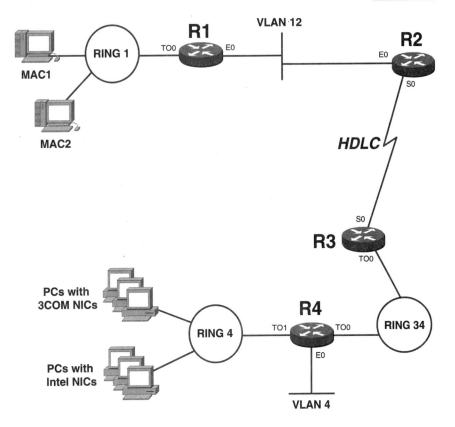

Figure 2-9
A sample scenario for protocol type code and vendor code.

pass through R1, and likewise the `access-list 201 deny 0x80F3 0x0000` command denies AppleTalk AARP packets (protocol type code 0x80F3). The last line, `access-list 201 permit 0x0000 0xFFFF`, permits all other protocol type codes. Note that a wildcard mask bit of "0" means check and preserve the corresponding bit; a "1" means don't care.

2. The interface subcommand `source-bridge input-type-list 201` activates the protocol type code filter on TO0, in the inbound direction.

■ ■

Code Listing 2-28
Vendor code filter
configuration for R4.

```
hostname C4700-R4
!
source-bridge ring-group 88
!
interface TokenRing1
 ring-speed 16
 source-bridge 4 4 88
 source-bridge spanning
 source-bridge input-address-list 704
!
access-list 704 deny 0260.8C00.0000 0000.00FF.FFFF
access-list 704 permit 0000.0000.0000 FFFF.FFFF.FFFF
```

1. Code Listing 2-28 illustrates the vendor code filter configuration for R4. Assume all the PCs with the Intel NICs have MAC address prefixes 00AA.00XX.XXXX, and the PCs with the 3Com NICs have MAC address prefixes 0260.8CXX.XXXX. The `access-list 704 deny 0260.8C00.0000 0000.00FF.FFFF` command denies access to all the PCs with the 3Com NICs (or with vendor code 0260.8CXX.XXXX), while the `access-list 704 permit 0000.0000.0000 FFFF.FFFF.FFFF` command permits all other vendor codes. Note that a wildcard mask bit of "0" means check and preserve the corresponding bit; a "1" means don't care.

2. The interface subcommand `source-bridge input-address-list 704` activates the vendor code filter on TO1, in the inbound direction.

In Code Listings 2-27 and 2-28, MAC1 and MAC2 are confined to RING 1. In other words, AppleTalk traffic generated by these two stations will not propagate out of RING 1. Likewise, the PCs with 3Com NICs are confined to RING 4; they cannot be accessed anywhere in the network other than RING 4.

Access Expressions

An access expression is a powerful tool used to combine different administrative filters together to establish complex conditions under which bridged frames can enter or leave a particular interface. Access expressions are built from individual access lists that define administrative filters based on the following fields in the frames:

■ *LSAP (DSAP/SSAP) type codes* Table 2-3a illustrates a snapshot of an 802.2 LLC frame. The upper-layer processes use IEEE 802.2 services through service access points (SAPs). The 802.2 header starts with a Destination Service Access Point (DSAP) field that identifies the receiving upper-layer process. Following the DSAP field is the Source Service Access Point (SSAP) address that identifies the sending upper-layer process. The DSAP and SSAP together form a Local Service Access Point (LSAP). Table 2-3b lists some of the common LSAP type codes assigned to the various protocols.

- MAC addresses
- NetBIOS station names
- NetBIOS arbitrary byte values

TABLE 2-3a
802.2 LLC frame format

1 byte	1 byte	1-2 bytes
DSAP	SSAP	Control
DDDDDDD I/G	SSSSSS C/R	Control
I/G: Individual/Group 0 = Individual DSAP 1 = Group DSAP	C/R: Command/Response 0 = Command 1 = ResponseControl	

TABLE 2-3b
Some common LSAP type codes

Address (in hex)	Assignment
00	Null LSAP
04, 08, 0C	SNA
06	IP
AA	Sub-Network Access Protocol (SNAP)
BC	Banyan VINES
E0	Novell
F0	NetBIOS

Note that for any given interface, an access expression and an access list are mutually exclusive for a given direction. For example, if an input access list is defined for MAC addresses on an interface, no access expression can be specified for the input side of that interface.

TABLE 2-4
Logical operators used in access expressions

Logical Operators	Symbol
AND	&
OR	|
NOT	!
Parenthesis	(...)

Administrative filters are combined into an access expression using logical operators. Table 2-4 lists the logical operators used by access expressions.

Figure 2-10
A sample mixed-protocols scenario.

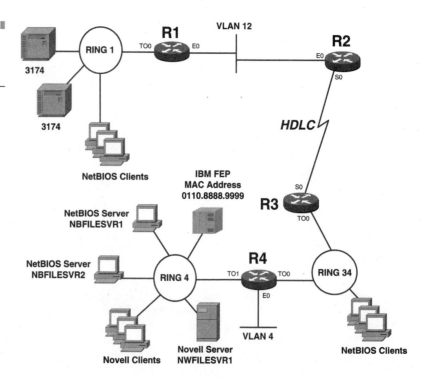

Figure 2-10 illustrates a complex mixed-protocol environment where:

i) NetBIOS clients on RING 1 must communicate only with Net-BIOS server NBFILESVR1 on RING 4. However, the two 3174 cluster controllers on RING 1 must communicate only with the FEP on RING 4 with a MAC address 0110.8888.9999.

ii) NetBIOS clients on RING 34 can communicate with any NetBIOS server (NBFILESVR1 or NBFILESVR2) on RING 4.

iii) Novell's traffic is not propagated out of RING 4.

iv) Without access expressions, condition i) cannot be achieved, since a filter on R1 restricting access to only the FEP would also restrict access of the NetBIOS clients to NBFILESVR1. Conditions ii) and iii) can be implemented using access expressions or administrative filters.

Code Listings 2-29 and 2-30 illustrate these.

Code Listing 2-29

Access expression configuration for R1.

```
hostname C2500-R1
!
source-bridge ring-group 12
!
interface TokenRing0
 ring-speed 16
 source-bridge 1 1 12
 source-bridge spanning
 access-expression in netbios-host(FSLIST) | (lsap(211) & dmac(711))
!
access-list 211 permit 0x0404 0x0101
access-list 211 permit 0x0004 0x0001
access-list 711 permit 0110.8888.9999 0000.0000.0000
netbios access-list host FSLIST permit NBFILESVR1
```

To satisfy condition i):

1. Code Listing 2-29 illustrates the access expression configuration for R1. The `access-list 211 permit 0x0404 0x0101` command allows SNA frames (LSAP=0x0404) to pass, and the `access-list 211 permit 0x0004 0x0001` command allows SNA explorers with NULL DSAP (LSAP=0x0004) to pass. The `0x0101` mask allows individual/group DSAP and command/response frames to pass equally. Refer to Table 2-3a and Table 2-3b for more details on LSAPs.

2. The `access-list 711 permit 0110.8888.9999 0000.0000.0000` command permits the FEP MAC address.

3. The `netbios access-list host FSLIST permit NBFILESVR1` command allows NetBIOS packets with station name NBFILESVR1 to pass through R1.

4. On TO0, the `access-expression in netbios-host(FSLIST) | (lsap(211) & dmac(711))` command combines all the administrative filters defined earlier into a single expression.

5. The operand `netbios-host(FSLIST)` uses the NetBIOS station name filter, FSLIST.

6. The operand `lsap(211)` uses the LSAP type-code filter, access-list 211, and the operand `dmac(711)` uses the destination MAC address filter, access-list 711. The symbol "&" is a logical AND operator (refer to Table 2-4) that performs an AND operation on these two operands using the expression `(lsap(211) & dmac(711))`. This expression means: "Must be SNA frames and destined to MAC address 0110.8888.9999."

7. The symbol "|" is a logical OR operator (refer to Table 2-4) that performs an OR operation on the operand `netbios-host(FSLIST)` and the expression `(lsap(211) & dmac(711))`. This expression means: "Allows NetBIOS packets with station name NBFILESVR1 to pass, or must be SNA frames and destined to MAC address 0110.8888.9999."

Code Listing 2-30

Access expression configuration for R4.

```
hostname C4700-R4
!
source-bridge ring-group 88
!
interface TokenRing0
 ring-speed 16
 source-bridge 34 4 88
 source-bridge spanning
 access-expression in lsap(204)
!
interface TokenRing1
 ring-speed 16
 source-bridge 4 4 88
 source-bridge spanning
 access-expression in ~lsap(214)
!
access-list 204 permit 0xF0F0 0x0101
access-list 214 permit 0xE0E0 0x0101
```

To satisfy conditions ii) and iii):

1. Code Listing 2-30 illustrates the access expression configuration for R4. The `access-list 204 permit 0xF0F0 0x0101` command allows NetBIOS packets (LSAP=0xF0F0) to pass, and the `access-list 214 permit 0xE0E0 0x0101` command allows Novell packets (LSAP=0xE0E0) to pass. The `0x0101` mask allows individual/group DSAP and command/response frames to pass equally. Refer to Table 2-3a and Table 2-3b for more details on LSAPs.

2. On TO0, the `access-expression in lsap(204)` command uses the LSAP type code filter, access-list 204, as the only operand or expression. This expression allows only NetBIOS packets to be source-route bridged between RING 34 and RING 4. Note that the `source-bridge input-lsap-list 204` command can also be used in place of the access expression. However, for any given interface, an access expression and an access list are mutually exclusive for a given direction.

3. On TO1, the `access-expression in ~lsap(214)` command uses the LSAP type-code filter, access-list 214, as the only operand. The symbol "~" is a logical NOT operator (refer to Table 2-4) that performs a NOT operation on this operand using the expression `~lsap(214)`. This expression means: "Allow any packets but not Novell packets." The access-list 214 permits only Novell packets to pass; however, the NOT operation reverses the matching condition to deny Novell packets and permit the rest.

SRB Performance Tuning

Explorer Processing Optimization

Efficient explorer processing is crucial to the smooth operation of SRB. The default configuration is satisfactory for most situations. However, unexpected broadcast storms will still occur when an unfavorable situation takes place. In cases like these, the default configuration can be modified to optimize the handling of explorer frames, thereby reducing the router's CPU processing and increasing explorer throughput. Consequently, the router's overall performance degrades less significantly during explorer broadcast storms. In this section, duplicate explorer filtering,

explorer byte rate, and explorer queue depth are configured in R4 for opti-
mum explorer processing, as illustrated in Code Listing 2-31.

■ |

Code Listing 2-31
Performance-tuning
configuration for R4.

```
hostname C4700-R4
!
source-bridge ring-group 88
source-bridge explorer-dup-ARE-filter
source-bridge explorerq-depth 100
source-bridge explorer-maxrate 100000
!
interface TokenRing0
 ip address 130.13.34.4 255.255.255.0
 ring-speed 16
 source-bridge 34 4 88
 source-bridge spanning
!
interface TokenRing1
 ring-speed 16
 source-bridge 4 4 88
 source-bridge spanning
```

1. Code Listing 2-31 illustrates the performance-tuning configuration
   for R4. The `source-bridge explorer-dup-ARE-filter` global
   command filters duplicate explorers (explorers that have already
   been forwarded once) to prevent excessive forwarding of these
   explorers, especially in redundant network topologies.

2. The `source-bridge explorer-maxrate 100000` global command sets the maximum byte rate of explorers per ring (RING 4
   and RING 34) to 100000 bytes per second (the default is 38400
   bytes per second). Note that the valid range for the explorer maximum byte rate is 100-1000000000.

3. The `source-bridge explorerq-depth 100` global command
   sets the maximum explorer queue depth to 100. In this implementation, the limitation is on a per-interface basis such that each
   interface (TO0 and TO1) can have, at most, 100 (the default is 30)
   outstanding explorer packets on the queue before explorers from
   that particular interface are dropped. Note that the valid range for
   the explorer queue depth is 1-500.

Proxy Explorer

Proxy explorers can limit excessive explorer traffic from propagating
through the SRB network, especially across low-speed serial links. Proxy

explorers are most ideal for multiple connections to a single node. In general, they reduce explorer traffic by half. A Cisco router does not forward proxy responses for a station. Rather, the RIF path is obtained from the RIF cache, the explorer is converted to a specific frame based on this information, and the frame is forwarded to the destination.

In instances when there are no responses from an end station before the validation timer expires, the RIF entry is marked as invalid. The invalid RIF entry is flushed from the cache table when another explorer for this station is received, and an explorer is forwarded to discover a path to this station. In this section, proxy explorer is configured on interface TO0 of R3 to reduce unnecessary explorer traffic going out of interface S0. Code Listing 2-32 illustrates this.

Code Listing 2-32
Proxy explorer configuration for R3.

```
hostname C2500-R3
!
source-bridge ring-group 23
source-bridge remote-peer 23 tcp 130.13.12.2
source-bridge remote-peer 23 tcp 130.13.34.3
!
interface Serial0
 ip address 130.13.23.3 255.255.255.0
 bandwidth 56
!
interface TokenRing0
 ip address 130.13.34.3 255.255.255.0
 ring-speed 16
 source-bridge 34 3 23
 source-bridge spanning
 multiring ip
 source-bridge proxy-explorer
!
router eigrp 130
 network 130.13.0.0
 no auto-summary
```

In Code Listing 2-32, the `source-bridge proxy-explorer` interface subcommand enables TO0 to convert explorer packets to specifically routed frames and forward these frames to the destination if that particular destination is in the RIF cache.

Summary

This chapter covered Source-Route Bridging (SRB), which was developed by IBM to interconnect multiple physical Token Rings into one logical network segment.

In the initial scenario, SRB was implemented on all the routers' active Token Ring interfaces, and Transparent Bridging (TB) was implemented on all the active Ethernet interfaces. Source-Route Translational Bridging (SR/TLB) was then configured, enabling the SRB and TB networks to interoperate.

Next, Remote Source-Route Bridging (RSRB) was configured using TCP/IP encapsulation, allowing traffic to be bridged between two Token Rings from two remote routers. Then IP packets were bridged across an SRB network.

The access control section discussed in-depth the three types of filters typically used to secure SRB networks and optimize their performance: NetBIOS access filters, administrative filters, and access expressions (a logical combination of administrative filters).

Finally, in the performance-tuning section, some SRB performance-tuning techniques—duplicate explorer filtering, explorer byte rate, explorer queue depth, and proxy explorers—were demonstrated.

References

1. Black, U. *Physical Level Interfaces and Protocols*. Los Alamitos, California: IEEE Computer Society Press, 1988.

2. Clark, W. "SNA Internetworking." *ConneXions: The Interoperability Report*, Vol. 6, No. 3. March 1992.

3. Documentation CD-ROM, Cisco Systems, Inc., 1998.

4. IEEE 802.1D Standard for Local Area Network MAC Bridges, ANSI/IEEE Standard, October 1985.

5. IEEE 802.2–Local Area Networks Standard, 802.2 Logical Link Control, ANSI/IEEE Standard, October 1985.

6. IEEE 802.5–Local Area Networks Standard, 802.5 Token Ring Access Method, ANSI/IEEE Standard, October 1985.

7. Martin, J. *SNA: IBM's Networking Solution*. Englewood Cliffs, New Jersey: Prentice Hall, 1987.

8. Miller, M.A. *LAN Protocol Handbook*. San Mateo, California: MT&T Books, 1990.

9. Perlman, R. *Interconnections: Bridges and Routers*. Reading, Massachusetts: Addison-Wesley Publishing Company, Inc., 1992.

10. Stallings, W. *Data and Computer Communications*. New York: Macmillan Publishing Company, 1991.

11. Tannenbaum, A.S. *Computer Networks*, 2nd ed. Englewood Cliffs, New Jersey: Prentice Hall, 1988.

CHAPTER 3

DLSw+

Introduction

IBM protocols like Systems Network Architecture (SNA) and Network Basic Input Output Services (NetBIOS) can be forwarded using Data Link Switching Plus (DLSw+) as an alternative to Remote Source-Route Bridging (RSRB). Data link switches use the Switch-to-Switch Protocol (SSP) to communicate with each other. SSP provides switching at the data link layer and encapsulation in TCP/IP for transport over the Internet. SSP uses TCP as the preferred reliable transport among data link switches.

A data link switch can support SNA Physical Unit (PU) 2, 2.1, and 4; SNA primary or secondary PU 2 systems attached to IBM Synchronous Data Link Control (SDLC) links, as well as NetBIOS systems attached to IEEE 802.2 bridged LANs.

For the SDLC attached systems, each SDLC PU is presented to the SSP protocol as a unique MAC/SAP address pair. For the Token-Ring-attached systems, the data link switch resembles a source-routing bridge. Token Ring systems that are accessed remotely through the data link switch appear as systems attached to an adjacent virtual ring.

DLSw+ Overview

Primarily, SNA and NetBIOS are connection-oriented protocols that use the IEEE 802.2 LLC Type 2 (LLC2) Data Link Control (DLC) procedure to establish a session. LLC2 is connection-oriented and uses a fixed timer for detecting lost frames; however, it will encounter some problems over lower speed WAN links, since the delay varies with congestion. The situation is such that if a frame is delayed but not lost, and the delay exceeds the timeout value, LLC2 will retransmit. However, LLC2 procedures will become confused when LLC2 eventually receives the delayed frame while retransmitting a new one. This may cause the link to go down.

Figures 3-1 and 3-2 illustrate the main difference between bridging and DLSw+ with two end systems. The contrast is DLSw+ terminates the LLC2 DLC locally for connection-oriented frames, while bridging does not.

DLSw+ can also support SNA protocols over WANs via the SDLC protocol.

Figure 3-1
Bridging and LLC2.

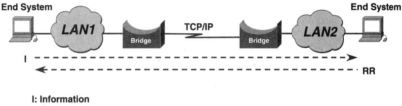

I: Information
RR: Receive Ready

Figure 3-2
DLSw+ and LLC2.

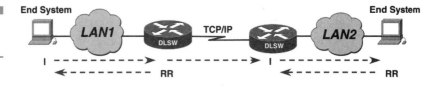

I: Information
RR: Receive Ready

Advantages of DLSw+

DLSw+ is developed primarily to address the following bridging limitations:

- DLC timeouts and DLC acknowledgements over WAN links: in bridging, the DLC is end-to-end, as illustrated in Figure 3-1. DLSw+ terminates the LLC2 connection at the switch, as shown in Figure 3-2; LLC2 connections do not traverse across the WAN but are terminated locally at each end. The data link switch will have to deliver frames that it receives from an LLC connection to the other end. The switch accomplishes this by multiplexing traffic from multiple LLC connections to TCP pipes, and transports the data reliably across an IP backbone. In this case, the LLC2 DLC timeouts and acknowledgements (Receive Ready) do not traverse the WAN. As a result, traffic across the WAN links is minimized. Similarly, polling and poll response occur locally for SDLC links.

- Flow and congestion control: the data link switch uses an adaptive windowing mechanism to provide flow and congestion control. The window size can be repeated, increased, decreased, halved, or reset to zero. The flow control is performed on a per-circuit basis, unidirectional, and applicable to both connection-oriented and connectionless data.

- Broadcast control of search packets: data link switches can control broadcast of search frames (Source-Route Bridging explorer frames or NetBIOS name queries) when the switch knows the designated system.

- Source-Route Bridging (SRB) hop count limits: IBM Token Ring specifies a maximum of 8 rings and 7 bridges. Consider Figure 3-3. In this scenario, Remote Source-Route Bridging (RSRB) is used and supports Routing Information Field (RIF) pass-through. That is, the whole WAN cloud is regarded as a single virtual ring; therefore, the entire path can only have a maximum of seven SRB hops.

In Figure 3-4, DLSw+ is used. It is more scalable than RSRB, as the RIF now terminates locally in the virtual ring, allowing a maximum of seven SRB hops on each side of the WAN cloud. However, this also means that the end-to-end RIF visibility is lost here.

Note that for connectionless LLC1 services, DLSw+ will only address the last two problems in the preceding list.

Figure 3-3
RIF pass-through.

RIF = R6-B1-R25-B2-R73-B3-R19   RIF = R6-B1-R25-B2-R73-B3-R19

Figure 3-4
RIF termination.

RIF = R6-B1-R25-B2-R73   RIF = R73-B3-R19

DLSw and DLSw+

DLSw+ is Cisco's implementation of DLSw. The "+" stands for extended and enhanced features to the DLSw standard; these include:

- transport options like TCP, Fast-Sequenced Transport (FST), and direct encapsulation
- resiliency enhancements like backup routers
- scalability features like peer groups, border peers, on-demand peers, explorer firewalls, and location learning
- media conversion between LANs and SDLC or Qualified Logical Link Control (QLLC)

Establishing Connections

Before two routers can forward SNA or NetBIOS traffic, they must first establish two TCP connections (port 2065 for read and port 2067 for write) between them. For Cisco routers, the peer connection may be TCP, FST, or direct encapsulation.

Capabilities Exchange

After the TCP connections are established, the routers exchange their capabilities. Capabilities include version number, vendor ID, initial pacing windows (receive window size), list of unsupported SAPs, the number of TCP connections supported, reachable MAC addresses, and NetBIOS names. To reduce explorer traffic, static resources capabilities exchange can be configured. A particular peer can send other peers a list of resources for which it has information (ICANREACH) or does not have information (ICANNOTREACH), and the information is exchanged as part of the capabilities exchange process. Additional information like group number, border peer, cost, Cisco version, and prioritization is exchanged for Cisco routers. After the capabilities exchange, the DLSw+ peers are ready to establish circuits between SNA or NetBIOS end systems.

SNA Circuit Establishment

DLSw+ uses LAN addressing to set up connections between SNA systems. For LLC2 circuit establishment, SNA systems send TEST or XID frames to the null (0x00) SAP to determine the source route information. SAP values for SNA are 0x04, 0x08, and 0x0C. These SAPs also help to ensure that SNA frames are not both bridged and switched. Typically SNA uses a DSAP and SSAP of 0x04. Figure 3-5 illustrates how a SNA circuit is established using the following steps. (Refer to Tables 3-1 and 3-2 for a list of common LLC2 and DLSw+ messages.)

1. SNA_SYS1 sends a TEST frame specifying the MAC address of the SNA_SYS2 to ROUTER1.

2. ROUTER1 forwards the CANUREACH_ex frame to each border peer in its group (if there is any) and to every configured peer outside its group.

3. When ROUTER2 receives the CANUREACH_ex frame, it forwards a TEST frame to its Token Ring LAN. Note that the default SNA retry interval is 30 seconds, and the default SNA explorer timeout is 3 minutes.

Figure 3-5

Establishing an SNA session.

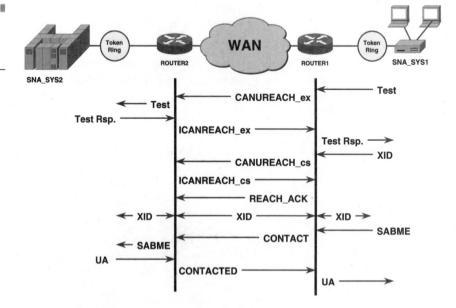

4. ROUTER2 caches the first RIF with a positive TEST Response for each port. The first port with a positive response is the preferred route, and any others (up to three additional) are capable.

5. ROUTER2 sends an ICANREACH_ex frame back to ROUTER1.

6. ROUTER1 sends a TEST Response frame to SNA_SYS1 and updates its cache for the first four positive responses. The preferred peer is the router with the least cost. If all costs are equal, the tie-breaker will be the router that responded first.

7. SNA_SYS1 responds to the TEST Response with an Exchange Identifier (XID).

8. ROUTER1 sends a CANUREACH_cs requesting the start of a session, and ROUTER2 responds with an ICANREACH_cs acknowledging the start of a session. ROUTER 1 then responds with a REACH_ACK, indicating that each side is now in sync.

9. XID flows back and forth. SNA_SYS1 then sends a SABME frame to ROUTER1, indicating that it is ready to send data. After receiving the CONTACTED frame, data starts to flow.

Table 3-1 lists some of the common LLC2 DLC commands and responses.

TABLE 3-1

Some common
LLC2 DLC
commands (C) and
responses (R)

Name	Function	Description
Information (I)	C/R	Exchange user data
Supervisory (S)		
Receive Ready (RR)	C/R	Positive acknowledgement; ready to receive I-frame
Receive Not Ready (RNR)	C/R	Positive acknowledgement; not ready to receive
Unnumbered (UI)		
Set Asynchronous Balanced/ Extended Mode (SABM/SABME)	C	Set mode; extended uses two-octet control field
Unnumbered Acknowledgement (UA)	R	Acknowledge acceptance of the above set mode commands
Unnumbered Information (UI)	C/R	Used to exchange control information
Exchange Identification (XID)	C/R	Used to request/report identity and status
Test (TEST)	C/R	Exchange identical information fields for testing

TABLE 3-2

Some common
DLSw+ messages

Command	Type	Description
CANUREACH_ex	0x03	Can you reach station-explorer
CANUREACH_cs	0x03	Can you reach station-circuit start
ICANREACH_ex	0x04	I can reach station-explorer
ICANREACH_cs	0x04	I can reach station-circuit start
REACH_ACK	0x05	Reach acknowledgment
XIDFRAME	0x07	XID frame
CONTACT	0x08	Contact remote station
CONTACTED	0x09	Remote station contacted
NETBIOS_NQ_ex	0x12	NETBIOS name query-explorer
NETBIOS_NR_ex	0x13	NETBIOS name recognized-explorer
TEST_CIRCUIT_REQ	0x7A	Test circuit request
TEST_CIRCUIT_RSP	0x7B	Test circuit response

Table 3-2 lists some of the common DLSw+ messages.

NetBIOS Circuit Establishment

Figure 3-6 illustrates how a NetBIOS circuit is established. LLC2 circuit establishment is achieved using Name Query and Name Recognized-frames (refer to Table 3-2). These frames are used for both address resolution and source route determination. NetBIOS always uses a link SAP value of 0xF0. The main difference between SNA and NetBIOS sessions is that XIDs do not flow for the NetBIOS stations, and the DLSw+ routers exchange Name Query and Name Recognized frames.

NetBIOS Name Queries are typically sent by an end station multiple times. DLSw+ only forwards one Name Query across the WAN but duplicates the Name Query on the remote LAN. Using the default timer values, the Name Queries are sent on the LAN once per session for up to 6 seconds.

Lastly, SDLC attached devices are defined with MAC and SAP addresses to enable them to communicate with LAN attached devices.

In the subsequent sections, the focus will be on using DLSw+ to transport SNA and NetBIOS traffic between remote LANs.

Figure 3-6
Establishing a Net-
BIOS session.

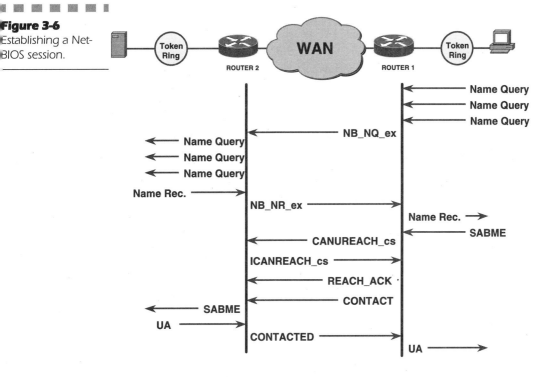

Case Scenario

Figure 3-7 illustrates the overall network scenario referenced throughout this chapter. This enterprise network spans four sites: Houston, Philadelphia, New York, and Chicago. The Houston office is internetworked to the New York office by X.25 with an ISDN dial-up line that serves as backup in the event the X.25 connectivity becomes unavailable. The New York office is interconnected to the Philadelphia and the Chicago offices through a Frame Relay network. Houston, Philadelphia, and New York each has a Token Ring LAN where end systems running on IP, SNA, and NetBIOS reside. Similarly, Chicago has end systems running these protocols, but on a VLAN (Ethernet LAN) instead.

■ ■ ■ ■ ■ ■ ■ ■

Figure 3-7
The overall network topology.

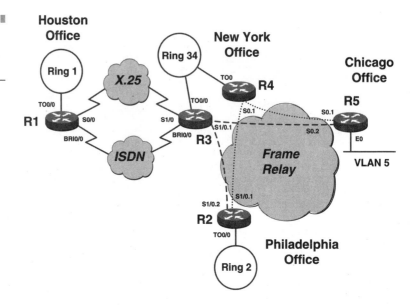

IP Setup

Figure 3-8 illustrates the underlying IP backbone that the enterprise network in Figure 3-7 uses. The whole network is under a single EIGRP routing domain with an autonomous system number of 256. This scenario uses VLSM extensively to form eight subnets with just three Class B IP addresses. Code Listings 3-1 through 3-10 illustrate the IP implementation.

Code Listing 3-1
IP configuration for R1.

```
Hostname C3640-R1
!
!
username C3640-R3 password 0 cisco
isdn switch-type basic-net3
!
interface TokenRing0/0
 ip address 150.25.13.33 255.255.255.224
 ring-speed 16
!
interface Serial1/0
 backup delay 10 30
 backup interface BRI0/0
 ip address 150.25.13.74 255.255.255.252
 encapsulation x25
 no ip split-horizon eigrp 256
 bandwidth 56
```

Code Listing 3-1
(continued)

```
x25 address 150251111
x25 map ip 150.25.13.73 150253333 broadcast
!
interface BRI0/0
 ip address 150.25.13.78 255.255.255.252
 encapsulation ppp
 dialer idle-timeout 60
 dialer map ip 150.25.13.77 name C3640-R3 broadcast 3245652
 dialer load-threshold 128 either
 dialer-group 1
 ppp authentication chap
!
dialer-list 1 protocol ip permit
!
router eigrp 256
 network 150.25.0.0
 no auto-summary
!
```

1. Code Listing 3-1 illustrates the IP configuration for R1. R1 is a
   Cisco 3600 series router. The hostname command sets the name of
   the router to C3640-R1. The username command uses the host
   name of R3, for PPP CHAP authentication. Note the password
   serves as the authentication key, and the password must be the
   same for both R1 and R3. The ISDN switch type used is basic-
   net3.

Figure 3-8
The overall IP net-
work.

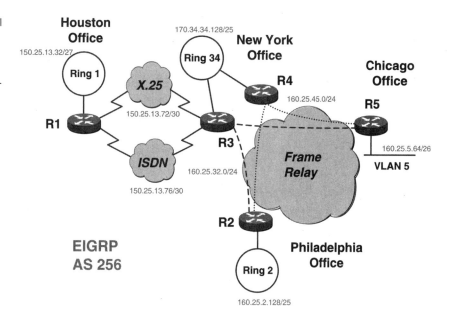

2. The Token Ring interface TO0/0 of R1 is in subnet 150.25.13.32 with a mask of 27 bits. The ring speed is 16Mbps.

3. The Serial interface S1/0 of R1 is in subnet 150.25.13.72 with a mask of 30 bits. S1/0 is connected to a X.25 cloud; its encapsulation type is X.25. R1's X.121 address is 150251111. The x25 map command creates a virtual circuit between R1 and R3 for routing IP. The IP and X.121 addresses used by the command are R3's. S1/0 is also backed up by ISDN interface BRI0/0. The backup delay command will control the backup link so it will only come up 10 seconds after the primary link is no longer available; the backup link will be disconnected after the primary link has reconnected for 30 seconds. In an NBMA (X.25) network, most IP routing protocols will encounter split-horizon problems. In this case, the routing protocol deployed is EIGRP, and the command no ip split-horizon eigrp 256 disables the split-horizon mechanism for this protocol.

4. The ISDN interface BRI0/0 (basic rate 2B+D) is in subnet 150.25.13.76 with a mask of 30 bits. Its encapsulation type is PPP, and the PPP authentication protocol used is CHAP. The dialer map command calls up R3 to establish a PPP connectivity when S1/0 becomes unavailable. The dialer idle-timeout command ensures that the ISDN line will be disconnected if it idles continuously for 60 seconds. This feature is used as a safeguard against unnecessary ISDN charges when the line is not in use. Initially, when a PPP connection is established, only one B channel is used. The dialer load-threshold command will bring up the second B channel when the threshold of the first channel has reached approximately 50% (128/255 x 100%). The either keyword configures the threshold to be applicable to both inbound and outbound traffic. The dialer-group 1 command refers to the dialer-list 1 command, and in this case, the list allows all IP traffic to pass. No refining on the dialer-list is required, as the purpose of the BRI0/0 interface is to back up S1/0.

5. R1 is running EIGRP in autonomous system 256 (AS 256). It spans interfaces TO0/0, S1/0, and BRI0/0. The no auto-summary command disables the default auto-summary feature of the protocol.

Code Listing 3-2 shows the IP routing table for R1.

Code Listing 3-2

IP routing table for
R1.

```
C3640-R1#show ip route
Codes: C - connected, S - static, I - IGRP, R - RIP, M - mobile, B - BGP
       D - EIGRP, EX - EIGRP external, O - OSPF, IA - OSPF inter area
       N1 - OSPF NSSA external type 1, N2 - OSPF NSSA external type 2
       E1 - OSPF external type 1, E2 - OSPF external type 2, E - EGP
       i - IS-IS, L1 - IS-IS level-1, L2 - IS-IS level-2, * - candidate default
       U - per-user static route, o - ODR

Gateway of last resort is not set

     170.34.0.0/25 is subnetted, 1 subnets
D       170.34.34.128 [90/46242304] via 150.25.13.73, 00:04:32, Serial1/0
     150.25.0.0/16 is variably subnetted, 3 subnets, 2 masks
C       150.25.13.32/27 is directly connected, TokenRing0/0
C       150.25.13.72/30 is directly connected, Serial1/0
D       150.25.13.76/30 [90/46738176] via 150.25.13.73, 00:07:33, Serial1/0
     160.25.0.0/16 is variably subnetted, 4 subnets, 3 masks
D       160.25.2.128/25 [90/46754304] via 150.25.13.73, 00:07:33, Serial1/0
D       160.25.45.0/24 [90/46754304] via 150.25.13.73, 00:04:31, Serial1/0
D       160.25.32.0/24 [90/46738176] via 150.25.13.73, 00:07:33, Serial1/0
D       160.25.5.64/26 [90/46763776] via 150.25.13.73, 00:06:33, Serial1/0
```

Code Listing 3-3

IP configuration for
R2.

```
hostname C3640-R2
!
interface TokenRing0/0
 ip address 160.25.2.129 255.255.255.128
 ring-speed 16
!
interface Serial1/0
 no ip address
 encapsulation frame-relay
 frame-relay lmi-type ansi
!
interface Serial1/0.1 point-to-point
 ip address 160.25.45.2 255.255.255.0
 no ip split-horizon eigrp 256
 bandwidth 56
 frame-relay interface-dlci 204
!
interface Serial1/0.2 point-to-point
 ip address 160.25.32.2 255.255.255.0
 no ip split-horizon eigrp 256
 bandwidth 56
 frame-relay interface-dlci 203
!
router eigrp 256
 network 160.25.0.0
 no auto-summary
!
```

1. Code Listing 3-3 illustrates the IP configuration for R2. R2 is a
   Cisco 3600 series router. The hostname command sets the name of
   the router to C3640-R2.

2. The Token Ring interface TO0/0 of R2 is in subnet 160.25.2.128
   with a mask of 25 bits. The ring speed is 16Mbps.

3. R2 happens to be the spoke router for the 160.25.32.0 and 160.25.45.0 Frame Relay subnets. These are implemented through two point-to-point subinterfaces, S1/0.1 and S1/0.2. S1/0.1 is in subnet 160.25.45.0 with a mask of 24 bits, and S1/0.2 is in subnet 160.25.32.0 also with the same number of mask bits. Note the Frame Relay LMI type is ANSI. The `frame-relay interface-dlci` command defines which DLCI numbers are associated with S1/0.1 and S1/0.2. In an NBMA (Frame Relay) network, most IP routing protocols will encounter split-horizon problems. In this case, the routing protocol deployed is EIGRP, and the command `no ip split-horizon eigrp 256` disables the split-horizon mechanism for this protocol.

4. R2 is running EIGRP in autonomous system 256 (AS 256). It spans interfaces TO0/0, S1/0.1, and S1/0.2. The `no auto-summary` command disables the default auto-summary feature of the protocol.

Code Listing 3-4 shows the IP routing table for R2.

Code Listing 3-4

IP routing table for R2.

```
C3640-R2#show ip route
Codes: C - connected, S - static, I - IGRP, R - RIP, M - mobile, B - BGP
       D - EIGRP, EX - EIGRP external, O - OSPF, IA - OSPF inter area
       N1 - OSPF NSSA external type 1, N2 - OSPF NSSA external type 2
       E1 - OSPF external type 1, E2 - OSPF external type 2, E - EGP
       i - IS-IS, L1 - IS-IS level-1, L2 - IS-IS level-2, * - candidate default
       U - per-user static route, o - ODR

Gateway of last resort is not set

     170.34.0.0/25 is subnetted, 1 subnets
D       170.34.34.128 [90/46242304] via 160.25.45.4, 00:04:41, Serial1/0.1
                      [90/46242304] via 160.25.32.3, 00:04:41, Serial1/0.2
     150.25.0.0/16 is variably subnetted, 3 subnets, 2 masks
D       150.25.13.32/27 [90/46754304] via 160.25.32.3, 00:04:40, Serial1/0.2
D       150.25.13.72/30 [90/46738176] via 160.25.32.3, 00:04:40, Serial1/0.2
D       150.25.13.76/30 [90/46738176] via 160.25.32.3, 00:04:40, Serial1/0.2
     160.25.0.0/16 is variably subnetted, 4 subnets, 3 masks
C       160.25.2.128/25 is directly connected, TokenRing0/0
C       160.25.45.0/24 is directly connected, Serial1/0.1
C       160.25.32.0/24 is directly connected, Serial1/0.2
D       160.25.5.64/26 [90/46763776] via 160.25.32.3, 00:06:34, Serial1/0.2
                       [90/46763776] via 160.25.45.4, 00:06:34, Serial1/0.1
```

Code Listing 3-5
IP configuration for
R3.

```
hostname C3640-R3
!
username C3640-R1 password 0 cisco
isdn switch-type basic-net3
!
interface TokenRing0/0
ip address 170.34.34.130 255.255.255.128
 ring-speed 16
!
interface Serial1/0
 no ip address
 encapsulation frame-relay
 no fair-queue
 frame-relay lmi-type ansi
!
interface Serial1/0.1 multipoint
 ip address 160.25.32.3 255.255.255.0
 no ip split-horizon eigrp 256
 bandwidth 56
 frame-relay map ip 160.25.32.2 302 broadcast
 frame-relay map ip 160.25.32.5 305 broadcast
!
interface Serial1/1
 ip address 150.25.13.73 255.255.255.252
 encapsulation x25
 no ip split-horizon eigrp 256
 bandwidth 56
 x25 address 150253333
 x25 map ip 150.25.13.74 150251111 broadcast
!
interface BRI0/0
 ip address 150.25.13.77 255.255.255.252
 encapsulation ppp
 dialer idle-timeout 60
 dialer map ip 150.25.13.78 name C3640-R1 broadcast
 dialer load-threshold 128 either
 dialer-group 1
 ppp authentication chap
!
dialer-list 1 protocol ip permit
!
router eigrp 256
 network 160.25.0.0
 network 170.34.0.0
 network 150.25.0.0
 no auto-summary
!
```

1. Code Listing 3-5 illustrates the IP configuration for R3. R3 is a Cisco 3600 series router. The `hostname` command sets the name of the router to C3640-R3. The `username` command uses the host name of R1, for PPP CHAP authentication. Note the password serves as the authentication key and must be the same for both R3 and R1. The ISDN switch type is `basic-net3`.

2. The Token Ring interface TO0/0 of R3 is in subnet 170.34.34.128 with a mask of 25 bits. The ring speed is 16Mbps.

3. Figure 3-8 shows two subnets spanning across the Frame Relay cloud. R3 is the hub router belonging to one of these subnets, while R4 serves the other. R2 and R5 are the spoke routers. For R3, this is implemented through a multipoint subinterface, S1/0.1. S1/0.1 is in subnet 160.25.32.0 with a mask of 24 bits. Note the Frame Relay LMI type is ANSI. The `frame-relay map` command statically maps the IP addresses of the spoke routers to their respective DLCIs. In an NBMA (Frame Relay) network, most IP routing protocols will encounter split-horizon problems. In this case, the routing protocol deployed is EIGRP, and the command `no ip split-horizon eigrp 256` disables the split-horizon mechanism for this protocol.

4. The Serial interface S1/1 of R3 is in subnet 150.25.13.72 with a mask of 30 bits. S1/1 is connected to the same X.25 cloud as R1, and thus its encapsulation type is X.25. R3's X.121 address is `150253333`. The `x25 map` command creates a virtual circuit between R3 and R1 for routing IP. The IP and X.121 addresses used by the command are R1's. In an NBMA (X.25) network, most IP routing protocols will encounter split-horizon problems. In this case, the routing protocol deployed is EIGRP, and the command `no ip split-horizon eigrp 256` disables the split-horizon mechanism for this protocol.

5. The ISDN interface BRI0/0 (basic rate 2B+D) is in subnet 150.25.13.76 with a mask of 30 bits. Its encapsulation type is PPP, and the PPP authentication protocol used is CHAP. The `dialer map` command establishes a PPP connectivity when R1 makes a call. Note no ISDN number is supplied here, as R1 will initiate the call. The `dialer idle-timeout` command ensures that the ISDN line will be disconnected if it idles continuously for 60 seconds. This is used as a safeguard against unnecessary ISDN charges when the line is not in use. Initially, when a PPP connectivity is established, only one B channel is used. The `dialer load-threshold` command will bring up the second B channel when the threshold of the first channel has reached approximately 50% (128/255 x 100%). The `either` keyword means that the threshold is applicable to inbound and outbound traffic. The `dialer-group 1` command refers to the `dialer-list 1` command, and in this case, the list allows all IP traffic to pass.

6. R3 is running EIGRP in autonomous system 256 (AS 256). It spans interfaces TO0/0, S1/0.1, S1/1, and BRI0/0. The `no auto-summary` command disables the default auto-summary feature of the protocol.

Code Listing 3-6 shows the IP routing table for R3.

Code Listing 3-6

IP routing table for R3.

```
C3640-R3#show ip route
Codes: C - connected, S - static, I - IGRP, R - RIP, M - mobile, B - BGP
       D - EIGRP, EX - EIGRP external, O - OSPF, IA - OSPF inter area
       N1 - OSPF NSSA external type 1, N2 - OSPF NSSA external type 2
       E1 - OSPF external type 1, E2 - OSPF external type 2, E - EGP
       i - IS-IS, L1 - IS-IS level-1, L2 - IS-IS level-2, * - candidate default
       U - per-user static route, o - ODR

Gateway of last resort is not set

     170.34.0.0/25 is subnetted, 1 subnets
C       170.34.34.128 is directly connected, TokenRing0/0
     150.25.0.0/16 is variably subnetted, 3 subnets, 2 masks
D       150.25.13.32/27 [90/46242304] via 150.25.13.74, 00:06:50, Serial1/1
C       150.25.13.72/30 is directly connected, Serial1/1
C       150.25.13.76/30 is directly connected, BRI0/0
     160.25.0.0/16 is variably subnetted, 4 subnets, 3 masks
D       160.25.2.128/25 [90/46242304] via 160.25.32.2, 00:04:49, Serial1/0.1
D       160.25.45.0/24 [90/46242304] via 170.34.34.129, 00:04:49, TokenRing0/0
C       160.25.32.0/24 is directly connected, Serial1/0.1
D       160.25.5.64/26 [90/46251776] via 160.25.32.5, 00:04:49, Serial1/0.1
```

Code Listing 3-7

IP configuration for R4.

```
hostname C2500-R4
!
interface TokenRing0
 ip address 170.34.34.129 255.255.255.128
 ring-speed 16
!
interface Serial0
 no ip address
 encapsulation frame-relay
 frame-relay lmi-type ansi
!
interface Serial0.1 multipoint
 ip address 160.25.45.4 255.255.255.0
 no ip split-horizon eigrp 256
 bandwidth 56
 frame-relay map ip 160.25.45.2 402 broadcast
 frame-relay map ip 160.25.45.5 405 broadcast
!
router eigrp 256
 network 160.25.0.0
 network 170.34.0.0
 no auto-summary
!
```

1. Code Listing 3-7 illustrates the IP configuration for R4. R4 is a Cisco 2500 series router. The `hostname` command sets the name of the router to C2500-R4.

2. The Token Ring interface TO0 of R4 is in subnet 170.34.34.128 with a mask of 25 bits. The ring speed is 16Mbps.

3. Figure 3-8 shows two subnets spanning the Frame Relay cloud. R4 is the hub router belonging to one of these subnets, whereas R3 serves the other. R2 and R5 are the spoke routers. For R4 this is implemented through a multipoint subinterface, S0.1. S0.1 is in subnet 160.25.45.0 with a mask of 24 bits. Note the Frame Relay LMI type is ANSI. The `frame-relay map` command statically maps the IP addresses of the spoke routers into their respective DLCIs. In an NBMA (Frame Relay) network, most IP routing protocols will encounter split-horizon problems. In this case, the routing protocol deployed is EIGRP, and the command `no ip split-horizon eigrp 256` disables the split-horizon mechanism for this protocol.

4. R4 is running EIGRP in autonomous system 256 (AS 256). It spans interfaces TO0 and S0.1. The `no auto-summary` command disables the default auto-summary feature of the protocol.

Code Listing 3-8 shows the IP routing table for R4.

Code Listing 3-8

IP routing table for R4.

```
C2500-R4#show ip route
Codes: C - connected, S - static, I - IGRP, R - RIP, M - mobile, B - BGP
       D - EIGRP, EX - EIGRP external, O - OSPF, IA - OSPF inter area
       N1 - OSPF NSSA external type 1, N2 - OSPF NSSA external type 2
       E1 - OSPF external type 1, E2 - OSPF external type 2, E - EGP
       i - IS-IS, L1 - IS-IS level-1, L2 - IS-IS level-2, * - candidate default
       U - per-user static route, o - ODR

Gateway of last resort is not set

     170.34.0.0/25 is subnetted, 1 subnets
C       170.34.34.128 is directly connected, TokenRing0
     150.25.0.0/16 is variably subnetted, 3 subnets, 2 masks
D       150.25.13.32/27 [90/46258432] via 170.34.34.130, 00:04:59, TokenRing0
D       150.25.13.72/30 [90/46242304] via 170.34.34.130, 00:04:59, TokenRing0
D       150.25.13.76/30 [90/40528128] via 170.34.34.130, 00:04:59, TokenRing0
     160.25.0.0/16 is variably subnetted, 4 subnets, 3 masks
D       160.25.2.128/25 [90/46242304] via 160.25.45.2, 00:04:59, Serial0.1
C       160.25.45.0/24 is directly connected, Serial0.1
D       160.25.32.0/24 [90/46242304] via 170.34.34.130, 00:05:00, TokenRing0
D       160.25.5.64/26 [90/46251776] via 160.25.45.5, 00:05:00, Serial0.1
```

Code Listing 3-9

IP configuration for R5.

```
hostname C2509-R5
!
interface Ethernet0
 ip address 160.25.5.65 255.255.255.192
!
interface Serial0
 no ip address
 encapsulation frame-relay
```

Code Listing 3-9
(continued)

```
frame-relay lmi-type ansi
!
interface Serial0.1 point-to-point
 ip address 160.25.45.5 255.255.255.0
 no ip split-horizon eigrp 256
 bandwidth 56
 frame-relay interface-dlci 504
!
interface Serial0.2 point-to-point
 ip address 160.25.32.5 255.255.255.0
 no ip split-horizon eigrp 256
 bandwidth 56
 frame-relay interface-dlci 503
!
router eigrp 256
 network 160.25.0.0
 no auto-summary
!
```

1. Code Listing 3-9 illustrates the IP configuration for R5. R5 is a Cisco 2500 series router. The `hostname` command sets the name of the router to C2509-R5.

2. The Ethernet interface E0 of R5 is in subnet 160.25.5.64 with a mask of 26 bits.

3. R5 happens to be the spoke router for the 160.25.32.0 and 160.25.45.0 Frame Relay subnets. These are implemented through two point-to-point subinterfaces, S0.1 and S0.2. S0.1 is in subnet 160.25.45.0 with a mask of 24 bits, and S0.2 is in subnet 160.25.32.0 also with the same number of mask bits. Note the Frame Relay LMI type is ANSI. The `frame-relay interface-dlci` command defines which DLCI numbers are associated with S0.1 and S0.2. In an NBMA (Frame Relay) network, most IP routing protocols will encounter split-horizon problems. In this case, the routing protocol deployed is EIGRP and the command `no ip split-horizon eigrp 256` disables the split-horizon mechanism for this protocol.

4. R5 is running EIGRP in autonomous system 256 (AS 256). It spans interfaces E0, S0.1, and S0.2. The `no auto-summary` command disables the default auto-summary feature of the protocol.

Code Listing 3-10 shows the IP routing table for R5.

Code Listing 3-10

IP routing table for R5.

```
C2509-R5#show ip route
Codes: C - connected, S - static, I - IGRP, R - RIP, M - mobile, B - BGP
       D - EIGRP, EX - EIGRP external, O - OSPF, IA - OSPF inter area
       N1 - OSPF NSSA external type 1, N2 - OSPF NSSA external type 2
       E1 - OSPF external type 1, E2 - OSPF external type 2, E - EGP
       i - IS-IS, L1 - IS-IS level-1, L2 - IS-IS level-2, * - candidate default
       U - per-user static route, o - ODR

Gateway of last resort is not set

     170.34.0.0/25 is subnetted, 1 subnets
D       170.34.34.128 [90/46242304] via 160.25.45.4, 00:05:18, Serial0.1
                      [90/46242304] via 160.25.32.3, 00:05:18, Serial0.2
     150.25.0.0/16 is variably subnetted, 3 subnets, 2 masks
D       150.25.13.32/27 [90/46754304] via 160.25.32.3, 00:05:16, Serial0.2
D       150.25.13.72/30 [90/46738176] via 160.25.32.3, 00:05:16, Serial0.2
D       150.25.13.76/30 [90/46738176] via 160.25.32.3, 00:05:16, Serial0.2
     160.25.0.0/16 is variably subnetted, 4 subnets, 3 masks
D       160.25.2.128/25 [90/46754304] via 160.25.32.3, 00:07:09, Serial0.2
                        [90/46754304] via 160.25.45.4, 00:07:10, Serial0.1
C       160.25.45.0/24 is directly connected, Serial0.1
C       160.25.32.0/24 is directly connected, Serial0.2
C       160.25.5.64/26 is directly connected, Ethernet0
```

Basic DLSw+ Configuration

Figure 3-9 shows the establishment of DLSw+ circuits between R1, R2, R3, and R4 using TCP encapsulation. Code Listings 3-11 through 3-22 illustrate this.

Code Listing 3-11

DLSw+ configuration for R1.

```
hostname C3640-R1
!
source-bridge ring-group 73
dlsw local-peer peer-id 150.25.13.33 promiscuous
dlsw port-list 1 TokenRing0/0
dlsw remote-peer 1 tcp 170.34.34.130
!
interface TokenRing0/0
 source-bridge 1 1 73
 source-bridge spanning
!
```

1. Code Listing 3-11 illustrates the DLSw+ configuration for R1. Locally the SNA and NetBIOS end systems on Ring 1 communicate with R1 through Source-Route Bridging. The command source-bridge ring-group 73 defines the target ring (virtual ring) number as 73. (Refer to Chapter 2 for more details on Source-Route

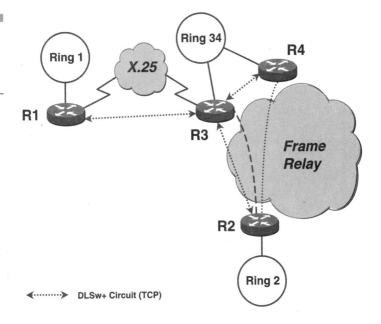

Figure 3-9
DLSw+ circuits
between R1, R2, R3,
and R4.

Bridging.) The interface command `source-bridge 1 1 73`
specifies the local ring connected to TO0/0 as Ring 1, the bridge
connecting the local and target rings as Bridge 1, and the target
ring defined earlier as Ring 73. In this scenario, spanning tree is
not run implicitly for bridging, so the spanning tree must be
explicitly configured on each forwarding Token Ring interface to
enable them to forward spanning explorers. In this case, the
`source-bridge spanning` command enables the spanning tree
algorithm for TO0/0.

2. To configure DLSw+ on R1, a local peer must first be defined. The
   command `dlsw local-peer peer-id 150.25.13.33` promiscuous sets the IP address of the local peer to the address of TO0/0.
   Note that any addresses on the current active interfaces can be
   assigned, not necessarily just TO0/0. If loopback addresses are used,
   they must be part of a subnet belonging to a routing domain. The
   keyword `promiscuous` means that R1 will accept connections from
   any remote peer requesting a peer startup. Hence, remote peers
   need not be defined in R1 using the `dlsw remote-peer` command.
   This will provide better control and manageability for R1.

3. Even though R1 is configured as a promiscuous peer, a DLSw+ circuit will be established only when a remote peer requests a peer

startup. The command `dlsw remote-peer` defines a remote peer if the establishment of a DLSw+ circuit with this specific remote peer is crucial. In R1 the full command is `dlsw remote-peer 1 tcp 170.34.34.130`, specifying R3 (whose TO0/0's IP address is 170.34.34.130) as the particular remote peer with which it would like to establish a DLSw+ circuit. The command also defines `tcp` as the encapsulation on the remote peer.

4. The `dlsw port-list 1 TokenRing0/0` command maps traffic on TO0/0 to the remote peer. This means that traffic received from the remote peer is only forwarded to TO0/0. The `port-list` controls the flooding of explorer frames by allowing the network to be segmented. The `port-list` must be configured before defining the remote peers. The 1 that follows after the `remote-peer` keyword is the `port-list` number and, in this case, refers to `port-list 1`. For all peers and all ports (Token Ring and Serial) to receive all traffic, specify 0 as the list number.

Code Listing 3-12 shows the DLSw+ peer information for R1.

Code Listing 3-12
DLSw+ peer information for R1.

```
C3640-R1#show dlsw peers
Peers:                      state   pkts_rx   pkts_tx  type  drops ckts TCP   uptime
  TCP 170.34.34.130  CONNECT   30        30      conf     0     0    0 00:03:58
```

From the `show dlsw peers` command in Code Listing 3-12, a DLSw+ circuit has been established and is in the CONNECT state. The encapsulation used is TCP. As the remote peer is explicitly specified using the `dlsw remote peer` command, the type of remote peer is reflected as `conf` (configured).

Code Listing 3-13 shows the DLSw+ capabilities information for R1.

Code Listing 3-13
DLSw+ capabilities information for R1.

```
C3640-R1#show dlsw capabilities
DLSw: Capabilities for peer 170.34.34.130(2065)
  vendor id (OUI)          : '00C' (cisco)
  version number           : 1
  release number           : 0
  init pacing window       : 20
  unsupported saps         : none
  num of tcp sessions      : 1
  loop prevent support     : no
  icanreach mac-exclusive  : no
  icanreach netbios-excl.  : no
```

Code Listing 3-13
(continued)

```
reachable mac addresses : none
reachable netbios names : none
cisco version number     : 1
peer group number        : 0
border peer capable       : no
peer cost                 : 3
biu-segment configured   : no
local-ack configured     : yes
priority configured      : no
peer type                 : prom
version string           :
Cisco Internetwork Operating System Software
IOS (tm) 3600 Software (C3640-J-M), Version 11.2(15)P,   RELEASE
SOFTWARE (fc1)
Copyright (c) 1986-1998 by cisco Systems, Inc.
Compiled Tue 14-Jul-98 02:28 by dschwart
```

As R1 has established a DLSw+ circuit with remote peer R3, the `show dlsw capabilities` command in Code Listing 3-13 can be used to gather the DLSw+ capabilities for R3.

Code Listing 3-14
DLSw+ configuration
for R2.

```
hostname C3640-R2
!
source-bridge ring-group 73
dlsw local-peer peer-id 160.25.2.129 promiscuous
dlsw ring-list 1 rings 2
dlsw remote-peer 1 tcp 170.34.34.130
!
interface TokenRing0/0
 source-bridge 2 1 73
 source-bridge spanning
!
```

1. Code Listing 3-14 illustrates the DLSw+ configuration for R2. Locally the SNA and NetBIOS end systems on Ring 2 communicate with R2 through Source-Route Bridging. The command `source-bridge ring-group 73` defines the target ring (virtual ring) number as 73. (Refer to Chapter 2 for more details on Source-Route Bridging.) The interface command `source-bridge 2 1 73` specifies the local ring connected to TO0/0 as Ring 2, the bridge connecting the local and target rings as Bridge 1, and the target ring defined earlier as Ring 73. In this scenario, spanning tree is not run implicitly for bridging, so the spanning tree must be explicitly configured on each forwarding Token Ring interface to enable spanning explorers forwarding. In this case, the `source-bridge spanning` command enables the spanning tree algorithm for TO0/0.

2. To configure DLSw+ on R2, a local peer must first be defined. The command `dlsw local-peer peer-id 160.25.2.129` promiscuous sets the IP address of the local peer to the address of TO0/0. Any addresses on the current active interfaces can be assigned, not necessarily just TO0/0, but if loopback addresses are used, they must be part of a subnet belonging to a routing domain. The keyword `promiscuous` means that R2 will accept connections from any remote peer requesting a peer startup. Hence, the remote peers need not be defined in R2 using the `dlsw remote-peer` command. This will provide better control and manageability for R2.

3. Even though R2 is configured as a promiscuous peer, a DLSw+ circuit will be established only when a remote peer requests a peer startup. The command `dlsw remote-peer` defines a remote peer if the establishment of a DLSw+ circuit with this specific remote peer is crucial. In R2 the full command is `dlsw remote-peer 1 tcp 170.34.34.130`, specifying R3 (whose TO0/0's IP address is 170.34.34.130) as the particular remote peer with which it would like to establish a DLSw+ circuit. The command also defines `tcp` as the encapsulation on the remote peer.

4. The `dlsw ring-list 1 rings 2` command maps traffic on Ring 2 to the remote peer. This means that traffic received from the remote peer is only forwarded to Ring 2. The `ring-list` controls the flooding of explorer frames by allowing the network to be segmented. The `ring-list` must be configured before defining the remote peers. The `1` that follows after the `remote-peer` keyword is the `ring-list` number and, in this case, refers to `ring-list 1`. For all peers and all rings to receive all traffic, specify `0` as the list number.

Code Listing 3-15 shows the DLSw+ peer information for R2.

Code Listing 3-15
DLSw+ peer information for R2.

```
C3640-R2#show dlsw peers
Peers:                     state  pkts_rx  pkts_tx   type  drops ckts TCP    uptime
  TCP 170.34.34.130  CONNECT  1475     1480  conf       0      0    0  00:04:19
```

Code Listing 3-16 shows the DLSw+ capabilities information for R2.

Code Listing 3-16

DLSw+ capabilities
information for R2.

```
C3640-R2#show dlsw capabilities
DLSw: Capabilities for peer 170.34.34.130(2065)
  vendor id (OUI)         : '00C' (cisco)
  version number          : 1
  release number          : 0
  init pacing window      : 20
  unsupported saps        : none
  num of tcp sessions     : 1
  loop prevent support    : no
  icanreach mac-exclusive : no
  icanreach netbios-excl. : no
  reachable mac addresses : none
  reachable netbios names : none
  cisco version number    : 1
  peer group number       : 0
  border peer capable     : no
  peer cost               : 3
  biu-segment configured  : no
  local-ack configured    : yes
  priority configured     : no
  peer type               : prom
  version string          :
Cisco Internetwork Operating System Software
IOS (tm) 3600 Software (C3640-J-M), Version 11.2(15)P,  RELEASE
SOFTWARE (fc1)
Copyright (c) 1986-1998 by cisco Systems, Inc.
Compiled Tue 14-Jul-98 02:28 by dschwart
```

Code Listing 3-17

DLSw+ configuration
for R3.

```
hostname C3640-R3
!
source-bridge ring-group 73
dlsw local-peer peer-id 170.34.34.130 promiscuous
dlsw ring-list 1 rings 34
dlsw remote-peer 1 tcp 170.34.34.129
!
interface TokenRing0/0
 source-bridge 34 1 73
 source-bridge spanning
!
```

1. Code Listing 3-17 illustrates the DLSw+ configuration for R3.
   Locally the SNA and NetBIOS end systems on Ring 34 communicate with R3 through Source-Route Bridging. The command
   source-bridge ring-group 73 defines the target ring (virtual
   ring) number as 73. The interface command source-bridge 34 1
   73 specifies the local ring connected to TO0/0 as Ring 34, the bridge
   connecting the local and target rings as Bridge 1, and the target

ring defined earlier as Ring 73. In this scenario, spanning tree is not run implicitly for bridging, so the spanning tree must be explicitly configured on each forwarding Token Ring interface to enable them to forward spanning explorers. In this case, the `source-bridge spanning` command enables the spanning tree algorithm for TO0/0.

2. To configure DLSw+ on R3, a local peer must be defined. The command `dlsw local-peer peer-id 170.34.34.130 promiscuous` sets the IP address of the local peer to the address of TO0/0. Any addresses on the current active interfaces can be assigned, not necessarily just TO0/0, but if loopback addresses are used, they must be part of a subnet belonging to a routing domain. The keyword `promiscuous` means that R3 will accept connections from any remote peer requesting a peer startup. Hence, the remote peers need not be defined in R3 using the `dlsw remote-peer` command. This will provide better control and manageability for R3.

3. Even though R3 is configured as a promiscuous peer, a DLSw+ circuit will be established only when a remote peer requests a peer startup. The command `dlsw remote-peer` defines a remote peer if the establishment of a DLSw+ circuit with this specific remote peer is crucial. In R3 the full command is `dlsw remote-peer 1 tcp 170.34.34.129`, specifying R4 (whose TO0's IP address is 170.34.34.129) as the particular remote peer with which it would like to establish a DLSw+ circuit. The command also defines `tcp` as the encapsulation on the remote peer.

4. The `dlsw ring-list 1 rings 34` command maps traffic on Ring 34 to the remote peer. This means that traffic received from the remote peer is only forwarded to Ring 34. The `ring-list` controls the flooding of explorer frames by allowing the network to be segmented. The `ring-list` must be configured before defining the remote peers. The 1 that follows after the `remote-peer` keyword is the `ring-list` number and, in this case, refers to `ring-list 1`. For all peers and all rings to receive all traffic, specify 0 as the list number.

Code Listing 3-18 shows the DLSw+ peer information for R3.

Code Listing 3-18

DLSw+ peer informa-
tion for R3.

```
C3640-R3#show dlsw peers
Peers:                    state   pkts_rx   pkts_tx type  drops ckts TCP   uptime
  TCP 170.34.34.129   CONNECT    971       977  conf      0     0    0  00:05:37
  TCP 150.25.13.33    CONNECT     11        11  prom      0     0    0  00:04:59
  TCP 160.25.2.129    CONNECT     11        11  prom      0     0    0  00:04:50
```

The show dlsw peers command in Code Listing 3-18 displays three DLSw+ circuits that have been established and are in the CONNECT state. The encapsulation used is TCP. Remote peer R4 is explicitly specified using the dlsw remote peer command, indicated by the type conf (configured). Remote peers R1 and R2 are not explicitly specified, but their peer startup connections will be accepted, since R3 is configured as a promiscuous peer. In show dlsw peers, the type of remote peer is prom (promiscuous).

Code Listing 3-19 shows the DLSw+ capabilities information for R3.

Code Listing 3-19

DLSw+ capabilities
information for R3.

```
C3640-R3#show dlsw capabilities
DLSw: Capabilities for peer 170.34.34.129(2065)
  vendor id (OUI)          : '00C' (cisco)
  version number           : 1
  release number           : 0
  init pacing window       : 20
  unsupported saps         : none
  num of tcp sessions      : 1
  loop prevent support     : no
  icanreach mac-exclusive  : no
  icanreach netbios-excl.  : no
  reachable mac addresses  : none
  reachable netbios names  : none
  cisco version number     : 1
  peer group number        : 0
  border peer capable      : no
  peer cost                : 3
  biu-segment configured   : no
  local-ack configured     : yes
  priority configured      : no
  peer type                : conf
  version string           :
Cisco Internetwork Operating System Software
IOS (tm) 2500 Software (C2500-JS-L), Version 11.2(4), RELEASE SOFTWARE
(fc1)
Copyright (c) 1986-1997 by cisco Systems, Inc.
Compiled Mon 10-Feb-97 14:11 by ajchopra

DLSw: Capabilities for peer 150.25.13.33(2065)
  vendor id (OUI)          : '00C' (cisco)
  version number           : 1
  release number           : 0
  init pacing window       : 20
  unsupported saps         : none
```

■ |

Code Listing 3-19
(continued)

```
num of tcp sessions      : 1
loop prevent support     : no
icanreach mac-exclusive  : no
icanreach netbios-excl.  : no
reachable mac addresses  : none
reachable netbios names  : none
cisco version number     : 1
peer group number        : 0
border peer capable      : no
peer cost                : 3
biu-segment configured   : no
local-ack configured     : yes
priority configured      : no
peer type                : conf
version string           :
Cisco Internetwork Operating System Software
IOS (tm) 3600 Software (C3640-J-M), Version 11.2(15)P,  RELEASE
SOFTWARE (fc1)
Copyright (c) 1986-1998 by cisco Systems, Inc.
Compiled Tue 14-Jul-98 02:28 by dschwart

DLSw: Capabilities for peer 160.25.2.129(2065)
vendor id (OUI)          : '00C' (cisco)
version number           : 1
release number           : 0
init pacing window       : 20
unsupported saps         : none
num of tcp sessions      : 1
loop prevent support     : no
icanreach mac-exclusive  : no
icanreach netbios-excl.  : no
reachable mac addresses  : none
reachable netbios names  : none
cisco version number     : 1
peer group number        : 0
border peer capable      : no
peer cost                : 3
biu-segment configured   : no
local-ack configured     : yes
priority configured      : no
peer type                : conf
version string           :
Cisco Internetwork Operating System Software
IOS (tm) 3600 Software (C3640-J-M), Version 11.2(15)P,  RELEASE
SOFTWARE (fc1)
Copyright (c) 1986-1998 by cisco Systems, Inc.
Compiled Tue 14-Jul-98 02:28 by dschwart
```

R3 has established three DLSw+ circuits with remote peers: R1, R2, and R4. The show dlsw capabilities command in Code Listing 3-19 can be used to gather the DLSw+ capabilities for these peers.

Code Listing 3-20
DLSw+ configuration
for R4.

```
hostname C2500-R4
!
source-bridge ring-group 73
dlsw local-peer peer-id 170.34.34.129 promiscuous
dlsw ring-list 1 rings 34
dlsw remote-peer 1 tcp 170.34.34.130
!
interface TokenRing0
 source-bridge 34 2 73
 source-bridge spanning
!
```

1. Code Listing 3-20 illustrates the DLSw+ configuration for R4. Locally the SNA and NetBIOS end systems on Ring 34 communicate with R4 through Source-Route Bridging. The command `source-bridge ring-group 73` defines the target ring (virtual ring) number as 73. The interface command `source-bridge 34 2 73` specifies the local ring connected to TO0 as Ring 34, the bridge connecting the local and target rings as Bridge 2, and the target ring defined earlier as Ring 73. In our scenario, spanning tree is not run implicitly for bridging, so the tree must be explicitly configured on each forwarding Token Ring interfaces to enable them to forward spanning explorers. In this case, the `source-bridge spanning` command enables the spanning tree algorithm for TO0.

2. To configure DLSw+ on R4, a local peer must be defined. The command `dlsw local-peer peer-id 170.34.34.129 promiscuous` sets the IP address of the local peer to the address of TO0. Any addresses on the current active interfaces can be assigned, not necessarily just TO0, but if loopback addresses are used, they must be part of a subnet belonging to a routing domain. The keyword `promiscuous` means that R4 will accept connections from any remote peer requesting a peer startup. Hence, the remote peers need not be defined in R4 using the `dlsw remote-peer` command. This will provide better control and manageability for R4.

3. Even though R4 is configured as a promiscuous peer, a DLSw+ circuit will be established only when a remote peer requests a peer startup. The command `dlsw remote-peer` defines a remote peer if the establishment of a DLSw+ circuit with this specific remote peer is crucial. In R4, the full command is `dlsw remote-peer 1 tcp 170.34.34.130`, specifying R3 (whose TO0/0's IP address is 170.34.34.130) as the particular remote peer with which it would like to establish a DLSw+ circuit. The command also defines `tcp` as the encapsulation on the remote peer.

4. The `dlsw ring-list 1 rings 34` command maps traffic on Ring 34 to the remote peer. This means that traffic received from the remote peer is only forwarded to Ring 34. The `ring-list` controls the flooding of explorer frames by allowing the network to be segmented. The `ring-list` must be configured before defining the remote peers. The `1` that follows after the `remote-peer` keyword is the `ring-list` number and, in this case, refers to `ring-list 1`. For all peers and all rings to receive all traffic, specify `0` as the list number.

Code Listing 3-21 shows the DLSw+ peer information for R4.

Code Listing 3-21
DLSw+ peer information for R4.

```
C2500-R4#show dlsw peers
Peers:                          state     pkts_rx   pkts_tx  type  drops ckts TCP    uptime
  TCP 170.34.34.130   CONNECT   1514      1524    conf        0        0    0  00:06:14
```

Code Listing 3-22 shows the DLSw+ capabilities information for R4.

Code Listing 3-22
DLSw+ capabilities information for R4.

```
C2500-R4#show dlsw capabilities
DLSw: Capabilities for peer 170.34.34.130(2065)
  vendor id (OUI)           : '00C' (cisco)
  version number            : 1
  release number            : 0
  init pacing window        : 20
  unsupported saps          : none
  num of tcp sessions       : 1
  loop prevent support      : no
  icanreach mac-exclusive   : no
  icanreach netbios-excl.   : no
  reachable mac addresses   : none
  reachable netbios names   : none
  cisco version number      : 1
  peer group number         : 0
  border peer capable       : no
  peer cost                 : 3
  biu-segment configured    : no
  local-ack configured      : yes
  priority configured       : no
  peer type                 : conf
  version string            :
Cisco Internetwork Operating System Software
IOS (tm) 3600 Software (C3640-J-M), Version 11.2(15)P,  RELEASE
SOFTWARE (fc1)
Copyright (c) 1986-1998 by cisco Systems, Inc.
Compiled Tue 14-Jul-98 02:28 by dschwart
```

DLSw+ & Ethernet

Consider Figure 3-10. R5 establishes one DLSw+ circuit each to R3 and R4. The encapsulation used for both circuits is TCP. Code Listings 3-23 through 3-31 illustrate this.

Code Listing 3-23
DLSw+ configuration for R3.

```
hostname C3640-R3
!
source-bridge ring-group 73
dlsw local-peer peer-id 170.34.34.130 cost 2 promiscuous
dlsw ring-list 1 rings 34
dlsw remote-peer 1 tcp 170.34.34.129
!
interface TokenRing0/0
 source-bridge 34 1 73
 source-bridge spanning
!
```

The default DLSw+ peer cost is 3. In this case, the peer cost of R3 has been explicitly set to 2, as illustrated in Code Listing 3-23.

Code Listing 3-24 illustrates the DLSw+ peer information for R3.

Code Listing 3-24
DLSw+ peer information for R3.

```
C3640-R3#show dlsw peers
Peers:                        state   pkts_rx  pkts_tx  type  drops ckts TCP   uptime
  TCP 170.34.34.129   CONNECT   971      977  conf      0     0    0  00:05:37
  TCP 150.25.13.33    CONNECT    11       11  prom      0     0    0  00:04:59
  TCP 160.25.2.129    CONNECT    11       11  prom      0     0    0  00:04:50
  TCP 160.25.5.65     CONNECT    77       11  prom      0     0    0  00:05:05
```

Figure 3-10
DLSw+ circuits between R3, R4, and R5.

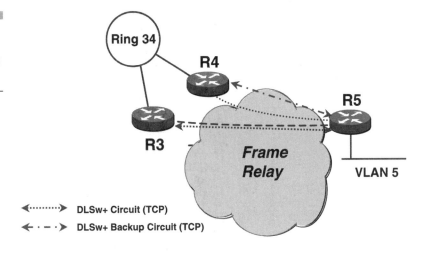

Ring 34

R4

R5

R3

Frame Relay

VLAN 5

◄··········► DLSw+ Circuit (TCP)

◄· — ·► DLSw+ Backup Circuit (TCP)

Code Listing 3-25 illustrates the DLSw+ capabilities information for R3.

Code Listing 3-25

DLSw+ capabilities
information for R3.

```
C3640-R3#show dlsw capabilities ip-address 160.25.5.65
DLSw: Capabilities for peer 160.25.5.65(2065)
  vendor id (OUI)           : '00C' (cisco)
  version number            : 1
  release number            : 0
  init pacing window        : 20
  unsupported saps          : none
  num of tcp sessions       : 1
  loop prevent support      : no
  icanreach mac-exclusive   : no
  icanreach netbios-excl.   : no
  reachable mac addresses   : none
  reachable netbios names   : none
  cisco version number      : 1
  peer group number         : 0
  border peer capable       : no
  peer cost                 : 3
  biu-segment configured    : no
  local-ack configured      : yes
  priority configured       : no
  peer type                 : conf
  version string            :
Cisco Internetwork Operating System Software
IOS (tm) 2500 Software (C2500-J-L), Version 11.2(7a), RELEASE SOFTWARE
(fc1)
Copyright (c) 1986-1997 by cisco Systems, Inc.
Compiled Tue 01-Jul-97 15:31 by kuong
```

Code Listing 3-26

DLSw+ configuration
for R4.

```
hostname C2500-R4
!
source-bridge ring-group 73
dlsw local-peer peer-id 170.34.34.129 cost 4 promiscuous
dlsw ring-list 1 rings 34
dlsw remote-peer 1 tcp 170.34.34.130
!
interface TokenRing0
 source-bridge 34 2 73
 source-bridge spanning
!
```

The default DLSw+ peer cost is 3. In this case, the peer cost of R4 has been explicitly set to 4, as illustrated in Code Listing 3-26. The bridge number defined for R3's TO0/0 is 1 and for R4's TO0 is 2. This is to prevent loops, since the Token Ring interfaces of both R3 and R4 are physically connected to the same ring.

Code Listing 3-27 illustrates the DLSw+ peer information for R4.

Code Listing 3-27

DLSw+ peer informa-
tion for R4.

```
C2500-R4#show dlsw peers
Peers:                     state   pkts_rx   pkts_tx  type  drops ckts TCP   uptime
  TCP 170.34.34.130   CONNECT   1514      1524     conf    0     0    0  00:06:14
  TCP 160.25.5.65     CONNECT    209       212     prom    0     0    0  01:42:37
```

Code Listing 3-28 illustrates the DLSw+ capabilities information for R4.

Code Listing 3-28

DLSw+ capabilities
information for R4.

```
C2500-R4#show dlsw capabilities ip-address 160.25.5.65
DLSw: Capabilities for peer 160.25.5.65(0)
    vendor id (OUI)          : '00C' (cisco)
    version number           : 1
    release number           : 0
    init pacing window       : 20
    unsupported saps         : none
    num of tcp sessions      : 1
    loop prevent support     : no
    icanreach mac-exclusive  : no
    icanreach netbios-excl.  : no
    reachable mac addresses  : none
    reachable netbios names  : none
    cisco version number     : 1
    peer group number        : 0
    border peer capable      : no
    peer cost                : 3
    biu-segment configured   : no
    local-ack configured     : yes
    priority configured      : no
    peer type                : conf
    version string           :
Cisco Internetwork Operating System Software
IOS (tm) 2500 Software (C2500-J-L), Version 11.2(7a), RELEASE SOFTWARE
(fc1)
Copyright (c) 1986-1997 by cisco Systems, Inc.
Compiled Tue 01-Jul-97 15:31 by kuong
```

Code Listing 3-29

DLSw+-over-Ethernet
configuration for R5.

```
hostname C2509-R5
!
dlsw local-peer peer-id 160.25.5.65 promiscuous
dlsw bgroup-list 1 bgroups 1
dlsw remote-peer 1 tcp 170.34.34.129
dlsw remote-peer 1 tcp 170.34.34.130
dlsw bridge-group 1
dlsw timer explorer-wait-time 5
!
interface Ethernet0
 bridge-group 1
!
bridge 1 protocol ieee
!
```

1. Code Listing 3-29 illustrates the DLSw+-over-Ethernet configuration for R5. Locally the SNA and NetBIOS end systems on VLAN 5 communicate with R5 through Transparent Bridging. The command `bridge 1 protocol ieee` defines the bridge number as 1 using the IEEE 802.1D-compatible spanning tree algorithm. The interface command `bridge-group 1` specifies E0 as a port of Bridge 1.

2. To configure DLSw+ on R5, a local peer must be defined. The command `dlsw local-peer peer-id 160.25.5.65 promiscuous` sets the IP address of the local peer to the address of E0. Any addresses on the current active interfaces can be assigned, not necessarily just E0, but if loopback addresses are used, they must be part of a subnet belonging to a routing domain. The keyword `promiscuous` means that R5 will accept connections from any remote peer requesting a peer startup. Hence, the remote peers need not be defined in R5 using the `dlsw remote-peer` command. This will provide better control and manageability for R5.

3. Even though R5 is configured as a promiscuous peer, a DLSw+ circuit will be established only when a remote peer requests a peer startup. The command `dlsw remote-peer` defines a remote peer if the establishment of a DLSw+ circuit with this specific remote peer is crucial. In R5 the commands `dlsw remote-peer 1 tcp 170.34.34.130` and `dlsw remote-peer 1 tcp 170.34.34.129` specify R3 and R4 as the particular remote peers with which R5 would like to establish a DLSw+ circuit. The commands also define `tcp` as the encapsulation on the remote peers. The DLSw+ routers will convert Ethernet frames to Token Ring frames. The encapsulation must be TCP for the conversion to take place, since FST and direct encapsulation do not support media translation.

4. The command `dlsw bridge-group 1` links the Ethernet segment that is currently serviced by Bridge 1 to the DLSw+ process. The `dlsw bgroup-list 1 bgroups 1` command maps traffic on bridge group 1 to the remote peer. Traffic received from the remote peer is only forwarded to bridge group 1. The `bgroup-list` controls the flooding of explorer frames by allowing the network to be segmented. The `bgroup-list` must be configured before defining the remote peers. The 1 that follows after the `remote-peer` keyword is the `bgroup-list` number and, in this case, refers to

bgroup-list 1. For all peers and all bridge groups to receive all traffic, specify 0 as the list number.

5. The two costs explicitly defined for R3 and R4 set up the scenario for DLSw+ cost peers. Cost peers add resiliency to the DLSw+ circuit establishment in R5 when a peer connection is lost. When both peers (R3 and R4) are active, R5 will select the peer with the least cost—in this case R3—as the preferred router for CANUREACH_cs and directed CANUREACH_ex frames. The command dlsw timer explorer-wait-time 5 sets a time buffer of five seconds to wait for all the explorers to return to R5, to prevent the problem with costs that can occur when R5 uses the first explorer (but not necessarily the one with the lowest cost) that comes back.

Code Listing 3-30 illustrates the DLSw+ peer information for R5.

Code Listing 3-30
DLSw+ peer information for R5.

```
C2509-R5#show dlsw peers
Peers:                    state    pkts_rx   pkts_tx type drops ckts TCP   uptime
  TCP 170.34.34.129   CONNECT   209      214    conf    0     0    0 01:43:14
  TCP 170.34.34.130   CONNECT   165     1802    conf    0     0    0 00:06:20
```

Code Listing 3-31 illustrates the DLSw+ capabilities information for R5.

Code Listing 3-31
DLSw+ capabilities information for R5.

```
C2509-R5#show dlsw capabilities
DLSw: Capabilities for peer 170.34.34.129(0)
  vendor id (OUI)          : '00C' (cisco)
  version number           : 1
  release number           : 0
  init pacing window       : 20
  unsupported saps         : none
  num of tcp sessions      : 1
  loop prevent support     : no
  icanreach mac-exclusive  : no
  icanreach netbios-excl.  : no
  reachable mac addresses  : none
  reachable netbios names  : none
  cisco version number     : 1
  peer group number        : 0
  border peer capable      : no
  peer cost                : 4
  biu-segment configured   : no
  local-ack configured     : no
  priority configured      : no
  peer type                : prom
  version string           :
Cisco Internetwork Operating System Software
```

■ |

Code Listing 3-31
(continued)

```
IOS (tm) 2500 Software (C2500-JS-L), Version 11.2(4), RELEASE SOFTWARE
(fc1)
Copyright (c) 1986-1997 by cisco Systems, Inc.
Compiled Mon 10-Feb-97 14:11 by ajchopra

DLSw: Capabilities for peer 170.34.34.130(2065)
    vendor id (OUI)        : '00C' (cisco)
    version number         : 1
    release number         : 0
    init pacing window     : 20
    unsupported saps       : none
    num of tcp sessions    : 1
    loop prevent support   : no
    icanreach mac-exclusive : no
    icanreach netbios-excl. : no
    reachable mac addresses : none
    reachable netbios names : none
    cisco version number   : 1
    peer group number      : 0
    border peer capable    : no
    peer cost              : 2
    biu-segment configured : no
    local-ack configured   : yes
    priority configured    : no
    peer type              : prom
    version string         :
Cisco Internetwork Operating System Software
IOS (tm) 3600 Software (C3640-J-M), Version 11.2(15)P,  RELEASE
SOFTWARE (fc1)
Copyright (c) 1986-1998 by cisco Systems, Inc.
Compiled Tue 14-Jul-98 02:28 by dschwart
```

DLSw+ Backup

Consider Figure 3-11. R1 and R2 both establish one primary DLSw+ circuit to R3 and one backup DLSw+ circuit to R4. In this case, R4 is the backup peer for R1 and R2. The encapsulation used for the backup circuit between R1 and R4 is TCP, and that between R2 and R4 is FST. Note that FST, unlike TCP, does not have local acknowledgement and is used for Token-Ring-to-Token-Ring connections only. Code Listings 3-32 through 3-35 illustrate all of these.

Figure 3-11
Backup peer circuits
for R1 and R2.

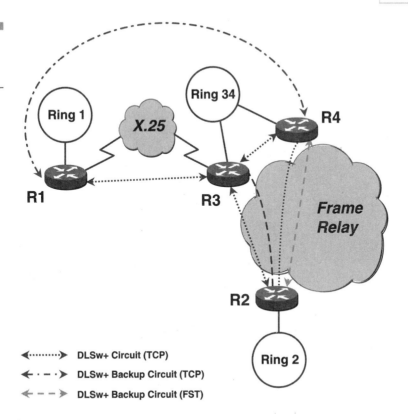

Code Listing 3-32
DLSw+ backup peer
configuration for R1.

```
hostname C3640-R1
!
source-bridge ring-group 73
dlsw local-peer peer-id 150.25.13.33 promiscuous
dlsw port-list 1 TokenRing0/0
dlsw remote-peer 1 tcp 170.34.34.130
dlsw remote-peer 1 tcp 170.34.34.129 backup-peer 170.34.34.130
!
interface TokenRing0/0
 source-bridge 1 1 73
 source-bridge spanning
!
```

Code Listing 3-32 illustrates the DLSw+ backup peer configuration for
R1. The command dlsw remote-peer 1 tcp 170.34.34.129
backup-peer 170.34.34.130 specifies R4 (170.34.34.129) as the
backup peer for R3 (170.34.34.130). That is, when the primary circuit
between R1 and R3 becomes unavailable, a backup circuit between R1
and R4 will be established. Once the primary circuit becomes operational

again, all subsequent new sessions will use this circuit, and the backup circuit will be torn down when data is no longer flowing through the old LLC2 connections. The `linger` option can be used to specify an uptime (in minutes) for the backup peer after the primary circuit is reestablished. Once the uptime expires, the backup circuit is disconnected.

Code Listing 3-33

DLSw+ peers information for R1.

```
C3640-R1#show dlsw peers
Peers:                     state   pkts_rx   pkts_tx   type   drops ckts TCP   uptime
  TCP 170.34.34.130  CONNECT    30        30     conf      0       0    0  00:03:58
  TCP 170.34.34.129  DISCONN    17        17     conf      0       0    -       -
```

The `show dlsw peers` command in Code Listing 3-33 illustrates that the backup peer is disconnected when the primary peer is connected.

Code Listing 3-34

DLSw+ backup peer configuration for R2.

```
hostname C3640-R2
!
source-bridge ring-group 73
dlsw local-peer peer-id 160.25.2.129 promiscuous
dlsw ring-list 1 rings 2
dlsw remote-peer 1 tcp 170.34.34.130
dlsw remote-peer 1 fst 170.34.34.129 backup-peer 170.34.34.130
!
interface TokenRing0/0
 source-bridge 2 1 73
 source-bridge spanning
!
```

Code Listing 3-34 illustrates the DLSw+ backup peer configuration for R2. The command `dlsw remote-peer 1 tcp 170.34.34.129 backup-peer 170.34.34.130` specifies R4 (170.34.34.129) as the backup peer for R3 (170.34.34.130). When the primary circuit between R2 and R3 becomes unavailable, a backup circuit between R2 and R4 will be established.

Code Listing 3-35 illustrates the DLSw+ peer information for R2.

Code Listing 3-35

DLSw+ peer information for R2.

```
C3640-R2#show dlsw peers
Peers:                     state   pkts_rx   pkts_tx   type   drops ckts TCP   uptime
  TCP 170.34.34.130  CONNECT  1475      1480     conf      0       0    0  00:04:19
  FST 170.34.34.129  DISCONN   353       343     conf      0       -    -       -
Expected: 0  Next Send: 0  Seq errors: 0
```

In Figure 3-12, the Token Ring connectivity between R3 and Ring 34 fails, thereby causing the primary circuits of R1 and R2 to become unavailable.

The `debug dlsw peers` command in Code Listing 3-36 shows what happens when R1's primary circuit goes down.

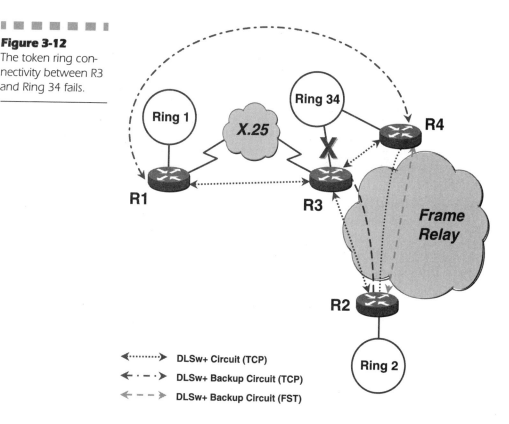

Figure 3-12
The token ring connectivity between R3 and Ring 34 fails.

◄········► DLSw+ Circuit (TCP)

◄ · — · ► DLSw+ Backup Circuit (TCP)

◄ — — ► DLSw+ Backup Circuit (FST)

Code Listing 3-36
Debugging output for DLSw+ peer events on R1.

```
C3640-R1#debug dlsw peers
DLSw: Keepalive Request sent to peer 170.34.34.130(2065))
DLSw: Keepalive Response sent to peer 170.34.34.130(2065))
DLSw: Keepalive Response sent to peer 170.34.34.130(2065))
DLSw: Keepalive Response sent to peer 170.34.34.130(2065))
DLSw: dlsw_tcpd_fini() for peer 170.34.34.130(2065)
DLSw: tcp fini closing connection for peer 170.34.34.130(2065)
DLSw: action_d(): for peer 170.34.34.130(2065)
DLSw: peer 170.34.34.130(2065), old state CONNECT, new state DISCONN
DLSw: action_a() attempting to connect peer 170.34.34.129(2065)
DLSw: action_a(): Write pipe opened for peer 170.34.34.129(2065)
DLSw: peer 170.34.34.129(2065), old state DISCONN, new state WAIT_RD
DLSw: passive open 170.34.34.129(11014) -> 2065
```

```
DLSw: action_c(): for peer 170.34.34.129(2065)
DLSw: peer 170.34.34.129(2065), old state WAIT_RD, new state CAP_EXG
DLSw: CapExId Msg sent to peer 170.34.34.129(2065)
DLSw: Recv CapExPosRsp Msg from peer 170.34.34.129(2065)
DLSw: action_e(): for peer 170.34.34.129(2065)
DLSw: Recv CapExId Msg from peer 170.34.34.129(2065)
DLSw: Pos CapExResp sent to peer 170.34.34.129(2065)
DLSw: action_e(): for peer 170.34.34.129(2065)
DLSw: peer 170.34.34.129(2065), old state CAP_EXG, new state CONNECT
DLSw: peer_act_on_capabilities() for peer 170.34.34.129(2065)
DLSw: dlsw_tcpd_fini() for peer 170.34.34.129(2065)
DLSw: dlsw_tcpd_fini() closing write pipe for peer 170.34.34.129
DLSw: action_g(): for peer 170.34.34.129(2065)
DLSw: closing write pipe tcp connection for peer 170.34.34.129(2065)
DLSw: action_a() attempting to connect peer 170.34.34.130(2065)
DLSw: CONN: peer 170.34.34.130 open failed, timed out [10]
DLSw: action_a(): CONN failed - retries 1
DLSw: peer 170.34.34.130(2065), old state DISCONN, new state DISCONN
DLSw: Keepalive Request sent to peer 170.34.34.129(2065))
DLSw: Keepalive Response from peer 170.34.34.129(2065)
```

In the preceding debug output, as illustrated in Code Listing 3-36, R3 did not respond to the keepalives R1 sent. R1 determined the primary peer, R3, must be down and changed R3's state to DISCONN. At the same time, the backup peer, R4, was changed from the DISCONN state to the WAIT_RD state, waiting for R1 to open the read port 2065. Afterwards R4 went into the CAP_EXG state, exchanging capabilities with R1, and finally into the CONNECT state when the backup circuit was established.

Note the DLSw+ peer information for R1, R2, R3 and R4, as illustrated in Code Listings 3-37 through 3-40.

```
C3640-R1#show dlsw peers
Peers:                      state   pkts_rx pkts_tx type  drops ckts TCP  uptime
  TCP 170.34.34.129 CONNECT   227     227 conf      0     0    0  01:23:24
  TCP 170.34.34.130 DISCONN    29      30 conf      0     0    -     -
```

In Code Listing 3-37, the backup peer, R4, is up and running (in the CONNECT state), while the primary peer, R3, is now in the DISCONN state.

Code Listing 3-38

DLSw+ peer information for R2.

```
C3640-R2#show dlsw peers
Peers:                        state  pkts_rx  pkts_tx  type  drops ckts TCP   uptime
  FST 170.34.34.129    CONNECT   662      646  conf     0     -    -    01:24:11
  Expected: 0  Next Send: 0  Seq errors: 0
  TCP 170.34.34.130    DISCONN  1522     1529  conf     0     0    -    -
```

In Code Listing 3-38, the backup peer, R4, is up and running (in the CONNECT state), while the primary peer, R3, is now in the DISCONN state.

Code Listing 3-39

DLSw+ peer information for R3.

```
C3640-R3#show dlsw peers
Peers:                        state  pkts_rx  pkts_tx  type  drops ckts TCP   uptime
  TCP 170.34.34.129    DISCONN   31       37  conf    *0     0    -    -
```

As R3 is unavailable, the circuit initially established between R3 and R4 is reported as down (or DISCONN) now, as illustrated in Code Listing 3-39.

Code Listing 3-40

DLSw+ peer information for R4.

```
C2500-R4#show dlsw peers
Peers:                        state  pkts_rx  pkts_tx  type  drops ckts TCP   uptime
  FST 160.25.2.129     CONNECT   170      170  prom     0     -    -    1:25:19
  Expected: 0  Next Send: 0  Seq errors: 0
  TCP 150.25.13.33     CONNECT   182      182  prom     0     0    0    01:24:56
  TCP 170.34.34.130    DISCONN  1566     1578  conf     0     0    -    -
```

In Code Listing 3-40, backup circuits have been established for R1 and R2.

The debug dlsw peers command in Code Listing 3-41 shows what happens when R1's primary circuit becomes available again.

Code Listing 3-41

Debugging output for DLSw+ peer events on R1.

```
C3640-R1#debug dlsw peers
DLSw: Keepalive Request sent to peer 170.34.34.129(2065))
DLSw: Keepalive Response from peer 170.34.34.129(2065)
DLSw: action_a() attempting to connect peer 170.34.34.130(2065)
DLSw: action_a(): Write pipe opened for peer 170.34.34.130(2065)
DLSw: peer 170.34.34.130(2065), old state DISCONN, new state WAIT_RD
DLSw: passive open 170.34.34.130(11017) -> 2065
DLSw: action_c(): for peer 170.34.34.130(2065)
DLSw: peer 170.34.34.130(2065), old state WAIT_RD, new state CAP_EXG
DLSw: CapExId Msg sent to peer 170.34.34.130(2065)
```

Code Listing 3-41
(continued)

```
DLSw: Recv CapExPosRsp Msg from peer 170.34.34.130(2065)
DLSw: action_e(): for peer 170.34.34.130(2065)
DLSw: Recv CapExId Msg from peer 170.34.34.130(2065)
DLSw: Pos CapExResp sent to peer 170.34.34.130(2065)
DLSw: action_e(): for peer 170.34.34.130(2065)
DLSw: peer 170.34.34.130(2065), old state CAP_EXG, new state CONNECT
DLSw Clear cache for 170.34.34.129
DLSw: peer_act_on_capabilities() for peer 170.34.34.130(2065)
DLSw: dlsw_tcpd_fini() for peer 170.34.34.130(2065)
DLSw: dlsw_tcpd_fini() closing write pipe for peer 170.34.34.130
DLSw: action_g(): for peer 170.34.34.130(2065)
DLSw: closing write pipe tcp connection for peer 170.34.34.130(2065)
DLSw: closing backup peer 170.34.34.129; no ckts
DLSw: action_d(): for peer 170.34.34.129(2065)
DLSw: aborting tcp connection for peer 170.34.34.129(11007)
DLSw: peer 170.34.34.129(2065), old state CONNECT, new state DISCONN
```

In the above debug output, the primary peer, R3, has become available again and changed from the DISCONN state to the WAIT_RD state, waiting for R1 to open the read port 2065. R3 then went into the CAP_EXG state, exchanging capabilities with R1, and finally into the CONNECT state when the primary circuit was reestablished. The backup circuit was torn down, since there were no LLC2 circuits using it. R4 then changed from the CONNECT state to the DISCONN state.

DLSw+ & DDR

In Figure 3-13, the X.25 link between R1 and R3 has been interrupted. This link has an ISDN dial-up line serving as backup. In the event X.25 connectivity becomes unavailable, the ISDN line is connected to maintain the connectivity between the two routers. Code Listings 3-42 and 3-43 illustrate the DDR implementation.

Code Listing 3-42
DLSw+ DDR configu-
ration for R1.

```
hostname C3640-R1
!
username C3640-R3 password 0 cisco
isdn switch-type basic-net3
source-bridge ring-group 73
dlsw local-peer peer-id 150.25.13.33 promiscuous
dlsw port-list 1 TokenRing0/0
dlsw remote-peer 1 tcp 170.34.34.130 dynamic no-llc 10
dlsw remote-peer 1 tcp 170.34.34.129 backup-peer 170.34.34.130 dynamic no-llc 10
dlsw netbios-keepalive-filter
```

Code Listing 3-42
(continued)

```
!
interface Serial1/0
 backup delay 10 30
 backup interface BRI0/0
!
interface BRI0/0
 encapsulation ppp
 dialer idle-timeout 60
 dialer map llc2  name C3640-R3 broadcast 3245652
 dialer load-threshold 128 either
 dialer-group 1
 ppp authentication chap
!
dialer-list 1 protocol llc2 permit
!
interface TokenRing0/0
 source-bridge 1 1 73
 source-bridge spanning
!
```

Figure 3-13
The X.25 connectivity between R1 and R3 fails.

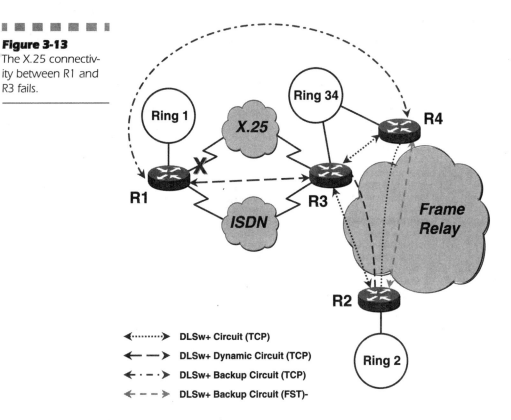

Ring 34

Ring 1

X.25

R4

Frame Relay

R1

ISDN

R3

R2

Ring 2

◄·········► DLSw+ Circuit (TCP)

◄ — ► DLSw+ Dynamic Circuit (TCP)

◄ · — · ► DLSw+ Backup Circuit (TCP)

◄ – – ► DLSw+ Backup Circuit (FST)-

1. Code Listing 3-42 illustrates the DLSw+ DDR configuration for R1. Note that SNA DDR technology allows DLSw+ links to be closed during idle periods. There are two ways to implement this:

   a. The `keepalive` option of the `dlsw remote-peer 1 tcp` command can be set to 0 seconds, and the `timeout` option can be configured accordingly. Normally a value lower than the default timeout of 90 seconds is used.

   b. The `dynamic` keyword may be used; in this case, the `keepalive` is set to 0 automatically, allowing the TCP connection to the remote peer to be established only when there is DLSw+ data to send. In this scenario, R1 establishes a TCP connection to R3 (or R4 when R3 is down) dynamically. In other words, R3 (or R4 when R3 is down) is configured as a dynamic peer. This configuration will provide some cost savings on the ISDN line charges. The TCP connection can be configured to terminate after a specified period of idle time on the peer using the `inactivity` option (default of five minutes), or after a specified period of no active LLC sessions on the peer using the `no-llc` option (default of five minutes, but in this instance, the value is specified as 10 minutes). Both options (`inactivity` and `no-llc`) are exclusive of each other. Even though a connection can be determined as idle for a certain period, the SNA sessions established for this connection may still be active; the `inactivity` option may cause these active sessions to be terminated.

2. The `dlsw netbios-keepalive-filter` command filters the NetBIOS Session Alive packets (LLC2 I-frames). These packets are redundant to a certain extent and add unnecessary traffic through the WAN. Filtering these packets will help to save some ISDN line charges. This command first appeared in Cisco IOS 11.2F.

3. The `dialer map` command dials R3 to establish a PPP connectivity when S1/0 becomes unavailable. The `dialer-group 1` command refers to the `dialer-list 1` command, and in this case, the list allows all LLC2 traffic to pass. No refining on the dialer-list is required, as the purpose of the BRI0/0 interface is to back up S1/0.

Code Listing 3-43
DLSw+ DDR configuration for R3.

```
hostname C3640-R3
!
username C3640-R1 password 0 cisco
isdn switch-type basic-net3
source-bridge ring-group 73
dlsw local-peer peer-id 170.34.34.130 cost 2 promiscuous
dlsw ring-list 1 rings 34
dlsw remote-peer 1 tcp 170.34.34.129
dlsw netbios-keepalive-filter
!
interface BRI0/0
 encapsulation ppp
 dialer idle-timeout 60
 dialer map llc2  name C3640-R1 broadcast
 dialer load-threshold 128 either
 dialer-group 1
 ppp authentication chap
!
dialer-list 1 protocol llc2 permit
!
interface TokenRing0/0
 source-bridge 34 1 73
 source-bridge spanning
!
```

1. Code Listing 3-43 illustrates the DLSw+ DDR configuration for R3. The `dlsw netbios-keepalive-filter` command filters the NetBIOS Session Alive packets (LLC2 I-frames). These packets are redundant to a certain extent and add unnecessary traffic through the WAN. Filtering these packets will help to save some ISDN line charges. This command first appeared in Cisco IOS 11.2F.

2. The `dialer map` command establishes a PPP connection when R1 makes a call. No ISDN number is supplied, as R1 will initiate the call. The `dialer-group 1` command refers to the `dialer-list 1` command, and in this case, the list allows all LLC2 traffic to pass.

DLSw+ & Frame Relay

Cisco IOS software for direct encapsulation of DLSw+ in Frame Relay is based on RFC 1490 that supports pass-through or local acknowledgement (LLC2 DLC termination). This feature requires a minimum number of PVCs and simplifies configuration, as multiple PUs can share a PVC without requiring the configuration of multiple SAPs.

The pass-through method generates little link overhead and requires minimal CPU cycles in the connecting DLSw+ routers, compared to TCP encapsulation, using local acknowledgement.

Local acknowledgement prevents DLC timeouts when congestion starts to build up in the WAN. It also reduces WAN traffic by terminating DLC acknowledgements and keepalives locally.

Figure 3-14 illustrates the two DLSw+ circuits R2 establishes over the Frame Relay cloud to R3 and R4 using the local acknowledgement method (also known as DLSw Lite). Code Listings 3-44 through 3-52 illustrate the Frame Relay implementation.

Figure 3-14
DLSw+ circuits over Frame Relay between R2, R3, and R4.

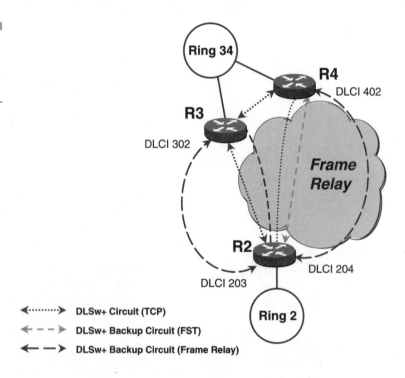

◀┄┄┄┄┄▶ **DLSw+ Circuit (TCP)**

◀ ─ ─ ▶ **DLSw+ Backup Circuit (FST)**

◀ ── ▶ **DLSw+ Backup Circuit (Frame Relay)**

Code Listing 3-44
DLSw+ Frame Relay
configuration for R2.

```
hostname C3640-R2
!
source-bridge ring-group 73
dlsw local-peer peer-id 160.25.2.129 promiscuous
dlsw ring-list 1 rings 2
dlsw remote-peer 1 frame-relay interface Serial1/0.1 204 lf 1500
dlsw remote-peer 1 frame-relay interface Serial1/0.2 203 lf 1500
dlsw remote-peer 1 tcp 170.34.34.130
dlsw remote-peer 1 fst 170.34.34.129 backup-peer 170.34.34.130
!
interface TokenRing0/0
 source-bridge 2 1 73
 source-bridge spanning
!
```

Code Listing 3-44 illustrates the DLSw+ Frame Relay configuration for R2. The commands `dlsw remote-peer 1 frame-relay interface Serial1/0.1 204 lf 1500` and `dlsw remote-peer 1 frame-relay interface Serial1/0.2 203 lf 1500` define direct encapsulation in Frame Relay for the DLSw+ circuits to R3 and R4. The `lf` option determines the largest frame that a peer can handle to prevent frame segmentation. In this example, the maximum frame size for the Frame Relay network is 1500 bytes.

Code Listing 3-45 illustrates the DLSw+ peer information for R2.

Code Listing 3-45
DLSw+ peer information for R2.

```
C3640-R2#show dlsw peers
Peers:                  state   pkts_rx  pkts_tx  type  drops ckts TCP     uptime
 FR  Se1/0.1    204  CONNECT  1328     1328  conf     0     0    -   10:59:43
 FR  Se1/0.2    203  CONNECT  1320     1321  conf     0     0    -   09:33:53
 TCP 170.34.34.130   CONNECT  1475     1480  conf     0     0    0   00:04:19
 FST 170.34.34.129   DISCONN   353      343  conf     0     -    -    -   ·
Expected: 0  Next Send: 0  Seq errors: 0
```

Code Listing 3-46 illustrates the DLSw+ capabilities information for R2.

Code Listing 3-46
DLSw+ capabilities
information for R2.

```
C3640-R2#show dlsw capabilities interface s1/0
DLSw: Capabilities for peer on interface Serial1/0
    vendor id (OUI)         : '00C' (cisco)
    version number          : 1
    release number          : 0
    init pacing window      : 20
    unsupported saps        : none
    num of tcp sessions     : 1
    loop prevent support    : no
    icanreach mac-exclusive : no
    icanreach netbios-excl. : no
```

Code Listing 3-46
(continued)

```
    reachable mac addresses : none
    reachable netbios names : none
    cisco version number    : 1
    peer group number       : 0
    border peer capable      : no
    peer cost                : 4
    biu-segment configured  : no
    local-ack configured     : yes
    priority configured     : no
    peer type                : conf
    version string          :
Cisco Internetwork Operating System Software
IOS (tm) 2500 Software (C2500-JS-L), Version 11.2(4), RELEASE SOFTWARE
(fc1)
Copyright (c) 1986-1997 by cisco Systems, Inc.
Compiled Mon 10-Feb-97 14:11 by ajchopra

DLSw: Capabilities for peer on interface Serial1/0
    vendor id (OUI)         : '00C' (cisco)
    version number          : 1
    release number          : 0
    init pacing window      : 20
    unsupported saps        : none
    num of tcp sessions     : 1
    loop prevent support    : no
    icanreach mac-exclusive : no
    icanreach netbios-excl. : no
    reachable mac addresses : none
    reachable netbios names : none
    cisco version number    : 1
    peer group number       : 0
    border peer capable      : no
    peer cost                : 2
    biu-segment configured  : no
    local-ack configured     : yes
    priority configured     : no
    peer type                : conf
    version string          :
Cisco Internetwork Operating System Software
IOS (tm) 3600 Software (C3640-J-M), Version 11.2(15)P,  RELEASE
SOFTWARE (fc1)
Copyright (c) 1986-1998 by cisco Systems, Inc.
Compiled Tue 14-Jul-98 02:28 by dschwart
```

Code Listing 3-47
DLSw+ Frame Relay
configuration for R3.

```
hostname C3640-R3
!
source-bridge ring-group 73
dlsw local-peer peer-id 170.34.34.130 cost 2 promiscuous
dlsw ring-list 1 rings 34
dlsw remote-peer 1 frame-relay interface Serial1/0.1 302 1f 1500
dlsw remote-peer 1 tcp 170.34.34.129
!
interface TokenRing0/0
 source-bridge 34 1 73
 source-bridge spanning
```

■ ■

Code Listing 3-47
(continued)

```
!
interface Serial1/0
 no ip address
 encapsulation frame-relay
 frame-relay lmi-type ansi
!
interface Serial1/0.1 multipoint
 bandwidth 56
 frame-relay map llc2   302 broadcast
!
```

1. Code Listing 3-47 illustrates the DLSw+ Frame Relay configuration for R3. The command `dlsw remote-peer 1 frame-relay interface Serial1/0.1 302 lf 1500` defines direct encapsulation in Frame Relay for the DLSw+ circuit from R3 to R2. Note that the `lf` option determines the largest frame that a peer can handle to prevent frame segmentation. In this example, the maximum frame size for the Frame Relay network is 1500 bytes.

2. The interface command `frame-relay map llc2 302 broadcast` is specified on the multipoint subinterface S1/0.1 to define the mapping between the DLSw+ circuit and the Frame Relay DLCI. The keyword `llc2` means local acknowledgement is used. This command is not required for point-to-point subinterfaces.

Code Listing 3-48 illustrates the DLSw+ peer information for R3.

■ ■

Code Listing 3-48
DLSw+ peer information for R3.

```
C3640-R3#show dlsw peers
Peers:                     state   pkts_rx   pkts_tx  type  drops ckts TCP   uptime
 TCP 160.25.5.65   CONNECT    77        11     prom     0     0    0  00:05:05
 TCP 170.34.34.129 CONNECT   971       977     conf     0     0    0  00:05:37
 FR   Se1/0.1  302 CONNECT  1134      1134     conf     0     0    -  09:34:24
 TCP 150.25.13.33  CONNECT    11        11     prom     0     0    0  00:04:59
 TCP 160.25.2.129  CONNECT    11        11     prom     0     0    0  00:04:50
```

Code Listing 3-49 illustrates the DLSw+ capabilities information for R3.

Code Listing 3-49

DLSw+ capabilities information for R3.

```
C3640-R3#show dlsw capabilities interface s1/0
DLSw: Capabilities for peer on interface Serial1/0
    vendor id (OUI)          : '00C' (cisco)
    version number           : 1
    release number           : 0
    init pacing window       : 20
    unsupported saps         : none
    num of tcp sessions      : 1
    loop prevent support     : no
    icanreach mac-exclusive  : no
    icanreach netbios-excl.  : no
    reachable mac addresses  : none
    reachable netbios names  : none
    cisco version number     : 1
    peer group number        : 0
    border peer capable      : no
    peer cost                : 3
    biu-segment configured   : no
    local-ack configured     : yes
    priority configured      : no
    peer type                : conf
    version string           :
Cisco Internetwork Operating System Software
IOS (tm) 3600 Software (C3640-J-M), Version 11.2(15)P,  RELEASE
SOFTWARE (fc1)
Copyright (c) 1986-1998 by cisco Systems, Inc.
Compiled Tue 14-Jul-98 02:28 by dschwart
```

Code Listing 3-50

DLSw+ Frame Relay configuration for R4.

```
hostname C2500-R4
!
source-bridge ring-group 73
dlsw local-peer peer-id 170.34.34.129 cost 4 promiscuous
dlsw ring-list 1 rings 34
dlsw remote-peer 1 frame-relay interface Serial0.1 402 1f 1500
dlsw remote-peer 1 tcp 170.34.34.130
!
interface Serial0
 no ip address
 encapsulation frame-relay
 frame-relay lmi-type ansi
!
interface Serial0.1 multipoint
 bandwidth 56
 frame-relay map llc2  402 broadcast
!
interface TokenRing0
 source-bridge 34 2 73
 source-bridge spanning
!
```

1. Code Listing 3-50 illustrates the DLSw+ Frame Relay configuration for R4. The command `dlsw remote-peer 1 frame-relay interface Serial0.1 402 lf 1500` defines direct encapsulation in Frame Relay for the DLSw+ circuit from R4 to R2. The `lf` option determines the largest frame that a peer can handle to prevent frame segmentation. In this example, the maximum frame size for the Frame Relay network is 1500 bytes.

2. The interface command `frame-relay map llc2 402 broadcast` is specified at the multipoint subinterface S0.1 to define the mapping between the DLSw+ circuit and the Frame Relay DLCI. The keyword `llc2` means local acknowledgement is used.

Code Listing 3-51 illustrates the DLSw+ peer information for R4.

Code Listing 3-51
DLSw+ peer information for R4.

```
C2500-R4#show dlsw peers
Peers:                        state  pkts_rx  pkts_tx type drops ckts TCP   uptime
 TCP 170.34.34.130  CONNECT    1514     1524  conf    0    0     0  00:06:14
 TCP 160.25.5.65    CONNECT     209      212  prom    0    0     0  01:42:37
 FR  Se0.1   402    CONNECT    1330     1330  conf    0    0     -  11:00:52
```

Code Listing 3-52 illustrates the DLSw+ capabilities information for R4.

Code Listing 3-52
DLSw+ capabilities information for R4.

```
C2500-R4#show dlsw capabilities interface s0
DLSw: Capabilities for peer on interface Serial0
  vendor id (OUI)          : '00C' (cisco)
  version number           : 1
  release number           : 0
  init pacing window       : 20
  unsupported saps         : none
  num of tcp sessions      : 1
  loop prevent support     : no
  icanreach mac-exclusive  : no
  icanreach netbios-excl.  : no
  reachable mac addresses  : none
  reachable netbios names  : none
  cisco version number     : 1
  peer group number        : 0
  border peer capable      : no
  peer cost                : 3
  biu-segment configured   : no
  local-ack configured     : yes
  priority configured      : no
  peer type                : conf
  version string           :
Cisco Internetwork Operating System Software
IOS (tm) 3600 Software (C3640-J-M), Version 11.2(15)P,  RELEASE
SOFTWARE (fc1)
Copyright (c) 1986-1998 by cisco Systems, Inc.
Compiled Tue 14-Jul-98 02:28 by dschwart
```

DLSw+ Peer Groups

Consider Figure 3-15. This network is divided into two DLSw+ peer groups: group 25 and group 6, with R3 and R4 configured as border peers. This is implemented in Code Listings 3-53 through 3-67.

Code Listing 3-53
DLSw+ peer group configuration for R1.

```
hostname C3640-R1
!
source-bridge ring-group 73
dlsw local-peer peer-id 150.25.13.33 group 25 promiscuous
dlsw port-list 1 TokenRing0/0
dlsw remote-peer 1 tcp 170.34.34.130
!
interface TokenRing0/0
 source-bridge 1 1 73
 source-bridge spanning
!
```

The command `dlsw local-peer peer-id 150.25.13.33 group 25 promiscuous` in Code Listing 3-53 sets R1 in peer group 25. The `promiscuous` keyword allows for any-to-any connections.

Figure 3-15
DLSw+ border peers and peer groups.

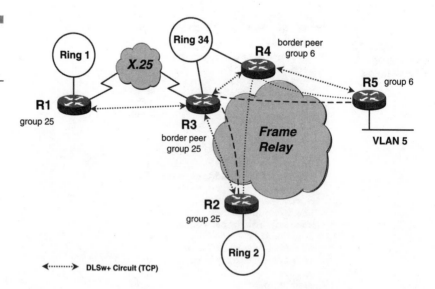

Code Listing 3-54 illustrates the DLSw+ peer information for R1.

Code Listing 3-54
DLSw+ peers information for R1.

```
C3640-R1#show dlsw peers
Peers:                          state  pkts_rx  pkts_tx  type  drops ckts TCP   uptime
  TCP 170.34.34.130   CONNECT     30       30    conf     0      0    0    00:03:58
```

Code Listing 3-55 illustrates the DLSw+ capabilities information for R1.

Code Listing 3-55
DLSw+ capabilities information for R1.

```
C3640-R1#sh dlsw capabilities
DLSw: Capabilities for peer 170.34.34.130(2065)
  vendor id (OUI)        : '00C' (cisco)
  version number         : 1
  release number         : 0
  init pacing window     : 20
  unsupported saps       : none
  num of tcp sessions    : 1
  loop prevent support   : no
  icanreach mac-exclusive : no
  icanreach netbios-excl. : no
  reachable mac addresses : none
  reachable netbios names : none
  cisco version number   : 1
  peer group number      : 25
  border peer capable    : yes
  peer cost              : 3
  biu-segment configured : no
  local-ack configured   : yes
  priority configured    : no
  peer type              : prom
  version string         :
Cisco Internetwork Operating System Software
IOS (tm) 3600 Software (C3640-J-M), Version 11.2(15)P,  RELEASE
SOFTWARE (fc1)
Copyright (c) 1986-1998 by cisco Systems, Inc.
Compiled Tue 14-Jul-98 02:28 by dschwart
```

Code Listing 3-56
DLSw+ peer group configuration for R2.

```
hostname C3640-R2
!
source-bridge ring-group 73
dlsw local-peer peer-id 160.25.2.129 group 25 promiscuous
dlsw ring-list 1 rings 2
dlsw remote-peer 1 tcp 170.34.34.130
!
interface TokenRing0/0
 source-bridge 2 1 73
 source-bridge spanning
!
```

The command `dlsw local-peer peer-id 160.25.2.129 group 25 promiscuous` in Code Listing 3-56 sets R2 in peer group 25. The promiscuous keyword allows for any-to-any connections.

Code Listing 3-57 illustrates the DLSw+ peer information for R2.

Code Listing 3-57

DLSw+ peer information for R2.

```
C3640-R2#show dlsw peers
Peers:                        state   pkts_rx pkts_tx   type  drops ckts TCP    uptime
  TCP 170.34.34.130  CONNECT  1475       1480  conf       0      0    0  0  00:04:19
```

Code Listing 3-58 illustrates the DLSw+ capabilities information for R2.

Code Listing 3-58

DLSw+ capabilities information for R2.

```
C3640-R2#show dlsw capabilities
DLSw: Capabilities for peer 170.34.34.130(2065)
  vendor id (OUI)          : '00C' (cisco)
  version number           : 1
  release number           : 0
  init pacing window       : 20
  unsupported saps         : none
  num of tcp sessions      : 1
  loop prevent support     : no
  icanreach mac-exclusive  : no
  icanreach netbios-excl.  : no
  reachable mac addresses  : none
  reachable netbios names  : none
  cisco version number     : 1
  peer group number        : 25
  border peer capable      : yes
  peer cost                : 3
  biu-segment configured   : no
  local-ack configured     : yes
  priority configured      : no.
  peer type                : prom
  version string           :
Cisco Internetwork Operating System Software
IOS (tm) 3600 Software (C3640-J-M), Version 11.2(15)P, RELEASE
SOFTWARE (fc1)
Copyright (c) 1986-1998 by cisco Systems, Inc.
Compiled Tue 14-Jul-98 02:28 by dschwart
```

■ |

Code Listing 3-59
DLSw+ border peer
configuration for R3.

```
hostname C3640-R3
!
source-bridge ring-group 73
dlsw local-peer peer-id 170.34.34.130 group 25 border promiscuous
dlsw ring-list 1 rings 34
dlsw remote-peer 1 tcp 170.34.34.129
!
interface TokenRing0/0
 source-bridge 34 1 73
 source-bridge spanning
!
```

The command `dlsw local-peer peer-id 170.34.34.130 group 25 border promiscuous` in Code Listing 3-59 sets R3 as a border peer in peer group 25. The `promiscuous` keyword allows for any-to-any connections.

Code Listing 3-60 illustrates the DLSw+ peer information for R3.

■ |

Code Listing 3-60
DLSw+ peer informa-
tion for R3.

```
C3640-R3#show dlsw peers
Peers:                      state    pkts_rx    pkts_tx   type  drops ckts TCP    uptime
TCP 170.34.34.129  CONNECT   971        977   conf      0      0    0  00:05:37
TCP 150.25.13.33   CONNECT    11         11   prom      0      0    0  00:04:59
TCP 160.25.2.129   CONNECT    11         11   prom      0      0    0  00:04:50
```

Code Listing 3-61 illustrates the DLSw+ capabilities information for R3.

■ |

Code Listing 3-61
DLSw+ capabilities
information for R3.

```
C3640-R3#show dlsw capabilities
DLSw: Capabilities for peer 170.34.34.129(2065)
  vendor id (OUI)         : '00C' (cisco)
  version number          : 1
  release number          : 0
  init pacing window      : 20
  unsupported saps        : none
  num of tcp sessions     : 1
  loop prevent support    : no
  icanreach mac-exclusive : no
  icanreach netbios-excl. : no
  reachable mac addresses : none
  reachable netbios names : none
  cisco version number    : 1
  peer group number       : 6
  border peer capable     : yes
  peer cost               : 3
  biu-segment configured  : no
  local-ack configured    : yes
  priority configured     : no
  border peer for group 6 : peer 170.34.34.129(2065) cost 3
```

```
peer type                    : conf
    version string           :
Cisco Internetwork Operating System Software
IOS (tm) 2500 Software (C2500-JS-L), Version 11.2(4), RELEASE SOFTWARE
(fc1)
Copyright (c) 1986-1997 by cisco Systems, Inc.
Compiled Mon 10-Feb-97 14:11 by ajchopra

DLSw: Capabilities for peer 150.25.13.33(2065)
    vendor id (OUI)          : '00C' (cisco)
    version number           : 1
    release number           : 0
    init pacing window       : 20
    unsupported saps         : none
    num of tcp sessions      : 1
    loop prevent support     : no
    icanreach mac-exclusive  : no
    icanreach netbios-excl.  : no
    reachable mac addresses  : none
    reachable netbios names  : none
    cisco version number     : 1
    peer group number        : 25
    border peer capable      : no
    peer cost                : 3
    biu-segment configured   : no
    local-ack configured     : yes
    priority configured      : no
    border peer for group 6  : peer 170.34.34.129(2065) cost 3
    peer type                : conf
    version string           :
Cisco Internetwork Operating System Software
IOS (tm) 3600 Software (C3640-J-M), Version 11.2(15)P,  RELEASE
SOFTWARE (fc1)
Copyright (c) 1986-1998 by cisco Systems, Inc.
Compiled Tue 14-Jul-98 02:28 by dschwart

DLSw: Capabilities for peer 160.25.2.129(2065)
    vendor id (OUI)          : '00C' (cisco)
    version number           : 1
    release number           : 0
    init pacing window       : 20
    unsupported saps         : none
    num of tcp sessions      : 1
    loop prevent support     : no
    icanreach mac-exclusive  : no
    icanreach netbios-excl.  : no
    reachable mac addresses  : none
    reachable netbios names  : none
    cisco version number     : 1
    peer group number        : 25
    border peer capable      : no
    peer cost                : 3
    biu-segment configured   : no
    local-ack configured     : yes
    priority configured      : no
    border peer for group 6  : peer 170.34.34.129(2065) cost 3
    peer type                : conf
    version string           :
```

Code Listing 3-61
(continued)

```
Cisco Internetwork Operating System Software
IOS (tm) 3600 Software (C3640-J-M), Version 11.2(15)P,  RELEASE
SOFTWARE (fc1)
Copyright (c) 1986-1998 by cisco Systems, Inc.
Compiled Tue 14-Jul-98 02:28 by dschwart
```

Code Listing 3-62
DLSw+ border peer
configuration for R4.

```
hostname C2500-R4
!
source-bridge ring-group 73
dlsw local-peer peer-id 170.34.34.129 group 6 border promiscuous
dlsw ring-list 1 rings 34
dlsw remote-peer 1 tcp 170.34.34.130
!
interface TokenRing0
 source-bridge 34 2 73
 source-bridge spanning
!
```

The command `dlsw local-peer peer-id 170.34.34.129 group
6 border promiscuous` in Code Listing 3-62 sets R4 as a border peer
in peer group 6. The `promiscuous` keyword allows for any-to-any connections.

Code Listing 3-63 illustrates the DLSw+ peer information for R4.

Code Listing 3-63
DLSw+ peer informa-
tion for R4.

```
C2500-R4#show dlsw peers
Peers:                    state   pkts_rx   pkts_tx  type  drops ckts TCP   uptime
  TCP 170.34.34.130   CONNECT   1514     1524  conf      0      0    0 00:06:14
  TCP 160.25.5.65     CONNECT    209      212  prom      0      0    0 01:42:37
```

Code Listing 3-64 illustrates the DLSw+ capabilities information for R4.

Code Listing 3-64
DLSw+ capabilities
information for R4.

```
C2500-R4#show dlsw capabilities
DLSw: Capabilities for peer 170.34.34.130(2065)
  vendor id (OUI)       : '00C' (cisco)
  version number        : 1
  release number        : 0
  init pacing window    : 20
  unsupported saps      : none
  num of tcp sessions   : 1
  loop prevent support  : no
  icanreach mac-exclusive : no
  icanreach netbios-excl. : no
  reachable mac addresses : none
  reachable netbios names : none
```

Code Listing 3-64
(continued)

```
    cisco version number    : 1
    peer group number       : 25
    border peer capable      : yes
    peer cost               : 3
    biu-segment configured  : no
    local-ack configured    : yes
    priority configured     : no
    border peer for group 25 : peer 170.34.34.130(2065) cost 3
    peer type               : conf
    version string          :
Cisco Internetwork Operating System Software
IOS (tm) 3600 Software (C3640-J-M), Version 11.2(15)P,  RELEASE
SOFTWARE (fc1)
Copyright (c) 1986-1998 by cisco Systems, Inc.
Compiled Tue 14-Jul-98 02:28 by dschwart

DLSw: Capabilities for peer 160.25.5.65(0)
    vendor id (OUI)         : '00C' (cisco)
    version number          : 1
    release number          : 0
    init pacing window      : 20
    unsupported saps        : none
    num of tcp sessions     : 1
    loop prevent support    : no
    icanreach mac-exclusive : no
    icanreach netbios-excl. : no
    reachable mac addresses : none
    reachable netbios names : none
    cisco version number    : 1
    peer group number       : 6
    border peer capable     : no
    peer cost               : 3
    biu-segment configured  : no
    local-ack configured    : yes
    priority configured     : no
    border peer for group 25 : peer 170.34.34.130(2065) cost 3
    peer type               : conf
    version string          :
Cisco Internetwork Operating System Software
IOS (tm) 2500 Software (C2500-J-L), Version 11.2(7a), RELEASE SOFTWARE
(fc1)
Copyright (c) 1986-1997 by cisco Systems, Inc.
Compiled Tue 01-Jul-97 15:31 by kuong
```

Code Listing 3-65
DLSw+ peer group
configuration for R5.

```
hostname C2509-R5
!
dlsw local-peer peer-id 160.25.5.65 group 6 promiscuous
dlsw bgroup-list 1 bgroups 1
dlsw remote-peer 1 tcp 170.34.34.129
dlsw bridge-group 1
!
interface Ethernet0
 bridge-group 1
!
bridge 1 protocol ieee
!
```

The command `dlsw local-peer peer-id 160.25.5.65 group 6 promiscuous` in Code Listing 3-65 sets R5 in peer group 6. The promiscuous keyword allows for any-to-any connections.

Code Listing 3-66 illustrates the DLSw+ peer information for R5.

Code Listing 3-66

DLSw+ peer information for R5.

```
C2509-R5#show dlsw peers
Peers:                     state    pkts_rx   pkts_tx  type  drops ckts TCP   uptime
  TCP 170.34.34.129  CONNECT   209       214  conf      0     0    0 01:43:14
```

Code Listing 3-67 illustrates DLSw+ the capabilities information for R5.

Code Listing 3-67

DLSw+ capabilities information for R5.

```
C2509-R5#sh dlsw capabilities
DLSw: Capabilities for peer 170.34.34.129(0)
  vendor id (OUI)          : '00C' (cisco)
  version number           : 1
  release number           : 0
  init pacing window       : 20
  unsupported saps         : none
  num of tcp sessions      : 1
  loop prevent support     : no
  icanreach mac-exclusive  : no
  icanreach netbios-excl.  : no
  reachable mac addresses  : none
  reachable netbios names  : none
  cisco version number     : 1
  peer group number        : 6
  border peer capable      : yes
  peer cost                : 4
  biu-segment configured   : no
  local-ack configured     : no
  priority configured      : no
  peer type                : prom
  version string           :
Cisco Internetwork Operating System Software
IOS (tm) 2500 Software (C2500-JS-L), Version 11.2(4), RELEASE SOFTWARE
(fc1)
Copyright (c) 1986-1997 by cisco Systems, Inc.
Compiled Mon 10-Feb-97 14:11 by ajchopra
```

The peer routers in each group, with the help of the promiscuous keyword, need only to establish a single DLSw+ circuit with their respective border peers to achieve any-to-any connections with the other peers in the network. These routers have become on-demand peers; required peer connections are not established until a session connection request is received.

The border peer in each group helps to reduce the processing cycles in the peer routers in the group while they are handling broadcast searches. These routers need only send one copy of broadcast to the border peer, instead of one copy to every peer, and the border peer will forward this broadcast to other peers in the peer group and to other border peers.

In Figure 3-15, when R1 forwards an explorer to border peer R3, searching for a resource, R3 will propagate the explorer to every peer in group 25 and to the border peer for group 6, where the explorer will in turn be forwarded to all peers in group 6. The process (assuming two SNA systems are connected one each to Ring 1 and VLAN 5) is as follows:

1. When R1 receives a TEST frame from SNA_SYS1 (on Ring 1) requesting to establish a session with SNA_SYS2 (on VLAN 5), it sends a CANUREACH frame to border peer R3.

2. When R3 receives the CANUREACH frame, it sends the frame to all its peers in group 25 and to R4, the border peer for group 6. R3 also sends a TEST frame to its local interfaces that are configured for DLSw+.

3. Similarly, when R4 receives the CANUREACH frame from R3, it sends the frame to all its peers in group 6 and a TEST frame to its local interfaces.

4. Likewise, when R5 receives the CANUREACH frame, it sends a TEST frame to local interface E0, where SNA_SYS2 is connected.

5. SNA_SYS2 replies with a positive TEST Response frame to R5. R5 returns the ICANREACH frame to R4, R4 sends it to R3, and R3 forwards it back to R1. Thereafter, R1 initiates a peer connection with R5 and establishes a session between the two hosts. R1 and R5 have become on-demand peers.

Assuming a NetBIOS host (Windows 95 PC) is connected to Ring 1 and its Network Neighborhood folder is opened to browse for available resources. The host's NetBIOS name is CHARLES, and its MAC address is 0001.6303.9e69. Using the `show dlsw reachability` command in Code Listings 3-68 through 3-72, the NetBIOS name and MAC address are shown to have propagated to all the routers in the two peer groups.

Code Listing 3-68

DLSw+ reachability
information for R1.

```
C3640-R1#show dlsw reachability
DLSw Remote MAC address reachability cache list
Mac Addr         status      Loc.     port              rif
0001.6303.9e69   FOUND       LOCAL    TokenRing0/0      06B0.0011.0490

DLSw Local MAC address reachability cache list
Mac Addr         status      Loc.     peer

DLSw Local NetBIOS Name reachability cache list
NetBIOS Name     status      Loc.     port              rif
CHARLES          FOUND       LOCAL    TokenRing0/0      06B0.0011.0490

DLSw Remote NetBIOS Name reachability cache list
NetBIOS Name     status      Loc.     Peer
```

Code Listing 3-69

DLSw+ reachability
information for R2.

```
C3640-R2#show dlsw reachability
DLSw Remote MAC address reachability cache list
Mac Addr         status      Loc.     port                    rif

DLSw Local MAC address reachability cache list
Mac Addr         status      Loc.     Peer
0001.6303.9e69   FOUND       REMOTE   150.25.13.33(2065)

DLSw Local NetBIOS Name reachability cache list
NetBIOS Name     status      Loc.     port                    rif

DLSw Remote NetBIOS Name reachability cache list
NetBIOS Name     status      Loc.     peer
CHARLES          FOUND       REMOTE   150.25.13.33(2065)
```

Code Listing 3-70

DLSw+ reachability
information for R3.

```
C3640-R3#show dlsw reachability
DLSw Remote MAC address reachability cache list
Mac Addr         status      Loc.     port                    rif

DLSw Local MAC address reachability cache list
Mac Addr         status      Loc.     peer
0001.6303.9e69   FOUND       REMOTE   150.25.13.33(2065)

DLSw Local NetBIOS Name reachability cache list
NetBIOS Name     status      Loc.     port                    rif

DLSw Remote NetBIOS Name reachability cache list
NetBIOS Name     status      Loc.     peer
CHARLES          FOUND       REMOTE   150.25.13.33(2065)
```

Code Listing 3-71
DLSw+ reachability information for R4.

```
C2500-R4#show dlsw reachability
DLSw Remote MAC address reachability cache list
Mac Addr          status     Loc.    port                    rif

DLSw Local MAC address reachability cache list
Mac Addr          status     Loc.    peer
0001.6303.9e69    FOUND      REMOTE  150.25.13.33(2065)

DLSw Local NetBIOS Name reachability cache list
NetBIOS Name      status     Loc.    port                    rif

DLSw Remote NetBIOS Name reachability cache list
NetBIOS Name      status     Loc.    peer
CHARLES           FOUND      REMOTE  150.25.13.33(2065)
```

Code Listing 3-72
DLSw+ reachability information for R5.

```
C2509-R5#show dlsw reachability
DLSw Remote MAC address reachability cache list
Mac Addr          status     Loc.    port                    rif

DLSw Local MAC address reachability cache list
Mac Addr          status     Loc.    peer
0001.6303.9e69    FOUND      REMOTE  150.25.13.33(2065)

DLSw Local NetBIOS Name reachability cache list
NetBIOS Name      status     Loc.    port                    rif

DLSw Remote NetBIOS Name reachability cache list
NetBIOS Name      status     Loc.    peer
CHARLES           FOUND      REMOTE  150.25.13.33(2065)
```

In Figure 3-15, the border peers R3 and R4 are defined using the IP addresses of their respective Token Ring interfaces. The border peer concept will fail if either of the Token Ring interfaces becomes unavailable. A better design would be to use loopback addresses to incorporate some resiliency for the border peer. Two or more border peers can be defined, with the preferred border peer having the lowest cost.

Static Resources Capabilities Exchange

Consider Figure 3-15. Explorer traffic destined for R5 can be reduced by configuring a static list of resources for which it has information. This information is part of the capabilities exchange between R5 and its configured remote peers.

In Code Listing 3-73, the command dlsw icanreach mac-address defines the MAC address of a resource that is locally reachable by R5, and the command `dlsw netbios-name` defines the NetBIOS name of a resource that is locally reachable by R5.

Code Listing 3-73

DLSw+ static resources capabilities exchange configuration for R5.

```
hostname C2509-R5
!
dlsw local-peer peer-id 160.25.5.65 group 6 promiscuous
dlsw bgroup-list 1 bgroups 1
dlsw remote-peer 1 tcp 170.34.34.129
dlsw bridge-group 1
dlsw icanreach mac-address 0006.e9db.31ce  mask ffff.ffff.ffff
dlsw icanreach mac-address 0006.e9dd.559c  mask ffff.ffff.ffff
dlsw icanreach netbios-name SALES_SYS*
!
interface Ethernet0
 bridge-group 1
!
bridge 1 protocol ieee
!
```

In Code Listing 3-74, a `show dlsw capabilities` at R4 verifies the reachable MAC addresses and NetBIOS names for R5.

Code Listing 3-74

DLSw+ capabilities information for R4.

```
C2500-R4#show dlsw capabilities
DLSw: Capabilities for peer 160.25.5.65(0)
  vendor id (OUI)          : '00C' (cisco)
  version number           : 1
  release number           : 0
  init pacing window       : 20
  unsupported saps         : none
  num of tcp sessions      : 1
  loop prevent support     : no
  icanreach mac-exclusive  : no
  icanreach netbios-excl.  : no
  reachable mac addresses  : 0006.e9db.31ce  <mask ffff.ffff.ffff>
                             0006.e9dd.559c  <mask ffff.ffff.ffff>
  reachable netbios names  : SALES_SYS*
  cisco version number     : 1
  peer group number        : 6
  border peer capable      : no
  peer cost                : 3
  biu-segment configured   : no
  local-ack configured     : yes
  priority configured      : no
  border peer for group 25 : peer 170.34.34.130(2065) cost 2
  peer type                : conf
  version string           :
Cisco Internetwork Operating System Software
IOS (tm) 2500 Software (C2500-J-L), Version 11.2(7a), RELEASE SOFTWARE
(fc1)
Copyright (c) 1986-1997 by cisco Systems, Inc.
Compiled Tue 01-Jul-97 15:31 by kuong
```

DLSw+ Access Control

Basically, DLSw+ access control can be gained through the following ways:

- Filtering by specific MAC addresses, achieved by using either the dest-mac option or the dmac-output-list option in the dlsw remote-peer tcp command. The dest-mac option permits the TCP connection to be established to the remote peer only when an explorer frame is sent to the specified 48-bit MAC address. The dmac-output-list option is more refined, since the explorer frame needs to pass the specified destination MAC address access list in order to establish the TCP connection. Valid access list numbers are in the range 700 to 799.

- Filtering by LSAP type codes, achieved by using the lsap-output-list option, filters output IEEE 802 encapsulated packets by DSAP/SSAP addresses. Valid access list numbers are in the range 200 to 299.

- Filtering by NetBIOS byte offset, achieved by using the bytes-net-bios-out option to configure NetBIOS bytes output filtering for this peer. The NetBIOS byte offset access list is used.

- Filtering by NetBIOS station names, achieved by using the host-netbios-out option to configure NetBIOS host output filtering for this peer. The NetBIOS station access list is used.

These methods can also be implemented using access expressions. Refer to Chapter 2 for more details on MAC address filtering, LSAP filtering, NetBIOS filtering, and access expressions.

In Figure 3-16, IBM FEPs and the NetBIOS servers attached to Ring 34 belong to the Finance Department. The two IBM 3174s in Ring 2 need to access the FEP with MAC address 0110.3333.4444, and the NetBIOS clients in Ring 1 need to access the NetBIOS server FILESVR34. The DLSw+ access filtering is implemented in Code Listings 3-75 and 3-76.

Code Listing 3-75 illustrates the DLSw+ access filtering configuration for R1. The option host-netbios-out in the dlsw remote-peer command uses the keyword FINANCE to reference the NetBIOS host access list. The list only permits access to the NetBIOS station FILESVR34. That is, the NetBIOS clients in Ring 1 can only access this NetBIOS server in Ring 34.

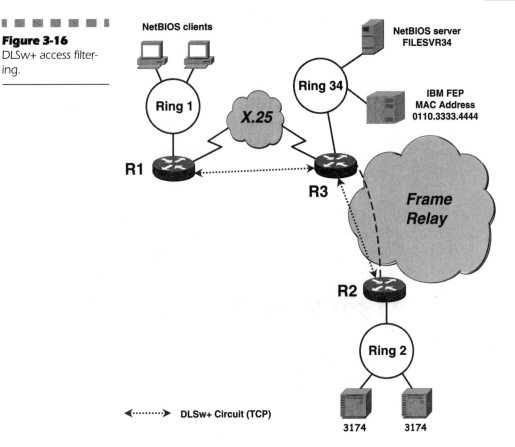

Figure 3-16
DLSw+ access filtering.

Code Listing 3-75
DLSw+ access filtering configuration for R1.

```
hostname C3640-R1
!
source-bridge ring-group 73
dlsw local-peer peer-id 150.25.13.33 promiscuous
dlsw port-list 1 TokenRing0/0
dlsw remote-peer 1 tcp 170.34.34.130 host-netbios-out FINANCE
!
netbios access-list host FINANCE permit FILESVR34
netbios access-list host FINANCE deny *
!
interface TokenRing0/0
 source-bridge 1 1 73
 source-bridge spanning
!
```

Code Listing 3-76
DLSw+ access filtering configuration for R2.

```
hostname C3640-R2
!
source-bridge ring-group 73
dlsw local-peer peer-id 160.25.2.129 promiscuous
dlsw ring-list 1 rings 2
dlsw remote-peer 1 tcp 170.34.34.130 dmac-output-list 700 lsap-output-list 200
!
access-list 200 permit 0x0404 0x0101
access-list 200 permit 0x0004 0x0001
access-list 700 permit 0110.3333.4444
!
interface TokenRing0/0
 source-bridge 2 1 73
 source-bridge spanning
!
```

Code Listing 3-76 illustrates the DLSw+ access filtering configuration for R2. The options `dmac-output-list 700` and `lsap-output-list 200` in the `dlsw remote-peer` command reference `access-list 700` and `access-list 200`. Access-list `700` permits the FEP MAC address 0110.3333.4444, and `access-list 200` permits SNA frames (individual/group DSAP and command/response frames) and SNA explorers (command/response frames) with Null DSAP. This means the two 3174s can only access the IBM FEP at MAC address 0110.3333.4444.

Summary

In chapter 3, the main focus is on using DLSw+ to transport SNA and NetBIOS traffic between remote LANs. DLSw+ is an improvement over RSRB, addressing most of RSRB's limitations. Today the most common nonroutable protocol happens to be SNA, followed by NetBIOS. In the case scenario, DLSw+ was implemented over an IP network.

DLSw+ was implemented based on a simple scenario, followed by progressively configuring cost peers, backup peers, dynamic peers, border peers, and on-demand peers. DLSw+ was also configured for different LAN and WAN media, including Ethernet, Token Ring, ISDN, X.25, and Frame Relay. In the last section, access control was configured using some of the DLSw+ command options.

These implementations demonstrate that DLSw+ possesses some powerful and robust features to help large corporations integrate new or existing SNA/NetBIOS networks with their existing IP backbones in a more flexible manner. With careful planning and proper execution, a DLSw+ transport network will carry nonroutable traffic like SNA and NetBIOS across enterprise networks more efficiently and effectively.

References

1. Black, U. *Physical Level Interfaces and Protocols.* Los Alamitos, California: IEEE Computer Society Press, 1988.

2. Clark, W. "SNA Internetworking." *ConneXions: The Interoperability Report*, Vol. 6, No. 3. March 1992.

3. Documentation CD-ROM, Cisco Systems, Inc., 1998.

4. IEEE 802.2 Local Area Networks Standard, 802.2 Logical Link Control, ANSI/IEEE Standard, October 1985.

5. IEEE 802.5–Local Area Networks Standard, 802.5 Token Ring Access Method, ANSI/IEEE Standard, October 1985.

6. Martin, J. *SNA: IBM's Networking Solution.* Englewood Cliffs, New Jersey: Prentice Hall, 1987.

7. Meijer, Anton. *Systems Network Architecture: A Tutorial.* New York: John Wiley & Sons, Inc., 1987.

8. Miller, M.A. *LAN Protocol Handbook.* San Mateo, California: MT&T Books, 1990.

9. Perlman, R. *Interconnections: Bridges and Routers.* Reading, Massachusetts: Addison-Wesley Publishing Company, Inc., 1992.

10. RFC 1795–Data Link Switching: Switch-to-Switch Protocol, April 1995.

11. RFC 1490–Multiprotocol Interconnect over Frame Relay, July 1993.

12. Stallings, W. *Data and Computer Communications.* New York: Macmillan Publishing Company, 1991.

13. Tannenbaum, A.S. *Computer Networks*, 2nd ed. Englewood Cliffs, New Jersey: Prentice Hall, 1988.

IPX

Introduction

Netware Servers operate on a proprietary Novell operating system. Users on workstations can redirect some of their operating system functions to these Netware servers. Novell's Network File Service (NFS) uses Netware Core Protocol (NCP) to transmit workstation commands or inquiries and to receive replies from file servers. NCP is Novell's application-level protocol for the exchange of commands and data among file servers and workstations. NCP makes use of Novell's implementation of the Xerox Network System (XNS) family of protocols developed by Xerox. These protocols handle the transmission and delivery of a packet but not its interpretation, which is left to the higher level protocol, NCP.

At the network level, Netware uses Internet Packet Exchange (IPX), a datagram (connectionless) protocol. IPX is the next most popular routed protocol after IP. It is derived from XNS's Internet Datagram Protocol (IDP). One main difference between IPX and XNS is they do not always use the same Ethernet encapsulation format. Another difference is IPX uses Novell's proprietary session-level Service Advertising Protocol (SAP) to advertise network services. IPX also uses ticks (1/18 seconds), while XNS uses hop count as the primary metric to determine the best path to a destination. Each IPX packet identifies the network, node, and socket of its source and destination. A socket may be a function within a node, and this can affect where the embedded NCP message is interpreted.

Netware also provides a connection-oriented transport-level virtual circuit protocol called Sequential Packet Exchange (SPX) that corresponds to Sequenced Packet Protocol (SPP) in the XNS protocol. However, NCP provides connection services without the use of SPX packets. In SPX each packet is identified in the same way as an IPX packet but with additional fields for the source and destination connection, a sequence number within that connection, an acknowledgement number, and an allocation of the number of unacknowledged SPX packets that the connection may tolerate.

IPX Overview

IPX is a network-level protocol that corresponds to XNS's IDP. Within this family of protocols, the following are identified:

- Sequential Packet Exchange (SPX): Novell's version of the XNS transport protocol called SPP.

- Routing Information Protocol (RIP): Novell's version of a routing protocol used to exchange routing information among gateways.

- Netware Link Services Protocol (NLSP): NLSP is a link-state protocol based on the Open System Interconnection (OSI) Intermediate-System-to-Intermediate-System (IS-IS) protocol. NLSP is designed for use in a hierarchical routing environment, where network systems are grouped into routing areas. These routing areas are, in turn, grouped into routing domains. NLSP improves the performance, reliability, scalability, and manageability of IPX traffic in large-scale internetworks.

- IPXWAN: IPXWAN is a startup end-to-end negotiation protocol. When a link comes up, the first IPX packets sent across are IPXWAN packets negotiating the options for the link. When the IPXWAN options have been successfully determined, normal IPX traffic starts. The three options negotiated are the link IPX network number, the internal network number, and link delay (ticks) characteristics. The end of the link with the higher internal network number gives the IPX network number and delay to use for the link on the other side. Once IPXWAN finishes, no IPXWAN packets are sent unless there is a link characteristic change or the connection fails.

IPX Routing

For IPX routing to work, it must be enabled explicitly, and an IPX network number must be configured on each interface.

IPX Addresses

An IPX network address is 80 bits long. It consists of a network number and a node number expressed in the format `network.node`.

The network number identifies a physical network. It is a 4-byte (32-bit) quantity that must be unique throughout the entire IPX internetwork. The network number is expressed as eight hexadecimal digits.

The node number identifies a node on the network. It is a 48-bit quantity, represented by dotted triplets of four-digit hexadecimal numbers.

Case Scenario

Figure 4-1 illustrates the overall network scenario referenced throughout this chapter. This enterprise network spans four sites: San Francisco, Oakland, Phoenix, and Sacramento. The San Francisco office is internetworked to the Oakland office by Frame Relay with an ISDN dial-up line that serves as backup in the event the Frame Relay connectivity becomes unavailable. Similarly the Oakland office is interconnected to the San Francisco and Sacramento offices through the same Frame Relay network. The Oakland office is also linked to the Sacramento office using X.25. The Phoenix office is linked to the Oakland office through HDLC. The Oakland and Sacramento offices both have a Virtual LAN connecting Netware clients and servers. Likewise, Netware clients and servers are found in the San Francisco and Phoenix offices, on Token Ring networks.

IPX Setup

Consider Figure 4-2. Altogether there are eight different IPX networks. The IPX routing protocol used is IPX RIP.

Basic IPX Configuration

This section will cover basic IPX configuration of the respective LANs connected to the five routers, as illustrated in Code Listings 4-1 to 4-5. Subsequent sections will cover the WAN configurations.

Figure 4-1
The overall network
topology.

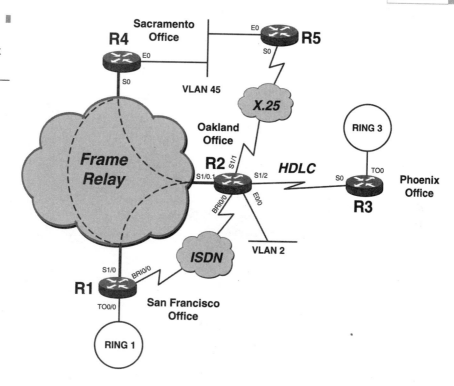

Code Listing 4-1
IPX configuration for
R1.

```
hostname C3640-R1
!
ipx routing 0010.7bb2.7761
!
interface TokenRing0/0
 ipx network 11
 ring-speed 16
```

1. Code Listing 4-1 illustrates the IPX configuration for R1. By
   default, IPX routing is not enabled. The global command ipx
   routing enables routing and the routing protocol IPX RIP. No
   other command is required to enable IPX RIP, since it is the default
   routing protocol. The value 0010.7bb2.7761 is the router's Burn-
   In-Address (BIA).

2. TO0/0 is configured with a ring speed of 16 Mbps and is part of IPX
   network 11. No specific frame encapsulation is specified, and the
   frame type used is SAP, the default for Token Ring.

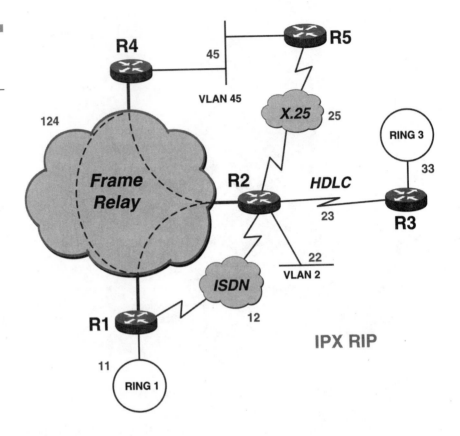

Figure 4-2
The overall IPX network.

Code Listing 4-2
IPX configuration for
R2.

```
hostname C3640-R2
!
ipx routing 00e0.1e6f.9821
!
interface Ethernet0/0
 ipx network 22
```

1. Code Listing 4-2 illustrates the IPX configuration for R2. By default, IPX routing is not enabled. The global command `ipx routing` enables routing and the routing protocol IPX RIP. No other command is required to enable IPX RIP, since it is the default routing protocol. The value `00e0.1e6f.9821` is the router's BIA.

2. E0/0 is part of IPX network 22. Since no specific frame encapsulation is specified, the frame type used is NOVELL-ETHER, the default for Ethernet.

Code Listing 4-3

IPX configuration for
R3.

```
hostname C2500-R3
!
ipx routing 00e0.1e5f.dd0d
!
interface TokenRing0
 ipx network 33
 ring-speed 16
```

1. Code Listing 4-3 illustrates the IPX configuration for R3. By default, IPX routing is not enabled. The global command `ipx routing` enables routing and the routing protocol IPX RIP. No other command is required to enable IPX RIP, since it is the default routing protocol. The value `00e0.1e5f.dd0d` is the router's BIA.

2. TO0 is part of IPX network 33. Since no specific frame encapsulation is specified, the frame type used is SAP, the default for Token Ring.

Code Listing 4-4

IPX configuration for
R4.

```
hostname C2500-R4
!
ipx routing 00e0.1e5f.de09
!
interface Ethernet0
ipx network 45
```

1. Code Listing 4-4 illustrates the IPX configuration for R4. By default, IPX routing is not enabled. The global command `ipx routing` enables routing and the routing protocol IPX RIP. No other command is required to enable IPX RIP, since it is the default routing protocol. The value `00e0.1e5f.de09` is the router's BIA.

2. E0 is part of IPX network 45. As no specific frame encapsulation is specified, the frame type used is NOVELL-ETHER, the default for Ethernet.

Code Listing 4-5

IPX configuration for
R5.

```
hostname C2509-R5
!
ipx routing 00e0.1e5d.3532
!
interface Ethernet0
 ipx network 45
```

1. Code Listing 4-5 illustrates the IPX configuration for R5. By default, IPX routing is not enabled. The global command `ipx routing` enables routing and the routing protocol IPX RIP. No other command is required to enable IPX RIP, since it is the default routing protocol. The value `00e0.1e5d.3532` is the router's BIA.

2. E0 is part of IPX network 45. As no specific frame encapsulation is specified, the frame type used is NOVELL-ETHER, the default for Ethernet.

IPX over Frame Relay

Figure 4-3 zooms into the full-mesh Frame Relay network where IPX is configured for R1, R2, and R4. Code Listings 4-6 through 4-8 illustrate the Frame Relay implementation. The number of PVCs required to achieve full-mesh is $N(N-1)/2 = 3(2)/2 = 3$, where N is the number of routers.

Figure 4-3
IPX over Frame Relay.

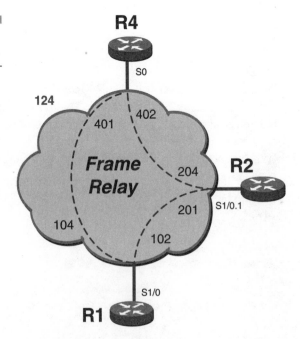

■ ■ ■ ■ ■ ■ ■ ■ ■ ▯

Code Listing 4-6
IPX-over-Frame Relay configuration for R1.

```
hostname C3640-R1
!
ipx routing 0010.7bb2.7761
!
interface Serial1/0
 encapsulation frame-relay
 bandwidth 56
 ipx network 124
 frame-relay map ipx 124.00e0.1e6f.9821 102 broadcast
 frame-relay map ipx 124.00e0.1e5f.de09 104 broadcast
 frame-relay lmi-type ansi
```

Code Listing 4-6 illustrates the IPX-over-Frame Relay configuration for R1. S1/0 is part of IPX network 124. The `frame-relay map` command statically maps the IPX addresses of R2 and R4 to their respective DLCIs. As the Frame Relay topology is fully meshed, R1 must implement a multipoint Serial interface. Note that a physical Frame Relay interface (in this case, S1/0) is by default multipoint.

■ ■ ■ ■ ■ ■ ■ ■ ▯

Code Listing 4-7
IPX-over-Frame Relay configuration for R2.

```
hostname C3640-R2
!
ipx routing 00e0.1e6f.9821
!
interface Serial1/0
 encapsulation frame-relay
 frame-relay lmi-type ansi
!
interface Serial1/0.1 multipoint
 bandwidth 56
 ipx network 124
 frame-relay map ipx 124.00e0.1e5f.de09 204 broadcast
 frame-relay map ipx 124.0010.7bb2.7761 201 broadcast
!
```

Code Listing 4-7 illustrates the IPX-over-Frame Relay configuration for R2. R2 implements a multipoint Serial subinterface S1/0.1 for the fully meshed Frame Relay topology. S1/0.1 is part of IPX network 124. The `frame-relay map` command statically maps the IPX addresses of R1 and R4 into their respective DLCIs.

Code Listing 4-8
IPX-over-Frame Relay
configuration for R4.

```
hostname C2500-R4
!
ipx routing 00e0.1e5f.de09
!
interface Serial0
 encapsulation frame-relay
 bandwidth 56
 ipx network 124
 frame-relay map ipx 124.00e0.1e6f.9821 402 broadcast
 frame-relay map ipx 124.0010.7bb2.7761 401 broadcast
 frame-relay lmi-type ansi
```

Code Listing 4-8 illustrates the IPX-over-Frame Relay configuration for R4. S0 is part of IPX network 124. The `frame-relay map` command statically maps the IPX addresses of R1 and R2 to their respective DLCIs. The Frame Relay topology is fully meshed; R4 must implement a multipoint Serial interface. Note that a physical Frame Relay interface (in this case, S0) is by default multipoint.

IPX over X.25

Figure 4-4 zooms into the X.25 network where IPX is implemented between R2 and R5. Code Listings 4-9 and 4-10 illustrate the X.25 implementation.

Figure 4-4
IPX over X.25.

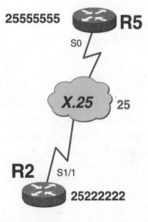

Code Listing 4-9
IPX-over-X.25 configuration for R2.

```
hostname C3640-R2
!
ipx routing 00e0.1e6f.9821
!
interface Serial1/1
 encapsulation x25
 bandwidth 56
 ipx network 25
 x25 address 25222222
 x25 map ipx 25.00e0.1e5d.3532 25555555 broadcast
```

Code Listing 4-9 illustrates the IPX-over-X.25 configuration for R2. S1/1 is part of IPX network 25. The command x25 map ipx creates a virtual circuit between R2 and R5 for IPX routing. The IPX and X.121 addresses used by the command are R5's.

Code Listing 4-10
IPX-over-X.25 configuration for R5.

```
hostname C2509-R5
!
ipx routing 00e0.1e5d.3532
!
interface Serial0
 encapsulation x25
 bandwidth 56
 ipx network 25
 x25 address 25555555
 x25 map ipx 25.00e0.1e6f.9821 25222222 broadcast
```

Code Listing 4-10 illustrates the IPX-over-X.25 configuration for R5. S0 is part of IPX network 25. The command x25 map ipx creates a virtual circuit between R5 and R2 for IPX routing. The IPX and X.121 addresses used by the command are R2's.

IPX over HDLC

Figure 4-5 shows the portion of network where IPX over HDLC is implemented between R2 and R3. Code Listings 4-11 and 4-12 illustrate this.

Figure 4-5
IPX over HDLC.

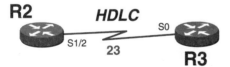

Code Listing 4-11
IPX-over-HDLC config-
uration for R2.

```
hostname C3640-R2
!
ipx routing 00e0.1e6f.9821
!
interface Serial1/2
 bandwidth 56
 ipx network 23
```

Code Listing 4-11 illustrates the IPX-over-HDLC configuration for R2. To configure IPX over HDLC, specify the IPX network number on the respective Serial interfaces. In this case, S1/2 is part of IPX network 23. The default encapsulation type for Serial interfaces is HDLC; however, Cisco's HDLC frame format is proprietary and may not be compatible with non-Cisco routers using HDLC.

Code Listing 4-12
IPX-over-HDLC config-
uration for R3.

```
hostname C2500-R3
!
ipx routing 00e0.1e5f.dd0d
!
interface Serial0
 bandwidth 56
 ipx network 23
```

Code Listing 4-12 illustrates the IPX-over-HDLC configuration for R3. To configure IPX over HDLC, specify the IPX network number on the respective Serial interfaces. In this case, S0 is part of IPX network 23.

IPX over DDR

Figure 4-6 shows the portion of network where IPX over DDR is implemented between R1 and R2. In this case, DDR backs up the Frame Relay-Serial interface S1/0 in R1 if it becomes unavailable. Code Listings 4-13 and 4-14 illustrate the DDR implementation.

Code Listing 4-13 illustrates the IPX-over-DDR configuration for R1. ISDN interface BRI0/0 is part of IPX network 12. The dialer map command dials up R2 to establish a PPP connection when S1/0 becomes unavailable. The IPX address, host name, and ISDN number used by the command are R2's. The dialer-group 1 command refers to the dialer-list 1 command and allows all IPX traffic to pass. No refining on the dialer-list is required, as the purpose of the BRI0/0 interface is to back up S1/0.

Figure 4-6
IPX over DDR.

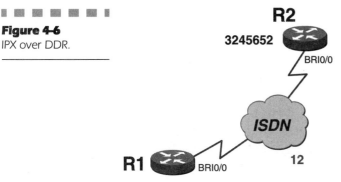

Code Listing 4-13
IPX-over-DDR configuration for R1.

```
hostname C3640-R1
username C3640-R2 password 0 cisco
isdn switch-type basic-net3
!
ipx routing 0010.7bb2.7761
!
 interface BRI0/0
 encapsulation ppp
 ipx network 12
 dialer idle-timeout 60
 dialer map ipx 12.00e0.1e6f.9821 name C3640-R2 broadcast 3245652
 dialer load-threshold 128 either
 dialer-group 1
 ppp authentication chap
!
dialer-list 1 protocol ipx permit
!
interface Serial1/0
 backup delay 10 30
 backup interface BRI0/0
```

Code Listing 4-14
IPX-over-DDR configuration for R2.

```
hostname C3640-R2
username C3640-R1 password 0 cisco
isdn switch-type basic-net3
!
ipx routing 00e0.1e6f.9821
!
interface BRI0/0
 encapsulation ppp
 ipx network 12
 dialer idle-timeout 60
 dialer map ipx 12.0010.7bb2.7761 name C3640-R1 broadcast
 dialer load-threshold 128 either
 dialer-group 1
 ppp authentication chap
!
dialer-list 1 protocol ipx permit
```

Code Listing 4-14 illustrates the IPX-over-DDR configuration for R2. The ISDN interface BRI0/0 is part of IPX network 12. The `dialer = 1 map` command establishes a PPP connection when R1 makes a call. No ISDN number is specified here, since R1 will initiate the call. The IPX address and host name used by the command are R1's. The `dialer-group 1` command refers to the `dialer-list 1` command and allows all IPX traffic to pass.

Note the routing tables for all five routers, as illustrated in Code Listings 4-15 to 4-19.

Code Listing 4-15

IPX routing table for R1.

```
C3640-R1#show ipx route
Codes: C - Connected primary network,     c - Connected secondary network
       S - Static, F - Floating static, L - Local (internal), W - IPXWAN
       R - RIP, E - EIGRP, N - NLSP, X - External, A - Aggregate
       s - seconds, u - uses

8 Total IPX routes. Up to 1 parallel paths and 16 hops allowed.

No default route known.

C           11 (SAP),        To0/0
C          124 (FRAME-RELAY),  Se1/0
R           12 [07/01] via    124.00e0.1e6f.9821,    29s, Se1/0
R           22 [07/01] via    124.00e0.1e6f.9821,    29s, Se1/0
R           23 [07/01] via    124.00e0.1e6f.9821,    29s, Se1/0
R           25 [07/01] via    124.00e0.1e6f.9821,    29s, Se1/0
R           33 [13/02] via    124.00e0.1e6f.9821,    29s, Se1/0
R           45 [07/01] via    124.00e0.1e5f.de09,    22s, Se1/0
```

Code Listing 4-16

IPX routing table for R2.

```
C3640-R2#show ipx route
Codes: C - Connected primary network,     c - Connected secondary network
       S - Static, F - Floating static, L - Local (internal), W - IPXWAN
       R - RIP, E - EIGRP, N - NLSP, X - External, A - Aggregate
       s - seconds, u - uses

8 Total IPX routes. Up to 1 parallel paths and 16 hops allowed.

No default route known.

C           12 (PPP),        BR0/0
C           22 (NOVELL-ETHER),  Et0/0
C           23 (HDLC),       Se1/2
C           25 (X25),        Se1/1
C          124 (FRAME-RELAY),  Se1/0.1
R           11 [07/01] via    124.0010.7bb2.7761,    44s, Se1/0.1
R           33 [07/01] via     23.00e0.1e5f.dd0d,    16s, Se1/2
R           45 [07/01] via    124.00e0.1e5f.de09,    28s, Se1/0.1
```

Code Listing 4-17
IPX routing table for R3.

```
C2500-R3#show ipx route
Codes: C - Connected primary network,     c - Connected secondary network
       S - Static, F - Floating static, L - Local (internal), W - IPXWAN
       R - RIP, E - EIGRP, N - NLSP, X - External, A - Aggregate
       s - seconds, u - uses

8 Total IPX routes. Up to 1 parallel paths and 16 hops allowed.

No default route known.

        C       23 (HDLC),        Se0
        C       33 (SAP),         To0
        R       11 [13/02] via    23.00e0.1e6f.9821,    19s, Se0
        R       12 [07/01] via    23.00e0.1e6f.9821,    19s, Se0
        R       22 [07/01] via    23.00e0.1e6f.9821,    19s, Se0
        R       25 [07/01] via    23.00e0.1e6f.9821,    19s, Se0
        R       45 [13/02] via    23.00e0.1e6f.9821,    19s, Se0
        R      124 [07/01] via    23.00e0.1e6f.9821,    19s, Se0
```

Code Listing 4-18
IPX routing table for R4.

```
C2500-R4#show ipx route
Codes: C - Connected primary network,     c - Connected secondary network
       S - Static, F - Floating static, L - Local (internal), W - IPXWAN
       R - RIP, E - EIGRP, N - NLSP, X - External, A - Aggregate
       s - seconds, u - uses

8 Total IPX routes. Up to 1 parallel paths and 16 hops allowed.

No default route known.

        C       45 (NOVELL-ETHER),   Et0
        C      124 (FRAME-RELAY),    Se0
        R       11 [07/01] via    124.0010.7bb2.7761,   58s, Se0
        R       12 [07/01] via    124.00e0.1e6f.9821,   50s, Se0
        R       22 [07/01] via    124.00e0.1e6f.9821,   50s, Se0
        R       23 [07/01] via    124.00e0.1e6f.9821,   50s, Se0
        R       25 [02/01] via     45.00e0.1e5d.3532,   55s, Et0
        R       33 [13/02] via    124.00e0.1e6f.9821,   50s, Se0
```

Code Listing 4-19
IPX routing table for R5.

```
C2509-R5#show ipx route
Codes: C - Connected primary network,     c - Connected secondary network
       S - Static, F - Floating static, L - Local (internal), W - IPXWAN
       R - RIP, E - EIGRP, N - NLSP, X - External, A - Aggregate
       s - seconds, u - uses

8 Total IPX routes. Up to 1 parallel paths and 16 hops allowed.

No default route known.

        C       25 (X25),         Se0
        C       45 (NOVELL-ETHER),   Et0
        R       11 [08/02] via     45.00e0.1e5f.de09,   23s, Et0
        R       12 [07/01] via     25.00e0.1e6f.9821,   20s, Se0
        R       22 [07/01] via     25.00e0.1e6f.9821,   20s, Se0
        R       23 [07/01] via     25.00e0.1e6f.9821,   20s, Se0
        R       33 [13/02] via     25.00e0.1e6f.9821,   20s, Se0
        R      124 [02/01] via     45.00e0.1e5f.de09,   24s, Et0
```

IPX RIP uses ticks (one tick is approximately equivalent to 1/18 seconds) and hops as metric. The default number of ticks for a LAN interface is one and for a WAN interface is six.

Consider Figure 4-7. The ISDN backup link will become operational when the Frame Relay connection between R1 and R2 fails. In this event, note the routing tables for R1 and R2, as illustrated in Code Listings 4-20 and 4-21.

Figure 4-7
The Frame Relay connectivity between R1 and R2 fails.

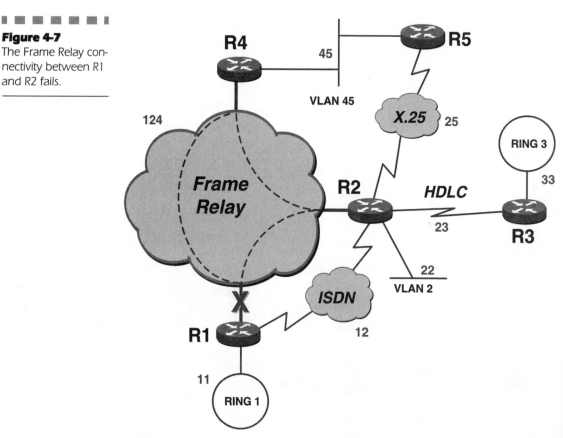

Code Listing 4-20
IPX routing table for R1.

```
C3640-R1#show ipx route
Codes: C - Connected primary network,    c - Connected secondary network
       S - Static, F - Floating static, L - Local (internal), W - IPXWAN
       R - RIP, E - EIGRP, N - NLSP, X - External, A - Aggregate
       s - seconds, u - uses

8 Total IPX routes. Up to 1 parallel paths and 16 hops allowed.

No default route known.

C        11 (SAP),            To0/0
C        12 (PPP),            BR0/0
R        22 [07/01] via       12.00e0.1e6f.9821,   33s, BR0/0
R        23 [07/01] via       12.00e0.1e6f.9821,   33s, BR0/0
R        25 [07/01] via       12.00e0.1e6f.9821,   33s, BR0/0
R        33 [13/02] via       12.00e0.1e6f.9821,   33s, BR0/0
R        45 [13/02] via       12.00e0.1e6f.9821,   33s, BR0/0
R       124 [07/01] via       12.00e0.1e6f.9821,   33s, BR0/0
```

R1 now learns all IPX routes through the ISDN interface BRI0/0.

Code Listing 4-21
IPX routing table for
R2.

```
C3640-R2#show ipx route
Codes: C - Connected primary network,    c - Connected secondary network
       S - Static, F - Floating static, L - Local (internal), W - IPXWAN
       R - RIP, E - EIGRP, N - NLSP, X - External, A - Aggregate
       s - seconds, u - uses

8 Total IPX routes. Up to 1 parallel paths and 16 hops allowed.

No default route known.

C          12 (PPP),          BR0/0
C          22 (NOVELL-ETHER), Et0/0
C          23 (HDLC),         Se1/2
C          25 (X25),          Se1/1
C         124 (FRAME-RELAY),  Se1/0.1
R          11 [07/01] via     12.0010.7bb2.7761,   107s, BR0/0
R          33 [07/01] via     23.00e0.1e5f.dd0d,    19s, Se1/2
R          45 [07/01] via    124.00e0.1e5f.de09,    31s, Se1/0.1
```

R2 now learns the route to IPX network 11 through its ISDN interface BRI0/0, as shown in Code Listing 4-21.

IPX EIGRP

Enhanced IGRP (EIGRP) is an enhanced version of the Interior Gateway Routing Protocol (IGRP). EIGRP uses the same distance vector algorithm and distance information as IGRP; however, convergence properties and operating efficiency of EIGRP are improved. The convergence technology uses the Diffusing Update Algorithm (DUAL). This algorithm ensures loop-free operation at every instant throughout route computations and allows all routers involved in a topology change to synchronize at the same time. Routers that are not affected by topology changes are not involved in recomputations.

Neighbor Discovery

Neighbor discovery is the process that routers use to dynamically learn about other routers on their directly attached networks. Routers must also discover when their neighbors become unreachable. Neighbor discovery is achieved with low overhead by periodically sending small hello packets. As long as a router receives these hello packets, it can determine that a neighbor is functioning. Once this status is determined, the neighboring devices exchange routing information. By default, hello packets are sent every five seconds. The exception is on low-speed NBMA media, where the default hello interval is 60 seconds. Low speed means a rate of T1 or slower. The hello interval remains at five seconds for high-speed NBMA networks. Hold time is advertised in hello packets and indicates to neighbors the length of time they should consider the sender valid. The default hold time is three times the hello interval.

Reliable Transport Protocol

The reliable transport protocol is responsible for guaranteed ordered delivery of EIGRP packets to all neighbors. It supports the transmission of multicast and unicast packets; reliability is provided only when necessary. On a multi-access network having multicast capabilities, such as Ethernet, EIGRP sends a single multicast hello with an indication that the packet need not be acknowledged. Other types of packets, such as updates, require acknowledgement, and this is also indicated in the packet. The reliable protocol has a provision to send multicast packets quickly when there are unacknowledged packets pending, helping to ensure convergence remains low with different link speeds.

Dual FSM

The DUAL finite-state machine (FSM) encompasses the decision process for route computations. It tracks routes advertised by all neighbors. DUAL uses the distance information (known as metric) to select efficient, loop-free paths. DUAL selects routes based on feasible successors. A successor is a neighbor that has the least path cost to a destination and is not part of a routing loop. When there are no feasible successors, but neighbors advertise the destination, recomputation must occur. This process selects a new successor. Recomputation uses up CPU cycles and affects convergence time, and should be avoided if unnecessary. When a topology change occurs, DUAL tests for feasible successors. If there are feasible successors, DUAL will select one to avoid unnecessary recomputation.

Protocol-Dependent Modules

The protocol-dependent modules are responsible for network-layer protocol-specific tasks, for parsing EIGRP packets and informing DUAL of the new information received. EIGRP uses DUAL to make routing decisions; however, the results are stored in the IPX routing table. EIGRP is also responsible for redistributing routes learned by other IPX routing protocols.

Configuring IPX EIGRP

Figure 4-8 illustrates IPX EIGRP for the Frame Relay, X.25, and ISDN networks. The rest are running IPX RIP. Traffic-management control techniques—like longer EIGRP hello interval and hold time, IPX and SPX spoofing, and disabling CDP on the ISDN interfaces of both R1 and R2—are implemented. These are illustrated in Code Listings 4-22 to 4-25.

Figure 4-8
Implementing IPX
EIGRP over Frame
Relay, X.25, and
ISDN.

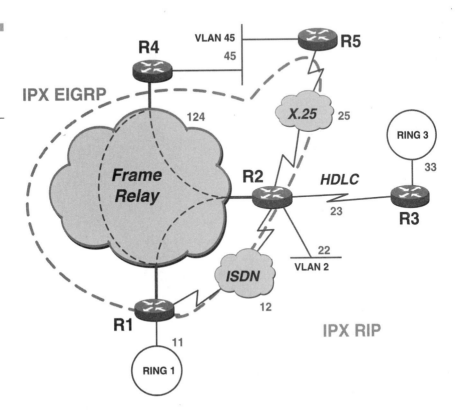

■ ▪

Code Listing 4-22

IPX configuration for R1.

```
hostname C3640-R1
!
username C3640-R2 password 0 cisco
ipx routing 0010.7bb2.7761
isdn switch-type basic-net3
!
interface BRI0/0
 encapsulation ppp
 ipx network 12
 dialer idle-timeout 60
 dialer map ipx 12.00e0.1e6f.9821 name C3640-R2 broadcast 3245652
 dialer load-threshold 128 either
 dialer-group 1
 ppp authentication chap
 no ipx route-cache
 ipx watchdog-spoof
 ipx spx-spoof
 ipx hello-interval eigrp 62 3600
 ipx hold-time eigrp 62 10800
 ipx sap-incremental eigrp 62
 no cdp enable
!
dialer-list 1 protocol ipx permit
!
interface Serial1/0
 backup delay 10 30
 backup interface BRI0/0
 encapsulation frame-relay
 bandwidth 56
 ipx network 124
 no ipx split-horizon eigrp 62
 ipx bandwidth-percent eigrp 62 25
 frame-relay map ipx 124.00e0.1e6f.9821 102 broadcast
 frame-relay map ipx 124.00e0.1e5f.de09 104 broadcast
 frame-relay lmi-type ansi
!
ipx router eigrp 62
 network 124
 network 12
!
ipx router rip
 no network 124
 no network 12
!
```

1. Code Listing 4-22 illustrates the IPX configuration for R1. The watchdog protocol belonging to one of the NCPs periodically queries for inactive workstation connections, and sends updates to the system when a workstation connection fails to respond accordingly. IPX watchdog packets are keepalive packets that servers send to clients after a client session has been idle for approximately five minutes. The system closes connections reported as unavailable. The `ipx watchdog-spoof` command implements

IPX spoofing, where the router responds to a server's Watchdog requests on behalf of remote clients. Fast switching and autonomous switching must be disabled on BRI0/0 using the command `no ipx route-cache`.

2. Some applications, such as Remote Console (RCONSOLE), Remote Printer (RPRINTER), and Systems Application Architecture (SAA), use the SPX protocol rather than IPX since they require guaranteed, sequenced delivery of packets. Servers send SPX keepalive packets to clients every 15 to 20 seconds after a client session has been idle for a period of time following the end of data transfer and after unsolicited acknowledgements are sent. Idle time may vary depending on client and server parameters. The command `ipx spx-spoof` implements SPX spoofing, where the router responds to the keepalive packets rather than the SPX applications. Fast switching and autonomous switching must be disabled on BRI0/0 using the command `no ipx route-cache`.

3. To prevent the EIGRP hello packets from keeping the ISDN line constantly active, the commands `ipx hello-interval eigrp` and `ipx hold-time eigrp` set the interval between hello packets to an hour and set the hold time to three times the hello interval, that is, three hours.

4. As EIGRP is implemented on the BRI0/0 interfaces of R1 and R2, SAP updates will be sent when the SAP table changes. This action is achieved through the default command `ipx sap-incremental eigrp 62`.

5. Cisco Discovery Protocol (CDP) is also disabled using the command `no cdp enable`.

6. Split horizon controls sending of EIGRP update and query packets. If split horizon is enabled on an interface, and this interface is the next hop to a particular destination, these packets are not sent. By default, split horizon is enabled on all interfaces; its mechanism optimizes communication among multiple routers, especially when links are broken. However, with NBMA networks like Frame Relay, situations can arise where this behavior is suboptimal The interface command `no ipx split-horizon eigrp 62` disables the split horizon mechanism for EIGRP on S1/0.

7. EIGRP packets consume a maximum of 50 percent of the link bandwidth by default. The command `ipx bandwidth-percent`

`eigrp 62 25` configures the bandwidth that EIGRP may use on S1/0 as 25 percent.

8. As IPX RIP and IPX EIGRP can coexist and their route redistribution is automatic, running just IPX EIGRP for an IPX network, IPX RIP must be disabled for that particular network.

9. The command `ipx router eigrp 62` defines the IPX EIGRP autonomous system number as 62 and goes to the `ipx router` configuration mode. The command `network 124` specifies the IPX network for Frame Relay, where EIGRP is running, and the command `network 12` specifies the IPX network for ISDN, where EIGRP is running.

10. Notice that IPX RIP is disabled on these networks by going to the `ipx router rip` configuration mode and using the `no network 124` and `no network 12` commands.

Code Listing 4-23
IPX configuration for R2.

```
hostname C3640-R2
!
username C3640-R1 password 0 cisco
ipx routing 00e0.1e6f.9821
isdn switch-type basic-net3
!
interface BRI0/0
 encapsulation ppp
 ipx network 12
 dialer idle-timeout 60
 dialer map ipx 12.0010.7bb2.7761 name C3640-R1 broadcast
 dialer load-threshold 128 either
 dialer-group 1
 ppp authentication chap
 no ipx route-cache
 ipx watchdog-spoof
 ipx spx-spoof
 ipx hello-interval eigrp 62 3600
 ipx hold-time eigrp 62 10800
 ipx sap-incremental eigrp 62
 no cdp enable
!
dialer-list 1 protocol ipx permit
!
interface Serial1/0
 encapsulation frame-relay
 frame-relay lmi-type ansi
!
interface Serial1/0.1 multipoint
 bandwidth 56
 ipx network 124
```

```
no ipx split-horizon eigrp 62
ipx bandwidth-percent eigrp 62 25
 frame-relay map ipx 124.00e0.1e5f.de09 204 broadcast
 frame-relay map ipx 124.0010.7bb2.7761 201 broadcast
 !
interface Serial1/1
 encapsulation x25
 bandwidth 56
 ipx network 25
 no ipx split-horizon eigrp 62
 ipx bandwidth-percent eigrp 62 25
 x25 address 25222222
 x25 map ipx 25.00e0.1e5d.3532 25555555 broadcast
 !
ipx router eigrp 62
 network 124
 network 12
 network 25
 !
ipx router rip
 no network 124
 no network 25
 no network 12
```

1. Code Listing 4-23 illustrates the IPX configuration for R2. The watchdog protocol belonging to one of the NCPs periodically queries for inactive workstation connections and sends updates to the system when a connection fails to respond accordingly. IPX watchdog packets are keepalive packets sent from servers to clients after a client session has been idle for approximately five minutes. The system closes connections reported as unavailable. The ipx watchdog-spoof command implements IPX spoofing. The router responds to a server's watchdog requests on behalf of a remote client. Fast switching and autonomous switching must be disabled on BRI0/0 using the command no ipx route-cache.

2. Some applications, such as Remote Console (RCONSOLE), Remote Printer (RPRINTER), and Systems Application Architecture (SAA), use the SPX protocol rather than IPX since they require guaranteed, sequenced delivery of packets. Servers send SPX keepalive packets to clients every 15 to 20 seconds after a client session has been idle for a period of time following the end of data transfer and after which only unsolicited acknowledgements are sent. Idle time may vary depending on client and server parameters. The command ipx spx-spoof implements SPX spoofing, where the router responds to the keepalive packets rather than the SPX applications. Fast switching and autonomous

switching must be disabled on BRI0/0 using the command `no ipx route-cache`.

3. To prevent EIGRP hello packets from keeping the ISDN line active, the commands `ipx hello-interval eigrp` and `ipx hold-time eigrp` set the interval between hello packets to an hour and set the hold time to three times the hello interval, that is, three hours.

4. As EIGRP is implemented on both BRI0/0 interfaces of R2 and R1, SAP updates will be sent when the SAP table changes. This action is achieved through the default command `ipx sap-incremental eigrp 62`.

5. Cisco Discovery Protocol (CDP) is also disabled using the command `no cdp enable`.

6. Split horizon controls sending of EIGRP update and query packets. If split horizon is enabled on an interface, and this interface is the next hop to a particular destination, these packets are not sent. By default, split horizon is enabled on all interfaces; its mechanism optimizes communication among multiple routers, especially when links are broken. However, with NBMA networks like Frame Relay and X.25, situations can arise where this behavior is suboptimal. The interface command `no ipx split-horizon eigrp 62` disables the split horizon mechanism for EIGRP on S1/0.1 and S1/1.

7. EIGRP packets consume a maximum of 50 percent of the link bandwidth by default. The command `ipx bandwidth-percent eigrp 62 25` configures the bandwidth that EIGRP may use on S1/0.1 and S1/1 as 25 percent.

8. As IPX RIP and IPX EIGRP can coexist and route redistribution is automatic, running just IPX EIGRP for an IPX network, IPX RIP must be disabled for that particular network.

9. The command `ipx router eigrp 62` defines the IPX EIGRP autonomous system number as 62 and goes to the ipx router configuration mode. We specify the IPX network where EIGRP is to run here. The command `network 124` specifies the IPX network for Frame Relay, where EIGRP is running, the command `network 25` specifies the IPX network for X.25, and the command `network 12` specifies the IPX network for ISDN.

10. Notice that IPX RIP is disabled on these networks by going to the `ipx router rip` configuration mode and using the `no network 124`, `no network 25`, and `no network 12` commands.

Code Listing 4-24
IPX configuration for R4.

```
hostname C2500-R4
!
ipx routing 00e0.1e5f.de09
!
interface Serial0
 encapsulation frame-relay
 bandwidth 56
 ipx network 124
 no ipx split-horizon eigrp 62
 ipx bandwidth-percent eigrp 62 25
 frame-relay map ipx 124.00e0.1e6f.9821 402 broadcast
 frame-relay map ipx 124.0010.7bb2.7761 401 broadcast
 frame-relay lmi-type ansi
!
ipx router eigrp 62
 network 124
!
ipx router rip
 no network 124
```

1. Code Listing 4-24 illustrates the IPX configuration for R4. Split horizon controls sending of EIGRP update and query packets. If split horizon is enabled on an interface, and this interface is the next hop to a particular destination, these packets are not sent. By default, split horizon is enabled on all interfaces; its mechanism optimizes communication among multiple routers, especially when links are broken. However, with NBMA networks like Frame Relay, situations can arise where this behavior is suboptimal. The interface command `no ipx split-horizon eigrp 62` disables the split horizon mechanism for EIGRP on S0.

2. EIGRP packets consume a maximum of 50 percent of the link bandwidth by default. The command `ipx bandwidth-percent eigrp 62 25` configures the bandwidth that EIGRP may use on S0 as 25 percent.

3. As IPX RIP and IPX EIGRP can coexist and route redistribution is automatic, running just IPX EIGRP for an IPX network, IPX RIP must be disabled for that particular network.

4. The command `ipx router eigrp 62` defines the IPX EIGRP autonomous system number as 62 and goes to the ipx router con-

figuration mode. The command `network 124` specifies the IPX network for Frame Relay, where EIGRP is running.

5. Notice that IPX RIP is disabled on these networks by going to the `ipx router rip` configuration mode and using the `no network 124` command.

Code Listing 4-25
IPX configuration for R5.

```
hostname C2509-R5
!
ipx routing 00e0.1e5d.3532
!
interface Serial0
 encapsulation x25
 bandwidth 56
 ipx network 25
 no ipx split-horizon eigrp 62
 ipx bandwidth-percent eigrp 62 25
 x25 address 25555555
 x25 map ipx 25.00e0.1e6f.9821 25222222 broadcast
!
ipx router eigrp 62
 network 25
!
ipx router rip
 no network 25
```

1. Code Listing 4-25 illustrates the IPX configuration for R5. Split horizon controls sending of EIGRP update and query packets. If split horizon is enabled on an interface, and this interface is the next hop to a particular destination, these packets are not sent. By default, split horizon is enabled on all interfaces; its mechanism optimizes communication among multiple routers, especially when links are broken. However, with NBMA networks like X.25, situations can arise where this behavior is suboptimal. The interface command `no ipx split-horizon eigrp 62` disables the split horizon mechanism for EIGRP on S0.

2. EIGRP packets consume a maximum of 50 percent of the link bandwidth by default. The command `ipx bandwidth-percent eigrp 62 25` configures the bandwidth that EIGRP may use on S0 as 25 percent.

3. As IPX RIP and IPX EIGRP can coexist and their route redistribution is automatic, running just IPX EIGRP for an IPX network, IPX RIP must be disabled for that particular network.

4. The command `ipx router eigrp 62` defines the IPX EIGRP autonomous system number as 62 and goes to the `ipx router` configuration mode. The command `network 25` specifies the IPX network for X.25, where EIGRP is running.

5. Notice IPX RIP is disabled on these networks by going into the `ipx router rip` configuration mode and using the `no network 25` command.

Code Listing 4-26 shows the IPX routing table for R1.

Code Listing 4-26
IPX routing table for R1.

```
C3640-R1#show ipx route
Codes: C - Connected primary network,    c - Connected secondary network
       S - Static, F - Floating static, L - Local (internal), W - IPXWAN
       R - RIP, E - EIGRP, N - NLSP, X - External, A - Aggregate
       s - seconds, u - uses

8 Total IPX routes. Up to 1 parallel paths and 16 hops allowed.

No default route known.

C          11 (SAP),          To0/0
C         124 (FRAME-RELAY),   Se1/0
E          12 [46738176/0] via      124.00e0.1e6f.9821, age 00:08:54,
   1u, Se1/0
E          22 [46251776/1] via      124.00e0.1e6f.9821, age 00:08:54,
   1u, Se1/0
E          23 [46738176/1] via      124.00e0.1e6f.9821, age 00:08:54,
   1u, Se1/0
E          25 [46738176/0] via      124.00e0.1e6f.9821, age 00:08:54,
   1u, Se1/0
E          33 [276864000/2] via      124.00e0.1e6f.9821, age 00:08:54,
   1u, Se1/0
E          45 [267008000/1] via      124.00e0.1e5f.de09, age 00:08:53,
   1u, Se1/0
```

Code Listing 4-27 shows the IPX routing table for R2.

Code Listing 4-27
IPX routing table for R2.

```
C3640-R2#show ipx route
Codes: C - Connected primary network,    c - Connected secondary network
       S - Static, F - Floating static, L - Local (internal), W - IPXWAN
       R - RIP, E - EIGRP, N - NLSP, X - External, A - Aggregate
       s - seconds, u - uses

8 Total IPX routes. Up to 1 parallel paths and 16 hops allowed.

No default route known.

C          12 (PPP),          BR0/0
C          22 (NOVELL-ETHER),  Et0/0
C          23 (HDLC),         Se1/2
C          25 (X25),          Se1/1
C         124 (FRAME-RELAY),   Se1/0.1
E          11 [46242304/1] via      124.0010.7bb2.7761, age 00:06:18,
   1u, Se1/0.1
R          33 [07/01] via      23.00e0.1e5f.dd0d,    19s, Se1/2
E          45 [267008000/1] via      124.00e0.1e5f.de09, age 00:05:07,
   1u, Se1/0.1
```

Note that in Code Listing 4-27, the route to IPX network 33 is still learned through IPX RIP, since IPX EIGRP is not configured on R3.

Code Listing 4-28 shows the IPX routing table for R3.

Code Listing 4-28

IPX routing table for R3.

```
C2500-R3#show ipx route
Codes: C - Connected primary network,    c - Connected secondary network
       S - Static, F - Floating static, L - Local (internal), W - IPXWAN
       R - RIP, E - EIGRP, N - NLSP, X - External, A - Aggregate
       s - seconds, u - uses

8 Total IPX routes. Up to 1 parallel paths and 16 hops allowed.

No default route known.

C         23 (HDLC),           Se0
C         33 (SAP),            To0
R         11 [13/02] via       23.00e0.1e6f.9821,    23s, Se0
R         12 [07/01] via       23.00e0.1e6f.9821,    23s, Se0
R         22 [07/01] via       23.00e0.1e6f.9821,    23s, Se0
R         25 [07/01] via       23.00e0.1e6f.9821,    23s, Se0
R         45 [07/02] via       23.00e0.1e6f.9821,    23s, Se0
R        124 [07/01] via       23.00e0.1e6f.9821,    23s, Se0
```

In Code Listing 4-28, the IPX route entries on R3 are all reflected as IPX RIP routes since IPX EIGRP is not configured.

Code Listing 4-29 shows the IPX routing table for R4.

Code Listing 4-29

IPX routing table for R4.

```
C2500-R4#show ipx route
Codes: C - Connected primary network,    c - Connected secondary network
       S - Static, F - Floating static, L - Local (internal), W - IPXWAN
       R - RIP, E - EIGRP, N - NLSP, X - External, A - Aggregate
       s - seconds, u - uses

8 Total IPX routes. Up to 1 parallel paths and 16 hops allowed.

No default route known.

C         45 (NOVELL-ETHER),   Et0
C        124 (FRAME-RELAY),    Se0
E         11 [46242304/1] via      124.0010.7bb2.7761, age 00:09:19,
   1u, Se0
E         12 [46738176/0] via      124.00e0.1e6f.9821, age 00:09:21,
   1u, Se0
E         22 [46251776/1] via      124.00e0.1e6f.9821, age 00:09:21,
   1u, Se0
E         23 [46738176/1] via      124.00e0.1e6f.9821, age 00:09:21,
   1u, Se0
E         25 [46738176/0] via      124.00e0.1e6f.9821, age 00:09:21,
   1u, Se0
E         33 [276864000/2] via     124.00e0.1e6f.9821, age 00:09:21,
   1u, Se0
```

Code Listing 4-30 shows the IPX routing table for R5.

Code Listing 4-30
IPX routing table for
R5.

```
C2509-R5#show ipx route
Codes: C - Connected primary network,    c - Connected secondary network
       S - Static, F - Floating static, L - Local (internal), W - IPXWAN
       R - RIP, E - EIGRP, N - NLSP, X - External, A - Aggregate
       s - seconds, u - uses

8 Total IPX routes. Up to 1 parallel paths and 16 hops allowed.

No default route known.

C         25 (X25),          Se0
C         45 (NOVELL-ETHER), Et0
E         11 [46754304/1] via       25.00e0.1e6f.9821, age 00:05:39,
 1u, Se0
E         12 [46738176/0] via       25.00e0.1e6f.9821, age 00:05:40,
 1u, Se0
E         22 [46251776/1] via       25.00e0.1e6f.9821, age 00:05:40,
 1u, Se0
E         23 [46738176/1] via       25.00e0.1e6f.9821, age 00:05:40,
 1u, Se0
E         33 [276864000/2] via       25.00e0.1e6f.9821, age 00:05:40,
 1u, Se0
E        124 [46738176/0] via       25.00e0.1e6f.9821, age 00:05:40,
 1u, Se0
```

Consider Figure 4-7. When Frame Relay connectivity between R1 and R2 becomes unavailable, the ISDN backup link will become active. See Code Listings 4-31 and 4-32 for the changes in the routing tables of R1 and R2.

Code Listing 4-31
IPX routing table for
R1.

```
C3640-R1#show ipx route
Codes: C - Connected primary network,    c - Connected secondary network
       S - Static, F - Floating static, L - Local (internal), W - IPXWAN
       R - RIP, E - EIGRP, N - NLSP, X - External, A - Aggregate
       s - seconds, u - uses

8 Total IPX routes. Up to 1 parallel paths and 16 hops allowed.

No default route known.

C         11 (SAP),          To0/0
C         12 (PPP),          BR0/0
E         22 [40537600/1] via       12.00e0.1e6f.9821, age 00:00:27,
 1u, BR0/0
E         23 [46738176/1] via       12.00e0.1e6f.9821, age 00:00:27,
 1u, BR0/0
E         25 [46738176/0] via       12.00e0.1e6f.9821, age 00:00:27,
 1u, BR0/0
E         33 [276864000/2] via       12.00e0.1e6f.9821, age 00:00:27,
 1u, BR0/0
E         45 [267520000/1] via       12.00e0.1e6f.9821, age 00:00:27,
 1u, BR0/0
E        124 [46738176/0] via       12.00e0.1e6f.9821, age 00:00:27,
 1u, BR0/0
```

In Code Listing 4-31, all route entries for R1, besides those directly connected, are now learned via BRI0/0.

```
C3640-R2#show ipx route
Codes: C - Connected primary network,    c - Connected secondary network
       S - Static, F - Floating static, L - Local (internal), W - IPXWAN
       R - RIP, E - EIGRP, N - NLSP, X - External, A - Aggregate
       s - seconds, u - uses

8 Total IPX routes. Up to 1 parallel paths and 16 hops allowed.

No default route known.

C         12 (PPP),         BR0/0
C         22 (NOVELL-ETHER), Et0/0
C         23 (HDLC),         Se1/2
C         25 (X25),          Se1/1
C        124 (FRAME-RELAY),  Se1/0.1
E         11 [40528128/1] via      12.0010.7bb2.7761, age 00:00:43,
   1u, BR0/0
R         33 [07/01] via     23.00e0.1e5f.dd0d,   12s, Se1/2
E         45 [267008000/1] via    124.00e0.1e5f.de09, age 00:08:00,
   1u, Se1/0.1
```

In Code Listing 4-32, the route to IPX network 11 is now learned via
BRI0/0.

NLSP

NLSP Databases

NLSP is a link-state protocol; every router in a routing area maintains an
identical copy of the link-state database containing all information about
the area topology. All routers synchronize their views of the database to
keep each copy of the link-state database consistent. NLSP has the following three major databases:

■ Adjacency database: keeps track of the router's immediate neighbors
and the operational status of directly attached links by exchanging
hello packets. Adjacencies are created upon receipt of hello packets. If
a link goes down, the adjacencies time out and are deleted from the
database.

■ Link-state database: tracks the connectivity of a routing area by
aggregating the immediate neighborhood information from all routers into link-state packets (LSPs) containing lists of adjacencies.
LSPs are flooded to other devices via a reliable flooding algorithm
each time a link state changes. LSPs are refreshed every two hours.
To keep the size of the link-state database reasonable, NLSP uses

pseudonodes—representing LAN as a whole—and designated routers, originating LSPs on behalf of the pseudonode.

- Forwarding database: calculated from the adjacency and link-state databases using Dijkstra's Shortest Path First (SPF) algorithm.

Level 1, 2, and 3 Routers

Level 1 routers connect systems within a given area. Level 2 routers connect areas, and Level 3 routers connect routing domains. A Level 2 router also acts as a Level 1 router within its area; likewise, a Level 3 router also acts as a Level 2 router within its routing domain.

The router at each level of the topology stores complete information for its level. For instance, Level 1 routers store complete link-state information about their area. This information includes a record of all routers in the area, the links connecting them, the operational status of the devices, and other related parameters. For each point-to-point link, the database records the end-point devices and the link state. For each LAN, the database records which routers are connected to the LAN. Similarly Level 2 routers store information about all areas in the routing domain, and Level 3 routers store information about all routing domains in the internetwork.

Although NLSP is designed for hierarchical routing environments containing Level 1, 2, and 3 routers, currently Novell's Netware Link Services Protocol (NLSP) Specification, Revision 1.1, defines only Level 1 routing with area route aggregation and route redistribution.

NLSP Areas

NLSP version 1.0 routers support only a single Level 1 area. Two routers form an adjacency only if they share at least one configured area address. The coalition of routers with adjacencies forms an area.

Each router within the NLSP area has its adjacencies, link state, and forwarding databases. Each router's link-state database is identical. Within the router, these databases operate collectively as a single process discovering, selecting, and maintaining area route information. NLSP version 1.0 routers and NLSP version 1.1 routers existing within a single area use a single NLSP instance.

With NLSP version 1.1, multiple instances of NLSP may exist on a router. Each instance discovers, selects, and maintains route information for a separate NLSP area. Each instance has a copy of the NLSP adjacency and link state database for its area, but all instances share a single copy of the forwarding table.

Configuring NLSP

In Figure 4-9, NLSP is configured for RING 3 and the HDLC link between R2 and R3.

In this scenario, the implementation of NLSP is based on revision 1.0 of the Novell NLSP specification, which specifies Level 1 routing. Code Listings 4-33 through 4-39 illustrate this.

Figure 4-9
Implementing NLSP over LAN and WAN.

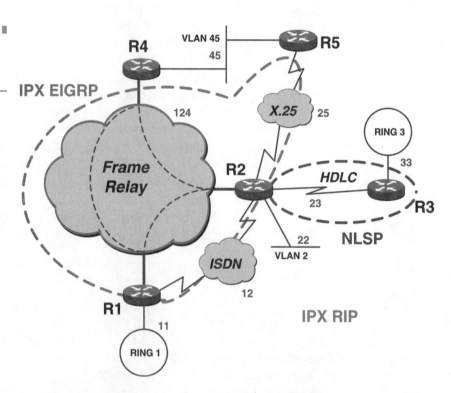

Code Listing 4-33
IPX NLSP configuration for R2.

```
hostname C3640-R2
!
ipx routing 00e0.1e6f.9821
ipx internal-network 2
!
interface Serial1/2
 bandwidth 56
 ipx ipxwan 2 23 C3640-R2
 ipx nlsp enable
!
ipx router eigrp 62
 redistribute nlsp
 network 124
 network 12
 network 25
!
ipx router nlsp
 area-address 0 0
 redistribute eigrp 62
```

1. Code Listing 4-33 illustrates the IPX NLSP configuration for R2. An internal network number is an IPX network number assigned to the router. For NLSP to operate, the internal network number must be configured for routers running NLSP. In this case, the internal network number is 2.

2. To enable NLSP on a WAN interface, IPXWAN must first be enabled on S1/2 by the command `ipx ipxwan 2 23 C3640-R2` (where 2 is the internal network number, 23 is the external network number, and C3640-R2 is the local server name or host name). IPXWAN is defined in RFC 1634, allowing a router running IPX routing to connect via a Serial link to another router, possibly from another manufacturer, that is also using IPXWAN. It is a connection startup protocol, and once a link has been established, IPXWAN incurs little overhead. IPXWAN can be used either over PPP or HDLC. However, for HDLC, both ends must be Cisco routers. The command `ipx nlsp enable` enables NLSP on the interface.

3. The command `ipx router nlsp` enables NLSP and goes to the `ipx router` configuration mode. An optional argument, `tag`, follows after the command, naming the NLSP processes that are assigned to the NLSP protocol. In this case, R2 has one process; therefore, defining a `tag` is optional. A maximum of three NLSP processes may be configured on one router simultaneously. The `tag` can be any combination of printable characters.

4. The command `area-address 0 0` defines an area address including all networks. The network range is refined with this command.

The following example defines an area address including networks CCCCBBC0 through CCCCBBDF: area-address CCCCBBC0 FFFFFFE0. Note that FFFFFFE0 is the mask. For NLSP filtering, a mask bit of 1 means check, and 0 means ignore.

5. Route redistribution between instances of NLSP (version 1.1 and 1.0) and EIGRP is disabled by default. Redistribution must be explicitly configured. From the ipx router configuration mode, enable redistribution of NLSP into EIGRP with the command redistribute nlsp and enable redistribution of EIGRP into NLSP using the command redistribute eigrp 62. Note that the route redistribution between NLSP (version 1.1 and 1.0) and RIP is enabled by default.

Code Listing 4-34

IPX NLSP configuration for R3.

```
hostname C2500-R3
!
ipx routing 00e0.1e5f.dd0d
ipx internal-network 3
!
interface Serial0
 bandwidth 56
 ipx ipxwan 3 23 C2500-R3
 ipx nlsp enable
!
interface TokenRing0
 ipx network 33
 ipx nlsp enable
 ring-speed 16
!
ipx router nlsp
 area-address 0 0
```

1. Code Listing 4-34 illustrates the IPX NLSP configuration for R3. An internal network number is an IPX network number assigned to the router. For NLSP to operate, the internal network number must be configured for the routers running NLSP. In this case, the internal network number is 3.

2. To enable NLSP on a WAN interface, IPXWAN must be enabled on S0, achieved by the command ipx ipxwan 3 23 C2500-R3 (where 3 is the internal network number, 23 is the external network number, and C2500-R3 is the local server name or host name).

3. The command ipx nlsp enable enables NLSP on S0 and TO0.

4. The command `ipx router nlsp` enables NLSP and goes to the
ipx router configuration mode. The command `area-address 0 0`
defines an area address that includes all networks.

Code Listing 4-35 shows the IPX routing table for R1.

Code Listing 4-35
IPX routing table for
R1.

```
C3640-R1#show ipx route
Codes: C - Connected primary network,    c - Connected secondary network
       S - Static, F - Floating static, L - Local (internal), W - IPXWAN
       R - RIP, E - EIGRP, N - NLSP, X - External, A - Aggregate
       s - seconds, u - uses

10 Total IPX routes. Up to 1 parallel paths and 16 hops allowed.

No default route known.

C        11 (SAP),        To0/0
C       124 (FRAME-RELAY),    Se1/0
E         2 [46354176/1] via        124.00e0.1e6f.9821, age 00:00:20,
 1u, Se1/0
E         3 [285312000/2] via       124.00e0.1e6f.9821, age 00:00:20,
 1u, Se1/0
E        12 [46738176/0] via        124.00e0.1e6f.9821, age 00:00:20,
 1u, Se1/0
E        22 [46251776/1] via        124.00e0.1e6f.9821, age 00:00:20,
 1u, Se1/0
E        23 [46738176/1] via        124.00e0.1e6f.9821, age 00:00:20,
 1u, Se1/0
E        25 [46738176/0] via        124.00e0.1e6f.9821, age 00:00:20,
 1u, Se1/0
E        33 [283904000/2] via       124.00e0.1e6f.9821, age 00:00:20,
 1u, Se1/0
E        45 [267008000/1] via       124.00e0.1e5f.de09, age 00:00:21,
 1u, Se1/0
```

Code Listing 4-36 shows the IPX routing table for R2.

Code Listing 4-36
IPX routing table for
R2.

```
C3640-R2#show ipx route
Codes: C - Connected primary network,    c - Connected secondary network
       S - Static, F - Floating static, L - Local (internal), W - IPXWAN
       R - RIP, E - EIGRP, N - NLSP, X - External, A - Aggregate
       s - seconds, u - uses

10 Total IPX routes. Up to 1 parallel paths and 16 hops allowed.

No default route known.

L         2 is the internal network
C        12 (PPP),        BR0/0
C        22 (NOVELL-ETHER),   Et0/0
W        23 (HDLC),       Se1/2
C        25 (X25),        Se1/1
C       124 (FRAME-RELAY),    Se1/0.1
N         3 [45][13/01] via        3.0000.0000.0001,  466s, Se1/2
E        11 [46242304/1] via       124.0010.7bb2.7761, age 00:00:32,
 1u, Se1/0.1
N        33 [45][12/01] via        3.0000.0000.0001,  466s, Se1/2
E        45 [267008000/1] via      124.00e0.1e5f.de09, age 00:00:44,
 1u, Se1/0.1
```

Code Listing 4-37 shows the IPX routing table for R3.

■ ■ ■ ■ ■ ■ ■　■ ▮

Code Listing 4-37

IPX routing table for R3.

```
C2500-R3#show ipx route
Codes: C - Connected primary network,    c - Connected secondary network
       S - Static, F - Floating static, L - Local (internal), W - IPXWAN
       R - RIP, E - EIGRP, N - NLSP, X - External, A - Aggregate
       s - seconds, u - uses

10 Total IPX routes. Up to 1 parallel paths and 16 hops allowed.

No default route known.

L        3 is the internal network
W       23 (HDLC),         Se0
C       33 (SAP),          To0
N        2 [45][13/01] via      2.0000.0000.0001,   425s, Se0
NX      11 [45][25/02][13/01] via    2.0000.0000.0001,   56s, Se0
N       12 [45][12/01]      via      2.0000.0000.0001,   73s, Se0
N       22 [45][12/01]      via      2.0000.0000.0001,  426s, Se0
N       25 [45][12/01]      via      2.0000.0000.0001,  426s, Se0
NX      45 [45][19/02][07/01] via    2.0000.0000.0001,   56s, Se0
N      124 [45][12/01]      via      2.0000.0000.0001,   56s, Se0
```

Code Listing 4-38 shows the IPX routing table for R4.

■ ■ ■ ■ ■ ■ ■　■ ▮

Code Listing 4-38

IPX routing table for R4.

```
C2500-R4#show ipx route
Codes: C - Connected primary network,    c - Connected secondary network
       S - Static, F - Floating static, L - Local (internal), W - IPXWAN
       R - RIP, E - EIGRP, N - NLSP, X - External, A - Aggregate
       s - seconds, u - uses

10 Total IPX routes. Up to 1 parallel paths and 16 hops allowed.

No default route known.

C       45 (NOVELL-ETHER),  Et0
C      124 (FRAME-RELAY),   Se0
E        2 [46354176/1] via       124.00e0.1e6f.9821, age 00:01:30,
  1u, Se0
E        3 [285312000/2] via      124.00e0.1e6f.9821, age 00:01:30,
  1u, Se0
E       11 [46242304/1] via       124.0010.7bb2.7761, age 00:01:15,
  1u, Se0
E       12 [46738176/0] via       124.00e0.1e6f.9821, age 00:01:30,
  1u, Se0
E       22 [46251776/1] via       124.00e0.1e6f.9821, age 00:01:30,
  1u, Se0
E       23 [46738176/1] via       124.00e0.1e6f.9821, age 00:01:30,
  1u, Se0
E       25 [46738176/0] via       124.00e0.1e6f.9821, age 00:01:30,
  1u, Se0
E       33 [283904000/2] via      124.00e0.1e6f.9821, age 00:01:30,
  1u, Se0
```

Code Listing 4-39 shows the IPX routing table for R5.

■ ■ ■ ■ ■ ■ ■   ■

Code Listing 4-39
IPX routing table for
R5.

```
C2509-R5#show ipx route
Codes: C - Connected primary network,    c - Connected secondary network
       S - Static, F - Floating static, L - Local (internal), W - IPXWAN
       R - RIP, E - EIGRP, N - NLSP, X - External, A - Aggregate
       s - seconds, u - uses

10 Total IPX routes. Up to 1 parallel paths and 16 hops allowed.

No default route known.

C        25 (X25),           Se0
C        45 (NOVELL-ETHER),  Et0
E         2 [46354176/1] via      25.00e0.1e6f.9821, age 00:26:09,
   1u, Se0
E         3 [285312000/2] via     25.00e0.1e6f.9821, age 00:08:51,
   1u, Se0
E        11 [46754304/1] via      25.00e0.1e6f.9821, age 00:01:26,
   1u, Se0
E        12 [46738176/0] via      25.00e0.1e6f.9821, age 00:57:41,
   1u, Se0
E        22 [46251776/1] via      25.00e0.1e6f.9821, age 00:26:09,
   1u, Se0
E        23 [46738176/1] via      25.00e0.1e6f.9821, age 00:08:55,
   1u, Se0
E        33 [283904000/2] via     25.00e0.1e6f.9821, age 00:08:51,
   1u, Se0
E       124 [46738176/0] via      25.00e0.1e6f.9821, age 00:57:41,
   1u, Se0
```

The two newly defined IPX internal networks are reflected in the IPX routing table for all the routers, as illustrated in Code Listings 4-35 to 4-39.

IPX Access Control

This section will examine three applications of IPX access lists:

- routing table filtering
- NetWare serialization packets filtering
- SAP filtering

Routing Table Filtering

Consider Figure 4-10. Eight new routes have been injected into VLAN 45.

Note the routing tables illustrated in Code Listings 4-40 to 4-44.

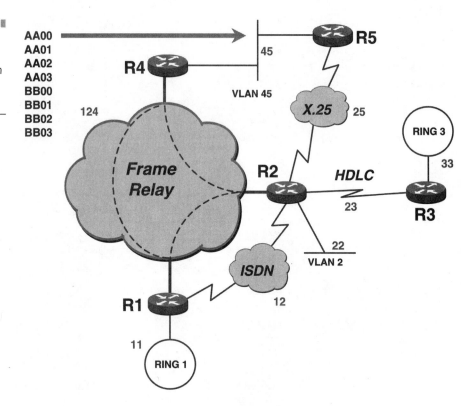

Figure 4-10
Eight additional IPX
RIP routes have been
injected into VLAN
45.

Code Listing 4-40
IPX routing table for
R1.

```
C3640-R1#show ipx route
Codes: C - Connected primary network,    c - Connected secondary network
       S - Static, F - Floating static, L - Local (internal), W - IPXWAN
       R - RIP, E - EIGRP, N - NLSP, X - External, A - Aggregate
       s - seconds, u - uses

18 Total IPX routes. Up to 1 parallel paths and 16 hops allowed.

No default route known.

C          11 (SAP),          To0/0
C         124 (FRAME-RELAY),  Se1/0
E           2 [46354176/1] via      124.00e0.1e6f.9821, age 00:03:20,
  1u, Se1/0
E           3 [285312000/2] via      124.00e0.1e6f.9821, age 00:03:20,
  1u, Se1/0
E          12 [46738176/0] via      124.00e0.1e6f.9821, age 00:03:20,
  1u, Se1/0
E          22 [46251776/1] via      124.00e0.1e6f.9821, age 00:03:20,
  1u, Se1/0
E          23 [46738176/1] via      124.00e0.1e6f.9821, age 00:03:20,
  1u, Se1/0
E          25 [46738176/0] via      124.00e0.1e6f.9821, age 00:03:20,
  1u, Se1/0
E          33 [283904000/2] via      124.00e0.1e6f.9821, age 00:03:20,
  1u, Se1/0
E          45 [267008000/1] via      124.00e0.1e5f.de09, age 00:00:23,
  1u, Se1/0
E        AA00 [269824000/2] via      124.00e0.1e5f.de09, age 00:00:22,
```

Code Listing 4-40
(continued)

```
            1u, Se1/0
E           AA01 [269824000/2] via      124.00e0.1e5f.de09, age 00:00:22,
            1u, Se1/0
E           AA02 [269824000/2] via      124.00e0.1e5f.de09, age 00:00:22,
            1u, Se1/0
E           AA03 [269824000/2] via      124.00e0.1e5f.de09, age 00:00:22,
            1u, Se1/0
E           BB00 [269824000/2] via      124.00e0.1e5f.de09, age 00:00:28,
            1u, Se1/0
E           BB01 [269824000/2] via      124.00e0.1e5f.de09, age 00:00:29,
            1u, Se1/0
E           BB02 [269824000/2] via      124.00e0.1e5f.de09, age 00:00:29,
            1u, Se1/0
E           BB03 [269824000/2] via      124.00e0.1e5f.de09, age 00:00:29,
            1u, Se1/0
```

Code Listing 4-41
IPX routing table for
R2.

```
C3640-R2#show ipx route
Codes: C - Connected primary network,    c - Connected secondary network
       S - Static, F - Floating static, L - Local (internal), W - IPXWAN
       R - RIP, E - EIGRP, N - NLSP, X - External, A - Aggregate
       s - seconds, u - uses

18 Total IPX routes. Up to 1 parallel paths and 16 hops allowed.

No default route known.

L          2 is the internal network
C         12 (PPP),          BR0/0
C         22 (NOVELL-ETHER), Et0/0
W         23 (HDLC),         Se1/2
C         25 (X25),          Se1/1
C        124 (FRAME-RELAY),  Se1/0.1
N          3 [45][13/01] via       3.0000.0000.0001, 4414s, Se1/2
E         11 [46242304/1] via      124.0010.7bb2.7761, age 00:03:24,
           1u, Se1/0.1
N         33 [45][12/01] via       3.0000.0000.0001, 4414s, Se1/2
E         45 [267008000/1] via     124.00e0.1e5f.de09, age 00:00:30,
           1u, Se1/0.1
E         AA00 [269824000/2] via   124.00e0.1e5f.de09, age 00:00:28,
           1u, Se1/0.1
E         AA01 [269824000/2] via   124.00e0.1e5f.de09, age 00:00:29,
           1u, Se1/0.1
E         AA02 [269824000/2] via   124.00e0.1e5f.de09, age 00:00:29,
           1u, Se1/0.1
E         AA03 [269824000/2] via   124.00e0.1e5f.de09, age 00:00:29,
           1u, Se1/0.1
E         BB00 [269824000/2] via   124.00e0.1e5f.de09, age 00:00:31,
           1u, Se1/0.1
E         BB01 [269824000/2] via   124.00e0.1e5f.de09, age 00:00:31,
           1u, Se1/0.1
E         BB02 [269824000/2] via   124.00e0.1e5f.de09, age 00:00:31,
           1u, Se1/0.1
E         BB03 [269824000/2] via   124.00e0.1e5f.de09, age 00:00:32,
           1u, Se1/0.1
```

Code Listing 4-42

IPX routing table for R3.

```
C2500-R3#show ipx route
Codes: C - Connected primary network,    c - Connected secondary network
       S - Static, F - Floating static, L - Local (internal), W - IPXWAN
       R - RIP, E - EIGRP, N - NLSP, X - External, A - Aggregate
       s - seconds, u - uses

18 Total IPX routes. Up to 1 parallel paths and 16 hops allowed.

No default route known.

L         3 is the internal network
W        23 (HDLC),           Se0
C        33 (SAP),            To0
N         2 [45][13/01] via        2.0000.0000.0001, 4353s, Se0
NX       11 [45][25/02][13/01] via 2.0000.0000.0001,   27s, Se0
N        12 [45][12/01]        via 2.0000.0000.0001,  206s, Se0
N        22 [45][12/01]        via 2.0000.0000.0001, 4354s, Se0
N        25 [45][12/01]        via 2.0000.0000.0001,   27s, Se0
NX       45 [45][19/02][07/01] via 2.0000.0000.0001,   27s, Se0
N       124 [45][12/01]        via 2.0000.0000.0001,   27s, Se0
NX     AA00 [45][20/03][08/02] via 2.0000.0000.0001,   27s, Se0
NX     AA01 [45][20/03][08/02] via 2.0000.0000.0001,   28s, Se0
NX     AA02 [45][20/03][08/02] via 2.0000.0000.0001,   28s, Se0
NX     AA03 [45][20/03][08/02] via 2.0000.0000.0001,   28s, Se0
NX     BB00 [45][20/03][08/02] via 2.0000.0000.0001,   28s, Se0
NX     BB01 [45][20/03][08/02] via 2.0000.0000.0001,   28s, Se0
NX     BB02 [45][20/03][08/02] via 2.0000.0000.0001,   28s, Se0
NX     BB03 [45][20/03][08/02] via 2.0000.0000.0001,   28s, Se0
```

Code Listing 4-43

IPX routing table for R4.

```
C2500-R4#show ipx route
Codes: C - Connected primary network,    c - Connected secondary network
       S - Static, F - Floating static, L - Local (internal), W - IPXWAN
       R - RIP, E - EIGRP, N - NLSP, X - External, A - Aggregate
       s - seconds, u - uses

18 Total IPX routes. Up to 1 parallel paths and 16 hops allowed.

No default route known.

C        45 (NOVELL-ETHER),  Et0
C       124 (FRAME-RELAY),   Se0
E         2 [46354176/1] via     124.00e0.1e6f.9821, age 00:00:53,
          1u, Se0
E         3 [285312000/2] via    124.00e0.1e6f.9821, age 00:00:53,
          1u, Se0
E        11 [46242304/1] via     124.0010.7bb2.7761, age 00:00:53,
          1u, Se0
E        12 [46738176/0] via     124.00e0.1e6f.9821, age 00:00:53,
          1u, Se0
E        22 [46251776/1] via     124.00e0.1e6f.9821, age 00:00:53,
          1u, Se0
E        23 [46738176/1] via     124.00e0.1e6f.9821, age 00:00:53,
          1u, Se0
E        25 [46738176/0] via     124.00e0.1e6f.9821, age 00:00:53,
          1u, Se0
E        33 [283904000/2] via    124.00e0.1e6f.9821, age 00:00:53,
          1u, Se0
R      AA00 [02/01] via      45.0060.2fa3.6848,  46s, Et0
R      AA01 [02/01] via      45.0060.2fa3.6848,  46s, Et0
R      AA02 [02/01] via      45.0060.2fa3.6848,  46s, Et0
R      AA03 [02/01] via      45.0060.2fa3.6848,  46s, Et0
R      BB00 [02/01] via      45.0060.2fa3.6848,  46s, Et0
R      BB01 [02/01] via      45.0060.2fa3.6848,  46s, Et0
R      BB02 [02/01] via      45.0060.2fa3.6848,  46s, Et0
R      BB03 [02/01] via      45.0060.2fa3.6848,  46s, Et0
```

Code Listing 4-44
IPX routing table for R5.

```
C2509-R5#show ipx route
Codes: C - Connected primary network,     c - Connected secondary network
       S - Static, F - Floating static, L - Local (internal), W - IPXWAN
       R - RIP, E - EIGRP, N - NLSP, X - External, A - Aggregate
       s - seconds, u - uses

18 Total IPX routes. Up to 1 parallel paths and 16 hops allowed.

No default route known.

C          25 (X25),          Se0
C          45 (NOVELL-ETHER),  Et0
E           2 [46354176/1] via        25.00e0.1e6f.9821, age 00:00:53,
   1u, Se0
E           3 [285312000/2] via        25.00e0.1e6f.9821, age 00:00:54,
   1u, Se0
E          11 [46754304/1] via        25.00e0.1e6f.9821, age 00:00:54,
   1u, Se0
E          12 [46738176/0] via        25.00e0.1e6f.9821, age 00:00:54,
   1u, Se0
E          22 [46251776/1] via        25.00e0.1e6f.9821, age 00:00:54,
   1u, Se0
E          23 [46738176/1] via        25.00e0.1e6f.9821, age 00:00:54,
   1u, Se0
E          33 [283904000/2] via        25.00e0.1e6f.9821, age 00:00:54,
   1u, Se0
E         124 [46738176/0] via        25.00e0.1e6f.9821, age 00:00:54,
   1u, Se0
R        AA00 [02/01] via        45.0060.2fa3.6848,     53s, Et0
R        AA01 [02/01] via        45.0060.2fa3.6848,     53s, Et0
R        AA02 [02/01] via        45.0060.2fa3.6848,     53s, Et0
R        AA03 [02/01] via        45.0060.2fa3.6848,     53s, Et0
R        BB00 [02/01] via        45.0060.2fa3.6848,     53s, Et0
R        BB01 [02/01] via        45.0060.2fa3.6848,     53s, Et0
R        BB02 [02/01] via        45.0060.2fa3.6848,     53s, Et0
R        BB03 [02/01] via        45.0060.2fa3.6848,     53s, Et0
```

Note that the eight newly discovered IPX networks are reflected in the IPX routing table for all routers, as illustrated in Code Listings 4-40 to 4-44. However, in this scenario, note the four new routes that begin with a network address prefix of AAxx, where xx can be any two hexadecimal digits. An IPX routing table filter can be used to fulfill this requirement. Code Listings 4-45 and 4-46 illustrate this.

■ ▮

Code Listing 4-45
IPX routing table filter
configuration for R4.

```
hostname C2500-R4
!
ipx routing 00e0.1e5f.de09
!
interface Ethernet0
 ipx input-network-filter 900
 ipx network 45
!
access-list 900 deny any BB00.0000.0000.0000 FF.ffff.ffff.ffff all any
all
access-list 900 permit any any
```

■ I

Code Listing 4-46
IPX routing table filter
configuration for R5.

```
hostname C2509-R5
!
ipx routing 00e0.1e5d.3532
!
interface Ethernet0
 ipx input-network-filter 900
 ipx network 45
!
access-list 900 deny any BB00.0000.0000.0000 FF.ffff.ffff.ffff all any
all
access-list 900 permit any any
```

In Code Listings 4-45 and 4-46, the command `access-list 900 deny any BB00.0000.0000.0000 FF.ffff.ffff.ffff all any all` denies any IPX packet with a source address prefix of BBxx, where xx can be any two hexadecimal digits. The access list is applied to E0 inbound for both R4 and R5 using the command `ipx input-network-filter 900`. This command controls which networks are added to the routing table when IPX RIP routing updates are received. The command `access-list 900 permit any any` permits packets that do not match the previous list. Note a more granular `access-list 900 permit any AA00.0000.0000.0000 C.ffff.ffff.ffff all any all` can be used to achieve the same results.

Note the routing tables, shown in Code Listings 4-47 to 4-51, after the access lists have been applied on both the Ethernet interfaces of R4 and R5.

■ I

Code Listing 4-47
IPX routing table for
R1.

```
C3640-R1#show ipx route
Codes: C - Connected primary network,    c - Connected secondary network
       S - Static, F - Floating static, L - Local (internal), W - IPXWAN
       R - RIP, E - EIGRP, N - NLSP, X - External, A - Aggregate
       s - seconds, u - uses

14 Total IPX routes. Up to 1 parallel paths and 16 hops allowed.

No default route known.

C        11 (SAP),            To0/0
C        12 (PPP),            BR0/0
E         2 [46354176/1] via       12.00e0.1e6f.9821, age 00:56:14,
  1u, BR0/0
E         3 [285312000/2] via      12.00e0.1e6f.9821, age 00:56:15,
  1u, BR0/0
E        22 [40537600/1] via       12.00e0.1e6f.9821, age 00:56:15,
  1u, BR0/0
E        23 [46738176/1] via       12.00e0.1e6f.9821, age 00:56:15,
  1u, BR0/0
E        25 [46738176/0] via       12.00e0.1e6f.9821, age 00:56:15,
  1u, BR0/0
E        33 [283904000/2] via      12.00e0.1e6f.9821, age 00:56:15,
  1u, BR0/0
E        45 [267520000/1] via      12.00e0.1e6f.9821, age 00:00:57,
  1u, BR0/0
E       124 [46738176/0] via       12.00e0.1e6f.9821, age 00:56:16,
```

Code Listing 4-47
(continued)

```
                1u, BR0/0
E           AA00 [270336000/2] via       12.00e0.1e6f.9821, age 00:00:57,
                1u, BR0/0
E           AA01 [270336000/2] via       12.00e0.1e6f.9821, age 00:00:57,
                1u, BR0/0
E           AA02 [270336000/2] via       12.00e0.1e6f.9821, age 00:00:57,
                1u, BR0/0
E           AA03 [270336000/2] via       12.00e0.1e6f.9821, age 00:00:57,
                1u, BR0/0
```

Code Listing 4-48
IPX routing table for
R2.

```
C3640-R2#show ipx route
Codes: C - Connected primary network,    c - Connected secondary network
       S - Static, F - Floating static, L - Local (internal), W - IPXWAN
       R - RIP, E - EIGRP, N - NLSP, X - External, A - Aggregate
       s - seconds, u - uses

14 Total IPX routes. Up to 1 parallel paths and 16 hops allowed.

No default route known.

L           2 is the internal network
C          12 (PPP),         BR0/0
C          22 (NOVELL-ETHER), Et0/0
W          23 (HDLC),        Se1/2
C          25 (X25),         Se1/1
C         124 (FRAME-RELAY),  Se1/0.1
N           3 [45][13/01] via        3.0000.0000.0001, 4084s, Se1/2
E          11 [40528128/1] via       12.0010.7bb2.7761, age 00:56:22,
                1u, BR0/0
N          33 [45][12/01] via        3.0000.0000.0001, 4084s, Se1/2
E          45 [267008000/1] via       25.00e0.1e5d.3532, age 00:01:05,
                1u, Se1/1
E          AA00 [269824000/2] via       124.00e0.1e5f.de09, age 00:00:58,
                1u, Se1/0.1
E          AA01 [269824000/2] via       124.00e0.1e5f.de09, age 00:00:58,
                1u, Se1/0.1
E          AA02 [269824000/2] via       124.00e0.1e5f.de09, age 00:00:59,
                1u, Se1/0.1
E          AA03 [269824000/2] via       124.00e0.1e5f.de09, age 00:00:59,
                1u, Se1/0.1
```

Code Listing 4-49
IPX routing table for
R3.

```
C2500-R3#show ipx route
Codes: C - Connected primary network,    c - Connected secondary network
       S - Static, F - Floating static, L - Local (internal), W - IPXWAN
       R - RIP, E - EIGRP, N - NLSP, X - External, A - Aggregate
       s - seconds, u - uses

14 Total IPX routes. Up to 1 parallel paths and 16 hops allowed.

No default route known.

L           3 is the internal network
W          23 (HDLC),        Se0
C          33 (SAP),         To0
N           2 [45][13/01] via        2.0000.0000.0001, 4025s, Se0
NX         11 [45][25/02][13/01] via       2.0000.0000.0001, 3381s, Se0
N          12 [45][12/01]       via       2.0000.0000.0001, 3381s, Se0
N          22 [45][12/01]       via       2.0000.0000.0001, 4025s, Se0
N          25 [45][12/01]       via       2.0000.0000.0001,   67s, Se0
NX         45 [45][19/02][07/01] via       2.0000.0000.0001,   67s, Se0
N         124 [45][12/01]       via       2.0000.0000.0001,   67s, Se0
NX        AA00 [45][20/03][08/02] via       2.0000.0000.0001,   67s, Se0
NX        AA01 [45][20/03][08/02] via       2.0000.0000.0001,   68s, Se0
NX        AA02 [45][20/03][08/02] via       2.0000.0000.0001,   68s, Se0
NX        AA03 [45][20/03][08/02] via       2.0000.0000.0001,   68s, Se0
```

Code Listing 4-50
IPX routing table for R4.

```
C2500-R4#show ipx route
Codes: C - Connected primary network,    c - Connected secondary network
       S - Static, F - Floating static, L - Local (internal), W - IPXWAN
       R - RIP, E - EIGRP, N - NLSP, X - External, A - Aggregate
       s - seconds, u - uses

14 Total IPX routes. Up to 1 parallel paths and 16 hops allowed.

No default route known.

C        45 (NOVELL-ETHER),   Et0
C       124 (FRAME-RELAY),    Se0
E         2 [46354176/1] via    124.00e0.1e6f.9821, age 00:01:20,
 1u, Se0
E         3 [285312000/2] via    124.00e0.1e6f.9821, age 00:01:21,
 1u, Se0
E        11 [46754304/1] via   124.00e0.1e6f.9821, age 00:01:21,
 1u, Se0
E        12 [46738176/0] via   124.00e0.1e6f.9821, age 00:01:21,
 1u, Se0
E        22 [46251776/1] via   124.00e0.1e6f.9821, age 00:01:21,
 1u, Se0
E        23 [46738176/1] via   124.00e0.1e6f.9821, age 00:01:21,
 1u, Se0
E        25 [46738176/0] via   124.00e0.1e6f.9821, age 00:01:21,
 1u, Se0
E        33 [283904000/2] via   124.00e0.1e6f.9821, age 00:01:21,
 1u, Se0
R      AA00 [02/01] via       45.0060.2fa3.6848,   14s, Et0
R      AA01 [02/01] via       45.0060.2fa3.6848,   14s, Et0
R      AA02 [02/01] via       45.0060.2fa3.6848,   14s, Et0
R      AA03 [02/01] via       45.0060.2fa3.6848,   14s, Et0
```

Code Listing 4-51
IPX routing table for R5.

```
C2509-R5#show ipx route
Codes: C - Connected primary network,    c - Connected secondary network
       S - Static, F - Floating static, L - Local (internal), W - IPXWAN
       R - RIP, E - EIGRP, N - NLSP, X - External, A - Aggregate
       s - seconds, u - uses

14 Total IPX routes. Up to 1 parallel paths and 16 hops allowed.

No default route known.

C        25 (X25),           Se0
C        45 (NOVELL-ETHER),   Et0
E         2 [46354176/1] via    25.00e0.1e6f.9821, age 00:01:46,
 1u, Se0
E         3 [285312000/2] via    25.00e0.1e6f.9821, age 00:01:47,
 1u, Se0
E        11 [46754304/1] via   25.00e0.1e6f.9821, age 00:01:47,
 1u, Se0
E        12 [46738176/0] via   25.00e0.1e6f.9821, age 00:01:47,
 1u, Se0
E        22 [46251776/1] via   25.00e0.1e6f.9821, age 00:01:47,
 1u, Se0
E        23 [46738176/1] via   25.00e0.1e6f.9821, age 00:01:47,
 1u, Se0
E        33 [283904000/2] via   25.00e0.1e6f.9821, age 00:01:47,
 1u, Se0
E       124 [46738176/0] via   25.00e0.1e6f.9821, age 00:01:47,
 1u, Se0
R      AA00 [02/01] via       45.0060.2fa3.6848,   20s, Et0
R      AA01 [02/01] via       45.0060.2fa3.6848,   20s, Et0
R      AA02 [02/01] via       45.0060.2fa3.6848,   20s, Et0
R      AA03 [02/01] via       45.0060.2fa3.6848,   20s, Et0
```

The four unwanted routes—BB00, BB01, BB02, and BB03—have been filtered in Code Listings 4-47 through 4-51.

NetWare Serialization Packets Filtering

The NetWare operating system has a built-in copy protection scheme to ensure that licensed copies of NetWare are not improperly copied to other servers. Each NetWare server transmits to all file servers a unicast packet containing its unique serialization number at an interval of approximately 66 seconds. When a server detects duplicate serialization identifiers, it broadcasts a copyright violation message to all users and the console log. These serialization packets pose the same problem as IPX watchdog updates and SPX keepalives, constantly keeping the dial-up link active.

Table 4-1 lists some of the common IPX protocol numbers and names.

TABLE 4-1

Some common IPX protocol numbers and names

IPX Protocol Number (Decimal)	IPX Protocol Name	Protocol (Packet Type)
-1	any	Wildcard; matches any packet type in 900 lists
0		Undefined; refer to the socket number to determine the packet type
1	rip	Routing Information Protocol (RIP)
4	sap	Service Advertising Protocol (SAP)
5	spx	Sequenced Packet Exchange (SPX)
17	ncp	NetWare Core Protocol (NCP)
20	netbios	IPX NetBIOS

TABLE 4-2

Some common IPX
socket numbers
and names

IPX Socket Number (Hexadecimal)	IPX Socket Name	Socket
0	all	All sockets; wildcard used to match all sockets
2	cping	Cisco IPX ping packet
451	ncp	NetWare Core Protocol (NCP) process
452	sap	Service Advertising Protocol (SAP) process
453	rip	Routing Information Protocol (RIP) process
455	netbios	Novell NetBIOS process
456	diagnostic	Novell diagnostic packet
457		Novell serialization socket
4000-7FFF		Dynamic sockets; used by workstations for interaction with file servers and other network servers
8000-FFFF		Sockets as assigned by Novell, Inc.
85BE	eigrp	IPX Enhanced Interior Gateway Routing Protocol (Enhanced IGRP)
9001	nlsp	NetWare Link Services Protocol
9086	nping	Novell standard ping packet

Table 4-2 lists some of the common IPX socket numbers and names.

In this scenario, the dialer list will be refined for R1 and R2, as illustrated in Code Listings 4-52 and 4-53, to filter out the serialization packets.

Code Listing 4-52

IPX configuration for R1.

```
hostname C3640-R1
!
username C3640-R2 password 0 cisco
ipx routing 0010.7bb2.7761
isdn switch-type basic-net3
!
interface BRI0/0
 encapsulation ppp
 ipx network 12
 dialer idle-timeout 60
 dialer map ipx 12.00e0.1e6f.9821 name C3640-R2 broadcast 3245652
 dialer load-threshold 128 either
 dialer-group 1
```

Code Listing 4-52
(continued)

```
ppp authentication chap
no ipx route-cache
ipx watchdog-spoof
ipx spx-spoof
ipx hello-interval eigrp 62 3600
ipx hold-time eigrp 62 10800
(ipx sap-incremental eigrp 62)
no cdp enable
!
dialer-list 1 list 900
access-list 900 deny 0 any all any 457
access-list 900 permit any any
```

Code Listing 4-53
IPX configuration for
R2.

```
hostname C3640-R2
!
username C3640-R1 password 0 cisco
ipx routing 00e0.1e6f.9821
isdn switch-type basic-net3
!
interface BRI0/0
 encapsulation ppp
 ipx network 12
 dialer idle-timeout 60
 dialer map ipx 12.0010.7bb2.7761 name C3640-R1 broadcast
 dialer load-threshold 128 either
 dialer-group 1
 ppp authentication chap
 no ipx route-cache
 ipx watchdog-spoof
 ipx spx-spoof
 ipx hello-interval eigrp 62 3600
 ipx hold-time eigrp 62 10800
 (ipx sap-incremental eigrp 62)
 no cdp enable
!
dialer-list 1 list 900
access-list 900 deny 0 any all any 457
access-list 900 permit any any
```

In Code Listings 4-52 and 4-53, the interface command `dialer-group 1` now refers to `dialer-list 1 list 900`, which in turn points to `access-list 900`. In `access-list 900 deny 0 any all any 457`, the 0 refers to the socket number determining the packet type (see Table 4-1); the first `any` refers to any source net; `all` is a wildcard used to match all source sockets (see Table 4-2); the second `any` refers to any destination net; and the destination socket number is 457, referring to the Novell serialization socket (see Table 4-2).

SAP Filtering

SAP allows service-providing nodes such as file servers, print servers, and gateway servers to advertise their services and addresses. This creates a dynamic process of adding and removing services on an IPX internetwork. Routers create and maintain a database (Server Information Table) of the service information on each server. This allows clients on the network to determine what services are available and to obtain the addresses of the servers (or nodes) where they can access these services. SAP updates, like RIP, are sent every 60 seconds—but periodic updates are often undesirable in a WAN environment.

In Figure 4-11, two Novell servers are interconnected to VLAN 2. The `ipx sap` command in R2 explicitly adds two servers to the Server Information Table (SAP table) so clients can always see and use the services of these servers. The command `ipx sap 4 FILESVR2 3C01.0000.0000.0001 451 1` defines the service type as 4–file server (see Table 4-3);

Figure 4-11
SAP filtering scenario.

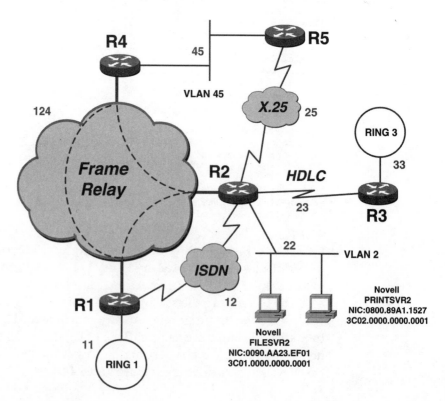

3C01.0000.0000.0001 is the internal IPX address; 451 is the socket number for NCP process see Table 4-2); and 1 is the number of hops to the server. Likewise, the command ipx sap 7 PRINTSVR2 3C02.0000.0000.0001 451 1 defines the service type as 7–print server (see Table 4-3); 3C02.0000.0000.0001 is the internal IPX address; 451 is the socket number for NCP process (see Table 4-2); and 1 is the number of hops to the server.

Static SAP assignments always override any identical dynamic entries in the SAP table, regardless of hop count. If a dynamic route that is associated with a static SAP entry is no longer available, the static SAP entry will not be advertised until the router relearns the route. To prevent this from happening, two static routes to the servers' internal network numbers (3C01 for FILESVR2 and 3C02 for PRINTSVR2) are defined. Note that 22.0090.aa23.ef01 (0090.aa23.ef01 is the NIC or MAC address for FILESVR2) and 22.0800.89a1.1527 (0800.89a1.1527 is the NIC or MAC address for PRINTSVR2) are the external IPX addresses for FILESVR2 and PRINTSVR2. The number 22 is the IPX network number for VLAN 2. NetWare version 3.11 and later use an internal network and node number as their address (3C01.0000.0000.0001 for FILESVR2 and 3C02.0000.0000.0001 for PRINTSVR2). Code Listing 4-54 illustrates all of these.

Code Listing 4-54
IPX static SAP configuration for R2.

```
hostname C3640-R2
!
ipx routing 00e0.1e6f.9821
!
interface Ethernet0/0
 ipx network 22
!
ipx route 3C02 22.0800.89a1.1527
ipx route 3C01 22.0090.aa23.ef01
!
ipx sap 4 FILESVR2 3C01.0000.0000.0001 451 1
ipx sap 7 PRINTSVR2 3C02.0000.0000.0001 451 1
```

Table 4-3 lists some of the common IPX SAP services.

	Service Type (Hexadecimal)	Description
TABLE 4-3 Some common IPX SAP services	1	User
	2	User group
	3	Print server queue
	4	File server
	5	Job server
	7	Print server
	9	Archive server
	A	Queue for job servers
	21	Network Application Support Systems Network Architecture (NAS SNA) gateway
	2D	Time Synchronization value-added process (VAP)
	2E	Dynamic SAP
	47	Advertising print server
	4B	Btrieve VAP 5.0
	4C	SQL VAP
	7A	TES—NetWare for Virtual Memory System (VMS)
	98	NetWare access server
	9A	Named Pipes server
	9E	Portable NetWare—UNIX
	107	RCONSOLE
	111	Test server
	166	NetWare management—Novell's Network Management Station (NMS)
	26A	NetWare management (NMS console)

The requirement is to allow clients on RING 1 to see and use PRINTSVR2's print service only. But first, note the service information (SAP Table) on all routers, as illustrated in Code Listings 4-55 through 4-59.

Code Listing 4-55

Server information table on R1.

```
C3640-R1#show ipx servers
Codes: S - Static, P - Periodic, E - EIGRP, N - NLSP, H - Holddown, + = detail
2 Total IPX Servers

Table ordering is based on routing and server info

      Type  Name         Net      Address     Port    Route Hops Itf
E     4     FILESVR2      3C01.0000.0000.0001:0451 267008000/02   2   Se1/0
E     7     PRINTSVR2     3C02.0000.0000.0001:0451 267008000/02   2   Se1/0
```

Code Listing 4-56

Server information table on R2.

```
C3640-R2#show ipx servers
Codes: S - Static, P - Periodic, E - EIGRP, N - NLSP, H - Holddown, + = detail
2 Total IPX Servers

Table ordering is based on routing and server info

      Type Name            Net      Address     Port    Route Hops Itf
S     4    FILESVR2         3C01.0000.0000.0001:0451    conn   1   Et0/0
S     7    PRINTSVR2        3C02.0000.0000.0001:0451    conn   1   Et0/0
```

Code Listing 4-57

Server information table on R3.

```
C2500-R3#show ipx servers
Codes: S - Static, P - Periodic, E - EIGRP, N - NLSP, H - Holddown, + = detail
2 Total IPX Servers

Table ordering is based on routing and server info

      Type Name            Net      Address     Port    Route Hops Itf
N     4    FILESVR2         3C01.0000.0000.0001:0451   13/02   2   Se0
N     7    PRINTSVR2        3C02.0000.0000.0001:0451   13/02   2   Se0
```

Code Listing 4-58

Server information table on R4.

```
C2500-R4#show ipx servers
Codes: S - Static, P - Periodic, E - EIGRP, N - NLSP, H - Holddown, + = detail
2 Total IPX Servers

Table ordering is based on routing and server info

      Type Name            Net      Address     Port    Route Hops Itf
E     4    FILESVR2         3C01.0000.0000.0001:0451 267008000/02   2   Se0
E     7    PRINTSVR2        3C02.0000.0000.0001:0451 267008000/02   2   Se0
```

Code Listing 4-59

Server information table on R5.

```
C2509-R5#show ipx servers
Codes: S - Static, P - Periodic, E - EIGRP, N - NLSP, H - Holddown, + = detail
2 Total IPX Servers

Table ordering is based on routing and server info

      Type Name            Net      Address     Port    Route Hops Itf
E     4    FILESVR2         3C01.0000.0000.0001:0451 267008000/02   2   Se0
E     7    PRINTSVR2        3C02.0000.0000.0001:0451 267008000/02   2   Se0
```

The IPX servers discovered through SAP advertisements are listed using the `show ipx servers` command, and servers are displayed numerically by SAP service type. In Code Listings 4-55 through 4-59, all routers see servers FILESVR2 and PRINTSVR2. SAP filters are configured on R1, as illustrated in Code Listing 4-60, so clients on RING 1 can only see PRINTSVR2.

Code Listing 4-60
IPX SAP filter configuration for R1.

```
hostname C3640-R1
!
username C3640-R2 password 0 cisco
ipx routing 0010.7bb2.7761
isdn switch-type basic-net3
!
interface BRI0/0
 encapsulation ppp
 ipx input-sap-filter 1000
 ipx network 12
 dialer idle-timeout 60
 dialer map ipx 12.00e0.1e6f.9821 name C3640-R2 broadcast 3245652
 dialer load-threshold 128 either
 dialer-group 1
 ppp authentication chap
 no ipx route-cache
 ipx watchdog-spoof
 ipx spx-spoof
 ipx hello-interval eigrp 62 3600
 ipx hold-time eigrp 62 10800
 ipx sap-incremental eigrp 62
 no cdp enable
!
dialer-list 1 list 900
access-list 900 deny 0 any all any 457
access-list 900 permit any any
access-list 1000 permit 3C02.0000.0000.0001 7 PRINTSVR2
!
interface Serial1/0
 backup delay 10 30
 backup interface BRI0/0
 encapsulation frame-relay
 bandwidth 56
 ipx input-sap-filter 1000
 ipx network 124
 no ipx split-horizon eigrp 62
 frame-relay map ipx 124.00e0.1e6f.9821 102 broadcast
 frame-relay map ipx 124.00e0.1e5f.de09 104 broadcast
 frame-relay lmi-type ansi
!
ipx router eigrp 62
 network 124
 network 12
!
ipx router rip
 no network 124
 no network 12
```

In Code Listing 4-60, the `access-list 1000 permit 3C02.0000.0000.0001 7 PRINTSVR2` command permits PRINTSVR2's print service and is made active on BRI0/0 and S1/0 in the inward direction by using the `ipx input-sap-filter 1000` command. In this case, all incoming service advertisements are filtered except service type 7—print server. Note the new service information (SAP Table) on all the routers, as shown in Code Listings 4-61 through 4-65.

Code Listing 4-61

Server information table on R1.

```
C3640-R1#show ipx servers
Codes: S - Static, P - Periodic, E - EIGRP, N - NLSP, H - Holddown, + = detail
1 Total IPX Servers

Table ordering is based on routing and server info

    Type Name       Net       Address     Port      Route Hops Itf
E     7 PRINTSVR2   3C02.0000.0000.0001:0451 267008000/02   2  Se1/0
```

Code Listing 4-62

Server information table on R2.

```
C3640-R2#show ipx servers
Codes: S - Static, P - Periodic, E - EIGRP, N - NLSP, H - Holddown, + = detail
2 Total IPX Servers

Table ordering is based on routing and server info

    Type Name                  Net       Address     Port    Route Hops Itf
S     4 FILESVR2               3C01.0000.0000.0001:0451      conn   1  Et0/0
S     7 PRINTSVR2              3C02.0000.0000.0001:0451      conn   1  Et0/0
```

Code Listing 4-63

Server information table on R3.

```
C2500-R3#show ipx servers
Codes: S - Static, P - Periodic, E - EIGRP, N - NLSP, H - Holddown, + = detail
2 Total IPX Servers

Table ordering is based on routing and server info

    Type Name                  Net       Address     Port    Route Hops Itf
N     4 FILESVR2               3C01.0000.0000.0001:0451      13/02   2  Se0
N     7 PRINTSVR2              3C02.0000.0000.0001:0451      13/02   2  Se0
```

Code Listing 4-64

Server information table on R4.

```
C2500-R4#show ipx servers
Codes: S - Static, P - Periodic, E - EIGRP, N - NLSP, H - Holddown, + = detail
2 Total IPX Servers

Table ordering is based on routing and server info

    Type Name                  Net       Address     Port    Route Hops Itf
E     4 FILESVR2               3C01.0000.0000.0001:0451 267008000/02   2  Se0
E     7 PRINTSVR2              3C02.0000.0000.0001:0451 267008000/02   2  Se0
```

Code Listing 4-65

Server information table on R5.

```
C2509-R5#sh ipx ser
Codes: S - Static, P - Periodic, E - EIGRP, N - NLSP, H - Holddown, + = detail
2 Total IPX Servers

Table ordering is based on routing and server info

    Type Name                  Net       Address     Port    Route Hops Itf
E     4 FILESVR2               3C01.0000.0000.0001:0451 267008000/02   2  Se0
E     7 PRINTSVR2              3C02.0000.0000.0001:0451 267008000/02   2  Se0
```

After applying SAP filters, the PRINTSVR2 entry is the only entry in R1's Server Information Table, as illustrated in Code Listing 4-61.

NETBIOS Over IPX

NetBIOS over IPX uses type-20 (see Table 4-1) propagation broadcast packets, flooded to all networks, to obtain information about the named nodes on the network. Since NetBIOS is a nonroutable protocol, it uses a broadcast mechanism to obtain this information. By default, routers block all local broadcasts. These IPX NetBIOS packets can be accepted and forwarded by enabling type-20 packet propagation on the IPX interfaces in the router.

Figure 4-12 shows how to allow type-20 broadcast between Novell Client A and Novell Server A, the `ipx type-20-propagation` interface command must be enabled on the respective interfaces of R2 and R3. Note that type-20 packets can be propagated for up to eight hops.

Figure 4-12
IPX NetBIOS propagation scenario.

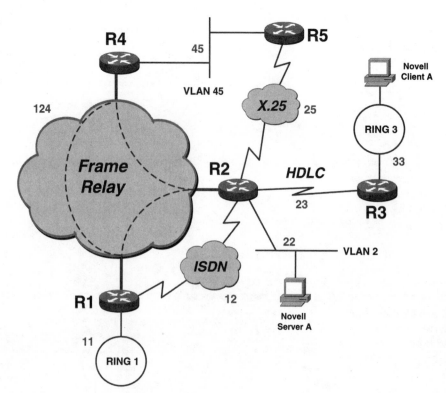

In Code Listing 4-66, the `ipx type-20-propagation` interface command is applied to E0/0 and S1/2 of R2.

■ ▮

Code Listing 4-66
IPX type-20-propagation configuration for R2.

```
hostname C3640-R2
!
ipx routing 00e0.1e6f.9821
!
interface Ethernet0/0
 ipx network 22
 ipx type-20-propagation
!
interface Serial1/2
 bandwidth 56
 ipx ipxwan 2 23 C3640-R2
 ipx nlsp enable
 ipx type-20-propagation
!
ipx router eigrp 62
 redistribute nlsp
 network 124
 network 12
 network 25
!
ipx router nlsp
 area-address 0 0
 redistribute eigrp 62
```

In Code Listing 4-67, the `ipx type-20-propagation` interface command is applied to S0 and TO0 of R3.

■ ▮

Code Listing 4-67
IPX type-20-propagation configuration for R3.

```
hostname C2500-R3
!
ipx routing 00e0.1e5f.dd0d
ipx internal-network 3
!
interface Serial0
 bandwidth 56
 ipx ipxwan 3 23 C2500-R3
 ipx nlsp enable
 ipz type-20-propagation
!
interface TokenRing0
 ipx network 33
 ipx nlsp enable
 ring-speed 16
 ipz type-20-propagation
!
ipx router nlsp
 area-address 0 0
```

Summary

This chapter covered Internet Packet Exchange (IPX), the next most popular routable protocol after IP. IPX is derived from Xerox's Internet Datagram Protocol (IDP). A wide variety of protocols like SPX, RIP, EIGRP, NLSP, and IPXWAN run on top of IPX.

In the initial scenario, IPX was configured for a LAN environment, then expanded to IPX over Frame Relay, X.25, HDLC, and DDR.

Next, IPX EIGRP was configured over Frame Relay, X.25, and ISDN networks, revisiting DDR by implementing a series of traffic-management control techniques like IPX and SPX spoofing.

As today's enterprise networks get bigger and more complex, parameters such as performance, reliability, scalability, and manageability have become increasingly important. Novell addresses these issues with Netware Link Services Protocol (NLSP), a link-state protocol based on the OSI IS-IS protocol. In the NLSP section, NLSP over a LAN and WAN scenario was implemented.

Novell's RIP and SAP updates are sent every 60 seconds. These periodic updates are often undesirable in a WAN environment. In the access control section, three applications of IPX access lists were implemented to limit IPX RIP routes, NetWare serialization packets, and service advertisements.

Finally, propagation of IPX NetBIOS packets across a routed network was controlled by enabling type-20 packet propagation on the IPX interfaces in the routers that are involved.

Altogether the implemented scenarios showed how IPX routing protocols coexist and complement each other; their pros and cons; and their characteristics. Knowing these points will give a better insight when you design, implement, or maintain large and complex IPX internetworks.

References

1. Chappell, L. *Novell's Guide to NetWare LAN Analysis*. San Jose, California: Novell Press, 1993.

2. Documentation CD-ROM, Cisco Systems, Inc., 1998.

3. Garcia-Luna-Aceves, J. J. "Loop-Free Routing Using Diffusing Computations." *IEEE/ACM Transactions on Networking*, Vol. 1, No. 1. 1993.

4. Malamud, C. *Analyzing Novell Networks*. New York: Van Nostrand Reinhold, 1991.

5. Novell, Inc. IPX Router Specification, Version 1.10. Part Number 107-000029-001. October 1992.

6. Novell, Inc. Netware Link Services Protocol (NLSP) Specification, Version 0.9. Part Number 100-001708-001. March 1993.

7. RFC 1634–Novell IPX Over WAN Media (IPXWAN), May 1995.

8. Stallings, W. *Data and Computer Communications*. New York: Macmillan Publishing Company, 1991.

9. Tannenbaum, A. S. *Computer Networks*, 2nd ed. Englewood Cliffs, New Jersey: Prentice Hall, 1988.

AppleTalk

Introduction

AppleTalk is intended to be a plug-and-play network protocol that allows AppleTalk users to plug a Macintosh into a network and communicate straightaway with minimal configuration. Users can access resources such as file servers and printers located anywhere in the AppleTalk network.

AppleTalk has two implementation phases—I and II. AppleTalk Phase I supports a single physical network with only one network number (nonextended) in a single zone. Phase I networks support 254 devices—127 end nodes and 127 servers. AppleTalk Phase II is designed for larger networks and has enhanced routing capabilities. Phase II supports multiple logical networks on a single physical network in a zone. One cable segment can have multiple network numbers (extended). Each logical network in Phase II supports 253 devices, with no limitations on the type of devices, end nodes, or servers. In Phase II a network can also exist in more than one zone.

In the following sections, discussions will center on AppleTalk Phase II extended networks.

AppleTalk Overview

Perhaps the most attractive feature of AppleTalk is its transparency to users. Users need only plug their Macintoshes into the network and they can access the various services available from the AppleTalk network. A rich suite of AppleTalk protocols enables these features. Some of these protocols are:

■ AppleTalk Filing Protocol (AFP) —AFP is a presentation-layer protocol used for access to remote files.

■ AppleTalk Transaction Protocol (ATP) —ATP is a transport-layer protocol that provides reliable transaction service between sockets, allowing exchanges between two socket clients, where one client requests the other to perform a particular task and report the result.

■ AppleTalk Session Protocol (ASP) —ASP is a session-layer protocol built upon ATP. ASP provides session establishment, maintenance, and tear-down, along with request sequencing.

- AppleTalk Data Stream Protocol (ADSP) —ADSP is a connection-oriented transport-layer protocol providing reliable, full-duplex, byte-stream service between any two sockets on an AppleTalk network, ensuring in-sequence, duplicate-free delivery of data over its connection.

- Name Binding Protocol (NBP) —NBP is a transport-layer protocol used in AppleTalk networks to associate network services and sockets to character names. NBP translates a character name within a zone to the corresponding socket address.

- Zone Information Protocol (ZIP) —ZIP is a transport-layer protocol used to maintain mapping of networks to zone names and as a resource for NBP to determine which networks belong to a given zone.

- Routing Table Maintenance Protocol (RTMP) —RTMP is AppleTalk's native routing protocol, sitting on the transport layer and allowing routers to dynamically discover routes to remote AppleTalk networks. RTMP is similar to RIP, using hop-count as its metric and an update-interval of 10 seconds.

- Datagram Delivery Protocol (DDP) —DDP is a network-layer protocol that provides a connectionless datagram delivery service.

AppleTalk Routing

For AppleTalk routing to work, it must be enabled explicitly (as it is disabled by default), and an AppleTalk cable range and zone name must be configured on each interface.

AppleTalk Addresses

An AppleTalk network address is 24 bits long. Addresses consist of a network number and a node number expressed in the format net-work.node.

The network number identifies a network, or cable segment, with a 16-bit decimal number, unique throughout the entire AppleTalk internetwork. In AppleTalk Phase II, a cable range corresponding to one or more logical networks identifies networks. Cable range resides on one network number or a contiguous sequence of several network numbers, but network number 0 is reserved.

The node number identifies all devices connected to the AppleTalk network. Node numbers are unique eight-bit decimal numbers. In Apple-Talk Phase II, node numbers 1 through 253 can be used for nodes attached to the network, but 0, 254, and 255 are reserved.

AppleTalk Zones

An AppleTalk zone is a logical grouping of AppleTalk networks. The networks in a zone may be contiguous or noncontiguous. Zones are identified by zone names up to 32 characters long. Zone names can include standard characters and AppleTalk special characters. To include a special character, type a colon followed by the two hexadecimal characters that represent the special character in the Macintosh character set. (For a list of Macintosh characters, refer to Apple Computer's *Inside AppleTalk* publication.) Note that in AppleTalk Phase II, an extended network has a 255-zone maximum.

Case Scenario

Figure 5-1 illustrates the overall network scenario referenced throughout this chapter. This enterprise network spans five sites: Atlanta, Bellevue, Boston, Charlotte, and Detroit. The Charlotte office is internetworked to the Atlanta office by Frame Relay, with an ISDN dial-up line serving as backup in the event the Frame Relay connectivity becomes unavailable. Similarly the Atlanta office is interconnected to the Charlotte and Boston offices through the same Frame Relay network. The Boston office is also connected to the Bellevue office using X.25. The Detroit office is linked to the Charlotte office through HDLC. Both Atlanta and Charlotte have their own Virtual LAN where Macintosh workstations are connected. Likewise, Macintoshes are found in the Bellevue and Detroit offices on Token Ring networks.

AppleTalk Setup

Consider Figure 5-2. There are altogether eight different AppleTalk cable ranges and seven different zone names. Note that RING 2 and RING 5

Figure 5-1
The overall network
topology.

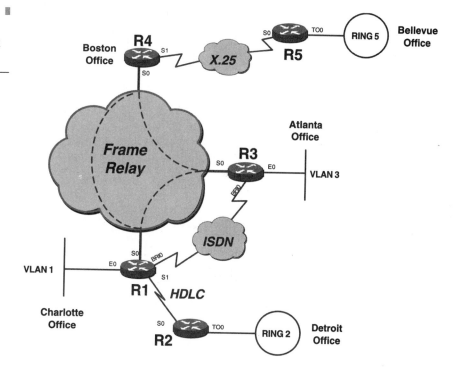

happen to share the same zone name. The routing protocol used is Apple-
Talk RTMP, the default.

Basic AppleTalk Configuration

For basic AppleTalk configuration, examine the configuration of the
respective LANs connected to R1, R2, R3, and R5, as illustrated in Code
Listings 5-1 through 5-4. Subsequent sections will cover WAN configurations.

Code Listing 5-1
AppleTalk configura-
tion for R1.

```
hostname C4700-R1
!
appletalk routing
!
interface Ethernet0
 media-type 10BaseT
 appletalk cable-range 10-19 17.175
 appletalk zone vlan1
```

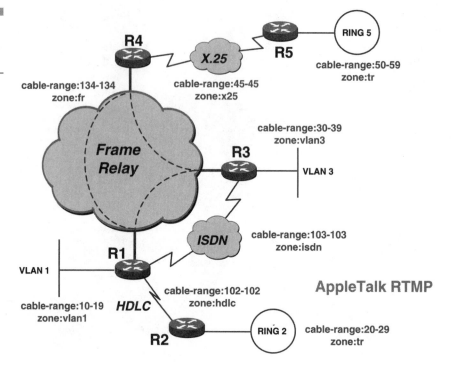

Figure 5-2
The overall AppleTalk
network.

1. Code Listing 5-1 illustrates the AppleTalk configuration for R1. By default, AppleTalk routing is not enabled. The global command `appletalk routing` explicitly enables AppleTalk routing and RTMP. No other commands are required to enable AppleTalk RTMP.

2. E0 is configured to use media type 10BaseT and has cable range 10-19 in zone "vlan1."

Code Listing 5-2
AppleTalk configuration for R2.

```
hostname C2500-R2
!
appletalk routing
!
interface TokenRing0
 appletalk cable-range 20-29 22.48
 appletalk zone tr
 ring-speed 16
```

1. Code Listing 5-2 illustrates the AppleTalk configuration for R2. By default, AppleTalk routing is not enabled. The global command `appletalk routing` explicitly enables AppleTalk routing and RTMP. No other commands are required to enable AppleTalk RTMP.

2. TO0 is assigned cable range 20-29 and appears in zone tr. Note that R5's TO0 is also in zone "tr."

Code Listing 5-3
AppleTalk configuration for R3.

```
hostname C4500-R3
!
appletalk routing
!
interface Ethernet0
 media-type 10BaseT
 appletalk cable-range 30-39 32.128
 appletalk zone vlan3
```

1. Code Listing 5-3 illustrates the AppleTalk configuration for R3. By default, AppleTalk routing is not enabled. The global command `appletalk routing` explicitly enables AppleTalk routing and RTMP. No other commands are required to explicitly enable Apple-Talk RTMP.

2. E0 is configured to use media type 10BaseT and has cable range 30-39 in zone "vlan3."

Code Listing 5-4
AppleTalk configuration for R5.

```
hostname C2500-R5
!
appletalk routing
!
interface TokenRing0
 appletalk cable-range 50-59 58.3
 appletalk zone tr
 ring-speed 16
```

1. Code Listing 5-4 illustrates the AppleTalk configuration for R5. By default, AppleTalk routing is not enabled. The global command `appletalk routing` explicitly enables AppleTalk routing and RTMP. No other commands are required to enable AppleTalk RTMP.

2. TO0 has cable range 50-59 in zone tr. Note that R2's TO0 is also in zone "tr."

AppleTalk over Frame Relay

Figure 5-3 zooms into the Frame Relay network where AppleTalk is configured for R1, R3, and R4. Code Listings 5-5 through 5-7 illustrate this. The three PVCs implement a fully meshed Frame Relay topology.

Figure 5-3
AppleTalk over Frame Relay.

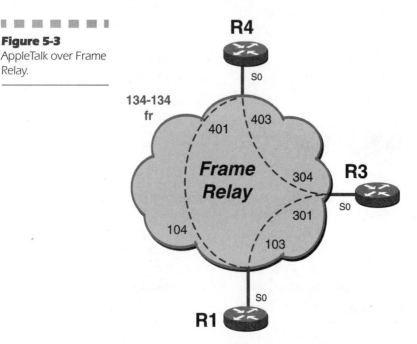

Code Listing 5-5
AppleTalk-over-Frame Relay configuration for R1.

```
hostname C4700-R1
!
appletalk routing
!
interface Serial0
 encapsulation frame-relay
 bandwidth 56
 appletalk cable-range 134-134 134.1
 appletalk zone fr
 no appletalk rtmp-splithorizon
 frame-relay map appletalk 134.3 103 broadcast
 frame-relay map appletalk 134.4 104 broadcast
 frame-relay lmi-type ansi
```

1. Code Listing 5-5 illustrates the AppleTalk-over-Frame Relay configuration for R1. S0 is assigned cable range 134-134 in zone "fr." The `frame-relay map` command statically maps the AppleTalk addresses of R3 and R4 to their respective DLCIs. Since the Frame Relay network has a fully meshed topology, R1 needs to implement a multipoint Serial interface. Note that a physical Frame Relay interface (in this case, S0) is by default multipoint.

2. Split horizon controls RTMP update and query packets. When split horizon is enabled on an interface, update and query packets are not sent if this interface is the next hop to a destination. By default, split horizon is enabled on all interfaces; its mechanism optimizes communication among multiple routers. However, with NBMA networks like Frame Relay, situations can arise where this behavior is suboptimal. The command `no appletalk rtmp-splithorizon` disables the split-horizon mechanism for RTMP on S0.

Code Listing 5-6

AppleTalk-over-Frame Relay configuration for R3.

```
hostname C4500-R3
!
appletalk routing
!
interface Serial0
 encapsulation frame-relay
 bandwidth 56
 appletalk cable-range 134-134 134.3
 appletalk zone fr
 no appletalk rtmp-splithorizon
 frame-relay map appletalk 134.1 301 broadcast
 frame-relay map appletalk 134.4 304 broadcast
 frame-relay lmi-type ansi
```

1. Code Listing 5-6 illustrates the AppleTalk-over-Frame Relay configuration for R3. S0 is assigned cable range 134-134 in zone "fr." The `frame-relay map` command statically maps the AppleTalk addresses of R1 and R4 to their respective DLCIs. Since the Frame Relay network has a fully meshed topology, R3 needs to implement a multipoint Serial interface. Note that a physical Frame Relay interface (in this case, S0) is by default multipoint.

2. Split horizon controls RTMP update and query packets. When split horizon is enabled on an interface, update and query packets are not sent if this interface is the next hop to a destination. By default, split horizon is enabled on all interfaces; its mechanism optimizes communication among multiple routers. However, with NBMA networks like Frame Relay, situations can arise where this behavior is

suboptimal. The command `no appletalk rtmp-splithorizon` disables the split-horizon mechanism for RTMP on S0.

■ ■

Code Listing 5-7
AppleTalk-over-Frame Relay configuration for R4.

```
hostname C2500-R4
!
appletalk routing
!
interface Serial0
 encapsulation frame-relay
 bandwidth 56
 appletalk cable-range 134-134 134.4
 appletalk zone fr
 no appletalk rtmp-splithorizon
 frame-relay map appletalk 134.1 401 broadcast
 frame-relay map appletalk 134.3 403 broadcast
 frame-relay lmi-type ansi
```

1. Code Listing 5-7 illustrates the AppleTalk-over-Frame Relay configuration for R4. S0 is assigned cable range 134-134 in zone "fr." The `frame-relay map` command statically maps the AppleTalk addresses of R1 and R3 to their respective DLCIs. Since the Frame Relay network has a fully meshed topology, R4 needs to implement a multipoint Serial interface. Note that a physical Frame Relay interface (in this case, S0) is by default multipoint.

2. Split horizon controls RTMP update and query packets. When split horizon is enabled on an interface, update and query packets are not sent if this interface is the next hop to a destination. By default, split horizon is enabled on all interfaces; its mechanism optimizes communication among multiple routers. However, with NBMA networks like Frame Relay, situations can arise where this behavior is suboptimal. The command `no appletalk rtmp-splithorizon` disables the split-horizon mechanism for RTMP on S0.

AppleTalk over X.25

Figure 5-4 zooms into the X.25 network where AppleTalk is implemented between R4 and R5. Code Listings 5-8 and 5-9 illustrate this.

Figure 5-4
AppleTalk over X.25.

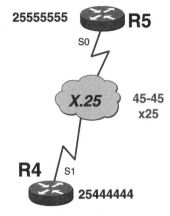

Code Listing 5-8
AppleTalk-over-X.25
configuration for R4.

```
hostname C2500-R4
!
appletalk routing
!
interface Serial1
 encapsulation x25
 bandwidth 56
 appletalk cable-range 45-45 45.4
 appletalk zone x25
 no appletalk rtmp-splithorizon
 x25 address 25444444
 x25 map appletalk 45.5 25555555 broadcast
```

1. Code Listing 5-8 illustrates the AppleTalk-over-X.25 configuration for R4. S1 is assigned cable range 45-45 in zone "x25." The command x25 map appletalk creates a virtual circuit between R4 and R5 for routing AppleTalk. The AppleTalk and X.121 (X.25) addresses used in the command are R5's.

2. Split horizon controls RTMP update and query packets. When split horizon is enabled on an interface, update and query packets are not sent if this interface is the next hop to a destination. By default, split horizon is enabled on all interfaces; its mechanism optimizes communication among multiple routers. However, with NBMA networks like X.25, situations can arise where this behavior is suboptimal. The command no appletalk rtmp-splithorizon disables the split-horizon mechanism for RTMP on S1.

Code Listing 5-9
AppleTalk-over-X.25
configuration for R5.

```
hostname C2500-R5
!
appletalk routing
!
interface Serial0
 encapsulation x25
 bandwidth 56
 appletalk cable-range 45-45 45.5
 appletalk zone x25
 no appletalk rtmp-splithorizon
 x25 address 25555555
 x25 map appletalk 45.4 25444444 broadcast
```

1. Code Listing 5-9 illustrates the AppleTalk-over-X.25 configuration for R5. S0 is assigned cable range 45-45 in zone "x25." The command `x25 map appletalk` creates a virtual circuit between R5 and R4 for routing AppleTalk. The AppleTalk and X.121 (X.25) addresses used in the command are R4's.

2. Split horizon controls RTMP update and query packets. When split horizon is enabled on an interface, these packets are not sent if this interface is the next hop to a destination. By default, split horizon is enabled on all interfaces; its mechanism optimizes communication among multiple routers. However, with NBMA networks like X.25, situations can arise where this behavior is suboptimal. The command `no appletalk rtmp-splithorizon` disables the split-horizon mechanism for RTMP on S0.

AppleTalk over HDLC

Figure 5-5 shows the portion of network where AppleTalk over HDLC is implemented between R1 and R2. Code Listings 5-10 and 5-11 illustrate this.

Figure 5-5
AppleTalk over HDLC.

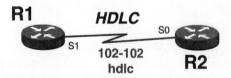

Code Listing 5-10
*AppleTalk-over-HDLC
configuration for R1.*

```
hostname C4700-R1
!
appletalk routing
!
interface Serial1
 bandwidth 56
 appletalk cable-range 102-102 102.161
 appletalk zone hdlc
```

Code Listing 5-10 illustrates the AppleTalk-over-HDLC configuration for R1. To configure AppleTalk over HDLC, specify the AppleTalk cable-range and zone on the respective Serial interfaces. In this case, R1's S1 has cable range 102-102 in zone "hdlc."

Code Listing 5-11
*AppleTalk-over-HDLC
configuration for R2.*

```
hostname C2500-R2
!
appletalk routing
!
interface Serial0
 bandwidth 56
 appletalk cable-range 102-102 102.120
 appletalk zone hdlc
```

Code Listing 5-11 illustrates the AppleTalk-over-HDLC configuration for R2. To configure AppleTalk over HDLC, specify the AppleTalk cable-range and zone on the respective Serial interfaces. In this case, R2's S0 has cable range 102-102 in zone "hdlc."

AppleTalk over DDR

Figure 5-6 shows the network where AppleTalk over DDR is implemented between R1 and R3. Code Listings 5-12 and 5-13 illustrate this. In this case, DDR backs up R1's Frame Relay Serial interface S0 if it becomes unavailable.

Figure 5-6
AppleTalk over DDR.

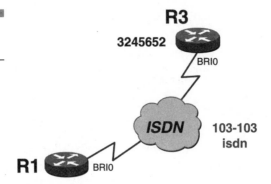

Code Listing 5-12
AppleTalk-over-DDR
configuration for R1.

```
hostname C4700-R1
!
username C4500-R3 password 0 cisco
appletalk routing
isdn switch-type basic-net3
!
interface Serial0
 backup delay 10 30
 backup interface BRI0
!
interface BRI0
 encapsulation ppp
 appletalk cable-range 103-103 103.1
 appletalk zone isdn
 dialer idle-timeout 60
 dialer map appletalk 103.3 name C4500-R3 broadcast 3245652
 dialer load-threshold 128 either
 dialer-group 1
 ppp authentication chap
!
dialer-list 1 protocol appletalk permit
```

Code Listing 5-12 illustrates the AppleTalk-over-DDR configuration for R1. The ISDN interface BRI0 has cable range 103-103 in zone "isdn." The `dialer map` command calls R3 to establish a PPP connection when S0 becomes unavailable. The AppleTalk address, host name, and ISDN number used by this command are R3's. The `dialer-group 1` command refers to `dialer-list 1` and allows all AppleTalk traffic to pass. No refining on the dialer-list is required, as the purpose of the BRI0 interface is to back up S0.

Code Listing 5-13
AppleTalk-over-DDR
configuration for R3.

```
hostname C4500-R3
!
username C4700-R1 password 0 cisco
appletalk routing
isdn switch-type basic-net3
!
interface BRI0
 encapsulation ppp
 appletalk cable-range 103-103 103.3
 appletalk zone isdn
 dialer idle-timeout 60
 dialer map appletalk 103.1 name C4700-R1 broadcast
 dialer load-threshold 128 either
 dialer-group 1
 ppp authentication chap
!
dialer-list 1 protocol appletalk permit
```

Code Listing 5-13 illustrates the AppleTalk-over-DDR configuration for R3. The ISDN interface BRI0 is assigned cable range 103-103 in zone "isdn." The `dialer map` command initiates a PPP connection when R1 makes a call. Note that no ISDN number is supplied, since R1 will initiate the call. The AppleTalk address and host name used in the `dialer map` command are R1's. The command `dialer-group 1` refers to `dialer-list 1` and allows all AppleTalk traffic to pass.

Now examine the routing tables and zone information tables on all five routers, as listed in Code Listings 5-14 through 5-23.

Code Listing 5-14
AppleTalk routing
table for R1.

```
C4700-R1#show appletalk route
Codes: R - RTMP derived, E - EIGRP derived, C - connected, A - AURP
       S - static  P - proxy
8 routes in internet

The first zone listed for each entry is its default (primary) zone.

C Net 10-19 directly connected, Ethernet0, zone vlan1
R Net 20-29 [1/G] via 102.120, 8 sec, Serial1, zone tr
R Net 30-39 [1/G] via 134.3, 0 sec, Serial0, zone vlan3
R Net 45-45 [1/G] via 134.4, 3 sec, Serial0, zone x25
R Net 50-59 [2/G] via 134.4, 3 sec, Serial0, zone tr
C Net 102-102 directly connected, Serial1, zone hdlc
R Net 103-103 [1/G] via 134.3, 0 sec, Serial0, zone isdn
C Net 134-134 directly connected, Serial0, zone fr
```

Code Listing 5-15

AppleTalk zone information on R1.

```
C4700-R1#show appletalk zone
Name                            Network(s)
hdlc                            102-102
isdn                            103-103
x25                               45-45
fr                              134-134
tr                           50-59 20-29
vlan1                             10-19
vlan3                             30-39
Total of 7 zones
```

Code Listing 5-16

AppleTalk routing table for R2.

```
C2500-R2#show appletalk route
Codes: R - RTMP derived, E - EIGRP derived, C - connected, A - AURP
       S - static  P - proxy
8 routes in internet

The first zone listed for each entry is its default (primary) zone.

R Net 10-19 [1/G] via 102.161, 6 sec, Serial0, zone vlan1
C Net 20-29 directly connected, TokenRing0, zone tr
R Net 30-39 [2/G] via 102.161, 6 sec, Serial0, zone vlan3
R Net 45-45 [2/G] via 102.161, 6 sec, Serial0, zone x25
R Net 50-59 [3/G] via 102.161, 6 sec, Serial0, zone tr
C Net 102-102 directly connected, Serial0, zone hdlc
R Net 103-103 [2/G] via 102.161, 7 sec, Serial0, zone isdn
R Net 134-134 [1/G] via 102.161, 7 sec, Serial0, zone fr
```

Code Listing 5-17

AppleTalk zone information on R2.

```
C2500-R2#show appletalk zone
Name                            Network(s)
hdlc                            102-102
isdn                            103-103
x25                               45-45
fr                              134-134
tr                           50-59 20-29
vlan1                             10-19
vlan3                             30-39
Total of 7 zones
```

Code Listing 5-18

AppleTalk routing table for R3.

```
C4500-R3#show appletalk route
Codes: R - RTMP derived, E - EIGRP derived, C - connected, A - AURP
       S - static  P - proxy
8 routes in internet

The first zone listed for each entry is its default (primary) zone.

R Net 10-19 [1/G] via 134.1, 3 sec, Serial0, zone vlan1
R Net 20-29 [2/G] via 134.1, 3 sec, Serial0, zone tr
C Net 30-39 directly connected, Ethernet0, zone vlan3
R Net 45-45 [1/G] via 134.4, 9 sec, Serial0, zone x25
```

Code Listing 5-18
(continued)

```
R Net 50-59 [2/G] via 134.4, 9 sec, Serial0, zone tr
R Net 102-102 [1/G] via 134.1, 3 sec, Serial0, zone hdlc
C Net 103-103 directly connected, BRI0, zone isdn
C Net 134-134 directly connected, Serial0, zone fr
```

Code Listing 5-19
AppleTalk zone information on R3.

```
C4500-R3#show appletalk zone
Name                         Network(s)
hdlc                           102-102
isdn                           103-103
x25                             45-45
fr                             134-134
tr                       20-29 50-59
vlan1                           10-19
vlan3                           30-39
Total of 7 zones
```

Code Listing 5-20
AppleTalk routing table for R4.

```
C2500-R4#show appletalk route
Codes: R - RTMP derived, E - EIGRP derived, C - connected, A - AURP
       S - static  P - proxy
8 routes in internet

The first zone listed for each entry is its default (primary) zone.

R Net 10-19 [1/G] via 134.1, 2 sec, Serial0, zone vlan1
R Net 20-29 [2/G] via 134.1, 2 sec, Serial0, zone tr
R Net 30-39 [1/G] via 134.3, 4 sec, Serial0, zone vlan3
C Net 45-45 directly connected, Serial1, zone x25
R Net 50-59 [1/G] via 45.5, 0 sec, Serial1, zone tr
R Net 102-102 [1/G] via 134.1, 2 sec, Serial0, zone hdlc
R Net 103-103 [1/G] via 134.3, 5 sec, Serial0, zone isdn
C Net 134-134 directly connected, Serial0, zone fr
```

Code Listing 5-21
AppleTalk zone information on R4.

```
C2500-R4#show appletalk zone
Name                         Network(s)
hdlc                           102-102
isdn                           103-103
x25                             45-45
fr                             134-134
tr                       50-59 20-29
vlan1                           10-19
vlan3                           30-39
Total of 7 zones
```

Code Listing 5-22

AppleTalk routing table for R5.

```
C2500-R5#show appletalk route
Codes: R - RTMP derived, E - EIGRP derived, C - connected, A - AURP
       S - static  P - proxy
8 routes in internet

The first zone listed for each entry is its default (primary) zone.

R Net 10-19 [2/G] via 45.4, 6 sec, Serial0, zone vlan1
R Net 20-29 [3/G] via 45.4, 6 sec, Serial0, zone tr
R Net 30-39 [2/G] via 45.4, 6 sec, Serial0, zone vlan3
C Net 45-45 directly connected, Serial0, zone x25
C Net 50-59 directly connected, TokenRing0, zone tr
R Net 102-102 [2/G] via 45.4, 6 sec, Serial0, zone hdlc
R Net 103-103 [2/G] via 45.4, 6 sec, Serial0, zone isdn
R Net 134-134 [1/G] via 45.4, 6 sec, Serial0, zone fr
```

Code Listing 5-23

AppleTalk zone information on R5.

```
C2500-R5#show appletalk zone
Name                           Network(s)
hdlc                            102-102
isdn                            103-103
x25                              45-45
fr                              134-134
tr                          50-59 20-29
vlan1                            10-19
vlan3                            30-39
Total of 7 zones
```

AppleTalk RTMP uses hop-count as its metric, and its default periodic update interval is 10 seconds.

Consider Figure 5-7. The ISDN backup link will be activated when the Frame Relay connectivity between R1 and R3 fails. Note the routing tables for R1 and R3, as listed in Code Listings 5-24 and 5-25.

Code Listing 5-24

AppleTalk routing table for R1.

```
C4700-R1#show appletalk route
Codes: R - RTMP derived, E - EIGRP derived, C - connected, A - AURP
       S - static  P - proxy
8 routes in internet

The first zone listed for each entry is its default (primary) zone.

C Net 10-19 directly connected, Ethernet0, zone vlan1
R Net 20-29 [1/G] via 102.120, 9 sec, Serial1, zone tr
R Net 30-39 [1/G] via 103.3, 2 sec, BRI0, zone vlan3
R Net 45-45 [2/G] via 103.3, 2 sec, BRI0, zone x25
R Net 50-59 [3/G] via 103.3, 2 sec, BRI0, zone tr
C Net 102-102 directly connected, Serial1, zone hdlc
C Net 103-103 directly connected, BRI0, zone isdn
R Net 134-134 [1/G] via 103.3, 3 sec, BRI0, zone fr
```

■ ■ ■ ■ ■ ■ ▮

Figure 5-7
The Frame Relay con-
nectivity between R1
and R3 fails.

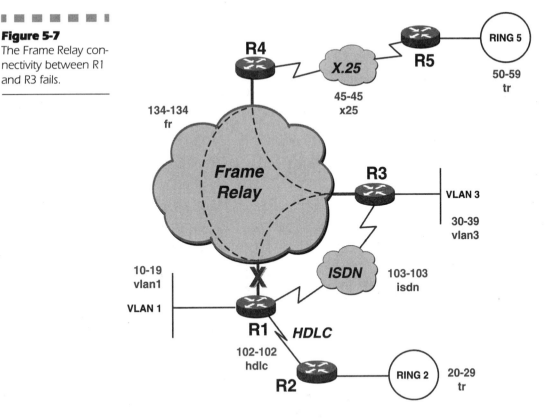

R1 now learns the routes to the AppleTalk cable-ranges 30-39, 45-45, 50-59, 103-103, and 134-134 through the ISDN interface BRI0.

■ ■ ▨ ▨ ■ ■ ▨ ▨ ■ ■ ■ ■ ■ ■ ■ ■ ■ ■ ■ ■ ■ ▨ ■ ■ ▨ ▨ ■ ▮

Code Listing 5-25
AppleTalk routing
table for R3.

```
C4500-R3#show appletalk route
Codes: R - RTMP derived, E - EIGRP derived, C - connected, A - AURP
       S - static  P - proxy
8 routes in internet

The first zone listed for each entry is its default (primary) zone.

R Net 10-19 [1/G] via 103.1, 8 sec, BRI0, zone vlan1
R Net 20-29 [2/G] via 103.1, 8 sec, BRI0, zone tr
C Net 30-39 directly connected, Ethernet0, zone vlan3
R Net 45-45 [1/G] via 134.4, 2 sec, Serial0, zone x25
R Net 50-59 [2/G] via 134.4, 2 sec, Serial0, zone tr
R Net 102-102 [1/G] via 103.1, 8 sec, BRI0, zone hdlc
C Net 103-103 directly connected, BRI0, zone isdn
C Net 134-134 directly connected, Serial0, zone fr
```

R3 now learns the routes to cable-ranges 10-19, 20-29, 103-103, and 102-102 through the ISDN interface BRI0.

AppleTalk Tunneling

When connecting two noncontiguous AppleTalk networks with a foreign backbone such as IP, the relatively high bandwidth consumed by RTMP updates (10-second interval) can seriously degrade the backbone network's overall performance. Tunneling tackles this performance issue. AppleTalk tunneling encapsulates AppleTalk packets inside IP protocol packets sent across the backbone to a destination router. The destination router does the reverse by de-encapsulating the AppleTalk packet and routes the packet to other AppleTalk networks near the remote end. Since the encapsulated AppleTalk packet is sent directly to a remote IP address, bandwidth consumption is reduced. Meanwhile, the encapsulated packet benefits from features normally enjoyed by IP packets, such as default routes and load balancing protocols.

There are two methods used to implement AppleTalk tunneling. The first method implements Cayman tunneling, designed by Cayman Systems, allowing routers to interoperate with Cayman GatorBoxes. For Cayman tunneling, Cisco routers may reside at both ends of the tunnel, or a GatorBox and a Cisco router on each end of a tunnel. Another method is a proprietary tunneling protocol, known as generic routing encapsulation (GRE). GRE tunneling requires Cisco routers on both ends of the tunnel connection.

In Figure 5-8, AppleTalk tunneling is configured over the Frame Relay 134.13.14.0/24 IP subnet, spanning across R1, R3 and R4. Note multiple GRE tunnels originate from R1. Tunnels are logical point-to-point links; hence, a separate tunnel is required for each virtual link. In this scenario, two tunnels are required - one from R1 to R3 and one from R1 to R4. Code Listings 5-26 through 5-28 illustrate this.

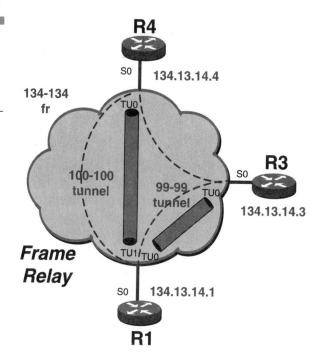

Figure 5-8
Tunneling AppleTalk through an IP backbone over Frame Relay.

Code Listing 5-26
AppleTalk tunneling configuration for R1.

```
hostname C4700-R1
!
appletalk routing
!
interface Serial0
 ip address 134.13.14.1 255.255.255.0
!
interface Tunnel0
 no ip address
 appletalk cable-range 99-99 99.1
 appletalk zone tunnel
 tunnel source Serial0
 tunnel destination 134.13.14.3
 tunnel mode gre ip
!
interface Tunnel1
 no ip address
 appletalk cable-range 100-100 100.1
 appletalk zone tunnel
 tunnel source Serial0
 tunnel destination 134.13.14.4
 tunnel mode gre ip
```

1. Code Listing 5-26 illustrates the AppleTalk tunneling configuration for R1. Two tunnel interfaces TU0 and TU1 are configured for R1.

TU0 has cable range 99-99 in zone "tunnel". TU1 has cable range
100-100 in the same zone as TU0.

2. The command `tunnel source` specifies S0 as the interface from
where the encapsulated AppleTalk packets will be sent.

3. The command `tunnel destination` specifies the tunnel's destination as the IP address of R3's S0 for TU0 and R4's S0 for TU1.

4. By default, the interface command `tunnel mode gre ip` enables
GRE tunneling.

Code Listing 5-27
AppleTalk tunneling
configuration for R3.

```
hostname C4500-R3
!
appletalk routing
!
interface Serial0
 ip address 134.13.14.3 255.255.255.0
!
interface Tunnel0
 no ip address
 appletalk cable-range 99-99 99.3
 appletalk zone tunnel
 tunnel source Serial0
 tunnel destination 134.13.14.1
 tunnel mode gre ip
```

1. Code Listing 5-27 illustrates the AppleTalk tunneling configuration
for R3. Only one tunnel interface TU0 is configured for R3. TU0 has
cable range 99-99 in zone "tunnel".

2. The command `tunnel source` specifies S0 as the interface from
where the encapsulated AppleTalk packets will be sent.

3. The command `tunnel destination` specifies TU0's destination
as the IP address of R1's S0.

4. By default, the interface command `tunnel mode gre ip` enables
GRE tunneling.

Code Listing 5-28
AppleTalk tunneling
configuration for R4.

```
hostname C2500-R4
!
appletalk routing
!
interface Serial0
 ip address 134.13.14.4 255.255.255.0
!
interface Tunnel0
```

Code Listing 5-28
(continued)

```
no ip address
appletalk cable-range 100-100 100.4
appletalk zone tunnel
tunnel source Serial0
tunnel destination 134.13.14.1
tunnel mode gre ip
```

1. Code Listing 5-28 illustrates the AppleTalk tunneling configuration for R4. Only one tunnel interface TU0 is configured for R4. TU0 has cable range 100-100 in zone "tunnel".

2. The command `tunnel source` specifies S0 as the interface from where the encapsulated AppleTalk packets will be sent.

3. The command `tunnel destination` specifies TU0's destination as the IP address of R1's S0.

4. By default, the interface command `tunnel mode gre ip` enables GRE tunneling.

Code Listing 5-29 illustrates the IP routing table for R1.

Code Listing 5-29
IP routing table for R1.

```
C4700-R1#show ip route
Codes: C - connected, S - static, I - IGRP, R - RIP, M - mobile, B - BGP
       D - EIGRP, EX - EIGRP external, O - OSPF, IA - OSPF inter area
       N1 - OSPF NSSA external type 1, N2 - OSPF NSSA external type 2
       E1 - OSPF external type 1, E2 - OSPF external type 2, E - EGP
       i - IS-IS, L1 - IS-IS level-1, L2 - IS-IS level-2, * - candidate default
       U - per-user static route, o - ODR

Gateway of last resort is not set

     134.13.0.0/24 is subnetted, 1 subnets
C       134.13.14.0 is directly connected, Serial0
```

Code Listing 5-30 illustrates the AppleTalk routing table for R1.

Code Listing 5-30
AppleTalk routing table for R1.

```
C4700-R1#show appletalk route
Codes: R - RTMP derived, E - EIGRP derived, C - connected, A - AURP
       S - static  P - proxy
10 routes in internet

The first zone listed for each entry is its default (primary) zone.

C Net 10-19 directly connected, Ethernet0, zone vlan1
R Net 20-29 [1/G] via 102.120, 7 sec, Serial1, zone tr
R Net 30-39 [1/G] via 134.3, 0 sec, Serial0, zone vlan3
R Net 45-45 [1/G] via 134.4, 3 sec, Serial0, zone x25
R Net 50-59 [2/G] via 134.4, 3 sec, Serial0, zone tr
C Net 99-99 directly connected, Tunnel0, zone tunnel
```

Code Listing 5-30
(continued)

```
C Net 100-100 directly connected, Tunnel1, zone tunnel
C Net 102-102 directly connected, Serial1, zone hdlc
R Net 103-103 [1/G] via 134.3, 0 sec, Serial0, zone isdn
C Net 134-134 directly connected, Serial0, zone fr
```

Code Listing 5-31 illustrates the AppleTalk zone information on R1.

Code Listing 5-31
AppleTalk zone information on R1.

```
C4700-R1#show appletalk zone
Name                              Network(s)
hdlc                              102-102
isdn                              103-103
x25                                45-45
fr                               134-134
tr                          50-59 20-29
tunnel                     100-100 99-99
vlan1                              10-19
vlan3                              30-39
Total of 8 zones
```

Code Listing 5-32 illustrates the AppleTalk routing table for R2.

Code Listing 5-32
AppleTalk routing table for R2.

```
C2500-R2#show appletalk route
Codes: R - RTMP derived, E - EIGRP derived, C - connected, A - AURP
       S - static  P - proxy
10 routes in internet

The first zone listed for each entry is its default (primary) zone.

R Net 10-19 [1/G] via 102.161, 6 sec, Serial0, zone vlan1
C Net 20-29 directly connected, TokenRing0, zone tr
R Net 30-39 [2/G] via 102.161, 6 sec, Serial0, zone vlan3
R Net 45-45 [2/G] via 102.161, 6 sec, Serial0, zone x25
R Net 50-59 [3/G] via 102.161, 6 sec, Serial0, zone tr
R Net 99-99 [1/G] via 102.161, 6 sec, Serial0, zone tunnel
R Net 100-100 [1/G] via 102.161, 6 sec, Serial0, zone tunnel
C Net 102-102 directly connected, Serial0, zone hdlc
R Net 103-103 [2/G] via 102.161, 6 sec, Serial0, zone isdn
R Net 134-134 [1/G] via 102.161, 6 sec, Serial0, zone fr
```

Code Listing 5-33 illustrates the AppleTalk zone information on R2.

Code Listing 5-33
AppleTalk zone infor-
mation on R2.

```
C2500-R2#show apple zone
Name                          Network(s)
hdlc                          102-102
isdn                          103-103
x25                             45-45
fr                            134-134
tr                       50-59 20-29
tunnel                   100-100 99-99
vlan1                           10-19
vlan3                           30-39
Total of 8 zones
```

Code Listing 5-34 illustrates the IP routing table for R3.

Code Listing 5-34
IP routing table for
R3.

```
C4500-R3#show ip route
Codes: C - connected, S - static, I - IGRP, R - RIP, M - mobile, B - BGP
       D - EIGRP, EX - EIGRP external, O - OSPF, IA - OSPF inter area
       N1 - OSPF NSSA external type 1, N2 - OSPF NSSA external type 2
       E1 - OSPF external type 1, E2 - OSPF external type 2, E - EGP
       i - IS-IS, L1 - IS-IS level-1, L2 - IS-IS level-2, * - candidate default
       U - per-user static route, o - ODR

Gateway of last resort is not set

     134.13.0.0/24 is subnetted, 1 subnets
C       134.13.14.0 is directly connected, Serial0
```

Code Listing 5-35 illustrates the AppleTalk routing table for R3.

Code Listing 5-35
AppleTalk routing
table for R3.

```
C4500-R3#show appletalk route
Codes: R - RTMP derived, E - EIGRP derived, C - connected, A - AURP
       S - static  P - proxy
10 routes in internet

The first zone listed for each entry is its default (primary) zone.

R Net 10-19 [1/G] via 134.1, 1 sec, Serial0, zone vlan1
R Net 20-29 [2/G] via 134.1, 1 sec, Serial0, zone tr
C Net 30-39 directly connected, Ethernet0, zone vlan3
R Net 45-45 [1/G] via 134.4, 7 sec, Serial0, zone x25
R Net 50-59 [2/G] via 134.4, 7 sec, Serial0, zone tr
C Net 99-99 directly connected, Tunnel0, zone tunnel
R Net 100-100 [1/G] via 134.1, 1 sec, Serial0, zone tunnel
R Net 102-102 [1/G] via 134.1, 1 sec, Serial0, zone hdlc
C Net 103-103 directly connected, BRI0, zone isdn
C Net 134-134 directly connected, Serial0, zone fr
```

Code Listing 5-36 illustrates the AppleTalk zone information on R3.

Code Listing 5-36
AppleTalk zone information on R3.

```
C4500-R3#show appletalk zone
Name                          Network(s)
hdlc                          102-102
isdn                          103-103
x25                            45-45
fr                            134-134
tr                          20-29 50-59
tunnel                      99-99 100-100
vlan1                          10-19
vlan3                          30-39
Total of 8 zones
```

Code Listing 5-37 illustrates the IP routing table for R4.

Code Listing 5-37
IP routing table for R4.

```
C2500-R4#show ip route
Codes: C - connected, S - static, I - IGRP, R - RIP, M - mobile, B - BGP
       D - EIGRP, EX - EIGRP external, O - OSPF, IA - OSPF inter area
       N1 - OSPF NSSA external type 1, N2 - OSPF NSSA external type 2
       E1 - OSPF external type 1, E2 - OSPF external type 2, E - EGP
       i - IS-IS, L1 - IS-IS level-1, L2 - IS-IS level-2, * - candidate default
       U - per-user static route, o - ODR

Gateway of last resort is not set

     134.13.0.0/24 is subnetted, 1 subnets
C       134.13.14.0 is directly connected, Serial0
```

Code Listing 5-38 illustrates the AppleTalk routing table for R4.

Code Listing 5-38
AppleTalk routing table for R4.

```
C2500-R4#show appletalk route
Codes: R - RTMP derived, E - EIGRP derived, C - connected, A - AURP
       S - static  P - proxy
10 routes in internet

The first zone listed for each entry is its default (primary) zone.

R Net 10-19 [1/G] via 134.1, 8 sec, Serial0, zone vlan1
R Net 20-29 [2/G] via 134.1, 8 sec, Serial0, zone tr
R Net 30-39 [1/G] via 134.3, 0 sec, Serial0, zone vlan3
C Net 45-45 directly connected, Serial1, zone x25
R Net 50-59 [1/G] via 45.5, 3 sec, Serial1, zone tr
R Net 99-99 [1/G] via 134.3, 0 sec, Serial0, zone tunnel
C Net 100-100 directly connected, Tunnel0, zone tunnel
R Net 102-102 [1/G] via 134.1, 8 sec, Serial0, zone hdlc
R Net 103-103 [1/G] via 134.3, 0 sec, Serial0, zone isdn
C Net 134-134 directly connected, Serial0, zone fr
```

Code Listing 5-39 illustrates the AppleTalk zone information on R4.

Code Listing 5-39
AppleTalk zone infor-
mation on R4.

```
C2500-R4#show appletalk zone
Name                          Network(s)
hdlc                          102-102
isdn                          103-103
x25                            45-45
fr                            134-134
tr                      50-59 20-29
tunnel                 100-100 99-99
vlan1                          10-19
vlan3                          30-39
Total of 8 zones
```

Code Listing 5-40 illustrates the AppleTalk routing table for R5.

Code Listing 5-40
AppleTalk routing
table for R5.

```
C2500-R5#show appletalk route
Codes: R - RTMP derived, E - EIGRP derived, C - connected, A - AURP
       S - static  P - proxy
10 routes in internet

The first zone listed for each entry is its default (primary) zone.

R Net 10-19 [2/G] via 45.4, 6 sec, Serial0, zone vlan1
R Net 20-29 [3/G] via 45.4, 6 sec, Serial0, zone tr
R Net 30-39 [2/G] via 45.4, 6 sec, Serial0, zone vlan3
C Net 45-45 directly connected, Serial0, zone x25
C Net 50-59 directly connected, TokenRing0, zone tr
R Net 99-99 [2/G] via 45.4, 6 sec, Serial0, zone tunnel
R Net 100-100 [1/G] via 45.4, 6 sec, Serial0, zone tunnel
R Net 102-102 [2/G] via 45.4, 6 sec, Serial0, zone hdlc
R Net 103-103 [2/G] via 45.4, 6 sec, Serial0, zone isdn
R Net 134-134 [1/G] via 45.4, 6 sec, Serial0, zone fr
```

Code Listing 5-41 illustrates the AppleTalk zone information on R5.

Code Listing 5-41
AppleTalk zone infor-
mation on R5.

```
C2500-R5#show appletalk zone
Name                          Network(s)
hdlc                          102-102
isdn                          103-103
x25                            45-45
fr                            134-134
tr                      50-59 20-29
tunnel                 100-100 99-99
vlan1                          10-19
vlan3                          30-39
Total of 8 zones
```

The two tunnels' cable ranges 99-99 and 100-100 are now reflected in the AppleTalk routing table for all routers. The zone name "tunnel" is also reflected in the AppleTalk zone information table on all routers.

AppleTalk EIGRP

AppleTalk EIGRP has the following features:

- By default, AppleTalk RTMP routes are automatically redistributed in EIGRP, and vice versa. Note that internal EIGRP routes are always preferred over external EIGRP routes, and redistributed RTMP routes are advertised as external EIGRP routes.

- AppleTalk interfaces can be configured to use both RTMP and EIGRP. If two adjacent routers are configured to use both RTMP and EIGRP, the EIGRP routing information supersedes the RTMP information. However, both devices continue to send RTMP updates.

Because EIGRP supersedes RTMP, disabling RTMP controls the bandwidth usage on WAN links. Using EIGRP on WAN links helps save valuable bandwidth and unnecessary traffic charges.

In Figure 5-9, AppleTalk EIGRP is configured on the Frame Relay, X.25, HDLC, and ISDN networks. Code Listings 5-42 through 5-46 illustrate this. Other networks are still running AppleTalk RTMP.

Code Listing 5-42
AppleTalk EIGRP configuration for R1.

```
hostname C4700-R1
!
username C4500-R3 password 0 cisco
appletalk routing eigrp 1
appletalk route-redistribution
isdn switch-type basic-net3
!
interface Tunnel0
 no ip address
 appletalk cable-range 99-99 99.1
 appletalk zone tunnel
 appletalk protocol eigrp
 no appletalk protocol rtmp
 tunnel source Serial0
 tunnel destination 134.13.14.3
!
interface Tunnel1
 no ip address
 appletalk cable-range 100-100 100.1
 appletalk zone tunnel
```

```
appletalk protocol eigrp
no appletalk protocol rtmp
tunnel source Serial0
tunnel destination 134.13.14.4
!
interface Serial0
 backup delay 10 30
 backup interface BRI0
 ip address 134.13.14.1 255.255.255.0
 encapsulation frame-relay
 bandwidth 56
 appletalk cable-range 134-134 134.1
 appletalk zone fr
 appletalk protocol eigrp
 no appletalk protocol rtmp
 no appletalk eigrp-splithorizon
 appletalk eigrp-bandwidth-percent 25
 frame-relay map appletalk 134.3 103 broadcast
 frame-relay map appletalk 134.4 104 broadcast
 frame-relay map ip 134.13.14.3 103 broadcast
 frame-relay map ip 134.13.14.4 104 broadcast
 frame-relay lmi-type ansi
!
interface Serial1
 bandwidth 56
 appletalk cable-range 102-102 102.161
 appletalk zone hdlc
 appletalk protocol eigrp
 no appletalk protocol rtmp
 appletalk eigrp-bandwidth-percent 25
!
interface BRI0
 encapsulation ppp
 appletalk cable-range 103-103 103.1
 appletalk zone isdn
 appletalk protocol eigrp
 no appletalk protocol rtmp
 dialer idle-timeout 60
 dialer map appletalk 103.3 name C4500-R3 broadcast 3245652
 dialer load-threshold 128 either
 dialer-group 1
 ppp authentication chap
!
dialer-list 1 protocol appletalk permit
```

1. Code Listing 5-42 illustrates the AppleTalk EIGRP configuration for R1. The global command `appletalk routing eigrp 1` starts an AppleTalk EIGRP routing process. Note that the `1` is the router number, not the autonomous system number for R1, and must be unique for each router.

2. The command `appletalk route-redistribution` redistributes AppleTalk RTMP routes into AppleTalk EIGRP automatically, and vice versa.

Figure 5-9
Implementing Apple-
Talk EIGRP over
Frame Relay, X.25,
HDLC, and ISDN.

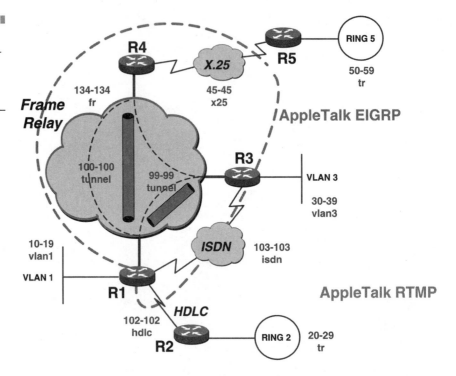

3. The interface command `appletalk protocol eigrp` enables
   EIGRP on interfaces TU0, TU1, S0, S1, and BRI0. By default,
   RTMP is enabled on these interfaces. Even though EIGRP supersedes RTMP, RTMP's routing updates will be sent out these interfaces. To prevent the bandwidth usage of RTMP on these links,
   disable RTMP on the respective interfaces with the interface command `no appletalk protocol rtmp`.

4. Split horizon controls AppleTalk EIGRP update and query packets.
   When split horizon is enabled on an interface, these packets are not
   sent to destinations for which this interface is the next hop. Split
   horizon is enabled on all interfaces, reducing the possibility of routing loops. The split-horizon mechanism optimizes communication
   among routers. With NBMA networks like Frame Relay, situations
   can arise where this behavior is suboptimal. The interface command `no appletalk eigrp-split horizon` disables the split-
   horizon mechanism for EIGRP on S0.

5. EIGRP packets consume, at most, 50 percent of link bandwidth by
   default. The command `appletalk eigrp-bandwidth-percent`

25 configures the bandwidth available for EIGRP on S0 and S1 as 25 percent.

```
hostname C2500-R2
!
appletalk routing eigrp 2
appletalk route-redistribution
!
interface Serial0
 bandwidth 56
 appletalk cable-range 102-102 102.120
 appletalk zone hdlc
 appletalk protocol eigrp
 no appletalk protocol rtmp
 appletalk eigrp-bandwidth-percent 25
```

1. Code Listing 5-43 illustrates the AppleTalk EIGRP configuration for R2. The global command `appletalk routing eigrp 2` starts an AppleTalk EIGRP routing process. Note that the 2 is the router number, not the autonomous system number for R2, and must be unique for each router.

2. By default, the command `appletalk route-redistribution` redistributes AppleTalk RTMP routes into AppleTalk EIGRP automatically, and vice versa.

3. The interface command `appletalk protocol eigrp` enables EIGRP on interface S0. By default, RTMP is enabled on this interface. Even though EIGRP supersedes RTMP, RTMP's routing updates will be sent out S0. To prevent the bandwidth usage of RTMP on the HDLC link, disable RTMP on S0 with the interface command `no appletalk protocol rtmp`.

4. EIGRP packets consume, at most, 50 percent of the link bandwidth by default. The command `appletalk eigrp-bandwidth-percent 25` configures the bandwidth available for EIGRP on S0 as 25 percent.

```
hostname C4500-R3
!
username C4700-R1 password 0 cisco
appletalk routing eigrp 3
appletalk route-redistribution
isdn switch-type basic-net3
!
```

■ l

Code Listing 5-44
(continued)

```
interface Tunnel0
 no ip address
 appletalk cable-range 99-99 99.3
 appletalk zone tunnel
 appletalk protocol eigrp
 no appletalk protocol rtmp
 tunnel source Serial0
 tunnel destination 134.13.14.1
!
interface Serial0
 ip address 134.13.14.3 255.255.255.0
 encapsulation frame-relay
 bandwidth 56
 appletalk cable-range 134-134 134.3
 appletalk zone fr
 appletalk protocol eigrp
 no appletalk protocol rtmp
 no appletalk eigrp-splithorizon
 appletalk eigrp-bandwidth-percent 25
 frame-relay map appletalk 134.1 301 broadcast
 frame-relay map appletalk 134.4 304 broadcast
 frame-relay map ip 134.13.14.1 301 broadcast
 frame-relay map ip 134.13.14.4 304 broadcast
 frame-relay lmi-type ansi
!
interface BRI0
 encapsulation ppp
 appletalk cable-range 103-103 103.3
 appletalk zone isdn
 appletalk protocol eigrp
 no appletalk protocol rtmp
 dialer idle-timeout 60
 dialer map ip 10.1.1.1 name C4700-R1 broadcast
 dialer map appletalk 103.1 name C4700-R1 broadcast
 dialer load-threshold 128 either
 dialer-group 1
 ppp authentication chap
!
dialer-list 1 protocol appletalk permit
```

1. Code Listing 5-44 illustrates the AppleTalk EIGRP configuration for R3. The global command `appletalk routing eigrp 3` starts an AppleTalk EIGRP routing process. Note that the 3 is the router number, not the autonomous system number for R3, and must be unique for each router.

2. By default, the command `appletalk route-redistribution` redistributes AppleTalk RTMP routes into AppleTalk EIGRP automatically, and vice versa.

3. The interface command `appletalk protocol eigrp` enables EIGRP on interfaces TU0, S0, and BRI0. By default, RTMP is enabled on these interfaces. Even though EIGRP supersedes RTMP,

RTMP's routing updates will be sent out these interfaces. To prevent the bandwidth usage of RTMP on these links, disable RTMP on the respective interfaces with the interface command `no appletalk protocol rtmp`.

4. Split horizon controls AppleTalk EIGRP update and query packets. When split horizon is enabled on an interface, these packets are not sent to destinations for which this interface is the next hop. By default, split horizon is enabled on all interfaces, reducing the possibility of routing loops. The split-horizon mechanism optimizes communication among routers. However, with NBMA networks like Frame Relay, situations can arise where this behavior is suboptimal. The interface command `no appletalk eigrp-split horizon` disables the split-horizon mechanism for EIGRP on S0.

5. EIGRP packets consume, at most, 50 percent of the link bandwidth by default. The command `appletalk eigrp-bandwidth-percent 25` configures the bandwidth available for EIGRP on S0 as 25 percent.

Code Listing 5-45
AppleTalk EIGRP configuration for R4.

```
hostname C2500-R4
!
appletalk routing eigrp 4
appletalk route-redistribution
!
interface Tunnel0
 no ip address
 appletalk cable-range 100-100 100.4
 appletalk zone tunnel
 appletalk protocol eigrp
 no appletalk protocol rtmp
 tunnel source Serial0
 tunnel destination 134.13.14.1
!
interface Serial0
 ip address 134.13.14.4 255.255.255.0
 encapsulation frame-relay
 bandwidth 56
 appletalk cable-range 134-134 134.4
 appletalk zone fr
 appletalk protocol eigrp
 no appletalk protocol rtmp
 no appletalk eigrp-splithorizon
 appletalk eigrp-bandwidth-percent 25
 frame-relay map appletalk 134.1 401 broadcast
 frame-relay map appletalk 134.3 403 broadcast
 frame-relay map ip 134.13.14.1 401 broadcast
 frame-relay map ip 134.13.14.3 403 broadcast
 frame-relay lmi-type ansi
!
```

```
interface Serial1
 encapsulation x25
 bandwidth 56
 appletalk cable-range 45-45 45.4
 appletalk zone x25
 appletalk protocol eigrp
 no appletalk protocol rtmp
 no appletalk eigrp-splithorizon
 appletalk eigrp-bandwidth-percent 25
 x25 address 25444444
 x25 map appletalk 45.5 25555555 broadcast
```

1. Code Listing 5-45 illustrates the AppleTalk EIGRP configuration for R4. The global command `appletalk routing eigrp 4` enables an AppleTalk EIGRP routing process. Note that the 4 is the router number, not the autonomous system number for R4, and must be unique for each router.

2. By default, the command `appletalk route-redistribution` redistributes AppleTalk RTMP routes into AppleTalk EIGRP automatically, and vice versa.

3. The interface command `appletalk protocol eigrp` enables EIGRP on interfaces TU0, S0, and S1. By default, RTMP is enabled on these interfaces. Even though EIGRP supersedes RTMP, RTMP's routing updates will be sent out these interfaces. To prevent the bandwidth usage of RTMP on these links, disable RTMP on the respective interfaces with the interface command `no appletalk protocol rtmp`.

4. Split horizon controls AppleTalk EIGRP update and query packets. When split horizon is enabled on an interface, these packets are not sent to destinations for which this interface is the next hop. By default, split horizon is enabled on all interfaces, reducing the possibility of routing loops. The split-horizon mechanism optimizes communication among routers. However, with NBMA networks like Frame Relay and X.25, situations can arise where this behavior is suboptimal. The interface command `no appletalk eigrp-splithorizon` disables the split-horizon mechanism for EIGRP on S0 and S1.

5. EIGRP packets consume a maximum of 50 percent of the link bandwidth by default. The command `appletalk eigrp-bandwidth-percent 25` configures the bandwidth available for EIGRP on S0 and S1 as 25 percent.

Code Listing 5-46
AppleTalk EIGRP con-
figuration for R5.

```
hostname C2500-R5
!
appletalk routing eigrp 5
appletalk route-redistribution
!
interface Serial0
 encapsulation x25
 bandwidth 56
 appletalk cable-range 45-45 45.5
 appletalk zone x25
 appletalk protocol eigrp
 no appletalk protocol rtmp
 no appletalk eigrp-splithorizon
 appletalk eigrp-bandwidth-percent 25
 x25 address 25555555
 x25 map appletalk 45.4 25444444 broadcast
```

1. Code Listing 5-46 illustrates the AppleTalk EIGRP configuration for R5. The global command `appletalk routing eigrp 5` starts an AppleTalk EIGRP routing process. Note that the 5 is the router number, not the autonomous system number for R5, and must be unique for each router.

2. By default, the command `appletalk route-redistribution` redistributes AppleTalk RTMP routes into AppleTalk EIGRP automatically, and vice versa.

3. The interface command `appletalk protocol eigrp` enables EIGRP on interface S0. By default, RTMP is enabled on this interface. Even though EIGRP supersedes RTMP, RTMP's routing updates will be sent out S0. To prevent the bandwidth usage of RTMP on the X.25 link, disable RTMP on S0 with the interface command `no appletalk protocol rtmp`.

4. Split horizon controls AppleTalk EIGRP update and query packets. When split horizon is enabled on an interface, these packets are not sent to destinations for which this interface is the next hop. By default, split horizon is enabled on all interfaces, reducing the possibility of routing loops. The split-horizon mechanism optimizes communication among routers. However, with NBMA networks like X.25, situations can arise where this behavior is suboptimal. The interface command `no appletalk eigrp-split horizon` disables the split-horizon mechanism for EIGRP on S0.

5. EIGRP packets consume, at most, 50 percent of the link bandwidth by default. The command `appletalk eigrp-bandwidth-per-cent 25` configures the bandwidth available for EIGRP on S0 as 25 percent.

Code Listings 5-47 through 5-51 illustrate the AppleTalk routing tables for R1 to R5.

Code Listing 5-47

AppleTalk routing table for R1.

```
C4700-R1#show appletalk route
Codes: R - RTMP derived, E - EIGRP derived, C - connected, A - AURP
       S - static  P - proxy
10 routes in internet

The first zone listed for each entry is its default (primary) zone.

C Net 10-19 directly connected, Ethernet0, zone vlan1
E Net 20-29 [1/G] via 102.120, 30834 sec, Serial1, zone tr
E Net 30-39 [1/G] via 134.3, 30835 sec, Serial0, zone vlan3
E Net 45-45 [1/G] via 134.4, 30835 sec, Serial0, zone x25
E Net 50-59 [2/G] via 134.4, 30835 sec, Serial0, zone tr
C Net 99-99 directly connected, Tunnel0, zone tunnel
C Net 100-100 directly connected, Tunnel1, zone tunnel
C Net 102-102 directly connected, Serial1, zone hdlc
E Net 103-103 [1/G] via 134.3, 30835 sec, Serial0, zone isdn
C Net 134-134 directly connected, Serial0, zone fr
```

Code Listing 5-48

AppleTalk routing table for R2.

```
C2500-R2#show appletalk route
Codes: R - RTMP derived, E - EIGRP derived, C - connected, A - AURP
       S - static  P - proxy
10 routes in internet

The first zone listed for each entry is its default (primary) zone.

E Net 10-19 [1/G] via 102.161, 31831 sec, Serial0, zone vlan1
C Net 20-29 directly connected, TokenRing0, zone tr
E Net 30-39 [2/G] via 102.161, 30872 sec, Serial0, zone vlan3
E Net 45-45 [2/G] via 102.161, 30843 sec, Serial0, zone x25
E Net 50-59 [3/G] via 102.161, 30843 sec, Serial0, zone tr
E Net 99-99 [1/G] via 102.161, 30897 sec, Serial0, zone tunnel
E Net 100-100 [1/G] via 102.161, 30895 sec, Serial0, zone tunnel
C Net 102-102 directly connected, Serial0, zone hdlc
E Net 103-103 [2/G] via 102.161, 30870 sec, Serial0, zone isdn
E Net 134-134 [1/G] via 102.161, 30897 sec, Serial0, zone fr
```

Code Listing 5-49

AppleTalk routing table for R3.

```
C4500-R3#show appletalk route
Codes: R - RTMP derived, E - EIGRP derived, C - connected, A - AURP
       S - static  P - proxy
10 routes in internet

The first zone listed for each entry is its default (primary) zone.

E Net 10-19 [1/G] via 134.1, 30850 sec, Serial0, zone vlan1
E Net 20-29 [2/G] via 134.1, 30850 sec, Serial0, zone tr
C Net 30-39 directly connected, Ethernet0, zone vlan3
```

Code Listing 5-49
(continued)

```
E Net 45-45 [1/G] via 134.4, 30850 sec, Serial0, zone x25
E Net 50-59 [2/G] via 134.4, 30850 sec, Serial0, zone tr
C Net 99-99 directly connected, Tunnel0, zone tunnel
E Net 100-100 [1/G] via 134.4, 30878 sec, Serial0, zone tunnel
E Net 102-102 [1/G] via 134.1, 30851 sec, Serial0, zone hdlc
C Net 103-103 directly connected, BRI0, zone isdn
C Net 134-134 directly connected, Serial0, zone fr
```

Code Listing 5-50
AppleTalk routing
table for R4.

```
C2500-R4#show appletalk route
Codes: R - RTMP derived, E - EIGRP derived, C - connected, A - AURP
       S - static  P - proxy
10 routes in internet

The first zone listed for each entry is its default (primary) zone.

E Net 10-19 [1/G] via 134.1, 30858 sec, Serial0, zone vlan1
E Net 20-29 [2/G] via 134.1, 30858 sec, Serial0, zone tr
E Net 30-39 [1/G] via 134.3, 30858 sec, Serial0, zone vlan3
C Net 45-45 directly connected, Serial1, zone x25
E Net 50-59 [1/G] via 45.5, 30858 sec, Serial1, zone tr
E Net 99-99 [1/G] via 134.3, 30858 sec, Serial0, zone tunnel
C Net 100-100 directly connected, Tunnel0, zone tunnel
E Net 102-102 [1/G] via 134.1, 30859 sec, Serial0, zone hdlc
E Net 103-103 [1/G] via 134.3, 30859 sec, Serial0, zone isdn
C Net 134-134 directly connected, Serial0, zone fr
```

Code Listing 5-51
AppleTalk routing
table for R5.

```
C2500-R5#sh app ro
Codes: R - RTMP derived, E - EIGRP derived, C - connected, A - AURP
       S - static  P - proxy
10 routes in internet

The first zone listed for each entry is its default (primary) zone.

E Net 10-19 [2/G] via 45.4, 30866 sec, Serial0, zone vlan1
E Net 20-29 [3/G] via 45.4, 30866 sec, Serial0, zone tr
E Net 30-39 [2/G] via 45.4, 31376 sec, Serial0, zone vlan3
C Net 45-45 directly connected, Serial0, zone x25
C Net 50-59 directly connected, TokenRing0, zone tr
E Net 99-99 [2/G] via 45.4, 31376 sec, Serial0, zone tunnel
E Net 100-100 [1/G] via 45.4, 31376 sec, Serial0, zone tunnel
E Net 102-102 [2/G] via 45.4, 30866 sec, Serial0, zone hdlc
E Net 103-103 [2/G] via 45.4, 31376 sec, Serial0, zone isdn
E Net 134-134 [1/G] via 45.4, 31376 sec, Serial0, zone fr
```

Consider Figure 5-7. When the Frame Relay connectivity between R1 and R3 becomes unavailable, the ISDN backup link will be established. Note the changes in the routing tables for R1 and R3, as illustrated in Code Listings 5-52 and 5-53.

Code Listing 5-52

AppleTalk routing table for R1.

```
C4700-R1#r1#show appletalk route
Codes: R - RTMP derived, E - EIGRP derived, C - connected, A - AURP
       S - static  P - proxy
10 routes in internet

The first zone listed for each entry is its default (primary) zone.

C Net 10-19 directly connected, Ethernet0, zone vlan1
E Net 20-29 [1/G] via 102.120, 17 sec, Serial1, zone tr
E Net 30-39 [1/G] via 103.3, 110 sec, BRIO, zone vlan3
E Net 45-45 [2/G] via 103.3, 110 sec, BRIO, zone x25
E Net 50-59 [3/G] via 103.3, 110 sec, BRIO, zone tr
E Net 99-99 [1/G] via 103.3, 110 sec, BRIO, zone tunnel
E Net 100-100 [2/G] via 103.3, 111 sec, BRIO, zone tunnel
C Net 102-102 directly connected, Serial1, zone hdlc
C Net 103-103 directly connected, BRIO, zone isdn
E Net 134-134 [1/G] via 103.3, 111 sec, BRIO, zone fr
```

R1 now learns the routes to AppleTalk cable ranges 30-39, 45-45, 50-59, 99-99, 100-100, 103-103, and 134-134 through the ISDN interface BRI0 using EIGRP.

Code Listing 5-53

AppleTalk routing table for R3.

```
C4500-R3#show appletalk route
Codes: R - RTMP derived, E - EIGRP derived, C - connected, A - AURP
       S - static  P - proxy
10 routes in internet

The first zone listed for each entry is its default (primary) zone.

E Net 10-19 [1/G] via 103.1, 33 sec, BRIO, zone vlan1
E Net 20-29 [2/G] via 103.1, 33 sec, BRIO, zone tr
C Net 30-39 directly connected, Ethernet0, zone vlan3
E Net 45-45 [1/G] via 134.4, 126 sec, Serial0, zone x25
E Net 50-59 [2/G] via 134.4, 126 sec, Serial0, zone tr
C Net 99-99 directly connected, Tunnel0, zone tunnel
E Net 100-100 [1/G] via 134.4, 126 sec, Serial0, zone tunnel
E Net 102-102 [1/G] via 103.1, 33 sec, BRIO, zone hdlc
C Net 103-103 directly connected, BRIO, zone isdn
C Net 134-134 directly connected, Serial0, zone fr
```

R3 now learns the routes to AppleTalk cable ranges 10-19, 20-29, 103-103, and 102-102 through the ISDN interface BRI0 using EIGRP.

AppleTalk Access Control

Service location traffic and frequent routing updates can create a significant amount of overhead traffic, especially in large AppleTalk networks. Access lists can be deployed to manage this excessive AppleTalk traffic. The next few sections discuss the five types of AppleTalk filtering—data packet filtering, route filtering, GetZoneList (GZL) filtering, Zone Information Protocol (ZIP) filtering, and NBP packet filtering.

Data Packet Filtering

In this section, access will be denied for an AppleTalk cable range. Figure 5-10 shows that data packet (DDP) filtering is executed on R3's S0, TU0, and BRI0 interfaces. Code Listing 5-54 illustrates this.

Figure 5-10
Data packet filtering.

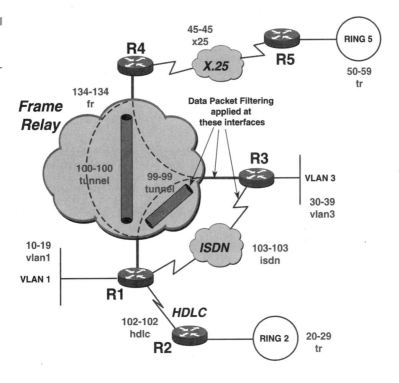

```
hostname C4500-R3
!
username C4700-R1 password 0 cisco
appletalk routing eigrp 3
appletalk route-redistribution
isdn switch-type basic-net3
!
interface Tunnel0
 no ip address
 appletalk cable-range 99-99 99.3
 appletalk zone tunnel
 appletalk protocol eigrp
 no appletalk protocol rtmp
 appletalk access-group 601
 tunnel source Serial0
 tunnel destination 134.13.14.1
!
interface Ethernet0
 media-type 10BaseT
 appletalk cable-range 30-39 32.128
 appletalk zone vlan3
!
interface Serial0
 ip address 134.13.14.3 255.255.255.0
 encapsulation frame-relay
 bandwidth 56
 appletalk cable-range 134-134 134.3
 appletalk zone fr
 appletalk protocol eigrp
 no appletalk protocol rtmp
 appletalk access-group 601
 no appletalk eigrp-splithorizon
 appletalk eigrp-bandwidth-percent 25
 frame-relay map appletalk 134.1 301 broadcast
 frame-relay map appletalk 134.4 304 broadcast
 frame-relay map ip 134.13.14.1 301 broadcast
 frame-relay map ip 134.13.14.4 304 broadcast
 frame-relay lmi-type ansi
!
interface BRI0
 encapsulation ppp
 appletalk cable-range 103-103 103.3
 appletalk zone isdn
 appletalk protocol eigrp
 no appletalk protocol rtmp
 appletalk access-group 601
 dialer idle-timeout 60
 dialer map appletalk 103.1 name C4700-R1 broadcast
 dialer load-threshold 128 either
 dialer-group 1
 ppp authentication chap
!
access-list 601 deny cable-range 30-39
access-list 601 permit other-access
!
dialer-list 1 protocol appletalk permit
```

1. Code Listing 5-54 illustrates the AppleTalk data packet filtering for R3. The `access-list 601 deny cable-range 30-39` command denies the cable range 30-39 on VLAN 3, and then the command `access-list 601 permit other-access` defines the default action to permit all other networks and cable ranges except 30-39.

2. The interface command `appletalk access-group 601` activates the access-list 601 on TU0, S0, and BRI0. Note that filtering is applied on the outward direction.

After applying data packet filtering on the respective interfaces, no longer does an AppleTalk ping from R1, R2, R4, or R5 succeed to the address 32.128 (that belongs to the cable range 30-39) on R3's E0. Code Listing 5-55 illustrates the AppleTalk ping results.

Code Listing 5-55
AppleTalk ping results.

```
C4700-R1#ping appletalk 32.128

Type escape sequence to abort.
Sending 5, 100-byte AppleTalk Echos to 32.128, timeout is 2 seconds:
.....
Success rate is 0 percent (0/5)


C2500-R2#ping appletalk 32.128

Type escape sequence to abort.
Sending 5, 100-byte AppleTalk Echos to 32.128, timeout is 2 seconds:
.....
Success rate is 0 percent (0/5)


C2500-R4#ping appletalk 32.128

Type escape sequence to abort.
Sending 5, 100-byte AppleTalk Echos to 32.128, timeout is 2 seconds:
.....
Success rate is 0 percent (0/5)


C2500-R5#ping appletalk 32.128

Type escape sequence to abort.
Sending 5, 100-byte AppleTalk Echos to 32.128, timeout is 2 seconds:
.....
Success rate is 0 percent (0/5)
```

Figure 5-11
Routing table update
filtering.

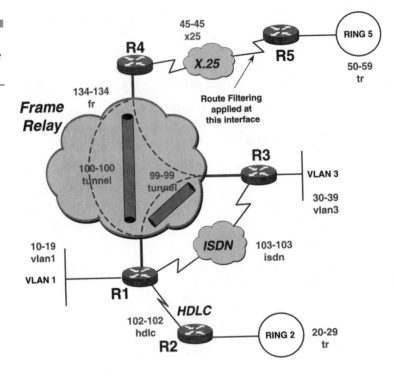

Route Filtering

This section demonstrates filtering an unwanted AppleTalk route. Figure
5-11 shows route filtering applied to R5's S0 interface. Code Listing 5-56
illustrates this

Code Listing 5-56
AppleTalk routing
table update filtering
configuration for R5.

```
hostname C2500-R5
!
appletalk routing eigrp 5
appletalk route-redistribution
!
interface Serial0
 encapsulation x25
 bandwidth 56
 appletalk cable-range 45-45 45.5
 appletalk zone x25
 appletalk protocol eigrp
 no appletalk protocol rtmp
 appletalk distribute-list 601 in
 no appletalk eigrp-splithorizon
 appletalk eigrp-bandwidth-percent 25
```

■ |

Code Listing 5-56
(continued)

```
 x25 address 25555555
 x25 map appletalk 45.4 25444444 broadcast
 !
interface TokenRing0
 appletalk cable-range 50-59 58.3
 appletalk zone tr
 ring-speed 16
 !
access-list 601 deny cable-range 20-29
access-list 601 permit other-access
```

1. Code listing 5-56 illustrates the AppleTalk routing table update-filtering configuration for R5. The `access-list 601 deny cable-range 20-29` command denies routes coming from the cable range 20-29, and then the command `access-list 601 permit other-access` defines the default action, permitting all routes from other networks and cable ranges except 20-29.

2. The interface command `appletalk distribute-list 601 in` activates the access-list 601 on S0. Note that filtering is applied to the inbound traffic.

R5's routing table, illustrated in Code Listing 5-57, no longer reflects the cable range 20-29.

■ |

Code Listing 5-57
AppleTalk routing table for R5.

```
C2500-R5#show appletalk route
Codes: R - RTMP derived, E - EIGRP derived, C - connected, A - AURP
       S - static  P - proxy
9 routes in internet

The first zone listed for each entry is its default (primary) zone.

E Net 10-19 [2/G] via 45.4, 221 sec, Serial0, zone vlan1
E Net 30-39 [2/G] via 45.4, 221 sec, Serial0, no zone set
C Net 45-45 directly connected, Serial0, zone x25
C Net 50-59 directly connected, TokenRing0, zone tr
E Net 99-99 [2/G] via 45.4, 221 sec, Serial0, zone tunnel
E Net 100-100 [1/G] via 45.4, 221 sec, Serial0, zone tunnel
E Net 102-102 [2/G] via 45.4, 222 sec, Serial0, zone hdlc
E Net 103-103 [2/G] via 45.4, 222 sec, Serial0, zone isdn
E Net 134-134 [1/G] via 45.4, 222 sec, Serial0, zone fr
```

Likewise, the cable range 20-29 no longer appears in the zone information table on R5, illustrated in Code Listing 5-58, as the route to it has been filtered.

```
C2500-R5#show appletalk zone
Name                    Network(s)
hdlc                      102-102
isdn                      103-103
x25                         45-45
fr                        134-134
tr                          50-59
tunnel             100-100 99-99
vlan1                       10-19
Total of 7 zones
```

GZL and ZIP Filtering

This section will configure GZL and ZIP reply filters and demonstrate differences between these types of filters. In Figure 5-12, GZL and ZIP filters are applied to R5's S0 and R3's S0, TU0, and BRI0.

Both GZL and ZIP reply filters control the zones seen on a particular network segment. GZL filters control zones seen by Macintoshes (1, 2, 3, and 5) on local network segments, and these filters have no effect on neighbor routers. GZL filters operate between Macintoshes and routers on local cable segments. Since a Macintosh chooses its router dynamically, GZL filtering must be implemented on all routers on that segment in order for it to work properly. GZL filtering only filters GZL requests on the network between the Macintosh's Chooser menu and the router. To filter zone information exchange between routers, ZIP reply filters are used. ZIP filters control zones seen by neighbor routers and by downstream routers. ZIP filters can even hide zones from all Macintoshes on all networks. In this scenario, GZL and ZIP reply filters will be implemented as illustrated in Code Listings 5-59 and 5-60.

```
hostname C4500-R3
!
username C4700-R1 password 0 cisco
appletalk routing eigrp 3
appletalk route-redistribution
isdn switch-type basic-net3
!
interface Tunnel0
 no ip address
 appletalk cable-range 99-99 99.3
 appletalk zone tunnel
 appletalk protocol eigrp
 no appletalk protocol rtmp
 appletalk getzonelist-filter 600
 appletalk zip-reply-filter 600
```

```
 tunnel source Serial0
 tunnel destination 134.13.14.1
 !
 interface Ethernet0
 media-type 10BaseT
 appletalk cable-range 30-39 32.128
 appletalk zone vlan3
 !
 interface Serial0
 ip address 134.13.14.3 255.255.255.0
 encapsulation frame-relay
 bandwidth 56
 appletalk cable-range 134-134 134.3
 appletalk zone fr
 appletalk protocol eigrp
 no appletalk protocol rtmp
 appletalk getzonelist-filter 600
 appletalk zip-reply-filter 600
 no appletalk eigrp-splithorizon
 appletalk eigrp-bandwidth-percent 25
 frame-relay map appletalk 134.1 301 broadcast
 frame-relay map appletalk 134.4 304 broadcast
 frame-relay map ip 134.13.14.1 301 broadcast
 frame-relay map ip 134.13.14.4 304 broadcast
 frame-relay lmi-type ansi
 !
 interface BRI0
 encapsulation ppp
 appletalk cable-range 103-103 103.3
 appletalk zone isdn
 appletalk protocol eigrp
 no appletalk protocol rtmp
 appletalk getzonelist-filter 600
 appletalk zip-reply-filter 600
 dialer idle-timeout 60
 dialer map ip 10.1.1.1 name C4700-R1 broadcast
 dialer map appletalk 103.1 name C4700-R1 broadcast
 dialer load-threshold 128 either
 dialer-group 1
 ppp authentication chap
 !
 access-list 600 deny zone vlan3
 access-list 600 permit additional-zones
 access-list 600 permit other-access
 !
 dialer-list 1 protocol appletalk permit
```

1. Code Listing 5-59 illustrates the AppleTalk GZL and ZIP filtering configuration for R3. The access-list 600 deny zone vlan3 command denies the zone "vlan3" in R3's GZL reply, making VLAN 3 invisible to the user. The next commands, access-list 600 permit additional-zones and access-list 600 permit other-access, allow other unfiltered zones to be accessible.

Figure 5-12
GZL and ZIP filtering.

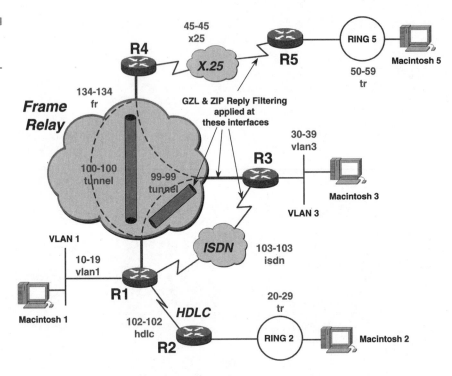

Figure 5-12
GZL and ZIP filtering.

2. The interface command `appletalk getzonelist-filter 600` activates the access-list 600 TU0, S0, and BRI0. Note that the filtering is applied to the outbound traffic. After applying the access-list on R3, users on other cable ranges (10-19, 20-29, 45-45, 50-59, 99-99, 100-100, 102-102, 103-103, and 134-134) will not see the zone "vlan3" in their Chooser.

3. ZIP reply filtering uses the same access-list 600. However, the interface command `appletalk zip-reply-filter 600` activates the access-list 600 on TU0, S0, and BRI0. R3 will include all zones except "vlan3" in its ZIP reply on interfaces TU0, S0, and BRI0. The zone "vlan3" will be invisible to R1, R2, R4, and R5.

■ ■

Code Listing 5-60
AppleTalk GZL and
ZIP filtering configuration for R5.

```
hostname C2500-R5
!
appletalk routing eigrp 5
appletalk route-redistribution
!
interface Serial0
 encapsulation x25
 bandwidth 56
 appletalk cable-range 45-45 45.5
 appletalk zone x25
 appletalk protocol eigrp
 no appletalk protocol rtmp
 appletalk getzonelist-filter 600
 appletalk zip-reply-filter 600
 no appletalk eigrp-splithorizon
 appletalk eigrp-bandwidth-percent 25
 x25 address 25555555
 x25 map appletalk 45.4 25444444 broadcast
!
interface TokenRing0
 appletalk cable-range 50-59 58.3
 appletalk zone tr
 ring-speed 16
!
access-list 600 deny zone tr
access-list 600 permit additional-zones
access-list 600 permit other-access
```

1. Code Listing 5-60 illustrates the AppleTalk GZL and ZIP filtering configuration for R5. The `access-list 600 deny zone tr` command denies the zone "tr" in R5's GZL reply and is thereby invisible to the user. The next commands, `access-list 600 permit additional-zones` and `access-list 600 permit other-access`, allow accessibility to all zones except "tr." Note that RING 2 and RING 5 share the same zone name, "tr"; the access-list 600 will deny zone information on RING 5 only.

2. The interface command `appletalk getzonelist-filter 600` activates the access-list 600 on S0. Note that filtering is applied to the outbound traffic. After applying access-list 600 on R5, users on other cable ranges (10-19, 20-29, 30-39, 45-45, 99-99, 100-100, 102-102, 103-103, and 134-134) will not see the zone "tr" belonging to RING 5 in their Chooser. However, users will be able to see the zone "tr" belonging to RING 2.

3. The same access-list 600 can be used for ZIP reply filtering. The interface command `appletalk zip-reply-filter 600` activates access-list 600 on S0. R5 will include all zones except "tr" (which belongs to RING 5) in its ZIP reply to these interfaces. The

zone "tr" that belongs to RING 5 will be invisible to R1, R2, R3, and R4.

From the zone information tables (ZIT) on the five routers illustrated in Code Listings 5-61 through 5-65, note that zone "vlan3" is now invisible to R1, R2, R4, and R5. Zone "tr" from RING 5 is now invisible to R1, R2, R3, and R4.

Code Listing 5-61

AppleTalk zone information on R1.

```
C4700-R1#show appletalk zone
Name                    Network(s)
hdlc                    102-102
isdn                    103-103
x25                      45-45
fr                      134-134
tr                       20-29
tunnel          100-100 99-99
vlan1                    10-19
Total of 7 zones
```

Code Listing 5-62

AppleTalk zone information on R2.

```
C2500-R2#show appletalk zone
Name                    Network(s)
hdlc                    102-102
isdn                    103-103
x25                      45-45
fr                      134-134
tr                       20-29
tunnel          100-100 99-99
vlan1                    10-19
Total of 7 zones
```

Code Listing 5-63

AppleTalk zone information on R3.

```
C4500-R3#show appletalk zone
Name                    Network(s)
hdlc                    102-102
isdn                    103-103
x25                      45-45
fr                      134-134
tr                       20-29
tunnel          100-100 99-99
vlan1                    10-19
vlan3                    30-39
Total of 8 zones
```

| **Code Listing 5-64**<br>*AppleTalk zone infor-<br>mation on R4.* | ```
C2500-R4#show appletalk zone
Name                    Network(s)
hdlc                       102-102
isdn                       103-103
x25                          45-45
fr                         134-134
tr                           20-29
tunnel              99-99 100-100
vlan1                        10-19
Total of 7 zones
``` |

| **Code Listing 5-65**<br>*AppleTalk zone infor-<br>mation on R5.* | ```
C2500-R5#show appletalk zone
Name                    Network(s)
hdlc                       102-102
isdn                       103-103
x25                          45-45
fr                         134-134
tr                        20-29 50-59
tunnel             100-100 99-99
vlan1                        10-19
Total of 7 zones
``` |

NBP Packet Filtering

NBP packet filtering can reduce unnecessary NBP overhead traffic or control access. NBP filtering has great flexibility; access can be permitted or denied to a single device in a zone, to all devices of one type (for example, AFPServer, LaserWriter, and Workstation) in a particular zone, or to all devices in a zone.

In this section, access will be denied to a specific device in a particular zone. Figure 5-13 shows NBP packet filtering applied on R2's S0 interface. Two devices—one a file server, the other a printer—are attached to VLAN 1. Code Listing 5-66 illustrates this.

| **Code Listing 5-66**<br>*AppleTalk NBP<br>packet-filtering con-<br>figuration for R2.* | ```
hostname C2500-R2
!
appletalk routing eigrp 2
appletalk route-redistribution
!
interface Serial0
 bandwidth 56
 appletalk access-group 602
 appletalk cable-range 102-102 102.120
 appletalk zone hdlc
 appletalk protocol eigrp
``` |
```

■ |

Code Listing 5-66
(continued)

```
no appletalk protocol rtmp
 appletalk eigrp-bandwidth-percent 25
 !
access-list 602 deny nbp 1 object Color Laser
access-list 602 deny nbp 1 type LaserWriter
access-list 602 deny nbp 1 zone vlan1
access-list 602 permit other-nbps
access-list 602 permit other-access
```

1. Code Listing 5-66 illustrates the AppleTalk NBP packet-filtering configuration for R2. In `access-list 602`, the number 1 after the keyword `nbp` is a sequence number used to link all three components (object, type, and zone) of a network-visible entity (NVE). An NVE is any device accessible over an AppleTalk network. In this case, the entity denied access is Color Laser:LaserWriter@vlan1. The `access-list 602 permit other-nbps` command allows users to access File Server 1, while the `access-list 600 permit other-access` command must be included to allow DDP traffic (AppleTalk data packets) to pass through.

■ ■ ■ ■ ■ ■ I

Figure 5-13
NBP packet filtering.

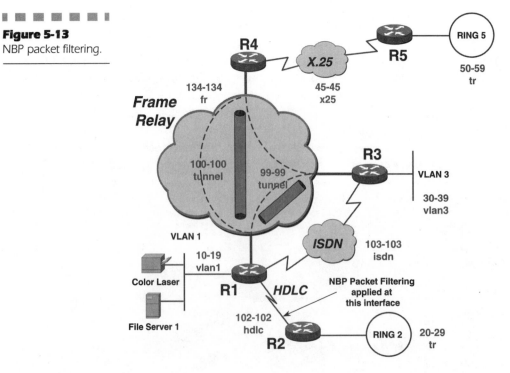

2. The interface command `appletalk access-group 602` activates the access-list 602 on S0. Note that filtering is applied against the inbound traffic. After applying access-list 602 on R2, users on RING 2 will no longer see "Color Laser" in their Chooser.

Summary

This chapter covered AppleTalk, a routable protocol well known for its ease of use and transparency to users. AppleTalk requires very little configuration from the users, but uses frequent periodic routing updates, which are often inappropriate for WAN links.

To configure AppleTalk on Cisco routers, AppleTalk routing must be enabled. This chapter focused on AppleTalk Phase II, so a cable range and zone need to be specified on each interface involved in routing.

In the initial scenario, AppleTalk was configured in a LAN environment, then expanded to Frame Relay, X.25, HDLC, and DDR. Tunneling and EIGRP were added to optimize network performance and reduce excessive or undesirable AppleTalk traffic in WANs.

Lastly, the five types of AppleTalk filtering—data, route, GZL, ZIP, and NBP—assist traffic management and control advertisements in a more efficient and effective manner.

References

1. Apple Computer, Inc. *AppleTalk Network System Overview*. Reading, Massachusetts: Addison-Wesley Publishing Company, Inc., 1989.

2. Apple Computer, Inc. *Planning and Managing AppleTalk Networks*. Reading, Massachusetts: Addison-Wesley Publishing Company, Inc., 1991.

3. Documentation CD-ROM, Cisco Systems, Inc., 1998.

4. Jones, N.E.H., and D. Kosiur. *Macworld Networking Handbook*. San Mateo, California: IDG Books Worldwide, Inc., 1992.

5. Sidhu, G.S., R.F. Andrews, and A.B. Oppenheimer. *Inside AppleTalk*, 2nd ed. Reading, Massachusetts: Addison-Wesley Publishing Company, Inc., 1990.

Banyan VINES

Introduction

The Banyan Virtual Network Service (VINES) protocol is a networking system for microcomputers. This proprietary protocol was developed by Banyan Systems, Inc., and derived from the Xerox Network System (XNS) protocol.

VINES uses a client-server architecture in which clients request certain services, such as file and printer access, from servers. Along with Novell's Netware, VINES is one of the popular distributed system environments for PC-based networks.

VINES Overview

VINES uses the VINES Internetwork Protocol (VIP) to perform Layer 3 functions. It also supports its own Address Resolution Protocol (ARP), and the Internet Control Protocol (ICP), providing exception handling and special routing cost information. Some of the protocols in the VINES protocol stack include the following:

■ *StreetTalk* is an application-layer protocol used to maintain a distributed directory of the names of network resources such as file and print servers. Note that these resource names are global across the VINES internetwork and autonomous to the network topology.

■ *Network Remote Procedure Call (Net RPC)* spans across the presentation and session layers. It provides advanced process-to-process communication and remote procedure calls. Net RPC is derived from the Courier protocol in the XNS protocol suite.

■ *Interprocess Communication Protocol (ICP)* is a transport-layer protocol that provides reliable message service and unreliable datagram service. The reliable service provides reliable sequenced and acknowledged delivery of messages between network nodes. This message can be transmitted in a maximum of four VIP packets. The unreliable service sends packets in a best-effort delivery but with no acknowledgement from the destination.

■ *Sequenced Packet Protocol (SPP)* is also a transport-layer protocol derived from the SPP protocol in the XNS protocol suite, providing virtual connectivity services.

- *Routing Table Update (RTP)* is a network-layer protocol used to distribute network topology information prior to Version 5.5 of Banyan VINES. Routing updates are broadcast periodically by both client and server nodes. These packets inform neighbors of a node's existence and indicate whether the node is a client or service node. Service nodes (or routers) also include in each routing update packet a list of all known networks and the cost factors associated with reaching specific networks.

- *Sequenced Routing Table Update (SRTP),* similar to RTP, is a network-layer protocol used to distribute network topology information in Version 5.5 of Banyan VINES.

- *Address Resolution Protocol (ARP)* is also a network-layer protocol used for finding a node's DLC addresses from its IP address. It is used prior to Version 5.5 of Banyan VINES. When a client starts up, it broadcasts query request packets. All servers hearing this request will respond. The client chooses the first response and requests a host address from that particular server. The server responds with an address consisting of its own network address concatenated with a host (subnetwork) address of its own choosing. Typically client host addresses are assigned sequentially, starting with 0x8001. Server host addresses are always 1.

- *Sequenced Address Resolution Protocol (SARP)* has the same functionality as ARP but is used in Version 5.5 of Banyan VINES.

- *Internet Control Protocol (ICP)* is a network-layer protocol that broadcasts notification of errors and to note changes in network topology. ICP defines exception notification and metric notification packets. Exception notification packets provide information about network-layer abnormalities; metric notification packets contain information about the final transmission used to reach a client node.

- *VINES Internet Protocol (VIP)* is the core network-layer protocol that transfers datagrams throughout the network.

VINES Routing

To configure VINES routing, it must first be enabled on the router and then on each interface. Enabling VINES routing on the router starts the VINES Routing Table Protocol (RTP) process by default.

VINES Addresses

A VINES network address is 48 bits long and consists of a network number and a host (or node) number expressed in the format *network:host*.

The network number identifies a VINES logical network, which comprises a single server and a group of client nodes. The network number is 32 bits (4 bytes) long and is the serial number of the server (or service) node. The host number is 16 bits (2 bytes) long. For server nodes, the host number is always 1. For client nodes, the host number can have a value ranging from 0x8001 through 0xFFFE.

Cisco VINES Network Numbers

Cisco addresses are created from the lower 21 bits of the Ethernet or Token Ring interface MAC address. These bits are placed behind an assigned block hexadecimal address of 300. The router uses the resulting value as its network number. Note how the five routers in the scenario derive their network addresses. Code Listings 6-1 through 6-5 illustrate the Burnt-In-Addresses (BIA) of these five routers.

Code Listing 6-1
Details on R1's interface E0.

```
C4500-R1#show interface e0
Ethernet0 is up, line protocol is up
  Hardware is Lance, address is 0010.7b47.9398 (bia 0010.7b47.9398)
  MTU 1500 bytes, BW 10000 Kbit, DLY 1000 usec, rely 128/255, load 1/255
  Encapsulation ARPA, loopback not set, keepalive not set
  ARP type: ARPA, ARP Timeout 04:00:00
  Last input never, output 00:00:31, output hang never
  Last clearing of "show interface" counters never
  Queueing strategy: fifo
  Output queue 0/40, 0 drops; input queue 0/75, 0 drops
  5 minute input rate 0 bits/sec, 0 packets/sec
  5 minute output rate 0 bits/sec, 0 packets/sec
     0 packets input, 0 bytes, 0 no buffer
     Received 0 broadcasts, 0 runts, 0 giants, 0 throttles
     0 input errors, 0 CRC, 0 frame, 0 overrun, 0 ignored, 0 abort
     0 input packets with dribble condition detected
     1051 packets output, 163923 bytes, 0 underruns
     1051 output errors, 0 collisions, 2 interface resets
     0 babbles, 0 late collision, 0 deferred
     1051 lost carrier, 0 no carrier
     0 output buffer failures, 0 output buffers swapped out
```

Given the MAC address 0010.7b47.9398 illustrated in Code Listing 6-1, the aggregate hexadecimal value of the lower 21 bits of this address is

0007.9398. After a host value of 0001 is assigned to the router, the final network address for R1 will be 30079398:0001.

Code Listing 6-2

Details on R2's Interface E0.

```
C4500-R2#show interface e0
Ethernet0 is up, line protocol is up
  Hardware is Lance, address is 00e0.b02c.48e0 (bia 00e0.b02c.48e0)
  MTU 1500 bytes, BW 10000 Kbit, DLY 1000 usec, rely 128/255, load 1/255
  Encapsulation ARPA, loopback not set, keepalive not set
  ARP type: ARPA, ARP Timeout 04:00:00
  Last input never, output 00:00:05, output hang never
  Last clearing of "show interface" counters never
  Queueing strategy: fifo
  Output queue 0/40, 0 drops; input queue 0/75, 0 drops
  5 minute input rate 0 bits/sec, 0 packets/sec
  5 minute output rate 0 bits/sec, 0 packets/sec
     0 packets input, 0 bytes, 0 no buffer
     Received 0 broadcasts, 0 runts, 0 giants
     0 input errors, 0 CRC, 0 frame, 0 overrun, 0 ignored, 0 abort
     0 input packets with dribble condition detected
     1012 packets output, 164304 bytes, 0 underruns
     1012 output errors, 0 collisions, 3 interface resets
     0 babbles, 0 late collision, 0 deferred
     1012 lost carrier, 0 no carrier
     0 output buffer failures, 0 output buffers swapped out
```

Given the MAC address 00e0.b02c.48e0 illustrated in Code Listing 6-2, the aggregate hexadecimal value of the lower 21 bits of this address is 000c.48e0. After a host value of 0001 is assigned to the router, the final network address for R2 will be 300c48e0:0001.

Code Listing 6-3

Details on R3's interface E0.

```
C2500-R3#show interface e0
Ethernet0 is administratively down, line protocol is down
  Hardware is Lance, address is 00e0.1e5f.dd0d (bia 00e0.1e5f.dd0d)
  MTU 1500 bytes, BW 10000 Kbit, DLY 1000 usec, rely 252/255, load 1/255
  Encapsulation ARPA, loopback not set, keepalive set (10 sec)
  ARP type: ARPA, ARP Timeout 04:00:00
  Last input never, output 03:39:58, output hang never
  Last clearing of "show interface" counters never
  Queueing strategy: fifo
  Output queue 0/40, 0 drops; input queue 0/75, 0 drops
  5 minute input rate 0 bits/sec, 0 packets/sec
  5 minute output rate 0 bits/sec, 0 packets/sec
     0 packets input, 0 bytes, 0 no buffer
     Received 0 broadcasts, 0 runts, 0 giants
     0 input errors, 0 CRC, 0 frame, 0 overrun, 0 ignored, 0 abort
     0 input packets with dribble condition detected
     41 packets output, 8681 bytes, 0 underruns
     41 output errors, 0 collisions, 2 interface resets
     0 babbles, 0 late collision, 0 deferred
     41 lost carrier, 0 no carrier
     0 output buffer failures, 0 output buffers swapped out
```

Given the MAC address 00e0.1e5f.dd0d illustrated in Code Listing 6-3, the aggregate hexadecimal value of the lower 21 bits of this address is 001f.dd0d. After a host value of 0001 is assigned to the router, the final network address for R3 will be 301fdd0d:0001.

Code Listing 6-4

Details on R4's interface E0.

```
C2509-R4#show interface e0
Ethernet0 is up, line protocol is up
  Hardware is Lance, address is 00e0.1e5d.2db9 (bia 00e0.1e5d.2db9)
  MTU 1500 bytes, BW 10000 Kbit, DLY 1000 usec, rely 128/255, load 1/255
  Encapsulation ARPA, loopback not set, keepalive not set
  ARP type: ARPA, ARP Timeout 04:00:00
  Last input never, output 00:00:02, output hang never
  Last clearing of "show interface" counters never
  Queueing strategy: fifo
  Output queue 0/40, 0 drops; input queue 0/75, 0 drops
  5 minute input rate 0 bits/sec, 0 packets/sec
  5 minute output rate 0 bits/sec, 0 packets/sec
     0 packets input, 0 bytes, 0 no buffer
     Received 0 broadcasts, 0 runts, 0 giants, 0 throttles
     0 input errors, 0 CRC, 0 frame, 0 overrun, 0 ignored, 0 abort
     0 input packets with dribble condition detected
     901 packets output, 126450 bytes, 0 underruns
     901 output errors, 0 collisions, 3 interface resets
     0 babbles, 0 late collision, 0 deferred
     901 lost carrier, 0 no carrier
     0 output buffer failures, 0 output buffers swapped out
```

Given the MAC address 00e0.1e5d.2db9 illustrated in Code Listing 6-4, the aggregate hexadecimal value of the lower 21 bits of this address is 001d.2db9. After a host value of 0001 is assigned to the router, the final network address for R4 will be 301d2db9:0001.

Code Listing 6-5

Details on R5's interface E0.

```
C2500-R5#show interface e0
Ethernet0 is administratively down, line protocol is down
  Hardware is Lance, address is 00e0.1e5f.de09 (bia 00e0.1e5f.de09)
  MTU 1500 bytes, BW 10000 Kbit, DLY 1000 usec, rely 252/255, load 1/255
  Encapsulation ARPA, loopback not set, keepalive set (10 sec)
  ARP type: ARPA, ARP Timeout 04:00:00
  Last input never, output 03:46:10, output hang never
  Last clearing of "show interface" counters never
  Queueing strategy: fifo
  Output queue 0/40, 0 drops; input queue 0/75, 0 drops
  5 minute input rate 0 bits/sec, 0 packets/sec
  5 minute output rate 0 bits/sec, 0 packets/sec
     0 packets input, 0 bytes, 0 no buffer
     Received 0 broadcasts, 0 runts, 0 giants, 0 throttles
     0 input errors, 0 CRC, 0 frame, 0 overrun, 0 ignored, 0 abort
     0 input packets with dribble condition detected
     134 packets output, 21029 bytes, 0 underruns
```

```
134 output errors, 0 collisions, 1 interface resets
0 babbles, 0 late collision, 0 deferred
134 lost carrier, 0 no carrier
0 output buffer failures, 0 output buffers swapped out
```

Given the MAC address 00e0.1e5f.de09 illustrated in Code Listing 6-5, the aggregate hexadecimal value of the lower 21 bits of this address is 001f.de09. After a host value of 0001 is assigned to the router, the final network address for R5 will be 301fde09:0001.

Case Scenario

Figure 6-1 illustrates the overall network scenario that will be referenced throughout the chapter. This enterprise network spans five sites: Cleveland, Indiana, Milwaukee, San Antonio, and Utah. The Indiana office is internetworked to the Cleveland office by Frame Relay with an ISDN dial-up line that serves as backup in the event the Frame Relay connectivity becomes unavailable. Similarly the Cleveland office is interconnected to the Indiana and San Antonio offices through the same Frame Relay network. The Cleveland office is also linked to the Milwaukee office using X.25. The Utah office is linked to the San Antonio office through HDLC. Cleveland, Indiana, and San Antonio each has its own Virtual LAN whereby VINES workstations are connected. These workstations are also found in Milwaukee and Utah, except they are on Token Rings.

VINES Setup

Consider Figure 6-2. There are five VINES networks altogether. The routing protocol used is VINES RTP (the default).

Basic VINES Configuration

For basic VINES configuration, the respective LANs connected to R1, R2, R3, R4, and R5 will be configured accordingly, as illustrated in Code Listings 6-6 through 6-10. Subsequent sections will cover the WAN configurations.

Figure 6-1
The overall network
topology.

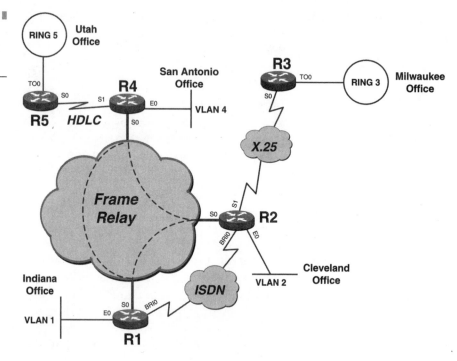

Figure 6-2
The overall VINES
network.

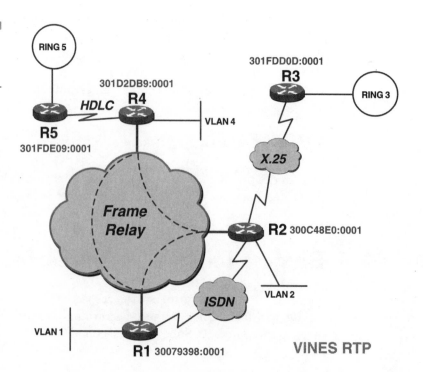

Code Listing 6-6
VINES configuration
for R1.

```
hostname C4500-R1
!
vines routing 30079398:0001
!
interface Ethernet0
 media-type 10BaseT
 vines metric 2
```

TABLE 6-1
Some delay metric
values

Interface Type	Default Delay Value	In Seconds
FDDI	1	0.2000
Ethernet	2	0.4000
16-Mb Token Ring	2	0.4000
4-Mb Token Ring	4	0.8000
T1 HDLC	35	7.0000
56-kb HDLC	45	9.0000
9600-baud HDLC	90	18.0000
4800-baud HDLC	150	30.0000
2400-baud HDLC	250	50.0000
1200-baud HDLC	450	90.0000
T1 X.25	45	9.0000
56-kb X.25	55	11.0000
9600-baud X.25	100	20.0000
4800-baud X.25	160	32.0000
2400-baud X.25	260	52.0000
1200-baud X.251	460	92.0000

1. Code Listing 6-6 illustrates the VINES configuration for R1. By default, VINES routing is not enabled. The global command `vines routing` enables VINES RTP routing on R1. To enable VINES SRTP (by default it is disabled), use the `vines srtp-enabled` global command after the `vines routing` command. When SRTP is enabled, the Cisco router will dynamically determine whether it needs to send RTP messages, SRTP messages, or both.

2. E0 is configured for 10BaseT media-type. The interface command `vines metric` enables VINES on E0. The optional delay metric parameter after the keyword `metric` can be set. If this parameter is not specified, the system will automatically choose a default value based on the interface type—in this case, Ethernet (see Table 6-1).

Code Listing 6-7
VINES configuration
for R2.

```
hostname C4500-R1
!
vines routing 30079398:0001
!
interface Ethernet0
 media-type 10BaseT
 vines metric 2
```

1. Code Listing 6-7 illustrates the VINES configuration for R2. By default, VINES routing is not enabled. The global command `vines routing` enables VINES RTP routing on R2.

2. E0 is configured for 10BaseT media-type. The interface command `vines metric` enables VINES on E0. The optional delay metric parameter after the keyword `metric` can be set. If this parameter is not specified, the system will automatically choose a default value based on the interface type—in this case, Ethernet (see Table 6-1).

Code Listing 6-8
VINES Configuration
for R3.

```
hostname C2500-R3
!
vines routing 301FDD0D:0001
!
interface TokenRing0
 vines metric 2
 ring-speed 16
```

1. Code Listing 6-8 illustrates the VINES configuration for R3. By default, VINES routing is not enabled. The global command `vines routing` enables VINES RTP routing on R3.

2. TO0 is configured for a ring speed of 16Mbps. The interface command `vines metric` enables VINES on TO0. The optional delay metric parameter after the keyword `metric` can be set. If this parameter is not specified, the system will automatically choose a default value based on the interface type—in this case, 16Mbps Token Ring (see Table 6-1).

Code Listing 6-9
VINES configuration
for R4.

```
hostname C2509-R4
!
vines routing 301D2DB9:0001
!
interface Ethernet0
 vines metric 2
```

1. Code Listing 6-9 illustrates the VINES configuration for R4. By default, VINES routing is not enabled. The global command `vines routing` enables VINES RTP routing on R4.

2. The interface command `vines metric` enables VINES on E0. The optional delay metric parameter after the keyword `metric` can be set. If this parameter is not specified, the system will automatically choose a default value based on the interface type—in this case, Ethernet (see Table 6-1).

Code Listing 6-10
VINES configuration for R5.

```
hostname C2500-R5
!
vines routing 301FDE09:0001
!
interface TokenRing0
 vines metric 2
 ring-speed 16
```

1. Code Listing 6-10 illustrates the VINES configuration for R5. By default, VINES routing is not enabled. The global command `vines routing` enables VINES RTP routing on R5.

2. TO0 is configured for a ring speed of 16Mbps. The interface command `vines metric` enables VINES on TO0. The optional delay metric parameter after the keyword `metric` can be set. If this parameter is not specified, the system will automatically choose a default value based on the interface type—in this case, 16Mbps Token Ring (see Table 6-1).

VINES over Frame Relay

Figure 6-3 zooms into the Frame Relay network where VINES is configured for R1, R2, and R4. Three PVCs are required to implement this fully meshed Frame Relay topology. Code Listings 6-11 through 6-13 illustrate this Frame Relay implementation.

Figure 6-3
VINES over Frame Relay.

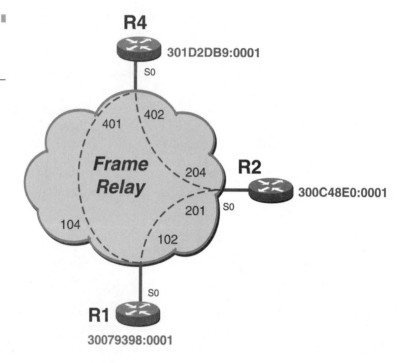

R4
301D2DB9:0001
S0

402
401
Frame Relay
204   R2
300C48E0:0001
201   S0
104
102

S0
R1
30079398:0001

Code Listing 6-11
VINES-over-Frame Relay configuration for R1.

```
hostname C4500-R1
!
vines routing 30079398:0001
!
interface Serial0
 encapsulation frame-relay
 bandwidth 56
 vines metric 45
 no vines split-horizon
 frame-relay map vines 300C48E0:0001 102 broadcast
 frame-relay map vines 301D2DB9:0001 104 broadcast
 frame-relay lmi-type ansi
```

1. Code Listing 6-11 illustrates the VINES-over-Frame Relay configuration for R1. The interface command `vines metric` enables VINES on S0. The `frame-relay map` command statically maps the VINES network addresses of R2 and R4 into their respective DLCIs. As the Frame Relay network has a fully meshed topology, R1 must implement a multipoint Serial interface. Note that a physical Frame Relay interface (in this case, S0) is by default multipoint.

2. Split horizon controls RTP update and query packets. If split horizon is enabled on an interface, these packets are not sent to a particular destination if this interface is the next hop to that destination. By default, split horizon is enabled on all interfaces; its mechanism optimizes communication among multiple routers, especially when links are broken. However, with NBMA networks like Frame Relay, situations can arise where this behavior is suboptimal. Even though the Frame Relay network is fully meshed, for illustration purposes, the interface command `no vines split-horizon` disables the split horizon mechanism for RTP on S0.

Code Listing 6-12
VINES-over-Frame
Relay configuration
for R2.

```
hostname C4500-R2
!
vines routing 300C48E0:0001
!
interface Serial0
 encapsulation frame-relay
 bandwidth 56
 vines metric 45
 no vines split-horizon
 frame-relay map vines 30079398:0001 201 broadcast
 frame-relay map vines 301D2DB9:0001 204 broadcast
 frame-relay lmi-type ansi
```

1. Code Listing 6-12 illustrates the VINES-over-Frame Relay configuration for R2. The interface command `vines metric` enables VINES on S0. The `frame-relay map` command statically maps the VINES network addresses of R1 and R4 into their respective DLCIs. As the Frame Relay network has a fully meshed topology, R2 must implement a multipoint Serial interface. Note that a physical Frame Relay interface (in this case, S0) is by default multipoint.

2. Split horizon controls RTP update and query packets. If split horizon is enabled on an interface, these packets are not sent to a particular destination if this interface is the next hop to that destination. By default, split horizon is enabled on all interfaces; its mechanism optimizes communication among multiple routers, especially when links are broken. However, with NBMA networks like Frame Relay, situations can arise where this behavior is suboptimal. Even though the Frame Relay network is fully meshed, for illustration purposes, the interface command `no vines split-horizon` disables the split horizon mechanism for RTP on S0.

```
hostname C2509-R4
!
vines routing 301D2DB9:0001
!
interface Serial0
 encapsulation frame-relay
 bandwidth 56
 vines metric 45
 no vines split-horizon
 frame-relay map vines 30079398:0001 401 broadcast
 frame-relay map vines 300C48E0:0001 402 broadcast
 frame-relay lmi-type ansi
```

1. Code Listing 6-13 illustrates the VINES-over-Frame Relay configuration for R4. The interface command `vines metric` enables VINES on S0. The `frame-relay map` command statically maps the VINES network addresses of R1 and R2 into their respective DLCIs. As the Frame Relay network has a fully meshed topology, R4 must implement a multipoint Serial interface. Note that a physical Frame Relay interface (in this case, S0) is by default multipoint.

2. Split horizon controls RTP update and query packets. If split horizon is enabled on an interface, these packets are not sent to a particular destination if this interface is the next hop to that destination. By default, split horizon is enabled on all interfaces; its mechanism optimizes communication among multiple routers, especially when links are broken. However, with NBMA networks like Frame Relay, situations can arise where this behavior is suboptimal. Even though the Frame Relay network is fully meshed, for illustration purposes, the interface command `no vines split-horizon` disable the split horizon mechanism for RTP on S0.

VINES over X.25

Figure 6-4 zooms into the X.25 network where VINES is implemented between R2 and R3. Code Listings 6-14 and 6-15 illustrate this.

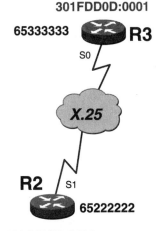

Figure 6-4
VINES over X.25.

301FDD0D:0001
65333333 R3
S0

X.25

R2 S1
65222222

300C48E0:0001

Code Listing 6-14
VINES-over-X.25 configuration for R2.

```
hostname C4500-R2
!
vines routing 300C48E0:0001
!
interface Serial1
 encapsulation x25
 bandwidth 56
 vines metric 55
 no vines split-horizon
 x25 address 65222222
 x25 map vines 301FDD0D:0001 65333333 broadcast
```

1. Code Listing 6-14 illustrates the VINES-over-X.25 configuration for R2. The interface command `vines metric` enables VINES on S1. The command `x25 map vines` creates a virtual circuit between R2 and R3 for routing VINES. The VINES and X.121 addresses used by the command are R3's.

2. Split horizon controls RTP update and query packets. If split horizon is enabled on an interface, these packets are not sent to a particular destination if this interface is the next hop to that destination. By default, split horizon is enabled on all interfaces; its mechanism optimizes communication among multiple routers, especially when links are broken. However, with NBMA networks like X.25, situations can arise where this behavior is suboptimal. The interface command `no vines split-horizon` disables the split horizon mechanism for RTP on S1.

```
hostname C2500-R3
!
vines routing 301FDD0D:0001
!
interface Serial0
 encapsulation x25
 bandwidth 56
 vines metric 55
 no vines split-horizon
 x25 address 65333333
 x25 map vines 300C48E0:0001 65222222 broadcast
```

1. Code Listing 6-15 illustrates the VINES-over-X.25 configuration for R3. The interface command `vines metric` enables VINES on S0. The command `x25 map vines` creates a virtual circuit between R3 and R2 for routing VINES. The VINES and X.121 addresses used by the command are R2's.

2. Split horizon controls RTP update and query packets. If split horizon is enabled on an interface, these packets are not sent to a particular destination if this interface is the next hop to that destination. By default, split horizon is enabled on all interfaces; its mechanism optimizes communication among multiple routers, especially when links are broken. However, with NBMA networks like X.25, situations can arise where this behavior is suboptimal. The interface command `no vines split-horizon` disables the split horizon mechanism for RTP on S0.

VINES over HDLC

Figure 6-5 shows the portion of network where VINES over HDLC is implemented between R4 and R5. Code Listings 6-16 and 6-17 illustrate this.

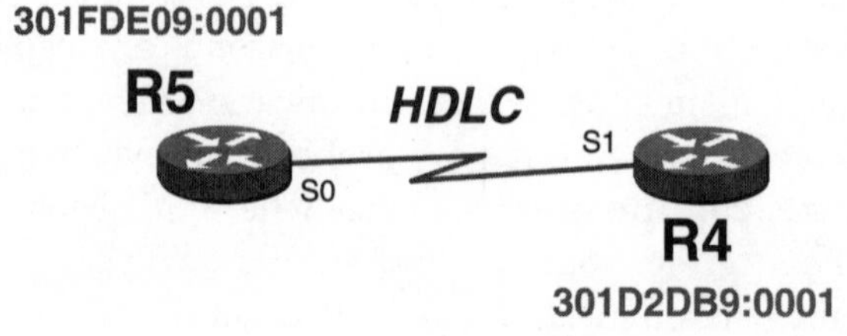

Figure 6-5
VINES over HDLC.

301FDE09:0001

R5 — HDLC — R4

301D2DB9:0001

Code Listing 6-16
VINES-over-HDLC
configuration for R4.

```
hostname C2509-R4
!
vines routing 301D2DB9:0001
!
interface Serial1
 bandwidth 56
 vines metric 45
```

To configure VINES over HDLC in R4, the interface command `vines metric` in Code Listing 6-16 enables VINES on S1.

Code Listing 6-17
VINES-over-HDLC
configuration for R5.

```
hostname C2500-R5
!
vines routing 301FDE09:0001
!
interface Serial0
 bandwidth 56
 vines metric 45
```

To configure VINES over HDLC in R5, the interface command `vines metric` in Code Listing 6-17 enables VINES on S0.

VINES over DDR

Figure 6-6 shows the portion of network where VINES over DDR is implemented between R1 and R2. DDR backs up the Frame Relay connectivity between R1 and R2. Code Listings 6-18 and 6-19 illustrate this DDR implementation.

Code Listing 6-18
VINES-over-DDR configuration for R1.

```
hostname C4500-R1
!
username C4500-R2 password 0 cisco
vines routing 30079398:0001
isdn switch-type basic-net3
!
interface Serial0
 backup delay 10 30
 backup interface BRI0
!
interface BRI0
 encapsulation ppp
 vines metric 45
```

Code Listing 6-18
(continued)

```
dialer map vines 300C48E0:0001 name C4500-R2 broadcast 3245652
dialer load-threshold 128 either
dialer-group 1
ppp authentication chap
!
dialer-list 1 protocol vines permit
```

Code Listing 6-18 illustrates the VINES-over-DDR configuration for R1. The interface command vines metric enables VINES on BRI0. The dialer map command dials up R2 to establish a PPP connection when S0 becomes unavailable. The VINES address, host name, and ISDN number used by the command are R2's. The dialer-group 1 command refers to dialer-list 1, and the list allows all VINES traffic to pass. No refining on the dialer-list is required, as the purpose of the BRI0 interface is to back up S0.

Code Listing 6-19
VINES-over-DDR configuration for R2.

```
hostname C4500-R2
!
username C4500-R1 password 7 0822455D0A16
vines routing 300C48E0:0001
isdn switch-type basic-net3
!
interface BRI0
 encapsulation ppp
 vines metric 45
 dialer idle-timeout 60
 dialer map vines 30079398:0001 name C4500-R1 broadcast
 dialer load-threshold 128 either
 dialer-group 1
 ppp authentication chap
!
dialer-list 1 protocol vines permit
```

Figure 6-6
VINES over DDR.

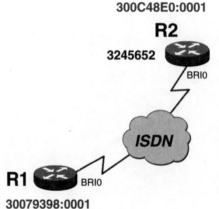

300C48E0:0001

R2

3245652

BRI0

ISDN

R1 BRI0

30079398:0001

Code Listing 6-19 illustrates the VINES-over-DDR configuration for R2. The interface command `vines metric` enables VINES on BRI0. The `dialer map` command establishes a PPP connectivity when R1 makes a call. Note that no ISDN number is supplied, as R1 will initiate the call. The VINES address and host name used by the command are R1's. The `dialer-group 1` command refers to `dialer-list 1`, and the list allows all VINES traffic to pass.

At this point, note the routing tables and neighbors' information on all the five routers in Code Listings 6-20 through 6-29.

Code Listing 6-20
VINES routing table for R1.

```
C4500-R1#show vines route
5 servers, 5 routes, version 67, next update 7 seconds

Network          Neighbor           Flags     Age     Metric     Uses
30079398         -                  C1        -        -          -
300C48E0         300C48E0:0001      RO*       19       02D0       0
301D2DB9         301D2DB9:0001      RO*       31       02D0       0
301FDD0D         300C48E0:0001      RO*       19       0640       34
301FDE09         301D2DB9:0001      RO*       31       05A0       0
```

Code Listing 6-21
R1's VINES neighbors.

```
C4500-R1#show vines neighbor
3 neighbors, 3 paths, version 6, next update 38 seconds

Address          Hardware Address   Type  Int    Flag Age  Metric   Uses
30079398:0001    -                  -     -      C    -    -        -
300C48E0:0001    102                FRAME Se0    RO*  78   02D0     66
301D2DB9:0001    104                FRAME Se0    RO*  0    02D0     83
```

Code Listing 6-22
VINES routing table for R2.

```
C4500-R2#show vines route.
5 servers, 5 routes, version 13, next update 4 seconds

Network          Neighbor           Flags     Age     Metric     Uses
30079398         30079398:0001      RO*       66       02D0       0
300C48E0         -                  C1        -        -          -
301D2DB9         301D2DB9:0001      RO*       38       02D0       -
301FDD0D         301FDD0D:0001      RO*       64       0370       0
301FDE09         301D2DB9:0001      RO*       38       05A0       0
```

Code Listing 6-23
R2's VINES neighbors.

```
C4500-R2#show vines neighbor
4 neighbors, 4 paths, version 6, next update 1 seconds

Address          Hardware Address   Type  Int    Flag Age  Metric   Uses
30079398:0001    201                FRAME Se0    RO*  62   02D0     60
300C48E0:0001    -                  -     -      C    -    -        -
301D2DB9:0001    204                FRAME Se0    RO*  10   02D0     12
301FDD0D:0001    65333333           X25   Se1    RO*  42   0370     164
```

Code Listing 6-24
VINES routing table for R3.

```
C2500-R3#show vines route
5 servers, 5 routes, version 25, next update 12 seconds
```

Network	Neighbor	Flags	Age	Metric	Uses
30079398	300C48E0:0001	R0*	33	0640	55
300C48E0	300C48E0:0001	R0*	33	0370	0
301D2DB9	300C48E0:0001	R0*	33	0640	12
301FDD0D	-	C1	-	-	-
301FDE09	300C48E0:0001	R0*	33	0910	0

Code Listing 6-25
R3's VINES neighbors.

```
C2500-R3#show vines neighbor
2 neighbors, 2 paths, version 2, next update 39 seconds
```

Address	Hardware Address	Type	Int	Flag	Age	Metric	Uses
300C48E0:0001	65222222	X25	Se0	R0*	6	0370	78
301FDD0D:0001	-	-	-	C	-	-	-

Code Listing 6-26
VINES routing table for R4.

```
C2509-R4#show vines route
5 servers, 5 routes, version 196, next update 37 seconds
```

Network	Neighbor	Flags	Age	Metric	Uses
30079398	30079398:0001	R0*	13	02D0	0
300C48E0	300C48E0:0001	R0*	39	02D0	0
301D2DB9	-	C1	-	-	-
301FDD0D	300C48E0:0001	R0*	39	0640	0
301FDE09	301FDE09:0001	R0*	21	02D0	0

Code Listing 6-27
R4's VINES neighbors.

```
C2509-R4#show vines neighbor
4 neighbors, 4 paths, version 5, next update 64 seconds
```

Address	Hardware Address	Type	Int	Flag	Age	Metric	Uses
30079398:0001	401	FRAME	Se0	R0*	76	02D0	7
300C48E0:0001	402	FRAME	Se0	R0*	12	02D0	89
301D2DB9:0001	-	-	-	C	-	-	-
301FDE09:0001	HDLC	HDLC	Se1	R0*	84	02D0	0

Code Listing 6-28
VINES routing table for R5.

```
C2500-R5#show vines route
5 servers, 5 routes, version 37, next update 60 seconds
```

Network	Neighbor	Flags	Age	Metric	Uses
30079398	301D2DB9:0001	R0*	60	05A0	26
300C48E0	301D2DB9:0001	R0*	60	05A0	0
301D2DB9	301D2DB9:0001	R0*	60	02D0	0
301FDD0D	301D2DB9:0001	R0*	60	0910	5
301FDE09	-	C1	-	-	-

Code Listing 6-29

R5's VINES neighbors.

```
C2500-R5#sh vines neighbor
2 neighbors, 2 paths, version 2, next update 86 seconds

Address          Hardware Address      Type  Int      Flag Age  Metric   Uses

301D2DB9:0001    HDLC                  HDLC  Se0      R0*  34   02D0     82
301FDE09:0001    -                     -     -        C    -    -        -
```

VINES RTP uses a delay metric and has a 90-second periodic update interval.

Consider Figure 6-7. The ISDN backup link will connect when the Frame Relay physical connectivity at R1 fails. Note the routing tables and neighbor information for R1 and R2 illustrated in Code Listings 6-30 through 6-33.

Figure 6-7

The Frame Relay physical connectivity at R1 becomes unavailable.

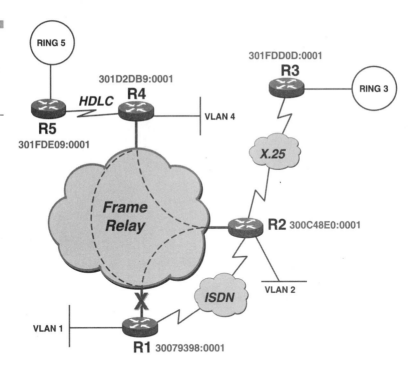

Code Listing 6-30
VINES Routing Table
for R1.

```
C4500-R1#show vines route
5 servers, 5 routes, version 107, next update 46 seconds

Network          Neighbor          Flags    Age      Metric    Uses
30079398         -                 C1       -        -         -
300C48E0         300C48E0:0001     R0*      225      02D0      0
301D2DB9         300C48E0:0001     R0*      225      05A0      0
301FDD0D         300C48E0:0001     R0*      225      0640      0
301FDE09         300C48E0:0001     R0*      225      0870      0
```

Code Listing 6-31
R1's VINES neighbors.

```
C4500-R1#sh vines neighbor
2 neighbors, 2 paths, version 7, next update 86 seconds

Address          Hardware Address    Type   Int      Flag Age  Metric   Uses
30079398:0001    -                   -      -        C    -    -        -
300C48E0:0001    PPP                 PPP    BR0      R0*  242  02D0     0
```

R1 now learns the VINES routes to the rest of the routers through its ISDN interface, BRI0, as illustrated in Code Listing 6-31.

Code Listing 6-32
VINES routing table
for R2.

```
C4500-R2#show vines route
5 servers, 5 routes, version 13, next update 10 seconds

Network          Neighbor          Flags    Age      Metric    Uses
30079398         30079398:0001     R0*      323      02D0      0
300C48E0         -                 C1       -        -         -
301D2DB9         301D2DB9:0001     R0*      1        02D0      0
301FDD0D         301FDD0D:0001     R0*      33       0370      0
301FDE09         301D2DB9:0001     R0*      1        05A0      0
```

Code Listing 6-33
R2's VINES neighbors.

```
C4500-R2#show vines neighbor
4 neighbors, 4 paths, version 7, next update 54 seconds

Address          Hardware Address    Type     Int    Flag Age  Metric   Uses
30079398:0001    PPP                 PPP      BR0    R0*  242  02D0     0
300C48E0:0001    -                   -        -      C    -    -        -
301D2DB9:0001    204                 FRAME    Se0    R0*  48   02D0     12
301FDD0D:0001    65333333            X25      Se1    R0*  79   0370     164
```

R2 now learns the VINES route to R1 through its ISDN interface, BRI0, as illustrated in Code Listing 6-33.

VINES Access Control

VINES has three types of access lists:

- Standard access lists have numbers ranging from 1 to 100. This type of access list restricts traffic based on: the protocol, source address, and mask; destination address and mask; and source and destination port numbers.

- Extended access lists have numbers ranging from 101 to 200. This type of access list restricts traffic in a manner similar to the standard access list, except the list can be further refined with masks for source and destination port numbers.

- Simple access lists have numbers ranging from 201 to 300. This type of access list restricts traffic just based on source address and source address mask. These access lists filter routing updates.

In this section, two applications of VINES access lists will be implemented: one uses a simple access list for route filtering, and the other uses a standard access list to deny access.

VINES Routing Table Filtering

Route filtering is applied on the S1 interface of R4 as shown in Figure 6-8. Code Listing 6-34 illustrates the implementation.

Code Listing 6-34
VINES route-filtering configuration for R4.

```
hostname C2509-R4
!
vines routing 301D2DB9:0001
!
interface Serial1
 bandwidth 56
 vines input-router-filter 201
 vines metric 45
!
vines access-list 201 deny    301FDE09:0001    00000000:0000
vines access-list 201 permit 00000000:0000    FFFFFFFF:FFFF
```

Code Listing 6-34 defines an access list that denies routing updates from R5 and permits routing updates from all other routers. The interface command `vines input-router-filter 201` filters incoming

Figure 6-8
VINES routing update
filtering.

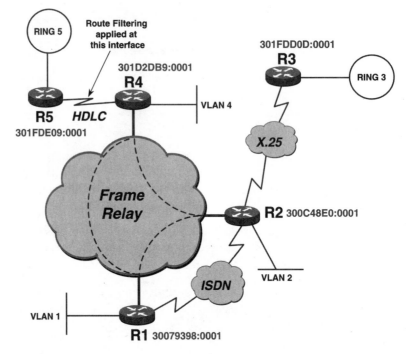

routing updates based on the source address of the received routing information—in this case, 301FDE09:0001.

Note the VINES routing tables in Code Listings 6-35 through 6-39. After router R4 applies the route filter on interface S1 of R4 against the incoming routing updates, R1, R2, R3, and R4 can no longer see the route 301FDE09:0001.

Code Listing 6-35
VINES routing table
for R1.

```
C4500-R1#show vines route
4 servers, 4 routes, version 66, next update 57 seconds

Network        Neighbor          Flags      Age    Metric    Uses
30079398       -                 C1         -      -         -
300C48E0       300C48E0:0001     RO*        59     02D0      0
301D2DB9       301D2DB9:0001     RO*        71     02D0      0
301FDD0D       300C48E0:0001     RO*        59     0640      34
```

Code Listing 6-36
VINES routing table
for R2.

```
C4500-R2#show vines route
4 servers, 4 routes, version 12, next update 22 seconds

Network          Neighbor          Flags     Age      Metric    Uses
30079398         30079398:0001     R0*       41       02D0      0
300C48E0         -                 C1        -        -         -
301D2DB9         301D2DB9:0001     R0*       80       02D0      0
301FDD0D         301FDD0D:0001     R0*       21       0370      0
```

Code Listing 6-37
VINES routing table
for R3.

```
C2500-R3#show vines route
4 servers, 4 routes, version 24, next update 58 seconds

Network          Neighbor          Flags     Age      Metric    Uses
30079398         300C48E0:0001     R0*       77       0640      55
300C48E0         300C48E0:0001     R0*       77       0370      0
301D2DB9         300C48E0:0001     R0*       77       0640      12
301FDD0D         -                 C1        -        -         -
```

Code Listing 6-38
VINES routing table
for R4.

```
C2509-R4#show vines route
4 servers, 4 routes, version 187, next update 81 seconds

Network          Neighbor          Flags     Age      Metric    Uses
30079398         30079398:0001     R0*       59       02D0      0
300C48E0         300C48E0:0001     R0*       86       02D0      0
301D2DB9         -                 C1        -        -         -
301FDD0D         300C48E0:0001     R0*       86       0640      79
```

Code Listing 6-39
VINES routing table
for R5.

```
C2500-R5#sh vines route
5 servers, 5 routes, version 37, next update 14 seconds

Network          Neighbor          Flags     Age      Metric    Uses
30079398         301D2DB9:0001     R0*       15       05A0      26
300C48E0         301D2DB9:0001     R0*       15       05A0      0
301D2DB9         301D2DB9:0001     R0*       15       02D0      0
301FDD0D         301D2DB9:0001     R0*       15       0910      5
301FDE09         -                 C1        -        -         -
```

VINES Traffic Filtering

In Figure 6-9, a VINES traffic filter is specified on the S1 interface of R2, permitting R1 to access R3. Code Listing 6-40 illustrates this.

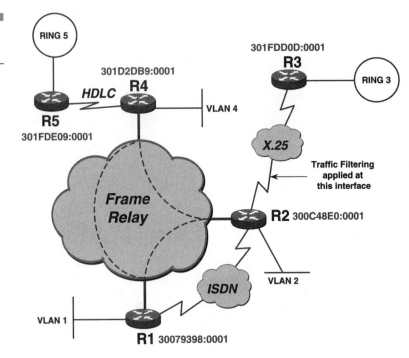

Figure 6-9
VINES traffic filtering.

Code Listing 6-40 VINES traffic-filtering configuration for R2.

```
hostname C4500-R2
!
vines routing 300C48E0:0001
!
interface Serial1
 encapsulation x25
 bandwidth 56
 vines access-group 1
 vines metric 55
 no vines split-horizon
 x25 address 65222222
 x25 map vines 301FDD0D:0001 65333333 broadcast
!
vines access-list 1   permit IP  30079398:0001   00000000:0000   301FDD0D:0001   00000000:0000
```

Code Listing 6-40 defines an access list that permits VINES Internet
Protocol (IP) traffic from R1 to R3, and vice versa. The interface command `vines access-group 1` filters outgoing VINES IP traffic based
on the source address 30079398:0001 (R1's address), and the destination
address 301FDD0D:0001 (R3's address).

In Code Listing 6-41, after applying the VINES IP traffic filter on interface S1 of R2 against the outgoing traffic, a VINES ping can no longer be performed from R4 and R5 to the R3's VINES address 301FDD0D:0001. Likewise, R3 cannot ping to R4 and R5 now. Note that R2 can still ping to R3, because standard and extended access lists are not designed to block packets that originate within the router. This means the outbound VINES standard access list does not prevent R2 from pinging R3, and vice versa.

■ |

Code Listing 6-41

VINES ping results.

```
C4500-R1#ping  301FDD0D:0001
Type escape sequence to abort.
Sending 5, 100-byte Vines Echoes to 301FDD0D:0001, timeout is 2 seconds:
!!!!!
Success rate is 100 percent (5/5), round-trip min/avg/max = 100/100/104 ms


C4500-R2#ping  301FDD0D:0001
Type escape sequence to abort.
Sending 5, 100-byte Vines Echoes to 301FDD0D:0001, timeout is 2 seconds:
!!!!!
Success rate is 100 percent (5/5), round-trip min/avg/max = 36/36/36 ms


C2509-R4#ping  301FDD0D:0001
Type escape sequence to abort.
Sending 5, 100-byte Vines Echoes to 301FDD0D:0001, timeout is 2 seconds:
.....
Success rate is 0 percent (0/5)


C2500-R5#ping  301FDD0D:0001
Type escape sequence to abort.
Sending 5, 100-byte Vines Echoes to 301FDD0D:0001, timeout is 2 seconds:
.....
Success rate is 0 percent (0/5)



C2500-R3#ping 30079398:0001
Type escape sequence to abort.
Sending 5, 100-byte Vines Echoes to 30079398:0001, timeout is 2 seconds:
!!!!!
Success rate is 100 percent (5/5), round-trip min/avg/max = 100/104/120 ms


C2500-R3#ping 300C48E0:0001
Type escape sequence to abort.
Sending 5, 100-byte Vines Echoes to 300C48E0:0001, timeout is 2 seconds:
!!!!!
Success rate is 100 percent (5/5), round-trip min/avg/max = 36/36/36 ms


C2500-R3#ping 301D2DB9:0001
Type escape sequence to abort.
Sending 5, 100-byte Vines Echoes to 301D2DB9:0001, timeout is 2 seconds:
.....
Success rate is 0 percent (0/5)


C2500-R3#ping 301FDE09:0001
Type escape sequence to abort.
Sending 5, 100-byte Vines Echoes to 301FDE09:0001, timeout is 2 seconds:
.....
Success rate is 0 percent (0/5)
```

Summary

This chapter covered VINES, a routable protocol that implements a distributed network operating system (NOS) based on a proprietary protocol family derived from the Xerox Network Systems (XNS) protocols.

In the scenario, VINES were first implemented in a LAN environment and expanded to VINES over Frame Relay, X.25, HDLC, and DDR.

In the final section, VINES access lists were used to filter unwanted VINES routes and excessive VINES IP traffic. These access lists can help to manage and control VINES traffic in a more efficient and effective manner. Moreover, they are useful for providing better network security.

References

1. Banyan Systems, Inc. VINES Protocol Definition. DA254-00, Rev. 1.0. February 1990.

2. Documentation CD-ROM, Cisco Systems, Inc., 1998.

3. Miller, M. A. *LAN Protocol Handbook*. San Mateo, California: MT&T Books, 1990.

4. Stallings, W. *Data and Computer Communications*. New York: Macmillan Publishing Company, 1991.

5. Sunshine, C. A., ed. *Computer Network Architectures and Protocols*, 2nd ed. New York: Plenum Press, 1989.

6. Tannenbaum, A. S. *Computer Networks*, 2nd ed. Englewood Cliffs, New Jersey: Prentice Hall, 1988.

DECnet

Introduction

The DECnet protocol family was developed by Digital Equipment Corporation (Digital) to provide a way for its computers to communicate with each other. DECnet is currently in its fifth generation, commonly referred to as DECnet Phase V or DECnet/OSI. DECnet Phase V is the superset of the OSI protocol suite and is compatible with Phase IV.

DECnet Overview

Both proprietary and standard protocols are defined in Digital's Digital Network Architecture (DNA). Some of the protocols in the DECnet protocol suite are:

■ Maintenance Operations Protocol (MOP): an application-layer protocol used for network maintenance services that include downline loading, upline dumping, remote testing, and problem diagnosis.

■ Local Area Transport (LAT): an application-layer protocol that handles multiplexed terminal (keyboard and screen) traffic to and from timesharing hosts.

■ Network Services Protocol (NSP): a transport-layer protocol providing reliable message transmission over virtual circuits. NSP's functions include establishing and tearing down logical links, error control, flow control, and segmentation and reassembly of messages.

■ Transport Protocol (TP): a transport-layer protocol supporting five different classes: Class 0 (TP0); Simple Class, for connectionless networks; Class 4 (TP4); Error Detection and Recovery Class, for connection-oriented networks; and the intermediate Class 2 (TP2), Multiplexing Class.

■ DECnet (Phase IV) Routing Protocol (DRP): a network layer protocol that moves packets from source nodes, through routers, between and within areas, and to end nodes.

■ Connectionless Network Service (CLNS): also known as ISO IP, functions at the network layer. CLNS provides a service interface to the transport layer in which a request to transfer data receives best-effort delivery.

- End-System-to-Intermediate-System Routing (ES-IS Routing): functions at the network layer and exchanges routing information between routers and hosts.

- Intermediate-System-to-Intermediate-System Routing (IS-IS Routing): functions at the network layer and exchanges routing information between routers.

DECnet Phase IV Routing

Before DECnet Phase IV routing can be configured, it must first be enabled on the router and then on each interface. Enabling DECnet Phase IV routing on the router starts the routing process and assigns an *area.node* address to the entire router.

DECnet identifies two types of nodes, end nodes and routing nodes. Both end nodes and routing nodes can transmit and receive network information, but only routing nodes can provide routing services for other DECnet nodes.

DECnet routing nodes are referred to as either Level 1 or Level 2 routers. A Level 1 router communicates with end nodes and with other Level 1 routers in a particular area. Level 2 routers communicate with Level 1 routers in the same area and with Level 2 routers in different areas. Together Level 1 and Level 2 routers form a hierarchical routing scheme. End systems send routing requests to a designated Level 1 router. The Level 1 router with the highest priority is elected to be the designated router. If two routers have the same priority, the one with the larger node number becomes the designated router. A router's priority can be manually configured to force it to become the designated router. Multiple Level 2 routers can exist in any area. When a Level 1 router wishes to send a packet outside its area, it forwards the packet to a Level 2 router in the same area.

DECnet routing decisions are based on cost, an arbitrary measure assigned and used in comparing various available paths in a DECnet internetwork. Cost is typically based on hop count, media bandwidth, or other measures. The best path is based on the lowest cost. When a network exception (or fault) happens, the DECnet Phase IV routing protocol uses cost values to recompute the best paths to each destination.

DECnet Addresses

A DECnet network address is 16 bits long and consists of an area and a node number expressed as decimal values in the format *area.node*.

DECnet addresses are not associated with the physical networks where nodes are connected. Rather, DECnet locates hosts using the *area.node* address pairs. The area is six bits long and can range from 1 to 63, inclusive. The node number is 10 bits in length and can range from 1 to 1023, inclusive. Therefore, each area can have a maximum of 1023 nodes, and approximately 65,000 nodes can be addressed in a DECnet network.

Determining DECnet MAC Addresses

DECnet hosts do not use manufacturer-assigned MAC addresses. Instead, network addresses are embedded in MAC addresses using an algorithm that multiples the area number by 1024 and then adds in the node number. The resulting 16-bit decimal is converted to a hexadecimal number and concatenated to the address AA00.0400 in byte-swapped order, with the least significant byte first. Note how the five routers in the scenario derive their DECnet MAC addresses.

R1's DECnet address is 8.1. The area number, 8, multiplied by 1024 gives 8192, and adding in the node number, 1, gives the aggregate decimal value of 8193. Converting 8193 to hexadecimal gives 0x2001. Appending this hexadecimal number to AA00.0400 in byte-swapped order, with the least significant byte first, results in DECnet MAC address AA00.0400.0120.

R2's DECnet address is 8.2. The area number, 8, multiplied by 1024 gives 8192, and adding in the node number, 2, gives the aggregate decimal value of 8194. Converting 8194 to hexadecimal gives 0x2002. Appending this hexadecimal number to AA00.0400 in byte-swapped order, with the least significant byte first, results in DECnet MAC address AA00.0400.0220.

R3's DECnet address is 8.3. The area number, 8, multiplied by 1024 gives 8192, and adding in the node number, 3, gives the aggregate decimal value of 8195. Converting 8195 to hexadecimal gives 0x2003. Appending this hexadecimal number to AA00.0400 in byte-swapped order, with the least significant byte first, results in DECnet MAC address AA00.0400.0320.

R4's DECnet address is 8.4. The area number, 8, multiplied by 1024 gives 8192, and adding in the node number, 4, gives the aggregate decimal value of 8196. Converting 8196 to hexadecimal gives 0x2004. Appending this hexadecimal number to AA00.0400 in byte-swapped order, with the least significant byte first, results in DECnet MAC address AA00.0400.0420.

R5's DECnet address is 8.5. The area number, 8, multiplied by 1024 gives 8192, and adding in the node number, 5, gives the aggregate decimal value of 8197. Converting 8197 to hexadecimal gives 0x2005. Appending this hexadecimal number to AA00.0400 in byte-swapped order, with the least significant byte first, results in DECnet MAC address AA00.0400.0520.

Note that these MAC address derivations are done automatically by the Cisco routers once DECnet Phase IV routing is enabled on them. Hence, no other forms of configuration are required.

Case Scenario

Figure 7-1 illustrates the overall network scenario that will be referenced throughout this chapter. This enterprise network spans five sites: Denver, Minnesota, New Orleans, Raleigh, and Washington. The Raleigh office is internetworked to the New Orleans office by HDLC with an ISDN dial-up line serving as backup in the event the HDLC connectivity becomes unavailable. The Raleigh office is also interconnected to the Denver and Minnesota offices through a Frame Relay network. Lastly, the New Orleans office is linked to the Washington office using X.25. Each office has its own Virtual LAN where VMS (Virtual Memory System) hosts are connected. Denver and Minnesota also have these hosts on Token Rings.

DECnet Setup

Consider Figure 7-2. There are five different DECnet nodes, all in the same Area 8. The routing protocol used is DECnet Phase IV routing.

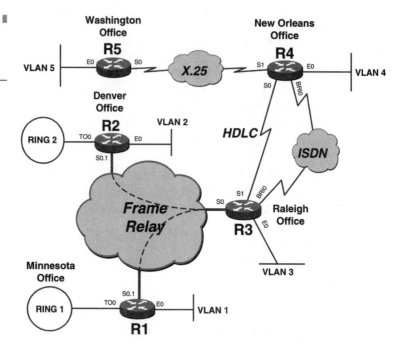

Figure 7-1
The overall network topology.

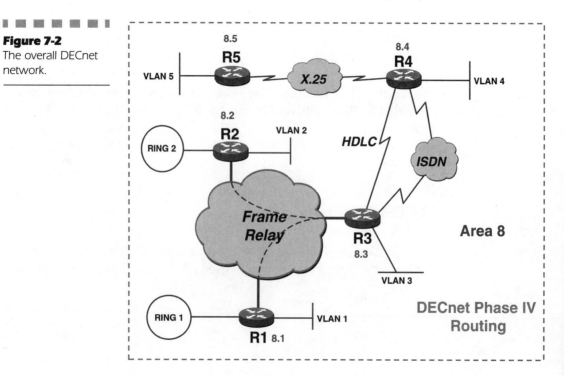

Figure 7-2
The overall DECnet network.

Basic DECnet Configuration

In this section, DECnet is configured for the respective LANs that are connected to R1, R2, R3, R4, and R5, as illustrated in Code Listings 7-1 through 7-5. Subsequent sections cover the WAN configurations.

Code Listing 7-1
DECnet configuration for R1.

```
hostname C2500-R1
!
decnet routing 8.1
decnet node-type routing-iv
!
interface Ethernet0
 decnet cost 1
!
interface TokenRing0
 decnet cost 1
 ring-speed 16
```

1. Code Listing 7-1 illustrates the DECnet configuration for R1. By default, DECnet routing is not enabled. The global command `dec-net routing` enables DECnet Phase IV routing on R1 and assigns a DECnet address, 8.1 (Area 8, Node 1), to the entire router. R1 is configured for Level 1 routing using the default command, `decnet node-type routing-iv`. Note that enabling DECnet changes the MAC addresses of the router's interfaces. If DECnet and IPX routing run concurrently on a router, the DECnet routing should be enabled first, followed by the IPX routing (without specifying the optional MAC address).

2. The interface command `decnet cost` enables DECnet on E0, and TO and assigns a cost (1 to 63) of 1 to these interfaces. Note that there are no default costs; therefore, it is mandatory to assign a cost to each interface.

Code Listing 7-2
DECnet configuration for R2.

```
hostname C2500-R2
!
decnet routing 8.2
decnet node-type routing-iv
!
interface Ethernet0
 decnet cost 2
!
interface TokenRing0
 decnet cost 2
 ring-speed 16
```

1. Code Listing 7-2 illustrates the DECnet configuration for R2. By default, DECnet routing is not enabled. The global command `decnet routing` enables DECnet Phase IV routing on R2 and assigns a DECnet address, 8.2 (Area 8, Node 2), to the entire router. R2 is configured for Level 1 routing using the default command, `decnet node-type routing-iv`.

2. The interface command `decnet cost` enables DECnet on E0, and TO0 and assigns a cost (1 to 63) of 2 to these interfaces.

Code Listing 7-3
DECnet configuration for R3.

```
hostname C4500-R3
!
decnet routing 8.3
decnet node-type routing-iv
!
interface Ethernet0
 media-type 10BaseT
 decnet cost 3
```

1. Code Listing 7-3 illustrates the DECnet configuration for R3. By default, DECnet routing is not enabled. The global command `decnet routing` enables DECnet Phase IV routing on R3 and assigns a DECnet address, 8.3 (Area 8, Node 3), to the entire router. R3 is configured for Level 1 routing using the default command, `decnet node-type routing-iv`.

2. E0 is configured for 10BaseT media-type. The interface command `decnet cost` enables DECnet on E0 and assigns a cost (1 to 63) of 3 to the interface.

Code Listing 7-4
DECnet configuration for R4.

```
hostname C4500-R4
!
decnet routing 8.4
decnet node-type routing-iv
!
interface Ethernet0
 media-type 10BaseT
 decnet cost 4
```

1. Code Listing 7-4 illustrates the DECnet configuration for R4. By default, DECnet routing is not enabled. The global command `decnet routing` enables DECnet Phase IV routing on R4 and assigns a DECnet address, 8.4 (Area 8, Node 4), to the entire router. R4 is

configured for Level 1 routing using the default command, decnet node-type routing-iv.

2. E0 is configured for 10BaseT media-type. The interface command decnet cost enables DECnet on E0 and assigns a cost (1 to 63) of 4 to the interface.

Code Listing 7-5
DECnet configuration for R5.

```
hostname C2509-R5
!
decnet routing 8.5
decnet node-type routing-iv
!
interface Ethernet0
 decnet cost 5
```

1. Code Listing 7-5 illustrates the DECnet configuration for R5. By default, DECnet routing is not enabled. The global command dec-net routing enables DECnet Phase IV routing on R5 and assigns a DECnet address, 8.5 (Area 8, Node 5), to the entire router. R5 is configured for Level 1 routing using the default command, decnet node-type routing-iv.

2. The interface command decnet cost enables DECnet on E0 and assigns a cost (1 to 63) of 3 to the interface.

DECnet over Frame Relay

Figure 7-3 zooms into the Frame Relay network where DECnet is configured for R1, R2, and R3. This is a hub-and-spoke Frame Relay topology, where R3 is the hub router interconnecting the two spoke routers, R1 and R2. Code Listings 7-6 through 7-8 illustrate this.

Code Listing 7-6 illustrates the DECnet-over-Frame Relay configuration for R1. In the Frame Relay scenario, R1 is a spoke router. Hence a point-to-point subinterface, S0.1, interconnects it to the hub router, R3. The interface command decnet cost enables DECnet on S0.1 and assigns a cost (1 to 63) of 3 to the interface. The frame-relay inter-face-dlci command defines the local DLCI, 103, for R1.

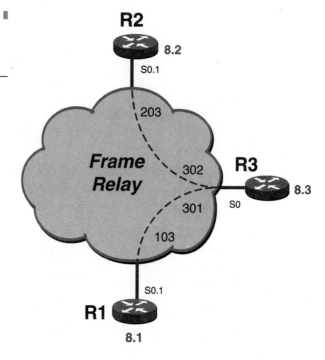

Figure 7-3
DECnet over Frame
Relay.

Code Listing 7-6
DECnet-over-Frame
Relay configuration
for R1.

```
hostname C2500-R1
!
decnet routing 8.1
decnet node-type routing-iv
!
interface Serial0
 encapsulation frame-relay
 frame-relay lmi-type ansi
!
interface Serial0.1 point-to-point
bandwidth 56
 decnet cost 3
 frame-relay interface-dlci 103
```

Code Listing 7-7
DECnet-over-Frame
Relay configuration
for R2.

```
hostname C2500-R2
!
decnet routing 8.2
decnet node-type routing-iv
!
interface Serial0
 encapsulation frame-relay
 frame-relay lmi-type ansi
```

Code Listing 7-7
(continued)

```
!
interface Serial0.1 point-to-point
 bandwidth 56
 decnet cost 3
 frame-relay interface-dlci 203
```

Code Listing 7-7 illustrates the DECnet-over-Frame Relay configuration for R2. R2 is also a spoke router. The point-to-point subinterface, S0.1, interconnects it to the hub router, R3. The interface command decnet cost enables DECnet on S0.1 and assigns a cost (1 to 63) of 3 to the interface. The frame-relay interface-dlci command specifies the local DLCI, 203, for R2.

Code Listing 7-8
DECnet-over-Frame
Relay configuration
for R3.

```
hostname C4500-R3
!
decnet routing 8.3
decnet node-type routing-iv
!
interface Serial0
 encapsulation frame-relay
 bandwidth 56
 decnet cost 3
 no decnet split-horizon
 frame-relay map decnet 8.1 301 broadcast
 frame-relay map decnet 8.2 302 broadcast
 frame-relay lmi-type ansi
```

1. Code Listing 7-8 illustrates the DECnet-over-Frame Relay configuration for R3. The interface command decnet cost enables DECnet on S0 and assigns a cost (1 to 63) of 3 to the interface. The frame-relay map command statically maps the DECnet node addresses of R1 and R2 into their respective DLCIs. As R3 is the hub router, a multipoint Serial interface is required to interconnect the spoke routers, R1 and R2. In this instance, the physical interface S0, which is by default multipoint, is used.

2. Split horizon controls DECnet Phase IV routing update and query packets. If split horizon is enabled on an interface, these packets are not sent to a particular destination if this interface is the next hop to that destination. By default, split horizon is enabled on all interfaces; its mechanism optimizes communication among multiple routers, especially when links are broken. However, with NBMA networks like Frame Relay, situations can arise where this behavior is suboptimal. The interface command no decnet split-

horizon disables the split-horizon mechanism for DECnet Phase IV routing on S0.

DECnet over X.25

Figure 7-4 zooms into the X.25 network where DECnet is implemented between R4 and R5. Code Listings 7-9 and 7-10 illustrate the X.25 implementation.

Code Listing 7-9
DECnet-over-X.25 configuration for R4.

```
hostname C4500-R4
!
decnet routing 8.4
decnet node-type routing-iv
!
interface Serial1
 encapsulation x25
 bandwidth 56
 decnet cost 5
 x25 address 6544444444
 x25 map decnet 8.5 6555555555 broadcast
```

Code Listing 7-9 illustrates the DECnet-over-X.25 configuration for R4. The interface command decnet cost enables DECnet on S1 and assigns a cost (1 to 63) of 5 to the interface. The command x25 map decnet creates a virtual circuit between R4 and R5 for routing DECnet packets. The DECnet and X.121 addresses used by the command are R5's.

Code Listing 7-10
DECnet-over-X.25 configuration for R5.

```
hostname C2509-R5
!
decnet routing 8.5
decnet node-type routing-iv
!
interface Serial0
 encapsulation x25
 decnet cost 5
 x25 address 6555555555
 x25 map decnet 8.4 6544444444 broadcast
```

Code Listing 7-10 illustrates the DECnet-over-X.25 configuration for R5. The interface command decnet cost enables DECnet on S0 and

Figure 7-4
DECnet over X.25.

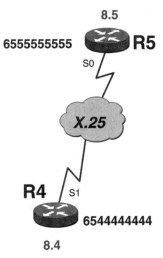

assigns a cost (1 to 63) of 5 to the interface. The command `x25 map decnet` creates a virtual circuit between R5 and R4 for routing DECnet packets. The DECnet and X.121 addresses used by the command are R4's.

DECnet over HDLC

Figure 7-5 shows the portion of network where DECnet over HDLC is implemented between R3 and R4. Code Listings 7-11 and 7-12 illustrate this.

Figure 7-5
DECnet over HDLC.

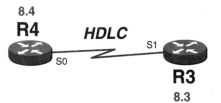

Code Listing 7-11
DECnet-over-HDLC
configuration for R3.

```
hostname C4500-R3
!
decnet routing 8.3
decnet node-type routing-iv
!
interface Serial1
 bandwidth 56
 decnet cost 4
```

Code Listing 7-11 illustrates the DECnet-over-HDLC configuration for R3. To configure DECnet over HDLC in R3, the interface command dec-net cost enables DECnet on S1 and assigns a cost (1 to 63) of 4 to this interface.

Code Listing 7-12
DECnet-over-HDLC
configuration for R4.

```
hostname C4500-R4
!
decnet routing 8.4
decnet node-type routing-iv
!
interface Serial0
 bandwidth 56
 decnet cost 4
```

Code Listing 7-12 illustrates the DECnet-over-HDLC configuration for R4. To configure DECnet over HDLC in R4, the interface command dec-net cost enables DECnet on S0 and assigns a cost (1 to 63) of 4 to this interface.

DECnet over DDR

Figure 7-6 shows the portion of the network where DECnet over DDR is implemented between R3 and R4. In this case, DDR backs up the HDLC link between R3 and R4 in the event it becomes unavailable. Code Listings 7-13 and 7-14 illustrate the DDR implementation.

Figure 7-6
DECnet over DDR.

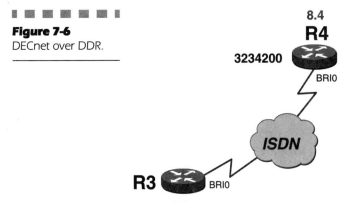

8.4
R4
3234200
BRI0

ISDN

R3 BRI0
8.3

Code Listing 7-13
DECnet-over-DDR
configuration for R3.

```
hostname C4500-R3
!
username C4500-R4 password 0 cisco
!
decnet routing 8.3
decnet node-type routing-iv
!
isdn switch-type basic-net3
!
interface Serial1
 backup delay 10 30
 backup interface BRI0
 decnet cost 4
!
interface BRI0
 encapsulation ppp
 decnet cost 4
 dialer idle-timeout 60
 dialer map decnet 8.4 name C4500-R4 broadcast 3234200
 dialer load-threshold 128 either
 dialer-group 1
 ppp authentication chap
!
dialer-list 1 protocol decnet permit
```

Code Listing 7-13 illustrates the DECnet-over-DDR configuration for R3. The interface command decnet cost enables DECnet on BRI0 and assigns a cost (1 to 63) of 4 to this interface. The dialer map command dials up R4 to establish a PPP connection when S1 becomes unavailable. The DECnet address, host name, and ISDN number used by the command are R4's. The dialer-group 1 command refers to dialer-list 1, and the list allows all DECnet traffic to pass. No refining on the dialer-list is required, as the purpose of the BRI0 interface is to back up S1.

Code Listing 7-14
DECnet-over-DDR
configuration for R4.

```
hostname C4500-R4
!
username C4500-R3 password 0 cisco
!
decnet routing 8.4
decnet node-type routing-iv
!
isdn switch-type basic-net3
!
interface BRI0
 encapsulation ppp
 decnet cost 4
 dialer idle-timeout 60
 dialer map decnet 8.3 name C4500-R3 broadcast
 dialer load-threshold 128 either
 dialer-group 1
 ppp authentication chap
!
dialer-list 1 protocol decnet permit
```

Code Listing 7-14 illustrates the DECnet-over-DDR configuration for R4. The interface command decnet cost enables DECnet on BRI0 and assigns a cost (1 to 63) of 4 to this interface. The dialer map command establishes a PPP connection when R3 makes a call. Note that no ISDN number is supplied here, as R3 will initiate the call. The DECnet address and host name used by the command are R3's. The dialer-group 1 command refers to dialer-list 1, and the list allows all DECnet traffic to pass.

Note the DECnet routing tables for all five routers in Code Listings 7-15 through 7-19.

Code Listing 7-15
DECnet routing table
for R1.

```
C2500-R1#show decnet route
  Node      Cost  Hops          Next Hop to Node Expires  Prio
 *8.1        0     0             (Local)  -> 8.1
 *8.2        6     2             Serial0.1 -> 8.3
 *8.3        3     1             Serial0.1 -> 8.3          35    64  V
 *8.4        7     2             Serial0.1 -> 8.3
 *8.5       12     3             Serial0.1 -> 8.3
```

Code Listing 7-16
DECnet routing table
for R2.

```
C2500-R2#show decnet route
  Node      Cost  Hops          Next Hop to Node Expires  Prio
 *8.1        6     2             Serial0.1 -> 8.3
 *8.2        0     0             (Local)  -> 8.2
 *8.3        3     1             Serial0.1 -> 8.3          45    64  V
 *8.4        7     2             Serial0.1 -> 8.3
 *8.5       12     3             Serial0.1 -> 8.3
```

Code Listing 7-17
DECnet routing table for R3.

```
C4500-R3#show decnet route
   Node      Cost   Hops       Next Hop to Node Expires   Prio
  *8.1        3      1         Serial0 -> 8.1   42         64   V
  *8.2        3      1         Serial0 -> 8.2   43         64   V
  *8.3        0      0         (Local) -> 8.3
  *8.4        4      1         Serial1 -> 8.4   42         64   V
  *8.5        9      2         Serial1 -> 8.4
```

Code Listing 7-18
DECnet routing table for R4.

```
C4500-R4#show decnet route
   Node      Cost   Hops       Next Hop to Node Expires   Prio
  *8.1        7      2         Serial0 -> 8.3
  *8.2        7      2         Serial0 -> 8.3
  *8.3        4      1         Serial0 -> 8.3   31         64   V
  *8.4        0      0         (Local) -> 8.4
  *8.5        5      1         Serial1 -> 8.5   31         64   V
```

Code Listing 7-19
DECnet routing table for R5.

```
C2509-R5#show decnet route
   Node      Cost   Hops       Next Hop to Node Expires   Prio
  *8.1       12      3         Serial0 -> 8.4
  *8.2       12      3         Serial0 -> 8.4
  *8.3        9      2         Serial0 -> 8.4
  *8.4        5      1         Serial0 -> 8.4            38         64   V
  *8.5        0      0         (Local) -> 8.5
```

In Code Listings 7-15 through 7-19, 64 denotes the default router priority of the DECnet node, and V represents an adjacent Level 1 router. DECnet Phase IV routing is a distance-vector routing protocol that uses path cost as its metric. It has a 40-second periodic update interval.

Consider Figure 7-7. The ISDN backup link will connect when the HDLC physical connectivity at R3 fails. Note the DECnet routing tables for R3 and R4 in Code Listings 7-20 and 7-21.

Code Listing 7-20
DECnet routing table for R3.

```
C4500-R3#show decnet route
   Node      Cost   Hops       Next Hop to Node Expires   Prio
  *8.1        3      1         Serial0 -> 8.1   44         64   V
  *8.2        3      1         Serial0 -> 8.2   45         64   V
  *8.3        0      0         (Local) -> 8.3
  *8.4        4      1             BRI0 -> 8.4   45         64   V
  *8.5        9      2             BRI0 -> 8.4
```

As illustrated in Code Listing 7-20, R3 now learns the DECnet routes to R4 and R5 through its ISDN interface, BRI0.

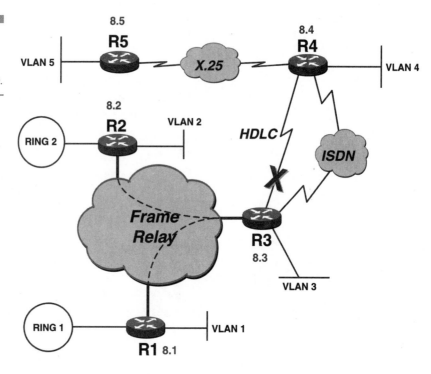

Figure 7-7
The HDLC link between R3 and R4 becomes unavailable.

Code Listing 7-21
DECnet routing table for R4.

```
C4500-R4#sh decnet route
   Node      Cost   Hops            Next Hop to Node Expires  Prio
*8.1         7      2                  BRI0 -> 8.3
*8.2         7      2                  BRI0 -> 8.3
*8.3         4      1                  BRI0 -> 8.3      44       64   V
*8.4         0      0               (Local) -> 8.4
*8.5         5      1               Serial1 -> 8.5      43       64   V
```

As illustrated in Code Listing 7-21, R4 now learns the DECnet route to R1, R2, and R3 through its ISDN interface, BRI0.

DECnet Level 1 and Level 2 Routing

In the previous sections, all the routers are in a single area, 8. These routers forward traffic within their own area and are referred to as Level 1 routers or routing-iv (DECnet Phase IV routing). Hence, R1, R2, R3, R4, and R5 have complete knowledge of all nodes within that area.

In Figure 7-8, R4 and R5 are segregated into Area 10, while R1, R2, and R3 remain in Area 8. In this case, R3 and R4 are known as Level 2 or area routers, while R1, R2, and R5 remain as Level 1 routers. Note that a Level 1 router will ignore Level 2 packets. R3 and R4 will be able to communicate between these two areas, and have knowledge of all nodes in their area and of the nodes that provide entry into other areas. Nevertheless, these two routers will still act as Level 1 routers in their own area. Hence, R1 and R2 will send packets destined for Area 10 to R3, which then forwards them to R4 in Area 10. Likewise, R5 will send packets destined for Area 8 to R4, which then forwards them to R3 in Area 8.

Note the router configurations for R3, R4, and R5 in Code Listings 7-22 through 7-24.

Figure 7-8
DECnet level 1 and
level 2 routing.

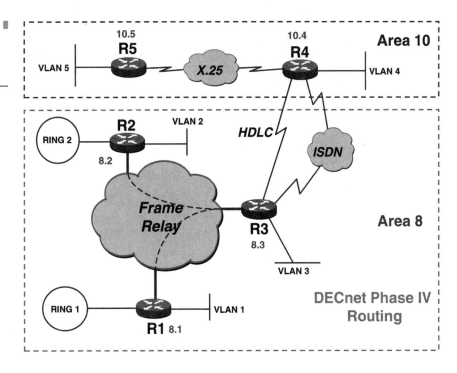

Code Listing 7-22
DECnet area router
configuration for R3.

```
hostname C4500-R3
!
username C4500-R4 password 0 cisco
!
decnet routing 8.3
decnet node-type area
!
isdn switch-type basic-net3
!
interface Ethernet0
 media-type 10BaseT
 decnet cost 3
!
interface Serial0
 encapsulation frame-relay
 bandwidth 56
 decnet cost 3
 no decnet split-horizon
 frame-relay map decnet 8.1 301 broadcast
 frame-relay map decnet 8.2 302 broadcast
 frame-relay lmi-type ansi
!
interface Serial1
 backup delay 20 60
 backup interface BRI0
 decnet cost 4
!
interface BRI0
 encapsulation ppp
 decnet cost 4
 decnet access-group 301
 dialer idle-timeout 60
 dialer map decnet 10.4 name C4500-R4 broadcast 3234200
 dialer load-threshold 128 either
 dialer-group 1
 ppp authentication chap
!
dialer-list 1 protocol decnet permit
```

Code Listing 7-22 illustrates the DECnet area router configuration for
R3. The global command `decnet node-type` sets R3 to an area router
by replacing the keyword `routing-iv` with `area`. Note that the `dialer
map` interface command defined on the BRI0 interface now uses 10.4 as
the DECnet address for R4.

Code Listing 7-23
DECnet area router
configuration for R4.

```
hostname C4500-R4
!
username C4500-R3 password 0 cisco
!
decnet routing 10.4
decnet node-type area
!
isdn switch-type basic-net3
!
interface Ethernet0
 media-type 10BaseT
 decnet cost 4
!
interface Serial0
 bandwidth 56
 decnet cost 4
!
interface Serial1
 encapsulation x25
 bandwidth 56
 decnet cost 5
 x25 address 6544444444
 x25 map decnet 10.5 6555555555 broadcast
!
interface BRI0
 encapsulation ppp
 decnet cost 4
 dialer idle-timeout 60
 dialer map decnet 8.3 name C4500-R3 broadcast
 dialer load-threshold 128 either
 dialer-group 1
 ppp authentication chap
!
dialer-list 1 protocol decnet permit
```

Code Listing 7-23 illustrates the DECnet area router configuration for R4. R4 is currently in Area 10. The global command decnet routing assigns a DECnet address, 10.4 (Area 10, Node 4), to the entire router. The global command decnet node-type sets R4 to an area router by replacing the keyword routing-iv with area. Note that the x25 map interface command defined in the S1 interface now uses 10.5 as the DECnet address for R5.

Code Listing 7-24
DECnet configuration for R5.

```
hostname C2509-R5
!
decnet routing 10.5
decnet node-type routing-iv
!
interface Ethernet0
 decnet cost 5
!
interface Serial0
 encapsulation x25
 bandwidth 56
 decnet cost 5
 x25 address 5555555555
 x25 map decnet 10.4 6544444444 broadcast
```

Code Listing 7-24 illustrates the DECnet configuration for R5. R5 is also in Area 10. The global command `decnet routing` assigns a DECnet address, `10.5` (Area 10, Node 5), to the entire router. Since R5 remains a Level 1 router, the `decnet node-type` is still `routing-iv`. Note that the `x25 map` interface command defined in the S0 interface now uses 10.4 as the DECnet address for R4.

Note the DECnet routing tables for the five routers in Code Listings 7-25 through 7-29.

Code Listing 7-25
DECnet routing table for R1.

```
C2500-R1#show decnet route
   Node      Cost  Hops           Next Hop to Node Expires   Prio
 *(Area)      3     1           Serial0.1 -> 8.3
 *8.1         0     0             (Local) -> 8.1
 *8.2         6     2           Serial0.1 -> 8.3
 *8.3         3     1           Serial0.1 -> 8.3          38      64  V+
```

Code Listing 7-25 shows the DECnet routing table for R1. R1 is a Level 1 router. The parameter (Area) under the Node field indicates the nearest Level 2 router, R3. Note that V indicates a Level 1 adjacency, and V+ indicates an adjacency is created with Level 2 router R3.

Code Listing 7-26
DECnet routing table for R2.

```
C2500-R2#show decnet route
   Node      Cost  Hops           Next Hop to Node Expires   Prio
 *(Area)      3     1           Serial0.1 -> 8.3
 *8.1         6     2           Serial0.1 -> 8.3
 *8.2         0     0             (Local) -> 8.2
 *8.3         3     1           Serial0.1 -> 8.3  44       64    V+
```

Code Listing 7-26 shows the DECnet routing table for R2. R2 is a Level 1 router. The parameter (Area) under the Node field indicates the nearest Level 2 router, R3. Note that V indicates a Level 1 adjacency, and V+ indicates an adjacency is created with Level 2 router R3.

Code Listing 7-27
DECnet routing table for R3.

```
C4500-R3#show decnet route
  Area      Cost  Hops      Next Hop to Node      Expires  Prio
*8            0     0        (Local) -> 8.3
*10           4     1        Serial1 -> 10.4          38      64  A+
  Node      Cost  Hops      Next Hop to Node      Expires  Prio
*(Area)       0     0        (Local) -> 8.3
*8.1          3     1        Serial0 -> 8.1          36      64  V
*8.2          3     1        Serial0 -> 8.2          41      64  V
*8.3          0     0        (Local) -> 8.3
```

Code Listing 7-27 shows the DECnet routing table for R3. R3 is a Level 2 router. Note that A indicates a Level 2 adjacency, and A+ indicates an adjacency is created with another Level 2 router, R4.

Code Listing 7-28
DECnet routing table for R4.

```
C4500-R4#show decnet route
  Area      Cost  Hops      Next Hop to Node      Expires  Prio
*8            4     1        Serial0 -> 8.3          37      64  A+
*10           0     0        (Local) -> 10.4
  Node      Cost  Hops      Next Hop to Node      Expires  Prio
*(Area)       0     0        (Local) -> 10.4
*10.4         0     0        (Local) -> 10.4
*10.5         5     1        Serial1 -> 10.5         35      64  V
```

Code Listing 7-28 shows the DECnet routing table for R4. R4 is a Level 2 router. Note that A indicates a Level 2 adjacency, and A+ indicates an adjacency is created with another Level 2 router, R3.

Code Listing 7-29
DECnet routing table for R5.

```
C2509-R5#show decnet route
  Node      Cost  Hops      Next Hop to Node      Expires  Prio
*(Area)       5     1        Serial0 -> 10.4
*10.4         5     1        Serial0 -> 10.4         31      64  V+
*10.5         0     0        (Local) -> 10.5
```

Code Listing 7-29 shows the DECnet routing table for R5. R5 is a Level 1 router. The parameter (Area) under the Node field indicates the nearest Level 2 router, R4. Note that V indicates a Level 1 adjacency, and V+ indicates an adjacency is created with Level 2 router R4.

DECnet Access Control

In this section, two applications of DECnet access lists will be implemented, one using standard access lists for route filtering, and the other using extended access lists to deny access.

DECnet Routing Filter

This section demonstrates DECnet route filtering by controlling the access to routing information sent out of an interface. Figure 7-9 shows the route filtering that is applied on R2's S0.1 interface. This route filtering is implemented in Code Listing 7-30.

Figure 7-9
DECnet routing filter.

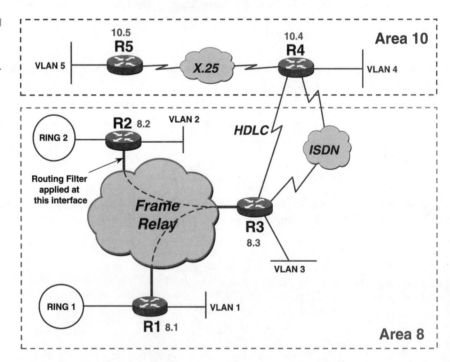

■ I

Code Listing 7-30
DECnet route filtering configuration for R2.

```
hostname C2500-R2
!
decnet routing 8.2
decnet node-type routing-iv
!
interface Serial0
 encapsulation frame-relay
 frame-relay lmi-type ansi
!
interface Serial0.1 point-to-point
 decnet cost 3
 decnet out-routing-filter 301
!
access-list 301 deny   8.2 0.0
access-list 301 permit 0.0 63.1023
```

Code Listing 7-30 defines a standard access-list 301. (The standard and extended access list numbers for DECnet use the range 300-399.) In this instance, the source address is in the form *area.node*, that is, 8.2. Note that in other cases, the source address can be an entire area. The wildcard masks match bit-for-bit with the DECnet *area.node* address. A zero in the wildcard mask indicates the corresponding bit in the DECnet address to be checked, and a one indicates the corresponding bit to be ignored. However, in DECnet, the wildcard masks are expressed in decimal notation. A mask of 0.0 means check all the bits in the DECnet address 8.2, and the access list will need to match this specific address. A mask of 63.1023 means don't care, and the access list will match any address.

In other words, access-list 301 denies the DECnet routing information for node 8.2 from going out of interface S0.1 of R2, and permits routing updates from all other nodes. The interface command decnet out-routing-filter 301 filters outgoing routing information based on the source node address, 8.2.

After applying the outbound routing filter on interface S0.1 of R2, the route to node 8.2 is no longer reflected in the DECnet routing tables for R1, R2, and R3, as illustrated in Code Listings 7-31 through 7-33.

■ I

Code Listing 7-31
DECnet routing table for R1.

```
C2500-R1#show decnet route
   Node       Cost  Hops        Next Hop to Node Expires  Prio
 *(Area)        3     1         Serial0.1 -> 8.3
 *8.1           0     0           (Local) -> 8.1
 *8.3           3     1         Serial0.1 -> 8.3          35    64  V+
```

▪ |

Code Listing 7-32
DECnet routing table for R2.

```
C2500-R2#show decnet route
  Node       Cost  Hops        Next Hop to Node Expires   Prio
*(Area)       3     1          Serial0.1 -> 8.3
*8.1          6     2          Serial0.1 -> 8.3
*8.2          0     0          (Local)  -> 8.2
*8.3          3     1          Serial0.1 -> 8.3          43      64  V+
```

▪ |

Code Listing 7-33
DECnet routing table for R3.

```
C4500-R3#show decnet route
  Area       Cost  Hops        Next Hop to Node Expires   Prio
*8            0     0          (Local)  -> 8.3
*10           4     1          Serial1  -> 10.4          32      64  A+
  Node       Cost  Hops        Next Hop to Node Expires   Prio
*(Area)       0     0          (Local)  -> 8.3
*8.1          3     1          Serial0  -> 8.1          31      64  V
*8.3          0     0          (Local)  -> 8.3
```

DECnet Traffic Filtering

In Figure 7-10, a DECnet traffic filter is specified on interfaces S1 and BRI0 of R3, permitting access to R2 only. Code Listing 7-34 illustrates this.

▪ |

Code Listing 7-34
DECnet traffic filter configuration for R3.

```
hostname C4500-R3
!
decnet routing 8.3
decnet node-type area
!
interface Serial1
 decnet cost 4
 decnet access-group 301
!
interface BRI0
 encapsulation ppp
 decnet cost 4
 decnet access-group 301
 dialer idle-timeout 60
 dialer map decnet 10.4 name C4500-R4 broadcast 3234200
 dialer load-threshold 128 either
 dialer-group 1
 ppp authentication chap
!
access-list 301 permit 8.2 0.0  0.0 63.1023
```

Code Listing 7-34 defines an extended access-list 301 allowing only traffic from node 8.2 to be forwarded out of interfaces S1 and BRI0 to any destination. The list also implies that no other traffic will be per-

Figure 7-10
DECnet traffic filtering.

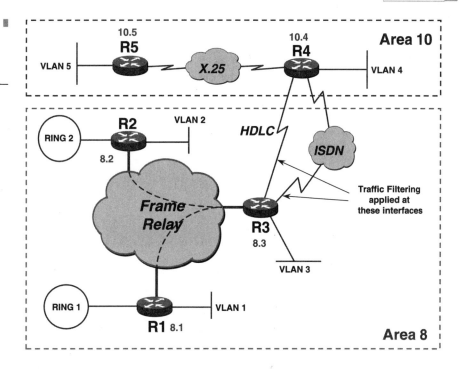

mitted. The interface command `decnet access-group 301` activates access-list 301 on interfaces S1 and BRI0 in the outbound direction.

After applying the DECnet outbound traffic filter at S1 and BRI0 of R3, executing a DECnet ping from R4 and R5 will return a positive ping (echo) reply from node 8.2 but not from node 8.1. Likewise, R2 will be able to ping to R4 and R5, whereas R1 will not. Code Listing 7-35 illustrates these DECnet ping results.

Code Listing 7-35
DECnet ping results.

```
C4500-R4#ping decnet 8.2
Type escape sequence to abort.

Sending 5, 100-byte DECnet echos to 8.2, timeout is 5 seconds:
!!!!!
Success rate is 100 percent (5/5), round-trip min/avg/max = 60/64/72
ms


C4500-R4#ping decnet 8.1

Type escape sequence to abort.
Sending 5, 100-byte DECnet echos to 8.1, timeout is 5 seconds:
.....
```

■ |

Code Listing 7-35
(continued)

```
Success rate is 0 percent (0/5)


C2509-R5#ping decnet 8.2

Type escape sequence to abort.
Sending 5, 100-byte DECnet echos to 8.2, timeout is 5 seconds:
!!!!!
Success rate is 100 percent (5/5), round-trip min/avg/max = 88/157/436
ms


C2509-R5#ping decnet 8.1

Type escape sequence to abort.
Sending 5, 100-byte DECnet echos to 8.1, timeout is 5 seconds:
.....
Success rate is 0 percent (0/5)
```

Phase IV-to-Phase V Conversion

DECnet Phase V, commonly known as DECnet/OSI, is the fifth generation of the Digital Network Architecture (DNA). It has been designed to
address the limitations of DECnet Phase IV. The Phase IV architecture is
considered proprietary and is reaching the limit of its address space (of
approximately 65,000 nodes). Moreover, the Phase IV routing algorithm
is unable to cope with large growing networks, and its network management is not capable of being extended.

The Phase V implementation is more powerful, as it has a larger
address space and is easier to manage. It uses DECdns, a name service
that has centralized administration of node databases which reduces
local management overhead and removes risk of address duplication.
DECdns also has an end-node auto-configuration feature whereby end
systems can automatically obtain their full address information without
manual intervention, hence simplifying the process of adding a new node
to the network. Besides the ease of management, Phase V supports the
International Standards Organization (ISO) standards and has full inte-
gration of OSI protocols, which makes it more open and less proprietary
while maintaining interoperability to the Phase IV DNA. If there are
Phase IV hosts in Phase V networks and vice versa, the Phase IV-to-
Phase V conversion (and vice versa) must be enabled for all nodes to communicate with each other. Routers that have conversion enabled will

advertise node reachability to both Phase IV and V hosts in both types of routing updates (Phase IV and V). To enable this conversion, DECnet and ISO CLNS must be configured on the routers.

In Figure 7-11, DECnet Phase V is configured for the HDLC and ISDN links between R3 and R4. The OSI protocol to be used for the Phase V routing between the two routers is the CLNS IS-IS protocol.

The IS-IS routing protocol uses a special kind of Network Service Access Point (NSAP) address known as a Network Entity Title (NET). A NET has the same format as an NSAP address except for the last byte (SEL), which is set to 0x00. NSAP/NET addresses have a maximum length of 20 bytes and should be globally unique. A Phase V node may have up to three NETs, which is equivalent to three node addresses.

Figure 7-11
DECnet Phase IV-to-
Phase V conversion.

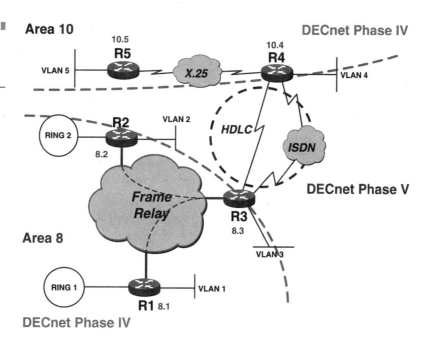

TABLE 7-1

NSAP groupings

1 byte	Variable	Variable	2 bytes	6 bytes	1 byte
AFI	IDI	PRE-DSP	LOC_AREA	ID	SEL
NSAP/NET					
IDP		DSP			
DECnet Area				ID	SEL
Phase IV Address Prefix			Phase IV Area	AA-04-00-XX-YY	SEL

As listed in Table 7-1, an NSAP/NET address consists of the following two major fields:

■ The initial domain part (IDP) consists of a one-byte authority and format identifier (AFI), and a variable-length initial domain identifier (IDI). The length of the IDI and the encoding format for the domain-specific part (DSP) are based on the value of the AFI.

■ The DSP consists of a variable-length high-order DSP (PRE-DSP), a two-byte area identifier (LOC_AREA), a six-byte system identifier (ID), and a one-byte N-selector (SEL).

The Phase V address (NSAP) structure requires a minimum DSP size of nine bytes: *LOC_AREA (2 bytes) + ID (6 bytes) + SEL (1 byte)*.

The DECnet area address is all of the NSAP/NET except the last seven bytes (ID + SEL). The LOC_AREA field is only significant in differentiating Phase IV and Phase V addresses as follows:

■ LOC_AREA = 0 (not allowed)

■ LOC_AREA = 65535 (not allowed)

■ LOC_AREA = 1 to 63 (Phase IV area)

■ LOC_AREA = 64 to 65534 (Phase V area)

The IDI is of variable length, depending on the AFI. The PRE-DSP is also of variable length, depending on the AFI and the total length of the NSAP.

In the scenario, the default Phase IV NSAPs are constructed for the five routers using the following criteria:

■ AFI = 49, which signifies local addressing with a null IDI (0 bytes). The length of the PRE-DSP field (typically 0 to 10 bytes) when AFI = 49 is limited by the NSAP length. In this case, the PRE-DSP has a value of zero.

- LOC_AREA = area (in hexadecimal), which is extracted from the Phase IV *area.node* address.■ ID = AA-00-04-00-XX-YY, which is the DECnet MAC address derived from the Phase IV *area.node* address by multiplying the area number by 1024 and then adding in the node number. The resulting 16-bit decimal is converted to a hexadecimal number (YY-XX) and concatenated to the address AA00.0400 in byte-swapped order, with the least significant byte (XX) first.

- SEL = 00 (for NET)

Note the router configuration for R3 and R4 in Code Listings 7-36 and 7-37.

Code Listing 7-36
DECnet Phase IV-to-Phase V conversion configuration for R3.

```
hostname C4500-R3
!
username C4500-R4 password 0 cisco
isdn switch-type basic-net3
!
decnet routing 8.3
decnet node-type area
decnet conversion 49
!
clns routing
!
interface Ethernet0
 media-type 10BaseT
 decnet cost 3
 clns router isis 8
!
interface Serial0
 encapsulation frame-relay
 bandwidth 56
 decnet cost 3
 no decnet split-horizon
 clns router isis 8
 frame-relay map decnet 8.1 301 broadcast
 frame-relay map decnet 8.2 302 broadcast
 frame-relay lmi-type ansi
!
interface Serial1
 backup delay 10 30
 backup interface BRI0
 clns router isis 8
!
interface BRI0
 encapsulation ppp
 dialer idle-timeout 60
 dialer map clns 49.000a.aa00.0400.0428.00 name C4500-R4 broadcast 3234200
 dialer load-threshold 128 either
 dialer-group 1
```

■ ▪ |

Code Listing 7-36
(continued)

```
ppp authentication chap
 clns router isis 8
 !
router isis 8
 net 49.0008.aa00.0400.0320.00
 !
dialer-list 1 protocol clns permit
```

1. Code Listing 7-36 illustrates the DECnet Phase IV-to-Phase V conversion configuration for R3. To enable Phase IV-to-Phase V conversion, DECnet Phase IV routing must first be enabled as usual together with ISO CLNS routing, which the global command `clns routing` enables. This is followed by the `decnet conversion 49` global command, which enables DECnet Phase IV-to-Phase V (and vice versa) conversion on the router.

2. As DECnet Phase V implements full OSI routing, IS-IS is adopted as the Phase V routing protocol here. The router command, `router isis 8`, enables IS-IS. The value 8 is the optional tag used for identifying the IS-IS routing process. If it is not specified, a null tag is assumed. In this case, the NET value of `49.0008.aa00.0400.0320.00` is defined for the IS-IS routing process. The value 49, which ties in with the value of the NSAP-prefix in the `decnet conversion` command, is the AFI that signifies local addressing with a null IDI (0 bytes), defined earlier in this section. The value 0008 is the LOC_AREA or area (in hexadecimal), which is extracted from the Phase IV node address, 8.3 (*area.node*). The value aa00.0400.0320 represents the system identifier (ID), which is the DECnet MAC address derived from the Phase IV node address, 8.3 (*area.node*) by multiplying the area number by 1024 and then adding in the node number. The resulting 16-bit decimal is converted to a hexadecimal number (2003) and concatenated to the address AA00.0400 in byte-swapped order, with the least significant byte (03) first. Since NET is used for the IS-IS routing process, the value of the SEL is set to 00.

3. CLNS must be enabled on all interfaces using the interface command `clns router isis 8` even if the router has only Phase IV hosts/routers on some of these interfaces. This facilitates R3 converting Phase IV adjacency information into Phase V, thus enabling other routers to be informed about the hosts/routers connected by these interfaces.

4. Since Phase V is also implemented across the ISDN backup link, the interface command `dialer map` dials up R4 to establish a PPP

connectivity when S1 becomes unavailable. The CLNS NSAP (NET) address, host name, and ISDN number used by the command are R4's. The `dialer-group 1` command refers to `dialer-list 1`, and the list allows all CLNS traffic to pass. No refining on the dialer-list is required, as the purpose of the BRI0 interface is to back up S1.

■ ■

Code Listing 7-37
DECnet Phase IV-to-Phase V conversion configuration for R4.

```
hostname C4500-R4
!
username C4500-R3 password 0 cisco
isdn switch-type basic-net3
!
decnet routing 10.4
decnet node-type area
decnet conversion 49
!
clns routing
!
interface Ethernet0
 media-type 10BaseT
 decnet cost 4
 clns router isis 8
!
interface Serial0
 bandwidth 56
 clns router isis 8
!
interface Serial1
 encapsulation x25
 bandwidth 56
 decnet cost 5
 x25 address 6544444444
 x25 map decnet 10.5 6555555555 broadcast
 clns router isis 8
!
interface BRI0
 encapsulation ppp
 dialer idle-timeout 60
 dialer map clns 49.0008.aa00.0400.0320.00 name C4500-R3 broadcast
 dialer load-threshold 128 either
 dialer-group 1
 ppp authentication chap
 clns router isis 8
!
router isis 8
 net 49.000a.aa00.0400.0428.00
!
dialer-list 1 protocol clns permit
```

1. Code Listing 7-37 illustrates the DECnet Phase IV-to-Phase V conversion configuration for R4. To enable Phase IV-to-Phase V conversion, DECnet Phase IV routing must first be enabled as usual

together with ISO CLNS routing, which the global command `clns routing` enables. This is followed by the `decnet conversion 49` global command, which enables DECnet Phase IV-to-Phase V (and vice versa) conversion on the router.

2. As DECnet Phase V implements full OSI routing, IS-IS is adopted as the Phase V routing protocol here. The router command, `router isis 8`, enables IS-IS. The value 8 is the optional tag used to identify the IS-IS routing process. If it is not specified, a null tag is assumed. In this case, the NET value of `49.000a.aa00.0400.0428.00` is defined for the IS-IS routing process. Let us do some interpretation on this address. The value `49`, which ties in with the value of the NSAP-prefix in the `decnet conversion` command, is the AFI that signifies local addressing with a null IDI (zero bytes) defined earlier in this section. The value `000a` is the LOC_AREA or area (in hexadecimal), which is extracted from the Phase IV node address, `10.4` (*area.node*). The value `aa00.0400.0428` represents the system identifier (ID), which is the DECnet MAC address derived from the Phase IV node address, `10.4` (*area.node*), by multiplying the area number by 1024 and then adding in the node number. The resulting 16-bit decimal is converted to a hexadecimal number (`2804`) and concatenated to the address `AA00.0400` in byte-swapped order, with the least significant byte (`04`) first. Since a NET is used for the IS-IS routing process, the value of the SEL is set to `00`.

3. CLNS must be enabled on all interfaces using the interface command `clns router isis 8` even if the router has only Phase IV hosts/routers on some of these interfaces. This facilitates R3 converting Phase IV adjacency information into Phase V, thus, enabling other routers to be informed about the hosts/routers connected by these interfaces.

4. Since Phase V is implemented across the ISDN backup link, the interface command `dialer map` establishes a PPP connection when R3 makes a call. Note that no ISDN number is supplied here, as R3 will initiate the call. The CLNS NSAP (NET) address and host name used by the command are R3's. The `dialer-group 1` command refers to `dialer-list 1`, and the list allows all CLNS traffic to pass.

Using the `show decnet` exec command in Code Listing 7-38, note that the Phase IV-to-Phase V conversion has been enabled on R3 and R4, and the conversion NSAP prefix (AFI) is 49.

Code Listing 7-38
Global DECnet information for R3 and R4.

```
C4500-R3#show decnet
Global DECnet parameters for network 0:
  Local address is 8.3, node type is area
  Level-2 'Attached' flag is TRUE
  Maximum node is 1023, maximum area is 63, maximum visits is 63
  Maximum paths is 1, path split mode is normal
  Local maximum cost is 1022, maximum hops is 30
  Area maximum cost is 1022, maximum hops is 30
  Static routes *NOT* being sent in routing updates
  Phase IV <-> Phase V Conversion Enabled
      Conversion prefix is: 49
  Areas being advertised :


C4500-R4#show decnet
Global DECnet parameters for network 0:
  Local address is 10.4, node type is area
  Level-2 'Attached' flag is TRUE
  Maximum node is 1023, maximum area is 63, maximum visits is 63
  Maximum paths is 1, path split mode is normal
  Local maximum cost is 1022, maximum hops is 30
  Area maximum cost is 1022, maximum hops is 30
  Static routes *NOT* being sent in routing updates
  Phase IV <-> Phase V Conversion Enabled
      Conversion prefix is: 49
  Areas being advertised :
```

Using the show clns protocol exec command in Code Listing 7-39, note that CLNS has been enabled on all the active interfaces of R3 and R4. Note also the system identifier and area address configured.

Code Listing 7-39
CLNS protocol information for R3 and R4.

```
C4500-R3#show clns protocol
IS-IS Router: 8
  System Id: AA00.0400.0320.00  IS-Type: level-1-2
  Manual area address(es):
      49.0008
  Routing for area address(es):
      49.0008
  Interfaces supported by IS-IS:
      BRI0 - OSI
      Ethernet0 - OSI
      Serial0 - OSI
      Serial1 - OSI
  Redistributing:
    static
  Distance: 110
```

```
C4500-R4#show clns protocol
IS-IS Router: 8
  System Id: AA00.0400.0428.00   IS-Type: level-1-2
  Manual area address(es):
        49.000a
  Routing for area address(es):
        49.000a
  Interfaces supported by IS-IS:
        BRI0 - OSI
        Ethernet0 - OSI
        Serial1 - OSI
        Serial0 - OSI
  Redistributing:
    static
  Distance: 110
```

Using the show clns neighbors exec command in Code Listing 7-40, note that the Level 2 (L2) router adjacency that has been established across the HDLC link between R3 and R4 is now learned through the OSI routing protocol, IS-IS. The rest of the end-system (ES) adjacencies (with R1, R2, and R5) are discovered via DECnet.

```
C4500-R3#show clns neighbors
```

System Id Protocol	SNPA	Interface	State	Holdtime	Type
AA00.0400.0120 Decnet	DLCI 301	Se0	Up	45	ES
AA00.0400.0220 Decnet	DLCI 302	Se0	Up	35	ES
AA00.0400.0428 IS-IS	***HDLC***	**Se1**	**Up**	**29**	**L2**

```
C4500-R4#show clns neighbors
```

System Id Protocol	SNPA	Interface	State	Holdtime	Type
AA00.0400.0320 IS-IS	***HDLC***	**Se0**	**Up**	**29**	**L2**
AA00.0400.0528 Decnet	5555555555	Se1	Up	37	ES

Code Listing 7-41 shows the DECnet routing table for R1.

Code Listing 7-41
DECnet routing table for R1.

```
C2500-R1#show decnet route
  Node         Cost   Hops            Next Hop to Node Expires  Prio
*(Area)          3      1             Serial0.1 -> 8.3
*8.1             0      0              (Local) -> 8.1
*8.2             6      2             Serial0.1 -> 8.3
*8.3             3      1             Serial0.1 -> 8.3             36    64   V
```

Code Listing 7-42 shows the DECnet routing table for R2.

Code Listing 7-42
DECnet routing table for R2.

```
C2500-R2#show decnet route
  Node         Cost   Hops            Next Hop to Node Expires  Prio
*(Area)          3      1             Serial0.1 -> 8.3
*8.1             6      2             Serial0.1 -> 8.3
*8.2             0      0              (Local) -> 8.2
*8.3             3      1             Serial0.1 -> 8.3             42    64   V
```

Code Listing 7-43 shows the DECnet routing table for R3.

Code Listing 7-43
DECnet routing table for R3.

```
C4500-R3#show decnet route
  Area         Cost   Hops          Next Hop to Node      Expires  Prio
*8               0      0            (Local) -> 8.3
  Node         Cost   Hops          Next Hop to Node      Expires  Prio
*(Area)          0      0            (Local) -> 8.3
*8.1             3      1            Serial0 -> 8.1          32     64   V
*8.2             3      1            Serial0 -> 8.2          38     64   V
*8.3             0      0            (Local) -> 8.3
```

The DECnet routing table for R3 in Code Listing 7-43 no longer reflects any entry for Area 10, since Area 10 is now learned via IS-IS. However, a DECnet ping from R3 to the valid nodes on Area 10 will still return a positive ping (or echo) reply.

Code Listing 7-44 shows the DECnet routing table for R4.

Code Listing 7-44
DECnet routing table for R4.

```
C4500-R4#show decnet route
  Area         Cost   Hops          Next Hop to Node      Expires  Prio
*10              0      0            (Local) -> 10.4
  Node         Cost   Hops          Next Hop to Node      Expires  Prio
*(Area)          0      0            (Local) -> 10.4
*10.4            0      0            (Local) -> 10.4
*10.5            5      1            Serial1 -> 10.5         45     64   V
```

The DECnet routing table for R4 in Code Listing 7-44 no longer reflects any entry for Area 8, since Area 8 is now learned via IS-IS. However, a DECnet ping from R4 to the valid nodes on Area 8 will still return a positive ping (or echo) reply.

Code Listing 7-45 shows the DECnet routing table for R5.

Code Listing 7-45
DECnet routing table for R5.

```
C2509-R5#show decnet route
   Node      Cost  Hops            Next Hop to Node Expires   Prio
 *(Area)       5     1             Serial0 -> 10.4
 *10.4         5     1             Serial0 -> 10.4           41      64  V
 *10.5         0     0             (Local) -> 10.5
```

The CLNS routing tables for R3 and R4 in Code Listing 7-46 will supplement the DECnet routing tables for these two routers in Code Listings 7-43 and 7-44. From the CLNS routing tables, note that Area 8 (49.0008) and Area 10 (49.000a) are now learned via IS-IS.

Code Listing 7-46
CLNS routing tables for R3 and R4.

```
C4500-R3#show clns route
CLNS Prefix Routing Table
49.0008.aa00.0400.0320.00, Local NET Entry
49.0008 [110/0]
   via AA00.0400.0320, IS-IS, Up
49.000a [110/10]
   via AA00.0400.0428, IS-IS, Up, Serial1


C4500-R4#show clns route
CLNS Prefix Routing Table
49.000a.aa00.0400.0428.00, Local NET Entry
49.0008 [110/10]
   via AA00.0400.0320, IS-IS, Up, Serial0
49.000a [110/0]
   via AA00.0400.0428, IS-IS, Up
```

Local Area Transport (LAT)

The Digital Equipment Corporation (Digital) Local Area Transport (LAT) is often used to connect to Digital's (VMS) hosts. LAT is a Digital-proprietary protocol that allows a user to establish a LAT connection to a host at another site, then passes the keystrokes from one system to the other. A user can establish a LAT connection through the router to a LAT host by entering the host name.

Unlike TCP/IP, LAT was designed for LANs and cannot be routed because it does not have a network layer address. However, it can be bridged across a WAN or protocol translation and carry LAT traffic over a WAN by first translating LAT to X.25 or Telnet.

Consider Figure 7-12. In this scenario, a plain LAT session will be established from R3 to R5 using X.25 translation. This is followed by a direct LAT session from R4 to R3, whereby R3 provides a simple LAT service showing the DECnet routing table for R3. Code Listings 7-47 through 7-49 illustrate these LAT implementations.

Figure 7-12
LAT sessions between the two pairs of routers, R3-R5 and R4-R3.

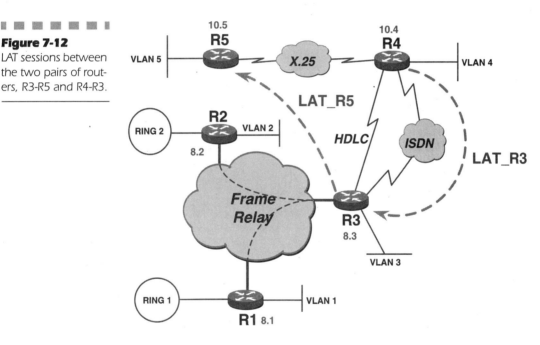

Code Listing 7-47
LAT configuration for R3.

```
hostname C4500-R3
!
interface Serial1
 lat enabled
!
lat service LAT_R3 autocommand show decnet route
lat service LAT_R3 password CISCO
lat service LAT_R3 enabled
```

1. Code Listing 7-47 illustrates the LAT configuration for R3. The `lat enabled` interface command enables the LAT protocol on interface S1 so that a LAT session can be initiated through this interface.

2. Since R3 provides the LAT service, LAT_R3, this service must be enabled using the `lat service LAT_R3 enabled` global command. This command enables inbound connections to the service, LAT_R3. An authenticating password is also being set for this service using the `lat service LAT_R3 password CISCO` global command. In addition, an exec command is associated with this service for auto-execution using the `lat service LAT_R3 autocommand show decnet route` global command so that when the service is executed, it will show the current DECnet routing table of R3.

■ |

Code Listing 7-48
LAT configuration for R4.

```
hostname C4500-R4
!
interface Serial0
 lat enabled
!
interface Serial1
 encapsulation x25
 bandwidth 56
 lat enabled
 decnet cost 5
 x25 address 6544444444
!
translate lat LAT_R5 x25 6555555555
```

1. Code Listing 7-48 illustrates the LAT configuration for R4. The `lat enabled` interface command enables the LAT protocol on interfaces S0 and S1 so that a LAT session can be initiated through either of these interfaces.

2. When R4 receives a LAT connection request to the LAT service, LAT_R5, R4 will automatically translate the request to another outgoing protocol connection type. In this case, the connection type is X.25 and the X.121 address, 6555555555 (which is R5's X.121 address), is used as the outgoing address. The global command `translate lat LAT_R5 x25 6555555555` configures this.

Code Listing 7-49
LAT configuration for R5.

```
hostname C2509-R5
!
interface Serial0
 encapsulation x25
 bandwidth 56
 lat enabled
 decnet cost 5
 x25 address 6555555555
!
lat service LAT_R5 enabled
!
line vty 0 4
 password cisco
 login
```

1. Code Listing 7-49 illustrates the LAT configuration for R5. The `lat enabled` interface command enables the LAT protocol on interface S0 so that a LAT session can be initiated through this interface.

2. Since R5 provides the LAT service, LAT_R5, this service must be enabled using the `lat service LAT_R5 enabled` global command. This command enables inbound connections to the service, LAT_R5. Note that enabling a service is mandatory; however, this does not mean all the other attributes (password and autocommand) in R3 are necessary in a particular environment.

A LAT session is a bidirectional logical connection between a LAT service and the router. The two-way connection is transparent to the user at a console connected to a LAT session. To the user, it appears that the connection has been made to the desired device or application program.

The LAT protocol is asymmetrical; it has a master and slave functionality. First, the LAT master initiates a LAT circuit by sending a circuit start message, and then a LAT slave responds with its own circuit start message. A range of 1 to 255 LAT sessions can then be multiplexed on this circuit.

In a typical setup, where a user's terminal is connected to a router, the router acts as the master, and the target VMS host acts as the slave. A router can also act as a slave if the user connects from one router to another. In the above scenario, R3 acts as the master (server) and R5 acts as the slave (host). When the LAT_R5 service is invoked at R3, as illustrated in Code Listing 7-50, it is translated to a X.25 session to R5 using its X.121 address, 6555555555. In this case, the user access verification requires the virtual terminal password (cisco), which is defined in R5.

deep

en

single

all

LAT

7-50

7-51

LAT session listings and DECnet routing table

Code Listing 7-50
LAT session from R3 to R5.

```
C4500-R3#lat lat_r5
Trying LAT_R5...Open
Trying 6555555555...Open

User Access Verification

Password: <cisco>
C2509-R5>
C2509-R5>exit

[Connection to lat_r5 closed by foreign host]
C4500-R3#
```

Resources such as modems, computers, and application software are perceived as services in a LAT network that any users in the network can use. A LAT node can offer one or more such LAT services, and more than one LAT node can offer the equivalent service.

Services that are offered by a LAT node are known as advertised services. The LAT node advertises its services through messages called LAT service announcements. Furthermore, a LAT node can also listen for these LAT service announcements on the network. These messages are then cached in a dynamic table of known LAT services, known as learned services. In the above scenario, R3 offers the LAT service, LAT_R3, allowing a user to view the DECnet routing table of R3. When the LAT_R3 service is invoked at R4 as illustrated in Code Listing 7-51, a password is required, since it has been defined for the LAT_R3 service in the LAT configuration for R3. After entering the correct password (cisco), a snapshot of R3's DECnet routing table can be seen.

Code Listing 7-51
LAT session from R4 to R3.

```
C4500-R4#lat lat_r3
Trying LAT_R3...Password required

Password: <cisco>
Trying LAT_R3...Open

    Area     Cost  Hops        Next Hop to Node Expires  Prio
*8           0     0           (Local) -> 8.3
    Node     Cost  Hops        Next Hop to Node Expires  Prio
*(Area)      0     0           (Local) -> 8.3
*8.1         3     1           Serial0 -> 8.1       35      64  V
*8.2         3     1           Serial0 -> 8.2       40      64  V
*8.3         0     0           (Local) -> 8.3
[Connection to lat_r3 closed by foreign host]
C4500-R4#
```

Summary

This chapter 7 covered DECnet. Digital Equipment Corporation designed DECnet in the 1970s as part of its Digital Network Architecture (DNA).

In the initial scenario, DECnet Phase IV routing was configured over Ethernet and Token Ring, Frame Relay, X.25, HDLC, and DDR. Next, the differences between Level 1 and Level 2 routing were discussed; and subsequently, an environment for Level 1 and 2 routing was configured using the existing setup.

In the access control section, two applications of DECnet access lists were implemented: route and traffic filtering. These access lists provide a way to better secure and control a large scale DECnet internetwork in a more efficient and effective manner.

DECnet supports both connectionless and connection-oriented network layers implemented by Open System Interconnection (OSI) protocols. DECnet Phase IV is similar to OSI routing, but DECnet Phase V implements full OSI routing, which includes support for End System-to-Intermediate System (ES-IS) and Intermediate System-to-Intermediate System (IS-IS) connections. In the Phase IV-to-Phase V conversion section, DECnet Phase V was configured for the HDLC and ISDN links between two routers. The OSI routing protocol, IS-IS, was used for implementing the Phase V routing between these routers.

Finally, in the Local Area Transport (LAT) section, a plain but indirect LAT session was established between two routers using X.25 translation. Then a direct LAT session was established between another pair of routers, where one of them provided a simple LAT service showing its DECnet routing table.

References

1. Digital Equipment Corporation. DECnet/OSI Phase V: Making the Transition from Phase IV. EK-PVTRN-BR, 1989.

2. Digital Equipment Corporation. DECserver 200 Local Area Transport (LAT) Network Concepts. AA-LD84A-TK, June 1988.

3. Digital Equipment Corporation. DIGITAL Network Architecture (Phase V). EK-DNAPV-GD-001, September 1987.

4. Documentation CD-ROM, Cisco Systems, Inc., 1998.

5. Hagans, R. "Components of OSI: ES-IS Routing." *ConnecXions: The Interoperability Report*, Vol. 3, No. 8. August 1989.

6. Malamud, C. *Analyzing DECnet/OSI Phase V.* New York: Van Nostrand Reinhold, 1991.

7. Rose, M. T. *The Open Book: A Practical Perspective on OSI.* Englewood Cliffs, New Jersey: Prentice Hall, 1990.

8. Tsuchiya, P. "Components of OSI: IS-IS Intra-Domain Routing." *ConnecXions: The Interoperability Report*, Vol. 3, No. 8. August 1989.

9. Tsuchiya, P. "Components of OSI: Routing (An Overview)." *ConnecXions: The Interoperability Report*, Vol. 3, No. 8. August 1989.

10. Zimmerman, H. "OSI Reference Model—The ISO Model Architecture for Open Systems Interconnection." *IEEE Transactions on Communications COM-28*, No. 4. April 1980.

ISO CLNS

Introduction

Under the OSI protocol suite, there are two types of network-layer services: connectionless and connection-oriented. In this chapter, focus is on the International Organization for Standardization (ISO) Connectionless Network Protocol (CLNP–ISO 8473). CLNP is a connectionless datagram protocol used to carry data and error indications. Functionally, it is analogous to IP. It has no error detection or correction mechanism. Instead it relies on the upper layers (typically the transport layer) to provide these services when necessary.

While CLNP performs network-layer functions, ISO Connectionless Network Services (CLNS) specifies a service provided to the transport layer whereby data gets sent using best-effort delivery. CLNS assumes that the transport layer will correct lost, corrupted, out of sequence, or duplicated data packets. CLNS and CLNP are often used interchangeably and discussed together because CLNS provides transport layers with the service interface to CLNP.

Subsequent sections will show the use of the ISO-developed Intermediate System-to-Intermediate System Routing Exchange Protocol (IS-IS– ISO 10589) for the dynamic routing of ISO CLNS packets.

CLNS Overview

ISO Routing Terminology

End system (ES) refers to any network node that does not have routing functionality, and intermediate system (IS) refers to a router. Together these terms form the basis for the OSI protocols: ES-IS (ISO 9542), which allows ESs and ISs to discover each other, and IS-IS, which provides routing between ISs.

The lowest level of routing hierarchy is the area, which comprises a set of end systems interconnected by intermediate systems (routers). Areas are interconnected to other areas to form routing domains. Each domain is an independently administered region, similar to an autonomous system.

Intermediate systems that keep track of how to communicate with all the end systems in their areas are known as Level 1 (or local) routers.

Other intermediate systems that keep track of how to communicate with other areas in the domain are known as Level 2 (or area) routers. End systems communicate with intermediate systems using the ISO ES-IS protocol, while Level 1 and Level 2 intermediate systems communicate with each other using the ISO IS-IS protocol.

ISO ES-IS Protocol

The ISO ES-IS protocol helps ESs and ISs to learn about each other. This process is known as configuration and must happen before routing between ESs can occur. ES-IS supports three different types of subnetworks: point-to-point (e.g., HDLC), broadcast (e.g., Ethernet), and general-topology (e.g., X.25).

Configuration information is transmitted periodically through two types of messages: ES hello messages (originated by ESs and sent to every IS on the subnetwork) and IS hello messages (originated by ISs and sent to all ESs on the subnetwork). These hello messages allow the subnetwork and network-layer addresses of the systems that generate them to communicate.

ES-IS conveys both network-layer addresses and subnetwork addresses. In OSI terminology, a network-layer address is known as the service access point (NSAP–ISO 8348/Ad2)—which is the interface between Layer 3 and Layer 4—or the network entity title (NET)—which is the network-layer entity (the address of a routing node or router) in an OSI IS. OSI subnetwork addresses, commonly referred to as the subnetwork point-of-attachment addresses (SNPA), are the points at which an ES or IS is physically attached to a subnetwork. The SNPA address (such as an Ethernet address, a X.121 address, or a Frame Relay DLCI) uniquely identifies each system attached to the subnetwork.

ISO IS-IS Protocol

The ISO IS-IS is a link-state routing protocol. To construct a consistent network topology database, it floods the network with link-state information. IS-IS supports two levels of routing: station (Level 1) routing within an area and area (Level 2) routing between areas. In other words, Level 1 routers form Level 1 areas and Level 2 routers form an intradomain routing backbone between Level 1 areas. Therefore Level 1 routers need only to have information on how to reach the nearest Level 2 router.

In IS-IS routing, each ES resides in a specific area. The ESs learn the nearest router (IS) by listening to IS hello packets. When an ES has some data to send to another ES, it forwards the packet to one of the routers on the network to which it is directly attached. The router determines the destination address and routes the packet out the best path. If the destination ES is on the same subnetwork or on another subnetwork in the same area, the local router will forward the packet accordingly. If the destination ES is in another area, the Level 1 router sends the packet to the nearest Level 2 router, and the traversing across Level 2 routers continues until the packet reaches a Level 2 router in the destination area. Within the destination area, routers forward the packet along the best path until it reaches the destination ES.

IS-IS uses a single default metric with a maximum path value of 1024. The metric is arbitrary and any link can have a maximum value of 64. The path lengths are computed by aggregating link values. IS-IS also specifies three other optional metrics (costs): delay cost (indicating the amount of delay on the link), expense cost (indicating the communications cost associated with using the link), and error cost (indicating the error rate of the link).

CLNS Addresses

Addresses in the ISO network architecture are known as Network Entity Titles (NETs) and Network Service Access Points (NSAPs). Each node in an ISO network can have one or more NETs. In addition, each node can have many NSAPs. Each NSAP varies from one of the NETs for a specific node in only the last byte, known as the n-selector.

An IS-IS NSAP address consists of two parts: an area and a system ID. Level 2 routing (routing between areas) uses the area address, while Level 1 routing (routing within an area) uses the system address. Table 8-1 illustrates the IS-IS NSAP addressing structure.

TABLE 8-1

IS-IS NSAP addressing structure

1 byte	Variable	2 bytes	6 bytes	1 byte
AFI	IDI	AREA ID	SYSTEM ID	SEL
NSAP/NET				
IDP		DSP		
IS-IS Area Address			System Address	SEL

Note the following in Table 8-1:

- The NSAP address consists of the Initial Domain Part (IDP) and the Domain-Specific Part (DSP).

- The first field of the IDP is a one-byte Authority and Format Identifier (AFI). The AFI defines the format and length of the Initial Domain Identifier (IDI), which has a variable length.

- The DSP is a nine-byte structure containing a two-byte area ID, a six-byte system ID, and a one-byte n-selector (SEL) field.

- The portion of the address from the AFI through the two-byte area ID forms the area address. IS-IS does not require all areas in one routing domain to have the same AFI or IDI.

- IS-IS supports multihoming; that is, one area may comprise more than one address. Each host in a multihomed area can have a maximum of three addresses, and these addresses must have the same system ID.

Case Scenario

Figure 8-1 illustrates the overall network scenario that will be referenced throughout this chapter. This enterprise network spans five sites: Cincinnati, Madison, Miami, Orlando, and St. Louis. The Madison office is internetworked to the St. Louis office via HDLC and to the Miami office by Frame Relay. The Miami and Madison offices are also linked up by an ISDN dial-up line, serving as backup in the event the Frame Relay connectivity between these two offices fails. The Miami office is also interconnected to the Orlando office through a Frame Relay network, which in turn links up the Cincinnati office using X.25. Cincinnati, Orlando, and St. Louis each has its own Virtual LAN whereby end systems (ESs) running on the OSI protocol stack are connected. Meanwhile, the Madison and Miami offices have these hosts on Token Rings.

CLNS Setup

In Figure 8-2, there are five NETs defined for the five routers. These NETs correspond to the same Area 0x470001. The CLNS IS-IS routing protocol is adopted here.

Figure 8-1
The overall network topology.

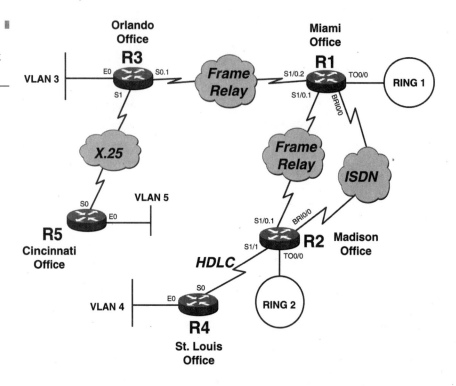

Basic CLNS Configuration

In the initial setup, CLNS is configured for the respective LANs connecting to the five routers as illustrated in Code Listings 8-1 through 8-5. Subsequent sections cover the WAN configurations.

Code Listing 8-1
CLNS configuration for R1.

```
hostname C3640-R1
!
clns routing
!
interface TokenRing0/0
 ring-speed 16
 clns router isis
!
router isis
 net 47.0001.0111.1111.1111.00
```

ISO CLNS

Figure 8-2
The overall CLNS net-
work.

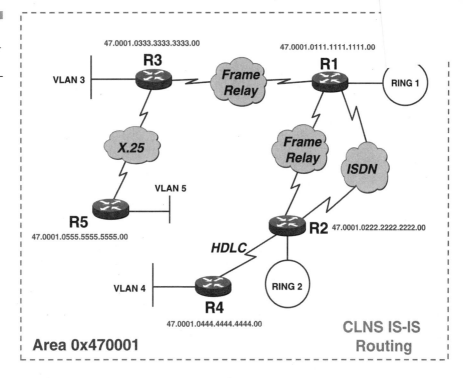

1. Code Listing 8-1 illustrates the CLNS configuration for R1. By default, CLNS routing is not enabled. The global command `clns routing` enables the routing of CLNS packets. However, CLNS routing is enabled by default when the interface subcommand `clns router isis` configures IS-IS dynamic routing for the routing of CLNS packets on the router's interfaces.

2. The `router isis` global command configures the IS-IS process. An optional tag serving as a later reference is associated with this process. Since no tag is specified here, a null tag is assumed.

3. The `net` router subcommand configures a Network Entity Title (NET) for the IS-IS routing process. In this case, the NET defines the area address for the IS-IS area as 47.0001 (AFI=47, IDI=NULL, AREA ID=0001), the system address as 0111.1111.1111, and the n-selector (SEL) as 00. Note that a maximum of three NETs per router can be configured for IS-IS.

4. The interface subcommand `clns router isis` enables IS-IS routing for CLNS packets on interface TO0/0.

Code Listing 8-2
CLNS configuration
for R2.

```
hostname C3640-R2
!
clns routing
!
interface TokenRing0/0
 ring-speed 16
 clns router isis
!
router isis
 net 47.0001.0222.2222.2222.00
```

1. Code Listing 8-2 illustrates the CLNS configuration for R2. By default, CLNS routing is not enabled. The global command clns routing enables the routing of CLNS packets. However, CLNS routing is enabled by default when the interface subcommand clns router isis configures IS-IS dynamic routing on the interfaces.

2. The router isis global command configures the IS-IS process. Since no tag is specified here, a null tag is assumed.

3. The net router subcommand configures a Network Entity Title (NET) for the IS-IS routing process. In this case, the NET defines the area address for the IS-IS area as 47.0001 (AFI=47, IDI=NULL, AREA ID=0001), the system address as 0222.2222.2222, and the n-selector (SEL) as 00.

4. The interface subcommand clns router isis enables IS-IS routing for CLNS packets on interface TO0/0.

Code Listing 8-3
CLNS configuration
for R3.

```
hostname C4500-R3
!
clns routing
!
interface Ethernet0
 media-type 10BaseT
 clns router isis
!
router isis
 net 47.0001.0333.3333.3333.00
```

1. Code Listing 8-3 illustrates the CLNS configuration for R3. By default, CLNS routing is not enabled. The global command clns routing explicitly enables the routing of CLNS packets. However, CLNS routing is enabled by default when the interface subcommand clns router isis configures IS-IS dynamic routing on the interfaces.

2. The `router isis` global command configures the IS-IS process. Since no tag is specified here, a null tag is assumed.

3. The `net` router subcommand configures a Network Entity Title (NET) for the IS-IS routing process. In this case, the NET defines the area address for the IS-IS area as 47.0001 (AFI=47, IDI=NULL, AREA ID=0001), the system address as 0333.3333.3333, and the n-selector (SEL) as 00.

4. The interface subcommand `clns router isis` enables IS-IS routing for CLNS packets on interface E0.

■ |

Code Listing 8-4
CLNS configuration for R4.

```
hostname C4500-R4
!
clns routing
!
interface Ethernet0
 media-type 10BaseT
 clns router isis
!
router isis
 net 47.0001.0444.4444.4444.00
```

1. Code Listing 8-4 illustrates the CLNS configuration for R4. By default, CLNS routing is not enabled. The global command `clns routing` enables the routing of CLNS packets. However, CLNS routing is enabled by default when the interface subcommand `clns router isis` configures IS-IS dynamic routing on the interfaces.

2. The `router isis` global command configures the IS-IS process. Since no tag is specified here, a null tag is assumed.

3. The `net` router subcommand configures a Network Entity Title (NET) for the IS-IS routing process. In this case, the NET defines the area address for the IS-IS area as 47.0001 (AFI=47, IDI=NULL, AREA ID=0001), the system address as 0444.4444.4444, and the n-selector (SEL) as 00.

4. The interface subcommand `clns router isis` enables IS-IS routing for CLNS packets on interface E0.

Code Listing 8-5
CLNS configuration for R5.

```
hostname C2500-R5
!
clns routing
!
interface Ethernet0
 clns router isis
!
router isis
 net 47.0001.0555.5555.5555.00
```

1. Code Listing 8-5 illustrates the CLNS configuration for R5. By default, CLNS routing is not enabled. The global command `clns routing` enables the routing of CLNS packets. However, CLNS routing is enabled by default when the interface subcommand `clns router isis` configures IS-IS dynamic routing on the interfaces.

2. The `router isis` global command configures the IS-IS process. Since no tag is specified here, a null tag is assumed.

3. The `net` router subcommand configures a Network Entity Title (NET) for the IS-IS routing process. In this case, the NET defines the area address for the IS-IS area as 47.0001 (AFI=47, IDI=NULL, AREA ID=0001), the system address as 0333.3333.3333, and the n-selector (SEL) as 00.

4. The interface subcommand `clns router isis` enables IS-IS routing for CLNS packets on interface E0.

CLNS over Frame Relay

Figure 8-3 zooms into the Frame Relay network where CLNS is configured for R1, R2, and R3. R2 is interconnected to R1 through a point-to-point Frame Relay topology; likewise, R3 is interconnected to R1 in the same manner. Code Listings 8-6 through 8-8 illustrate this Frame Relay implementation.

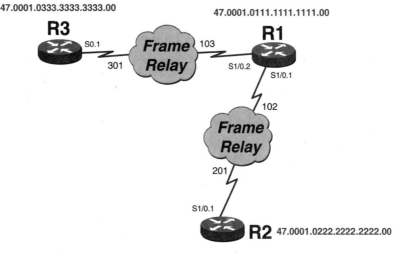

Figure 8-3
CLNS over Frame
Relay.

Code Listing 8-6
CLNS-over-Frame
Relay configuration
for R1.

```
hostname C3640-R1
!
clns routing
!
interface Serial1/0
 encapsulation frame-relay
 frame-relay lmi-type ansi
!
interface Serial1/0.1 point-to-point
 bandwidth 56
 clns router isis
 frame-relay interface-dlci 102
!
interface Serial1/0.2 point-to-point
 bandwidth 56
 clns router isis
 frame-relay interface-dlci 103
!
router isis
 net 47.0001.0111.1111.1111.00
```

1. Code Listing 8-6 illustrates the CLNS-over-Frame Relay configuration for R1. In Figure 8-3, the Frame Relay topology adopted in the scenario is implemented as two point-to-point links between R1-R2 and R1-R3. Hence, in R1 a point-to-point subinterface, S1/0.1, is used to connect to R2, and another point-to-point subinterface, S1/0.2, is used to connect to R3.

2. The interface subcommand clns router isis enables IS-IS routing for CLNS packets on subinterfaces S1/0.1 and S1/0.2.

3. The `frame-relay interface-dlci` interface subcommand defines the local DLCI, `102`, for R1-R2 and the local DLCI, `103`, for R1-R3.

Code Listing 8-7
CLNS-over-Frame Relay configuration for R2.

```
hostname C3640-R2
!
clns routing
!
interface Serial1/0
 encapsulation frame-relay
 frame-relay lmi-type ansi
!
interface Serial1/0.1 point-to-point
 bandwidth 56
 clns router isis
 frame-relay interface-dlci 201
!
router isis
 net 47.0001.0222.2222.2222.00
```

1. Code Listing 8-7 illustrates the CLNS-over-Frame Relay configuration for R2. On R2, Frame Relay point-to-point subinterface S1/0.1 is used to connect to R1.

2. The interface subcommand `clns router isis` enables IS-IS routing for CLNS packets on subinterface S1/0.1.

3. The `frame-relay interface-dlci` interface subcommand defines the local DLCI, `201`, for R2-R1.

Code Listing 8-8
CLNS-over-Frame Relay configuration for R3.

```
hostname C4500-R3
!
clns routing
!
interface Serial0
 encapsulation frame-relay
 frame-relay lmi-type ansi
!
interface Serial0.1 point-to-point
 bandwidth 56
 clns router isis
 frame-relay interface-dlci 301
!
router isis
 net 47.0001.0333.3333.3333.00
```

1. Code Listing 8-8 illustrates the CLNS-over-Frame Relay configuration for R3. On R3, Frame Relay point-to-point subinterface S0.1 is used to connect to R1.

2. The interface subcommand `clns router isis` enables IS-IS routing for CLNS packets on subinterface S0.1.

3. The `frame-relay interface-dlc` interface subcommand defines the local DLCI, `301`, for R3-R1.

CLNS over X.25

Figure 8-4 zooms into the X.25 network where CLNS is implemented between R3 and R5. Code Listings 8-9 and 8-10 illustrate this X.25 implementation.

Figure 8-4
CLNS over X.25.

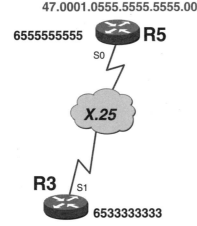

47.0001.0555.5555.5555.00

6555555555   R5

S0

X.25

R3   S1

6533333333

47.0001.0333.3333.3333.00

Code Listing 8-9
CLNS-over-X.25 configuration for R3.

```
hostname C4500-R3
!
clns routing
!
interface Serial1
 encapsulation x25
 bandwidth 56
 x25 address 6533333333
 x25 map clns 6555555555 broadcast
 clns router isis
!
router isis
 net 47.0001.0333.3333.3333.00
```

1. Code Listing 8-9 illustrates the CLNS-over-X.25 configuration for R3. The interface subcommand `clns router isis` enables IS-IS routing for CLNS packets on interface S1.

2. The interface subcommand `x25 map clns` creates a virtual circuit between R3 and R5 for the routing of CLNS packets. The X.121 (X.25) address, 6555555555, used by this subcommand belongs to R5.

Code Listing 8-10
CLNS-over-X.25 configuration for R5.

```
hostname C2500-R5
!
clns routing
!
interface Serial0
 encapsulation x25
 x25 address 6555555555
 x25 map clns 6533333333 broadcast
 clns router isis
!
router isis
 net 47.0001.0555.5555.5555.00
```

1. Code Listing 8-10 illustrates the CLNS-over-X.25 configuration for R5. The interface subcommand `clns router isis` enables IS-IS routing for CLNS packets on interface S0.

2. The interface subcommand `x25 map clns` creates a virtual circuit between R5 and R3 for the routing of CLNS packets. The X.121 (X.25) address, 6533333333, used by this subcommand belongs to R3.

CLNS over HDLC

Figure 8-5 shows the portion of the network where CLNS over HDLC is implemented between R2 and R4. Code Listings 8-11 and 8-12 illustrate this.

Figure 8-5
CLNS over HDLC.

47.0001.0444.4444.4444.00

R4　HDLC　S1/1
S0
R2
47.0001.0222.2222.2222.00

Code Listing 8-11
CLNS-over-HDLC con-
figuration for R2.

```
hostname C3640-R2
!
clns routing
!
interface Serial1/1
 bandwidth 56
 clns router isis
!
router isis
 net 47.0001.0222.2222.2222.00
```

Code Listing 8-11 illustrates the CLNS-over-HDLC configuration for R2. To configure CLNS over HDLC in R2, the interface subcommand `clns router isis` enables IS-IS routing for CLNS packets on interface S1/1.

Code Listing 8-12
CLNS-over-HDLC con-
figuration for R4.

```
hostname C4500-R4
!
clns routing
!
interface Serial0
 bandwidth 56
 clns router isis
!
router isis
 net 47.0001.0444.4444.4444.00
```

Code Listing 8-12 illustrates the CLNS-over-HDLC configuration for R4. To configure CLNS over HDLC in R4, the interface subcommand clns router isis enables IS-IS routing for CLNS packets on interface S0.

CLNS over DDR

Figure 8-6 shows the portion of the network where CLNS over DDR is implemented between R1 and R2. In this instance, the DDR backs up the Frame Relay physical connectivity between R1 and R2 when it fails. Code Listings 8-13 and 8-14 illustrate the DDR implementation.

■ ■ ■ ■ ■ ■ ■

Figure 8-6
CLNS over DDR.

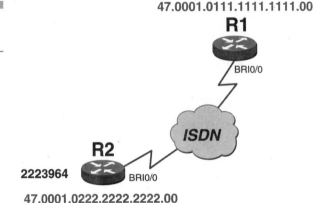

47.0001.0111.1111.1111.00

R1

BRI0/0

R2

2223964   BRI0/0

ISDN

47.0001.0222.2222.2222.00

Code Listing 8-13
CLNS-over-DDR configuration for R1.

```
hostname C3640-R1
!
username C3640-R2 password 0 cisco
clns routing
isdn switch-type basic-net3
!
interface BRI0/0
 encapsulation ppp
 dialer idle-timeout 60
 dialer map clns 47.0001.0222.2222.2222.00 name C3640-R2 broadcast 2223964
 dialer load-threshold 128 either
 dialer-group 1
 ppp authentication chap
 clns router isis
!
interface Serial1/0
 encapsulation frame-relay
 frame-relay lmi-type ansi
!
interface Serial1/0.1 point-to-point
 backup delay 10 30
 backup interface BRI0/0
 bandwidth 56
 clns router isis
 frame-relay interface-dlci 102
!
router isis
 net 47.0001.0111.1111.1111.00
!
dialer-list 1 protocol clns permit
```

1. Code Listing 8-13 illustrates the CLNS-over-DDR configuration for R1. The interface subcommand `clns router isis` enables IS-IS routing for CLNS packets on interface BRI0/0.

2. The `dialer map` interface subcommand calls up R2 to establish a PPP connection when S1/0.1 becomes unavailable. The CLNS address (NET), host name, and ISDN number used by the subcommand are R2's.

3. The `dialer-group 1` command refers to `dialer-list 1`, and the list allows all CLNS traffic to pass. No refining on the dialer-list is required, as the purpose of the BRI0/0 interface is to back up S1/0.1.

■ ■

Code Listing 8-14
CLNS-over-DDR configuration for R2.

```
hostname C3640-R2
!
username C3640-R1 password 0 cisco
clns routing
isdn switch-type basic-net3
!
interface BRI0/0
 encapsulation ppp
 dialer idle-timeout 60
 dialer map clns 47.0001.0111.1111.1111.00 name C3640-R1 broadcast
 dialer load-threshold 128 either
 dialer-group 1
 ppp authentication chap
 clns router isis
!
interface Serial1/0
 encapsulation frame-relay
 frame-relay lmi-type ansi
!
interface Serial1/0.1 point-to-point
 bandwidth 56
 clns router isis
 frame-relay interface-dlci 201
!
router isis
 net 47.0001.0222.2222.2222.00
!
dialer-list 1 protocol clns permit
```

1. Code Listing 8-14 illustrates the CLNS-over-DDR configuration for R2. The interface subcommand `clns router isis` enables IS-IS routing for CLNS packets on interface BRI0/0.

2. The `dialer map` command establishes a PPP connection when R1 makes a call. Note that no ISDN number is supplied here, as R1 will initiate the call. The CLNS address (NET) and host name used by the command are R1's.

3. The `dialer-group 1` command refers to `dialer-list 1`, and the list allows all CLNS traffic to pass.

Note the IS-IS and CLNS routing tables for all five routers in Code Listings 8-15 through 8-24.

Code Listing 8-15

IS-IS routing table for R1.

```
C3640-R1#show isis route
IS-IS Level-1 Routing Table - version 28
System Id        Next-Hop          SNPA       Interface    Metric
State
0111.1111.1111  0000.0000.0000    --         --           0      Up
0222.2222.2222  0222.2222.2222    DLCI 102   Se1/0.1      10     Up
0333.3333.3333  0333.3333.3333    DLCI 103   Se1/0.2      10     Up
0444.4444.4444  0222.2222.2222    DLCI 102   Se1/0.1      20     Up
0555.5555.5555  0333.3333.3333    DLCI 103   Se1/0.2      20          Up
```

Code Listing 8-16

CLNS routing table for R1.

```
C3640-R1#show clns route
CLNS Prefix Routing Table
47.0001.0111.1111.1111.00, Local NET Entry
47.0001 [110/0]
   via 0111.1111.1111, IS-IS, Up
```

Code Listing 8-17

IS-IS routing table for R2.

```
C3640-R2#show isis route
IS-IS Level-1 Routing Table - version 21
System Id        Next-Hop          SNPA       Interface    Metric
State
0111.1111.1111  0111.1111.1111    DLCI 201   Se1/0.1      10     Up
0222.2222.2222  0000.0000.0000    --         --           0      Up
0333.3333.3333  0111.1111.1111    DLCI 201   Se1/0.1      20     Up
0444.4444.4444  0444.4444.4444    *HDLC*     Se1/1        10     Up
0555.5555.5555  0111.1111.1111    DLCI 201   Se1/0.1      30          Up
```

Code Listing 8-18

CLNS routing table for R2.

```
C3640-R2#show clns route
CLNS Prefix Routing Table
47.0001.0222.2222.2222.00, Local NET Entry
47.0001 [110/0]
   via 0222.2222.2222, IS-IS, Up
```

Code Listing 8-19

IS-IS routing table for R3.

```
C4500-R3#show isis route
IS-IS Level-1 Routing Table - Version 16
System Id        Next-Hop          SNPA          Interface    Metric
State
0444.4444.4444  0111.1111.1111    DLCI 301      Se0.1        30     Up
0555.5555.5555  0555.5555.5555    6555555555    Se1          10     Up
0222.2222.2222  0111.1111.1111    DLCI 301      Se0.1        20     Up
0111.1111.1111  0111.1111.1111    DLCI 301      Se0.1        10     Up
0333.3333.3333  0000.0000.0000    --            --           0           Up
```

Code Listing 8-20
CLNS routing table for R3.

```
C4500-R3#show clns route
CLNS Prefix Routing Table
47.0001.0333.3333.3333.00, Local NET Entry
47.0001 [110/0]
    via 0333.3333.3333, IS-IS, Up
```

Code Listing 8-21
IS-IS routing table for R4.

```
C4500-R4#show isis route
IS-IS Level-1 Routing Table - Version 6
System Id         Next-Hop         SNPA           Interface   Metric
State
0555.5555.5555    0222.2222.2222   *HDLC*         Se0         40      Up
0333.3333.3333    0222.2222.2222   *HDLC*         Se0         30      Up
0111.1111.1111    0222.2222.2222   *HDLC*         Se0         20      Up
0222.2222.2222    0222.2222.2222   *HDLC*         Se0         10      Up
0444.4444.4444    0000.0000.0000   --             --          0           Up
```

Code Listing 8-22
CLNS routing table for R4.

```
C4500-R4#show clns route
CLNS Prefix Routing Table
47.0001.0444.4444.4444.00, Local NET Entry
47.0001 [110/0]
    via 0444.4444.4444, IS-IS, Up
```

Code Listing 8-23
IS-IS routing table for R5.

```
C2500-R5#show isis route
IS-IS Level-1 Routing Table - Version 6
System Id         Next-Hop         SNPA           Interface   Metric
State
0444.4444.4444    0333.3333.3333   6533333333     Se0         40      Up
0222.2222.2222    0333.3333.3333   6533333333     Se0         30      Up
0111.1111.1111    0333.3333.3333   6533333333     Se0         20      Up
0333.3333.3333    0333.3333.3333   6533333333     Se0         10      Up
0555.5555.5555    0000.0000.0000   --             --          0           Up
```

Code Listing 8-24
CLNS routing table for R5.

```
C2500-R5#show clns route
CLNS Prefix Routing Table
47.0001 [110/0]
    via 0555.5555.5555, IS-IS, Up
47.0001.0555.5555.5555.00, Local NET Entry
```

Note that only a single area is reflected in the CLNS routing tables illustrated in Code Listings 8-16, 8-18, 8-20, 8-22, and 8-24, because the only area defined is Area 0x470001.

Consider Figure 8-7. The ISDN backup link will connect when the physical Frame Relay connectivity between R1 and R2 becomes unavailable. Note the IS-IS routing tables for R1 and R2 in Code Listings 8-25 and 8-26.

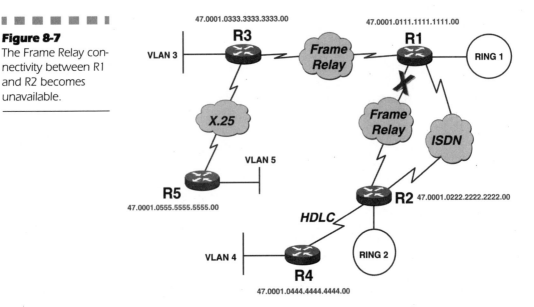

Figure 8-7
The Frame Relay connectivity between R1 and R2 becomes unavailable.

Code Listing 8-25
IS-IS routing table for R1.

```
C3640-R1#sh isis route
IS-IS Level-1 Routing Table - version 35
System Id       Next-Hop        SNPA            Interface    Metric
State
0111.1111.1111  0000.0000.0000  --              --           0      Up
0222.2222.2222  0222.2222.2222  *PPP*           BR0/0        10     Up
0333.3333.3333  0333.3333.3333  DLCI 103        Se1/0.2      10     Up
0444.4444.4444  0222.2222.2222  *PPP*           BR0/0        20     Up
0555.5555.5555  0333.3333.3333  DLCI 103        Se1/0.2      20        Up
```

As illustrated in Code Listing 8-25, R1 now learns the CLNS routes to R2 and R4 through its ISDN interface, BRI0/0.

Code Listing 8-26
IS-IS routing table for R2.

```
C3640-R2#show isis route
IS-IS Level-1 Routing Table - version 29
System Id       Next-Hop        SNPA            Interface    Metric
State
0111.1111.1111  0111.1111.1111  *PPP*           BR0/0        10     Up
0222.2222.2222  0000.0000.0000  --              --           0      Up
0333.3333.3333  0111.1111.1111  *PPP*           BR0/0        20     Up
0444.4444.4444  0444.4444.4444  *HDLC*          Se1/1        10     Up
0555.5555.5555  0111.1111.1111  *PPP*           BR0/0        30        Up
```

As illustrated in Code Listing 8-26, R2 now learns the CLNS routes to R1, R3, and R5 through its ISDN interface, BRI0/0.

CLNS IS-IS Level 1 and Level 2 Routing

In the previous sections, all the routers are in a single area, 0x470001. These routers forward traffic within their own area and function overall as Level 1 routers. Hence, the five routers have complete knowledge of each other within that area. In Figure 8-8, R4 is segregated into Area 0x470002; and R5 is segregated into Area 0x470003; and R1, R2, and R3 remain in Area 0x470001.

By default, the router acts as both a station (Level 1) router and an area (Level 2) router when it is configured for CLNS IS-IS routing. In other words, the five routers are all operating at IS Level 1-2 (Level 1 and 2). This means that a Level 1-2 adjacency is established if the neighbor is also configured as a Level 1-2, and there is at least one area in common. (See Figure 8-2, where Level 1-2 adjacencies are established for all the routers.) If there are no areas in common, a Level 2 adjacency is established.

In the scenario illustrated in Figure 8-8, R2 and R4 will form a Level 2 adjacency; likewise, R3 and R5 will also establish a Level 2 adjacency. However, R1 and R2 will form a Level 1-2 adjacency, and so will R1 and R3. Therefore, the five routers will forward intra-area (Level 1) CLNS packets to respective Level 1-2 routers, and forward inter-area (Level 2) CLNS packets to respective Level 1-2 or Level 2 routers.

Note the router configuration for R4 and R5 in Code Listings 8-27 and 8-28.

Code Listing 8-27
CLNS IS-IS level 2 routing configuration for R4.

```
hostname C4500-R4
!
clns routing
!
interface Ethernet0
 media-type 10BaseT
 clns router isis
!
interface Serial0
 bandwidth 56
 clns router isis
!
router isis
 net 47.0002.0444.4444.4444.00
```

Figure 8-8
CLNS IS-IS level 1 and
level 2 routing.

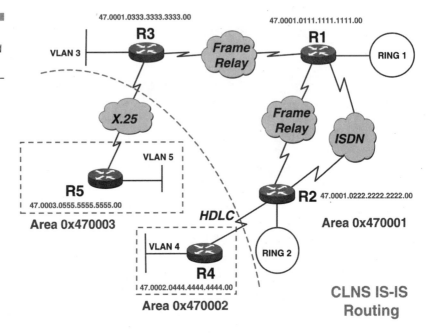

Code Listing 8-27 illustrates the CLNS IS-IS Level 2 routing configuration for R4. The `net` router subcommand configures the NET for the IS-IS routing process as 47.0002.0444.4444.4444.00. In this case, the NET defines the area address for the IS-IS area as 47.0002 (AFI=47, IDI=NULL, AREA ID=0002), the system address as 0444.4444.4444, and the n-selector (SEL) as 00.

Code Listing 8-28
CLNS IS-IS level 2 routing configuration for R5.

```
hostname C2500-R5
!
clns routing
!
interface Ethernet0
 clns router isis
!
interface Serial0
 encapsulation x25
 x25 address 6555555555
 x25 map clns 6533333333 broadcast
 clns router isis
!
router isis
 net 47.0003.0555.5555.5555.00
```

Code Listing 8-28 illustrates the CLNS IS-IS Level 2 routing configuration for R5. The `net` router subcommand configures the NET for the IS-IS routing process as 47.0003.0555.5555.5555.00. In this case, the NET defines the area address for the IS-IS area as 47.0003 (AFI=47, IDI=NULL, AREA ID=0003), the system address as 0555.5555.5555, and the n-selector (SEL) as 00.

Note the IS-IS and CLNS routing tables for the five routers in Code Listings 8-29 through 8-38.

Code Listing 8-29

IS-IS routing table for R1.

```
C3640-R1#show isis routes
IS-IS Level-1 Routing Table - version 71
System Id         Next-Hop          SNPA             Interface    Metric
State
0111.1111.1111   0000.0000.0000    --               --           0       Up
0222.2222.2222   0222.2222.2222    DLCI 102         Se1/0.1      10      Up
0333.3333.3333   0333.3333.3333    DLCI 103         Se1/0.2      10          Up
```

Code Listing 8-30

CLNS routing table for R1.

```
C3640-R1#show clns route
CLNS Prefix Routing Table
47.0001.0111.1111.1111.00, Local NET Entry
47.0003 [110/20]
   via 0333.3333.3333, IS-IS, Up, Serial1/0.2
47.0002 [110/20]
   via 0222.2222.2222, IS-IS, Up, Serial1/0.1
47.0001 [110/0]
   via 0111.1111.1111, IS-IS, Up
```

Code Listing 8-31

IS-IS routing table for R2.

```
C3640-R2#show isis routes
IS-IS Level-1 Routing Table - version 62
System Id         Next-Hop          SNPA             Interface    Metric
State
0111.1111.1111   0111.1111.1111    DLCI 201         Se1/0.1      10      Up
0222.2222.2222   0000.0000.0000    --               --           0       Up
0333.3333.3333   0111.1111.1111    DLCI 201         Se1/0.1      20          Up
```

Code Listing 8-32

CLNS routing table for R2.

```
C3640-R2#show clns route
CLNS Prefix Routing Table
47.0001.0222.2222.2222.00, Local NET Entry
47.0003 [110/30]
   via 0111.1111.1111, IS-IS, Up, Serial1/0.1
47.0002 [110/10]
   via 0444.4444.4444, IS-IS, Up, Serial1/1
47.0001 [110/0]
   via 0222.2222.2222, IS-IS, Up
```

Code Listing 8-33

IS-IS routing table for R3.

```
C4500-R3#show isis routes
IS-IS Level-1 Routing Table - Version 52
System Id       Next-Hop        SNPA        Interface   Metric
State
0222.2222.2222  0111.1111.1111  DLCI 301    Se0.1       20      Up
0111.1111.1111  0111.1111.1111  DLCI 301    Se0.1       10      Up
0333.3333.3333  0000.0000.0000  --          --          0           Up
```

Code Listing 8-34

CLNS routing table for R3.

```
C4500-R3#show cln route
CLNS Prefix Routing Table
47.0001.0333.3333.3333.00, Local NET Entry
47.0003 [110/10]
    via 0555.5555.5555, IS-IS, Up, Serial1
47.0002 [110/30]
    via 0111.1111.1111, IS-IS, Up, Serial0.1
47.0001 [110/0]
    via 0333.3333.3333, IS-IS, Up
```

Code Listing 8-35

IS-IS routing table for R4.

```
C4500-R4#show isis routes
IS-IS Level-1 Routing Table - Version 29
System Id       Next-Hop        SNPA        Interface   Metric
State
0444.4444.4444  0000.0000.0000  --          --          0       Up
```

Code Listing 8-36

CLNS routing table for R4.

```
C4500-R4#show clns route
CLNS Prefix Routing Table
47.0003 [110/40]
    via 0222.2222.2222, IS-IS, Up, Serial0
47.0002.0444.4444.4444.00, Local NET Entry
47.0002 [110/0]
    via 0444.4444.4444, IS-IS, Up
47.0001 [110/10]
    via 0222.2222.2222, IS-IS, Up, Serial0
```

Code Listing 8-37

IS-IS routing table for R5.

```
C2500-R5#show isis routes
IS-IS Level-1 Routing Table - Version 39
System Id       Next-Hop        SNPA        Interface   Metric
State
0555.5555.5555  0000.0000.0000  --          --          0       Up
```

■ I

Code Listing 8-38
CLNS routing table
for R5.

```
C2500-R5#show clns route
CLNS Prefix Routing Table
47.0003 [110/0]
   via 0555.5555.5555, IS-IS, Up
47.0002 [110/40]
   via 0333.3333.3333, IS-IS, Up, Serial0
47.0001 [110/10]
   via 0333.3333.3333, IS-IS, Up, Serial0
47.0003.0555.5555.5555.00, Local NET Entry
```

Note that the IS-IS routing tables in Code Listings 8-29, 8-31, 8-33, 8-35, and 8-37 reflect only the routes within an area—that is, the routes to Level 1 ISs (routers)—while the CLNS routing tables in Code Listings 8-30, 8-32, 8-34, 8-36, and 8-38 complement the IS-IS routing tables by reflecting the routes to the three different areas: 0x470001, 0x470002, and 0x470003.

Note the CLNS neighbors information for the five routers in Code Listings 8-39 through 8-43.

■ I

Code Listing 8-39
CLNS neighbors information for R1.

```
C3640-R1#show clns neighbors

System Id       SNPA              Interface  State  Holdtime  Type
Protocol
0222.2222.2222 DLCI 102          Se1/0.1    Up     23        L1L2
IS-IS
0333.3333.3333 DLCI 103          Se1/0.2    Up     28        L1L2
IS-IS
```

As illustrated in Code Listing 8-39, R1 establishes a Level 1-2 adjacency with R2 and R3.

■ I

Code Listing 8-40
CLNS neighbors information for R2.

```
C3640-R2#show clns neighbors

System Id       SNPA              Interface  State  Holdtime  Type
Protocol
0111.1111.1111 DLCI 201          Se1/0.1    Up     25        L1L2
IS-IS
0444.4444.4444 *HDLC*            Se1/1      Up     29        L2
IS-IS
```

As illustrated in Code Listing 8-40, R2 establishes a Level 1-2 adjacency with R1 and a Level 2 adjacency with R4.

Code Listing 8-41
CLNS neighbors infor-
mation for R3.

```
C4500-R3#show clns neighbors

System Id        SNPA            Interface   State   Holdtime   Type
Protocol
0555.5555.5555 6555555555       Se1         Up      8          L2
IS-IS
0111.1111.1111 DLCI 301         Se0.1       Up      23         L1L2
IS-IS
```

As illustrated in Code Listing 8-41, R3 establishes a Level 2 adjacency with R5 and a Level 1-2 adjacency with R1.

Code Listing 8-42
CLNS neighbors infor-
mation for R4.

```
C4500-R4#show clns neighbors

System Id        SNPA            Interface   State   Holdtime   Type
Protocol
0222.2222.2222 *HDLC*           Se0         Up      27         L2
IS-IS
```

As illustrated in Code Listing 8-42, R4 establishes a Level 2 adjacency with R2.

Code Listing 8-43
CLNS neighbors infor-
mation for R5.

```
C2500-R5#show clns neighbors

System Id        SNPA            Interface   State   Holdtime   Type
Protocol
0333.3333.3333 6533333333       Se0         Up      22         L2
IS-IS
```

As illustrated in Code Listing 8-43, R5 establishes a Level 2 adjacency with R3.

ISO CLNS ES-IS

ESs (end systems) need to know how to reach a Level 1 IS in their area, and Level 1 ISs need to know all of the ESs that are directly reachable through each of their interfaces. A Cisco router configured for CLNS IS-IS routing will dynamically learn all ESs running the ES-IS protocol. Note that ES-IS is enabled automatically on a specific interface if the clns router isis interface subcommand is configured on that interface. ESs that are not running the ES-IS protocol must be statically configured. In this case, NSAP/NET (protocol address) to SNPA (media address) mappings must be specified for these ESs.

In Figure 8-9, ES_HOST5 is an end system that does not support ES-IS. Therefore the ES-IS protocol must be statically configured, as illustrated in Code Listing 8-44.

Code Listing 8-44
CLNS static ES-IS configuration for R5.

```
hostname C2500-R5
!
clns routing
!
interface Ethernet0
 clns es-neighbor 47.0003.0666.6666.6666.00 0aaa.bbbb.cccc
 clns router isis
!
router isis
 net 47.0003.0555.5555.5555.00
```

Code Listing 8-44 illustrates the CLNS static ES-IS configuration for R5. The interface subcommand `clns es-neighbor` defines an NSAP/NET (with a value of 47.0003.0666.6666.6666.00) to SNPA (with a value of 0aaa.bbbb.cccc) mapping for ES_HOST5 on interface E0.

Figure 8-9
Configuring CLNS ES-IS statically for ES_HOST5.

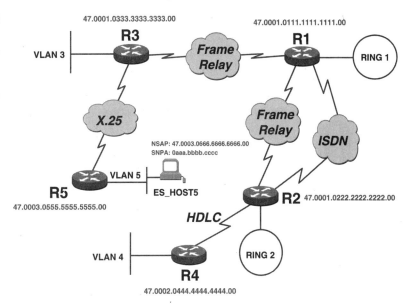

Note that the route to ES_HOST5 is now reflected in the IS-IS routing table shown in Code Listing 8-45, since R5 has discovered this ES through static configuration.

```
C2500-R5#show isis routes
IS-IS Level-1 Routing Table - Version 43
System Id      Next-Hop        SNPA            Interface   Metric
State
0666.6666.6666  0666.6666.6666  0aaa.bbbb.cccc  Et0          10      Up
0555.5555.5555  0000.0000.0000  --              --            0            Up
```

The CLNS neighbors information table in Code Listing 8-46 shows that R5 has established an ES adjacency with ES_HOST5. In this case, the ES adjacency is statically configured.

```
C2500-R5#show clns neighbors

System Id       SNPA            Interface   State   Holdtime  Type
Protocol
0666.6666.6666 0aaa.bbbb.cccc   Et0         Up      --        ES
Static
0333.3333.3333 6533333333       Se0         Up      27        L2
IS-IS
```

CLNS Access Control

CLNS access lists are in the form of filter expressions. These filter expressions are complex logical combinations of CLNS filter sets that are lists of address templates against which CLNS addresses are matched. In other words, these address templates are CLNS address patterns that are either simple CLNS addresses matched by just one address, or multiple CLNS addresses matched through the use of wildcard characters, prefixes, and suffixes. In this section, CLNS traffic filtering is implemented by using the CLNS filter expressions.

CLNS Traffic Filtering

In Figure 8-10, an inbound CLNS traffic filter is specified on the S0 interface of R5, permitting access to all the routers except R2. Code Listing 8-47 illustrates this.

Code Listing 8-47
CLNS traffic filtering configuration for R5.

```
hostname C2500-R5
!
clns routing
clns filter-set DENY-R2 deny 47.0001.0222.2222.2222.00
clns filter-set DENY-R2 permit default
clns filter-expr FILTER1 src DENY-R2
!
interface Serial0
 encapsulation x25
 x25 address 6555555555
 x25 map clns 6533333333 broadcast
 clns router isis
 clns access-group FILTER1 in
!
router isis
 net 47.0003.0555.5555.5555.00
```

1. Code Listing 8-47 illustrates the CLNS traffic filtering configuration for R5. The above router configuration demonstrates how to define a filter expression that matches addresses with a source address of anything besides 47.0001.0222.2222.2222.00.

Figure 8-10
CLNS traffic filtering.

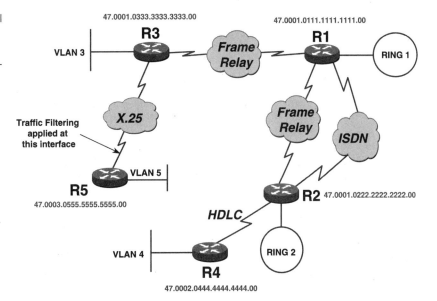

2. This is implemented through an address template (or filter set), DENY-R2, where the two lines of global configuration commands— `clns filter-set DENY-R2 deny 47.0001.0222.2222.2222.00` and `clns filter-set DENY-R2 permit default`—return a deny action if an address starts with 47.0001.0222.2222.2222.00, but return a permit action for any other addresses.

3. The filter expression, FILTER1, is then built using the global configuration command `clns filter-expr FILTER1 src DENY-R2` that matches the source NSAP addresses defined previously in the filter set, DENY-R2.

4. Finally, the filter expression is applied in the inbound direction at interface S0 using the interface subcommand `clns access-group FILTER1 in`.

After applying the CLNS inbound traffic filter at interface S0 of R5, all the rest of the routers except R2 can execute a positive CLNS ping to R5. Likewise, R5 can execute a positive CLNS ping to all the rest of the routers except R2. Code Listing 8-48 illustrates these CLNS ping results.

Code Listing 8-48
CLNS ping results.

```
C3640-R1#ping clns 47.0003.0555.5555.5555.00

Type escape sequence to abort.
Sending 5, 100-byte CLNS Echos with timeout 2 seconds
!!!!!
Success rate is 100 percent (5/5), round-trip min/avg/max = 116/235/
500 ms


C3640-R2#ping clns 47.0003.0555.5555.5555.00

Type escape sequence to abort.
Sending 5, 100-byte CLNS Echos with timeout 2 seconds
.....
Success rate is 0 percent (0/5)


C4500-R3#ping clns 47.0003.0555.5555.5555.00

Type escape sequence to abort.
Sending 5, 100-byte CLNS Echos with timeout 2 seconds
!!!!!
Success rate is 100 percent (5/5), round-trip min/avg/max = 44/88/268
ms


C4500-R4#ping clns 47.0003.0555.5555.5555.00

Type escape sequence to abort.
```

■ ■

Code Listing 8-48
(continued)

```
Sending 5, 100-byte CLNS Echos with timeout 2 seconds
!!!!!
Success rate is 100 percent (5/5), round-trip min/avg/max = 232/317/
404 ms




C2500-R5#ping clns 47.0001.0111.1111.1111.00

Type escape sequence to abort.
Sending 5, 100-byte CLNS Echos with timeout 2 seconds
!!!!!
Success rate is 100 percent (5/5), round-trip min/avg/max = 116/159/
260 ms


C2500-R5#ping clns 47.0001.0222.2222.2222.00

Type escape sequence to abort.
Sending 5, 100-byte CLNS Echos with timeout 2 seconds
.....
Success rate is 0 percent (0/5)


C2500-R5#ping clns 47.0001.0333.3333.3333.00

Type escape sequence to abort.
Sending 5, 100-byte CLNS Echos with timeout 2 seconds
!!!!!
Success rate is 100 percent (5/5), round-trip min/avg/max = 40/42/44
ms


C2500-R5#ping clns 47.0002.0444.4444.4444.00

Type escape sequence to abort.
Sending 5, 100-byte CLNS Echos with timeout 2 seconds
!!!!!
Success rate is 100 percent (5/5), round-trip min/avg/max = 232/272/
432 ms
```

Summary

This chapter covered the ISO CLNS protocol. ISO CLNS is a standard for the network layer of the OSI (Open Systems Interconnection) model, and the services provided by CLNS are analogous to the datagram services provided by IP.

In the initial scenario, CLNS IS-IS dynamic routing was configured over Ethernet, Token Ring, Frame Relay, X.25, HDLC, and DDR. Next, IS-IS Level 1, Level 1-2, and Level 2 routings were discussed. Subsequently, an environment for Level 1-2 and Level 2 routing was configured using the existing setup.

The nature of the ES-IS protocol was also investigated. It was configured statically on a router's interface for an end system that does not support ES-IS.

Finally, in the access control section, CLNS access lists were implemented using filter sets and filter expressions. An inbound CLNS traffic filter was configured based on the final derived filter expression built from earlier defined filter sets. These access lists (or filter expressions) provide a powerful tool to control excessive CLNS traffic and better secure a large CLNS internetwork.

References

1. Documentation CD-ROM, Cisco Systems, Inc., 1998.

2. Hagans, R. "Components of OSI: ES-IS Routing." *ConnecXions: The Interoperability Report*, Vol. 3, No. 8. August 1989.

3. Malamud, C. *Analyzing CLNS/OSI Phase V.* New York: Van Nostrand Reinhold, 1991.

4. Rose, M. T. *The Open Book: A Practical Perspective on OSI.* Englewood Cliffs, New Jersey: Prentice Hall, 1990.

5. Tsuchiya, P. "Components of OSI: IS-IS Intra-Domain Routing." *ConnecXions: The Interoperability Report*, Vol. 3, No. 8. August 1989.

6. Tsuchiya, P. "Components of OSI: Routing (An Overview)." *ConnecXions: The Interoperability Report*, Vol. 3, No. 8. August 1989.

7. Zimmerman, H. "OSI Reference Model—The ISO Model Architecture for Open Systems Interconnection." *IEEE Transactions on Communications COM-28*, No. 4. April 1980.

ACRONYMS

AFP	AppleTalk Filing Protocol
ARP	Address Resolution Protocol
AS	Autonomous Systems
ASBR	Autonomous System Border Router
ASP	AppleTalk Session Protocol
ATP	AppleTalk Transaction Protocol
BIA	Burn-In Address
BPDU	Bridge Protocol Data Unit
BVI	Bridge-Group Virtual Interface
CDP	Cisco Discovery Protocol
CLNP	Connectionless Network Protocol
CLNS	Connectionless Network Service
DDP	Datagram Delivery Protocol
DEC	Digital Equipment Corporation
DLC	Data Link Control
DLSw+	Data Link Switching Plus
DNA	Digital Network Architecture
DRP	DECnet Routing Protocol
DSAP	Destination Service Access Point
DSP	Domain Specific Part
DUAL	Diffusing Update Algorithm
EIGRP	Enhanced IGRP
ES	End System
ES-IS	End-System-to-Intermediate-System Routing

FSM	Finite-State Machine
FST	Fast Sequenced Transport
GRE	Generic Routing Encapsulation
GZL	Get Zone List
ICP	Internet Control Protocol
ICP	Interprocess Communication Protocol
ID	Identifier
IDI	Initial Domain Identifier
IDP	Initial Domain Part
IDP	Internet Datagram Protocol
IGRP	Interior Gateway Routing Protocol
IP	Internet Protocol
IPX	Internet Packet Exchange
IRB	Integrated Routing and Bridging
IS	Intermediate System
IS-IS	Intermediate-System-to-Intermediate-System Routing
ISO	International Organization for Standardization
LSAP	Local Service Access Point
LSP	Link-State Packet
LAT	Local Area Transport
MOP	Maintenance Operations Protocol
NAS	Network Application Support
NBMA	Non-Broadcast Multi-Access
NBP	Name Binding Protocol
NCP	Netware Core Protocol
NET RPC	Network Remote Procedure Call

NET	Network Entity Title
NetBIOS	Network Basic Input Output Services
NFS	Network File Service
NIC	Network Interface Card
NLSP	Netware Link Services Protocol
NMS	Network Management Station
NOS	Network Operating System
NSAP	Network Service Access Point
NSP	Network Services Protocol
NVE	Network Visible Entity
OSI	Open Systems Interconnection
Prom	Promiscuous
PU	Physical Unit
PVC	Permanent Virtual Circuit
QLLC	Qualified Logical Link Control
RC	Routing Control
RCONSOLE	Remote Console
RD	Routing Descriptor
RIF	Routing Information Field
RII	Routing Information Indicator
RPRINTER	Remote Printer
RSRB	Remote Source-Route Bridging
RTMP	Routing Table Maintenance Protocol
RTP	Routing Table Update
SAA	Systems Application Architecture
SAP	Service Access Point
SAP	Service Advertising Protocol

SARP	Sequenced Address Resolution Protocol
SDLC	Synchronous Data Link Control
SEL	N-Selector
SNA	Systems Network Architecture
SPF	Shortest Path First
SPP	Sequenced Packet Protocol
SPX	Sequential Packet Exchange
SR	Source-Route
SR/TLB	Source-Route Translational Bridging
SRB	Source-Route Bridging
SRTP	Sequenced Routing Table Update
SSAP	Source Service Access Point
SSP	Switch-to-Switch Protocol
STA	Spanning Tree Algorithm
TB	Transparent Bridging
TP	Transport Protocol
VINES	Virtual Network Service
VIP	VINES Internet Protocol
VMS	Virtual Memory System
VLSM	Variable Length Subnet Mask
XNS	XEROX Network System
ZIP	Zone Information Protocol
ZIT	Zone Information Table

INDEX

Software and Information License

The software and information on this diskette (collectively referred to as the "Product") are the property of The McGraw-Hill Companies, Inc. ("McGraw-Hill") and are protected by both United States copyright law and international copyright treaty provision. You must treat this Product just like a book, expect that you may copy it into a computer to be used and you may make archival copies of the Products for the sole purpose of backing up your software and protecting your investment from loss.

By saying "just like a book," McGraw-Hill means, for example, that the Product may be used by any number of people and may be freely moved from one computer location to another, so long as there is no possibility of the Product (or any part of the Product) being used at one location or on one computer while it is being used at another. Just as a book cannot be read by two different people in two different places at the same time, neither can the Product be used in two different places at the same time (unless, of course, McGraw-Hill's rights are being violated).

McGraw-Hill reserves the right to alter or modify the contents of the Product at any time.

This agreement is effective until terminated. The Agreement will terminate automatically without notice if you fail to comply with any provisions of this Agreement. In the event of termination by reason of your breach, you will destroy or erase all copies of the Product installed on any computer system or made for backup purposes and shall expunge the Product from your data storage facilities.

Limited Warranty

McGraw-Hill warrants the physical diskette(s) enclosed herein to be free of defects in materials and workmanship for a period of sixty days from the purchase date. If McGraw-Hill receives written notification within the warranty period of defects in materials or workmanship, and such notification is determined by McGraw-Hill to be correct, McGraw-Hill will replace the defective diskette(s). Send request to:

Customer Service
McGraw-Hill
Gahanna Industrial Park
860 Taylor Station Road
Blacklick, Ohio 43004-9615

The entire and exclusive liability and remedy for breach of this LimitedWarranty shall be limited to replacement of defective diskette(s) and shall not include or extend any claim for or right to cover any other damages, including but not limited to loss of profit, data, or use of the software, or special, incidental, or consequential damages or other similar claims, even if McGraw-Hill has been specifically advised as to the possibility of such damages. In no event will McGraw-Hill's liability for any damages to you or any other person ever exceed the lower of suggested list price or actual price paid for the license to use the Product, regardless of any form of the claim.

The McGraw-Hill Companies, Inc. specifically disclaims all other warranties, express or implied, including but not limited to, any implied warranty of merchantability or fitness for a particular purpose. Specifically, McGraw-Hill makes no representation or warranty that the Product is fit for any particular purpose and any implied warranty of merchantability is limited to the sixty day duration of the Limited Warranty covering the physical diskette(s) only (and not the software or information) and is otherwise expressly and specifically disclaimed.

This Limited Warranty gives you specific legal rights; you may have others which may vary from state to state. Some states do not allow the exclusion of incidental or consequential damages, or the limitation on how long an implied warranty lasts, so some of the above may not apply to you.

This agreement constitutes the entire agreement between the parties relating to use of the Product. The terms of any purchase order shall have no effect on the terms of this Agreement. Failure of McGraw-Hill to insist at any time on strict compliance with this Agreement shall not constitute a waiver of any rights under this Agreement. This Agreement shall be construed and governed in accordance with the laws of New York. If any provision of this Agreement is held to be contrary tolaw, that provision will be enforced to the maximum extent permissible and the remaining provisions will remain in force and effect.